DIES IN THE NATIVE LANGUAGES OF THE AMERICAS

ORS
las R. Parks
ond J. DeMallie

Topic and Discourse Struc
Greenlandic Agreement (

STU

EDIT
Doug
Raym

# Topic and Discourse Structure in West Greenlandic Agreement Constructions

ANNA BERGE

University of Nebraska Press | Lincoln and London

IN COOPERATION WITH THE AMERICAN INDIAN STUDIES
RESEARCH INSTITUTE, INDIANA UNIVERSITY, BLOOMINGTON

Library of Congress
Cataloging-in-Publication Data
Berge, Anna.
Topic and discourse structure
in West Greenlandic agreement
constructions / Anna Berge.
p.   cm.—(Studies in the native
languages of the Americas)
"In cooperation with the American
Indian Studies Research Institute,
Indiana University, Bloomington."
Includes bibliographical
references and index.
ISBN 978-0-8032-1645-7
(cloth: alk. paper)
1. Kalâtdlisut dialect—Discourse
analysis. 2. Kalâtdlisut dialect—
Syntax. I. Indiana University,
Bloomington. American Indian
Studies Research Institute. II. Title.
PM62.B46    2011
497'.12—dc22
2011001962

Set in Minion Pro by BookComp, Inc.
Designed by Nathan Putens.

*to Sweet Pea and Bjørni*
*and to my parents*

# CONTENTS

## PREFACE



This study is a slightly reworked version of my PhD dissertation, completed in 1997. Unfortunately, it has been held up in review for an unusually long period of time. The literature review in this work reflects the state of the field in 1997; since it was completed, many structural studies of discourse have been undertaken, and the field of discourse has gained in importance. The data and interpretations thereof, however, remain relevant today.

I initially began to study the Inuit language (specifically, the South-East Baffin Inuktitut dialect, and later West Greenlandic), with the intention of studying its syntax. After reviewing the texts I had collected, it seemed clear that there were important characteristics of Inuit that were only evident beyond the sentence level, and that the language's syntactic structures and their distribution and use in texts depended on as yet undescribed contextual factors. For example, an enormous amount had been written about ergative and antipassive structures in the Inuit dialects, which are relatively rare in oral texts. Yet little, if anything, had been written about the rather common use of the verb mood called causative in the Eskimo literature, as indicatives, beyond acknowledgment of its frequency and some discussion of possible environments in which it occurs. Scholars tended to explain syntactic structures that have figured prominently in contemporary linguistic analyses of European languages. Thus, early grammars of the Inuit dialects were modeled on European grammars; more modern syntactic descriptions dealt with the passive, the ergative, the dative, and other aspects of grammar that were currently the subject of scrutiny in more commonly studied languages. From a preliminary glance at my texts, I began to suspect that syntactic descriptions based solely on clause structure were failing to provide basic information about, let alone insight into, the language. For example, although many Eskimologists had noted the tendency for speakers of the Inuit dialects to use subordinate structures more frequently than English speakers do, no one to my knowledge had formally identified Eskimo as a clause-chaining language, the result being that typologists did not commonly cite Eskimo as a clause-chaining language. When noting characteristics of clause-chaining languages, linguists therefore were ignoring information available from Eskimo.

Syntactic descriptions of the Inuit dialects have also often been used to prove the validity of a linguistic theory, and the results have not been satisfactory. Clause-level analyses of Eskimo, for example, often require long explanations of rules and constraints on the construction of a clause, but rarely have I seen explanations of clause combination exceeding two or three clauses. Yet both my texts and personal communication with linguists and native speakers lead me to believe that multiple combinations of clauses are the normal method of sentence construction.

Examples of language in context are necessary to adequately understand the structure of the Inuit language. This notion is not new: S. T. Mallon and L. J. Dorais (personal communication) have previously expressed the belief that there is some kind of discourse grammar; I. Kalmár and A. Woodbury have since the 1970s discussed the relevance of discourse to grammatical descriptions; and grammars of West Greenlandic have from the first noted correlations between the uses of particular syntactic structures and pragmatics. What I propose is the systematic incorporation of discourse factors in the syntactic analysis of Eskimo. The present work is a functionalist study of West Greenlandic syntactic structures involving ergativity and switch-reference, but it is also a reanalysis of these structures within the context of discourse. It is a study of the effect that discourse roles may have on syntactic structures.

This project would not have been possible without the support and encouragement of my friends and colleagues. I have had help and support from many places throughout the various stages of production, from collecting data in the field, to writing my dissertation, and finally to turning it into this book. First, I would like to thank the members of my dissertation committee, Drs. Rich Rhodes, Gary Holland, Leanne Hinton, and Tom Shannon, who have guided and encouraged me, read the copious and verbose pages of my drafts, and believed in the quality of my work. The sometimes frustrating and never-ending work was made more pleasant by the good relations I have always had with each of my advisors. I would also like to thank Dr. Michael Fortescue and Maggie Fortescue, as well as Arnaq Grove, for their very generous help in checking my claims in the revision of this book.

None of my data and very little of my already scant knowledge of Greenlandic would have existed without the help and the good wishes of all the people I met while conducting fieldwork. I owe a special debt of gratitude to Kêrti Jeremiassen and Bodil Davidsen, who helped me find speakers to tape, transcribed and translated the texts for me, and welcomed me as a friend in their home and community; and to Per Langgård and his family, who so generously gave of his time to teach me the fundamentals of West Greenlandic and to review the morphological analyses of my texts. In addition, Karen Langgård and the staff of the University of Greenland, Karen Nielsen and Sakki, Rasmine Johansen and her family, Ole, Angut, and Olov, Sørine Petersen and her friends Lene Holm and Else Danielsen, Inge Hansen, and Paula Bekooy have all welcomed me, helped me, and extended their friendship to me, and I wish them to know how much I have appreciated them.

My work in West Greenland must properly be said to have started when I first began working in the Arctic. I first began my studies in Iqaluit, Baffin

Island, with the help of Susan Sammons, the Arctic College, Mick Mallon, Louis-Jacques Dorais, Shuvenai Mike, May Lonsdale, Debbie Qitsualik, Ashoona Kiliback, Sailua Attagujuk, and Sami Qaumariaq. It was there that I first was introduced to the culture and language of the Inuit Arctic, and there that I first developed a love and respect of the Arctic. It was in Greenland that I deepened it.

It was the support at home, however, that kept me from floundering during the writing of my dissertation, and I thank my good friends in the Bay Area, and particularly Trina Baker and the Feld family.

Above all, great thanks to my family from whom I learned the art of critical thinking, for their support and good wishes, even as they raised their eyebrows; and to Sweet Pea and Bjørn, who suffered my bouts of ill temper and neglect with stoicism and faith.

# ABBREVIATIONS

Single, full capital letters are used to refer to syntactic or semantic elements. Small capital abbreviations are used in morphological analyses.

| | | | |
|---|---|---|---|
| A | agent | LOC | locative |
| ABL | ablative | N | noun |
| ABS | absolutive | NC | noncoreferential |
| AGENT | agentive | NEG | negative |
| ANT | antipassive | NOM | nominalization |
| C | coreferential | NOMZ | nominalizer |
| CAUS | causative | O | object |
| COMPAR | comparative | OBJ | object |
| COND | conditional | P | patient |
| CONJ | conjunction | PART | participal/participle |
| CONSEQ | consequentiality | PASS | passive |
| COP | copula | PERF | perfective |
| CT | contemporative | PL | plural |
| DEIC | deictic | POS | possessor |
| DIM | diminutive | POSM | possessum |
| EQ | equalis | REL | relative |
| ERG | ergative | S | subject |
| FUT | future | SG | singular |
| HAB | habitual | SR | switch-reference |
| IND | indicative | SUBJ | subject |
| INST | instrumental | SUP | superlative |
| INT | interrogative | TERM | terminalis |
| INTNS | intensifier | TRANSR | transitivizer |
| INTRANS | intransitivizer | V | verb |
| IO | indirect object | VIA | vialis |

# ORTHOGRAPHIC CONVENTIONS

Greenlandic uses the roman alphabet, with all the letters that Danish uses; however, the phonology of native Greenlandic does not fully correspond with that of Danish. This is reflected in the general avoidance of certain letters in native words. The use of these letters is almost entirely due to loan words, as in <b>, <c>, <d>, <f>, word-initial <g>, <h>, word-initial <j>, word-initial <l>, word-initial <r>, word-initial <v>, <w>, <y>, <z>, <æ>, and <ø>. The phonetic value of these letters is as in Danish.

Letters representing native sounds in Greenlandic are listed in the vowel and consonant tables below, in the cells corresponding to their phonemic value. Orthographic representations of non-native sounds are listed in another table.

Most phonemes can be geminated; a few devoice or otherwise change quality as a result, and these are noted in the table below immediately following the corresponding single phoneme. Most vowels are subject to considerable modification in the neighborhood of uvulars.

**Table 0.1 Modern West Greenlandic orthographic representations of native phonemes**

<table>
<tr><td></td><td colspan="5">Vowels</td></tr>
<tr><td></td><td colspan="2">FRONT</td><td colspan="3">BACK</td></tr>
<tr><td></td><td colspan="2"><i>, <ii><br><e>, <ee> before uvular<br>consonants <q> and <r></td><td colspan="3"><u>, <uu><br><o>, <oo> before uvular<br>consonants <q> and <r><br><a>, <aa></td></tr>
<tr><td></td><td colspan="5">Consonants</td></tr>
<tr><td></td><td>LABIAL</td><td>DENTAL</td><td>PALATAL</td><td>VELAR</td><td>UVULAR</td></tr>
<tr><td>Stops<br>voiceless</td><td><p></td><td><t></td><td></td><td><k></td><td><q></td></tr>
<tr><td>Fricatives<br>voiceless</td><td><f>[1]</td><td><s></td><td><ss>[2]</td><td><gg></td><td><r>[3]</td></tr>
<tr><td>Fricatives<br>voiced</td><td><v>[4]</td><td></td><td></td><td><g></td><td><r></td></tr>
<tr><td>Laterals<br>voiceless</td><td></td><td><ll></td><td></td><td></td><td></td></tr>
<tr><td>Laterals<br>voiced</td><td></td><td><l></td><td></td><td></td><td></td></tr>
<tr><td>Glides</td><td></td><td></td><td><j></td><td></td><td></td></tr>
<tr><td>Nasals</td><td><m></td><td><n></td><td></td><td><ng>[5]</td><td></td></tr>
</table>

1. Usually a reflection of geminated [v].

2. Some dialects of West Greenlandic, particularly the more northern ones, still have a retroflex /s/ as the result of a sound change from /*t/ to [ʃ] after a vowel. Others have lost the retroflex quality and now have /s/ in all environments. The distinction is not made in the orthography.

3. Often allophone of /q/ before a consonant.

4. [w] or [b] according to some sources; often pronounced [b] by older speakers; written <f> when geminated.

5. Swadesh (1952) also includes in the list of nasals a palatal nasal; no other source to my knowledge suggests the existence of a palatal nasal in Greenlandic. The examples provided by Swadesh show clearly that his palatal nasals should in fact be the velar nasals.

Table 0.2  Orthographic conventions and phonemic values in loanwords

| ORTHOGRAPHY | PHONETIC VALUE | NOTES |
| --- | --- | --- |
| b | [b] or [p] | all voiced stops from Danish words tend to be devoiced |
| c | [s] | |
| d | [d] or [t] | |
| h | [h] | Only in one native word: *haa!* 'look!' |
| w | [v] | |
| y | [y] | |
| z | [z] | |
| æ | [æ] | |

# 1 Introduction

Since the 1950s, the study of syntax has been almost synonymous with the study of grammatical structure, and notions of constituent, phrase, and clause structure have proven useful in capturing linguistic universals and linguistic behavior. Several kinds of problems commonly arise from the study of decontextualized sentences, however, including those resulting from limitations of a particular theory of syntax applied to the description of a linguistic phenomenon. These problems are evident in syntactic studies of West Greenlandic, an Inuit language.

West Greenlandic long held the fascination of linguists, as much for its linguistic isolation as for its polysynthetic nature. From the earliest descriptions of the Inuit language, dating back to the seventeenth century in some cases, scholars have struggled to describe and explain structures and categories alien to Indo-European languages. Three or four issues in particular have figured prominently in discussions of Inuit syntax, highlighting typological differences between the European and Inuit languages. These issues generally relate to methods of tracking noun phrases within clauses, such as case marking, pronominal agreement marking on verbs, and referential agreement marking on both verbs and nouns, and they include studies of ergativity, transitivity, and switch-reference. Despite some very good linguistic descriptions, however, some elements of Inuit syntax have resisted a satisfactory explanation. Explanations of some structures, such as ergative or antipassive clauses, which make reference solely to syntactic rules, frequently result in many exceptions, and inevitably, nonsyntactic elements creep into these explanations. What governs ergative versus antipassive or accusative case marking and transitive or intransitive marking on verbs seems to have something to do with definiteness, givenness, or perhaps information flow; and coreferential or noncoreferential marking between noun phrases of two clauses seems to be governed by "psychological subject" rather than syntactic subject. Perhaps, then, the factor governing agreement marking is not strictly syntactic. If so, then what does determine agreement marking in West Greenlandic, and what implications does this have for syntactic theory? The consistency with which context is implicated in explanations of agreement constructions suggests that discourse is important, and if discourse can predictably affect syntactic constructions, then it must have predictable structural components, as do syntax and semantics, which are necessary to an adequate syntactic description of linguistic structure.

## 1.1 Overview of West Greenlandic grammar

Greenlandic is an Inuit dialect within the Eskimo branch of Eskimo-Aleut, which is spoken in the Arctic from the Chukchi Peninsula in Siberia to Greenland. Inuit consists of a continuum of closely related and relatively mutually intelligible dialects, spoken from Norton Sound in Alaska to East Greenland. Within Greenlandic, there are three major regional dialects, Polar Eskimo, West Greenlandic, and East Greenlandic. The dialect considered here is primarily the variety of West Greenlandic spoken in Nuuk and Sisimiut in Central West Greenland, although some data were also collected from speakers of Southern West Greenlandic.

The inventory of West Greenlandic phonemes is given in Table 0.1; for detailed phonological information on West Greenlandic, the reader is directed to Swadesh (1946) and especially Rischel (1974). There are a number of phonological and morphophonological processes that complicate the study of word formation and morphological parsing, including the reflexes of Proto-Eskimo phonemes that have disappeared but left traces, consonant and vowel assimilation in clusters (the practical effect of which has been to increase the number of homophonic lexemes and morphemes; see, for example, Dorais 1990:172), retention or dropping of initial and final elements of morphemes in word formation, allomorphic alternations of initial consonants of verbal inflectional endings (e.g., /p/ after consonants, /v/ after vowels in indicative inflectional endings), and so forth. For more on the morphophonology of Greenlandic, see Kleinschmidt (1851), Schultz-Lorenzen (1945), Bergsland (1955), and Fortescue (1984).

West Greenlandic words consist of a stem, from zero to five or more derivational suffixes (called postbases in the literature), and inflectional suffixes. There is only one prefix, *-ta-*, associated with anaphoric reference on deictic particles. The two most important word classes are nouns and verbs; there are smaller closed classes of particles and lexicalized adverbs, and demonstratives.

West Greenlandic is highly polysynthetic; indeed, it is considered extreme in comparison with other polysynthetic languages, preferring where possible a single lexical construction to a multilexical one. Both derivation and inflection are grammatically important. There are several hundred distinct derivational suffixes, many of which can be productively combined in multiple combinations (for more on the derivational suffixes, see Fortescue 1983). Many suffixes are class specific, being restricted to either nominal or verbal bases. They may elaborate the meaning of the stem without changing the part of speech, or they may change the part of speech, converting a noun stem to a verb stem or vice versa. This results in very productive processes of word formation, including the incorporation of nouns into the verbal structure.[1] Verbal possession and copular constructions are typically expressed through incorporation (example from Bergsland 1955:93):

(1.1)   palasinngorpoq
        *palasi -nngor-voq*
        priest-become-3SG.IND
        'he has become/became a priest'

Some complications arise from polysynthesis, including modifier stranding through the incorporation of the head of a noun phrase. In example 1.2 the stranded modifier of an incorporated noun is marked with the case the noun would otherwise have had, the instrumental, as an oblique object of an antipassive structure (about which there is more below) (example from Fortescue 1984:83):

(1.2)   *Nutaamik*      *umiarsuarnut*      *talittarviqarpoq*
        *nutaa-mik*     *umiarsuaq-nut*     *talittarvik-qaq-voq*
        new-INST        ship-TERM.PL        harbour-have-3SG.IND
        'There is a new harbour for ships'
        [lit. 'It has a new harbour for ships']

Tense and aspect are indicated via derivational morphemes. Tense morphemes are sparsely used and tend to have an aspectual component to

**Table 1.1** Nominal inflection

| CASE | FORM | PRIMARY FUNCTIONS |
| --- | --- | --- |
| Absolutive | o | Subject of intransitive clause, object of transitive clause |
| Relative | *-up* | Subject of transitive clause, possession |
| Localis | *-ni* | Location |
| Ablative | *-nit* | Movement from a location |
| Terminalis | *-nut* | Movement to a location |
| Vialis | *-gut* | Movement through a location or time |
| Equalis | *-tut* | Equality between two events, objects, etc. |
| Instrumental | *-nik* | Default case: instrumental construction, object of antipassive, stranded complement of incorporated noun, adverbial phrases, etc. |

their meaning; they occur immediately preceding the inflection. Far more common are the aspectual suffixes, which, through various combinations, allow fine aspectual distinctions to be made (see Fortescue 1983).

The inflectional system is every bit as rich. Within the nominal inflectional system, there are two grammatical cases, the absolutive and the relative (which functions both as the marker of the ergative and as the basis for marking possession). The absolutive marks subjects of intransitive clauses and objects of transitive clauses; subjects of transitive clauses are marked with the relative, or ergative, case. West Greenlandic is morphologically ergative: although they are case marked differently, subjects of transitive and intransitive clauses behave as a syntactic category for the purposes of clause combination. In addition to these, there are six oblique case markers: the instrumental, localis, ablative, terminalis, vialis, and equalis.[2] The morphophonemic forms of these case endings and their primary functions are shown in table 1.1; they are discussed in more detail in chapter 3. There are also possessive inflectional endings in all cases, and separate inflectional endings for demonstrative particles.

The verbal inflectional endings indicate mood, transitivity, person, and number. The latter two functions are largely fused, but mood and transitivity can often be identified through certain elements of the inflections. The first element of the inflectional ending indicates mood. There are four superordinate moods (indicative, interrogative, optative, and imperative) and four subordinate moods (causative, conditional, contemporative, and participial). The subordinate moods all tend to express temporal relationships to the main verb and may replace tense marking in some cases. The participial is closely related to nominalizations and relativizations. The identification of moods as superordinate or subordinate is somewhat misleading: the subordinate moods can occur as heads within a sentence (i.e., there is no superordinate mood). These sentences are explained by Bergsland (1955:62) as having particular discourse-relevant effects, as in the exclamatory force of a causative without a superordinate indicative, or as in the optative or imperative force of a contemporative in such circumstances. The morphophonemic forms of the moods and their primary functions are shown in table 1.2, and they are discussed in more detail in following chapters.

The second element of the inflectional ending indicates transitivity, at least in the superordinate moods. Transitive forms typically have the vowel-*a*-whereas intransitive forms have-*u*-. Person marking on verbs is linked with the transitivity of a clause. Greenlandic verbs can be transitive, intransitive, or reflexive; transitive clauses have pronominal marking indicating subject and object, whereas intransitive and reflexive clauses mark subject only. Transitivity in Greenlandic may be purely structural or mechanical; in this case, a verb may have transitive marking as a lexical requirement. It may, however, be syntactically motivated, in which case the speaker has a choice between a transitive or intransitive construction to express a concept. Verbs can be transitivized or detransitivized with derivational morphemes. Thus, verbs can be transitivized with the addition of a suffix (e.g.,-*uti*-, as in example 1.3), resulting in structures that are transitive or ditransitive (examples from P. Langgård, personal communication):

(1.3)    *majuarpoq*
        majuar-voq
        walk.upwards-3SG.IND
        'he walks upwards'

        majuuppaa
        *majuar-uti-vaa*
        walk.upwards-use.for-3SG.SUBJ/3SG.OBJ.IND
        'he brings it upwards'

**Table 1.2** Verbal inflection – moods

| SUPERORDINATE MOODS | FORM | PRIMARY FUNCTIONS |
|---|---|---|
| Indicative | *-p-/-v-* | Simple statements |
| Interrogative | *-p-/-v-* | Questions |
| Optative | *-l-* | Wishes |
| Imperative | *-g-* | Commands |
| Causative | *-ga-* | Past event relative to main clause; causation |
| Conditional | *-gu-* | Future event relative to main clause; condition |
| Participial | *-t-/-s* trans.*-g-* | Event simultaneous with that of main clause; nominalizations; switch reference |
| Contemporative | *-l-* | Default mood: event simultaneous with that of main clause, used for conjoining clauses in clause chain, for impersonal constructions, objects of transitive verbs, and manner of action, and to indicate subject coreference |

There are several ways to detransitivize verbs, with or without the use of detransitivizing postbases, resulting in structures that are reflexive, intransitive, passive, or antipassive. Example 1.5 illustrates a detransitivizing suffix, whereas examples 1.6 and 1.7 illustrate syntactic processes via modification of inflectional morphology:

(1.4)    Transitive (ergative)

> *Angutip*      *illu*            *takuaa*
> *Angut-p*     *illu-0*          *taku-va a*
> Angut-REL    house-ABS    see-3SG.SUBJ/3SG.OBJ.IND
> 'the man saw the house'

(1.5)   Intransitive
        *Angut*           *takusivoq*
        *angut-0*         *taku-si-voq*
        Angut-ABS    see-INTRANS-3SG.IND
        'the man sees

(1.6)   Passive
        *illu*            *(Angutimut)*        *takuneqarpoq*
        *illu-0*          *Angut-mut*          *taku-neqaq-voq*
        house-ABS    Angut-TERM    see-PASS-3SG.IND
        'The house is/was seen (by the man)'

(1.7)   Antipassive
        *Angut*           *illumik*            *takuvoq*
        *Angut-0*         *illu-mik*           *taku-voq*
        Angut-ABS    house-INST    see-3SG.IND
        The man saw a house'

Both passive and antipassive clauses are morphologically intransitive, as
the verb is marked for subject only. In passive structures, the subject has
been removed from its direct relationship with the verb, and the erstwhile
object has taken its place. In antipassive structures, the object has been
removed from its direct relationship with the verb, and no other nominal
has taken its place. The agents of passive clauses, if expressed, are case
marked with ablative or terminalis; the objects of antipassive structures
have instrumental rather than absolutive case marking.

Both nominal and verbal inflections mark four persons (1, 2, 3 coreferential, and 3 noncoreferential)[3] and two numbers (singular and plural,
with occasional vestiges of an old dual). In verbs, only subordinate moods
differentiate between 3 coreferential and noncoreferential persons. One
particularity of the contemporative is that in its transitive form, the inflectional suffix does not coindex the subject (example from Fortescue 1991:55):

(1.8)   *illu*            *tikillugu*       *Piitaq*          *takuaa*
        *illu-0*          *tikiC-lugu*      *Piitaq-0*        *taku-vaa*
        house-ABS    come.to-      Piitaq-ABS    see-3SG.SUBJ/
                          3NC.SG.CT                      3SG.OBJ.IND
        'Coming up to the house, he saw Piitaq'

The 3 noncoreferential inflectional ending coindexes the object, 'house', in the first clause. Because the subject of the contemporative is most often coreferential with that of the superordinate verb, as in example 1.5, it has been interpreted as a marker of coreference. The participial only differentiates between coreferential and noncoreferential person in the transitive inflectional endings. It is often found in subordinate clauses with a subject different from that of the main clause, hence its association with switch-reference in grammars of West Greenlandic.

Nominal and verbal marking of person and number are morphologically similar, if not identical in some cases. The similarity is more obvious between the nominal and intransitive verbal inflections, as the transitive forms show much more fusion between person and number.

West Greenlandic is clause chaining, stringing clauses together using subordinate verbal moods for all but one clause. This is opposed to the Indo-European method of forming complex sentences, which can consist of combinations of coordinated or subordinated clauses (or both). Head-final word order is typically preferred (i.e., SOV clause order, postpositions, postposed conjunctions, suffixation only, and so forth), although word order variations are common and may have semantic and pragmatic effects, such as signaling emphasis, focus, and other discourse-relevant concepts. Information structure in Greenlandic is also signaled by distinct intonational units and by the relative ordering of the intonationally distinct utterances (Fortescue 1984:174). More details about clause chaining in Greenlandic are provided in the relevant discussions in following chapters.

## 1.2 Inuit language in syntactic theory

Many of these characteristics have been addressed in linguistic descriptions of the Inuit language, but not always in comprehensive ways. For a language to be adequately described, all the information needed to speak or use that language should be described at all levels of linguistic complexity, from the levels of phonology, morphology, and syntax, to those of semantics, discourse, pragmatics, sociolinguistics, and more. What is or is not described in a language, however, depends greatly on the theory used to describe it and on the assumptions made by that theory. Looking specifically at syntax, traditional studies prior to Chomsky tended to focus on the inflectional morphology and had little to say about derivational morphology or about actual sentence formation beyond normal word order.[4] With the development of modern theories of syntax from the 1950s on, linguistic descriptions became more specialized, and syntactic descriptions have gained tremendously in importance in the literature.

The number of studies of Inuit syntax has increased dramatically since the 1970s. Several theoretical approaches are reflected in these studies, differing in important ways in their approach to the study of language in general and in their focus within Inuit syntax in particular. The most influential approach has probably been one version or another of Chomskian syntax (transformational grammar, government-binding theory, generalized phrase structure grammar, and so forth), in which the purpose of linguistic study is to formulate detailed descriptions, or grammars, of languages, as models of the linguistic knowledge of native speakers. These models of languages as abstract computational systems focus almost exclusively on the interaction of syntactic, semantic, and phonological structures, as opposed to pragmatic knowledge, which involves nonlinguistic background information (i.e., contextual knowledge). Early Chomskian approaches to linguistic description are concerned with the relationships of nominal arguments to the verb and the relationships between related clauses (e.g., active and corresponding passive clauses, etc.), and this is reflected in studies of Inuit syntax from the 1970s and 1980s (e.g., Smith 1981). Sentences are seen as expanded verb phrases, with subjects and objects defined and controlled by the verb and its lexical properties. They are assumed to be formed at a linguistically abstract level, and explanations of structure are aimed at describing abstract rather than actual linguistic forms. Discrepancies between abstract and actual structural forms are explained as the result of various processes that place constraints on the production of ungrammatical forms. Ungrammatical forms are the results of violations of these constraints. In the field of Inuit studies, scholars writing with this approach are Bok-Bennema, Smith, Creider, and Sadock; much of the theoretical work in the 1970s seems to have been influenced to some degree by this approach. In the mid-1980s, Sadock developed autolexical syntax as an outgrowth of and in reaction to generalized phrase structure grammar, especially because of problems posed by West Greenlandic in the application of theoretical rules. The theories differ especially in the incorporation of morphology as an integral part of the grammar by autolexical syntax, and in the assumption of three independent but interactive faces in the grammar, morphology, syntax, and semantics, but the essential goals of both approaches — to find a model of language — are similar.

Relational grammar was one of a number of syntactic theories developed in response to Chomsky's theory of transformational grammar, and it differs significantly in both its theoretical assumptions and in its goal. The aim is to characterize languages themselves, rather than a model of linguistic knowledge. In particular, the study of a wide range of languages, and especially non-European languages, has been important in the determination of linguistic universals. Like the Chomskian approaches, relational grammar focuses on the relationships of nominal arguments and verbs in related clauses; however, an important difference is in the theoretical understanding of the nature of verbs and their arguments. In relational grammar, subjects and objects are seen as entities in relationship to but independent of the verb. They are hierarchically ranked with respect to each other, with subjects and direct objects in a more direct relationship with the verb than other, oblique objects. Sentences are related via the promotion or demotion of nominal arguments on the hierarchy. Each argument is intimately connected with a semantic role, which is retained despite the promotion or demotion of the argument. Related clauses are thus definable according to the combination of syntactic and semantic roles of arguments in each clause. Partly because of its application to languages with typologically similar characteristics to those of the Inuit language, relational grammar has been the approach of choice for a number of Eskimologists, including early Woodbury (although he started with transformational grammar and moved toward a more prosodic approach in the 1980s), Johnson (although with the added component of Montague grammar, a theory of semantics), and others.

There are other theoretical approaches that have been applied to the study of the Inuit dialects, although these have figured less prominently in the general field of linguistics. The French theorist Guillaume's theory of psychoméchanique, which focuses on the psychology of speakers and which views language as a means of generalizing and particularizing about experience, is the basis for Lowe's descriptions of Western Canadian Inuit dialects. According to Lowe, sentences consist of a topic of speech, which can be either nominal or predicative under different conditions, and the similarities between nominal possessive morphology and verbal morphology is accounted for via the notion of topic and description. In functionally based approaches, form and function are studied together by including pragmatic factors. Kalmár in particular has written from this point of view, and Woodbury has written a number of articles on the effect of prosodic features on the syntax; both strive for a description of language in use rather than one of innate linguistic knowledge.

The differences in theoretical approaches to the study if the Inuit dialects have naturally led to very different analytical results. The study of the Inuit dialects suffers, paradoxically, both from attempts to show that the Inuit language is structurally compatible with theories developed for specific and structurally very different languages, and from notions of difference arising from the exoticism of "Eskimo." In the first case, fundamental structural differences are brushed aside, and in the second, fundamental similarities with other languages are not considered. Chomskian approaches have tended to analyze the Inuit structures as variations of those found in (for example) English. Relational grammar, based on a wider array of typologically different languages, has been more neutral in this respect. The more psychologically and pragmatically based approaches have tended to produce analyses that emphasize the otherness of the Inuit language.

The results of these theoretical leanings are evident in the interest or lack thereof evinced in particular aspects of Inuit. Although the nature of categories such as noun and verb in the Inuit language have been widely discussed because of some striking similarities in nominal and verbal inflection, other aspects of word formation have not. For example, polysynthesis and incorporation both involve derivational morphology, an aspect of language use largely ignored by most theories of syntax. Some Eskimologists have written morphological accounts in more than usual detail (e.g., Fortescue 1980), but these are more descriptive than theoretical, and there were few treatises outside the traditional grammars regarding polysynthesis or incorporation in the Inuit language until the mid- to late 1980s, as we see from Sadock (1984) and Baker (1988). Clause chaining as a phenomenon has also not been addressed in theoretical studies of the Inuit languages: sentence formation has largely been discussed in terms of word order and simple clause conjoining, and atheoretical descriptions of relative clause order and verb moods (Fortescue 1984 has provided the most complete atheoretical description of any of the Inuit dialects). However, this too is changing, as we see from studies of switch-reference, one of the phenomena known to co-occur with clause chaining (Fortescue 1991). As evidenced by the works of Lowe (1985), Kalmár (1979b), Woodbury (1977), and Bok-Bennema (1991), ergativity has been the most actively discussed from a theoretical point of view, and it is therefore presented in proportionately more detail below. The existence of ergativity has also fueled a number of separate but related discussions, including the problem of the formal, but not functional, identity of ergative and possessive constructions; the nominal or verbal character of Inuit verbs or nouns; the existence of both ergative and accusative-like (i.e., antipassive) structures; and the question of subjecthood.

Ergative case marking on the subjects of transitive clauses and transitive pronominal marking on the transitive verbs show obvious similarities with possessive marking:

(1.9)   Possessive
        *Angutip*       *illua*
        *Angut-p*       *illu-a*
        Angut-REL    house-3SG.POS.ABS
        'the man's house'

(1.10)  Ergative
        *Angutip*       *illu*          *takuaa*
        *Angut-p*       *illu-0*        *taku-va a*
        Angut-REL    house-ABS    see-3SG.SUBJ/3SG.OBJ.IND
        'the man saw the house'

This has led to proposals that ergative clauses are possessives or that possessives are simplified ergative clauses. Lowe (1985), for example, explains transitive sentences with ergative constructions as possessor relations: a sentence such as example 1.10 cannot be properly translated without taking possessive semantics into consideration. Thus, the above sentence is 'the man's house (is) the seen thing', in effect a verbless equational construction with a passive participle rather than a true transitive construction. Kalmár (1979b) argues along the same lines but reverses the equation: possessive constructions are clauses, the possessum being the predicator and the possessor the subject; the object is unexpressed. Thus, 'the man's house' above must be viewed as 'the *x* such that the man houses it'. The emphasis in these approaches is on a fundamentally different expressive capability between European languages and the Inuit language.

Bok-Bennema (1991), in perhaps the most exhaustive and also theory-dependent discussion of ergativity in Inuktitut, sees the different alignment of case in Inuktitut as a property of verb case-assignment capabilities: transitive verbs cannot always assign accusative case in Inuktitut; in other words, they vary from standard accusative case-assignment capabilities in language in general. Ergative case is renamed genitive, because of the similarity between genitive (i.e., possessive) and ergative inflection. Accusative, or antipassive, structures arise because in some cases transitive verbs can assign accusative case. None of these approaches seems to allow for the possibility that ergative case and possession are historically related but not necessarily synchronically linked (Fortescue 1995 in fact addresses this point).

The formal identity between ergative and possessive constructions is one of the reasons often given for claiming that Inuit verbs are in fact nouns (the nominalist theory, attributed to Hammerich 1951), or that nouns are in fact verbs (Kalmár 1979b). The identification of nominal and verbal categories in the Inuit language has seemed problematic for a number of reasons, including not only the relation between ergativity and possession but also the productivity of derivational processes. Thus, verbs can be readily nominalized and nouns verbalized, in some cases a number of times within a word:

(1.11)    *ajoqeqarsimannngitsuuppat*
          *ajoqi-qaq-sima-nngit-soq-u-ppat*
          catechist-have-PERF-NEG-PART-COP-3PL.NC.COND
          N-V-affix-affix-N-V-inflectional affix
          'if there hadn't been catechists . . .'

This easy and productive derivational means of word formation has led Lowe (1981) to suggest that words are formed at discourse level rather than at the level of thought in the Inuit dialects, in contrast to languages like English or French, in which words are fully formed at the level of thought before they are uttered. The issue continues to be raised from time to time, but current opinion holds that there are independent noun and verb stems.

Further, many derivational suffixes are obsolescent, only mildly productive, or limited in scope of applicability, and some combinations of suffixes are now regarded as lexicalized or semilexicalized (see Fortescue 1980). The existence of such constructions suggests that although speakers of Inuit dialects may have a great deal of freedom in word formation, there is nevertheless a level that includes words as they are conceptualized in less morphologically productive languages.

In addition to ergative structures, the Inuit language also has passive and antipassive[5] structures (see examples 1.6 and 1.7), all of which have also been the subject of a number of studies. Woodbury (1977) and Bok-Bennema (1991) explain the occurrence of both structures within a generative theoretical framework, but their explanations require many rules and constraints. Bok-Bennema links the two structures to the case-assigning abilities of the verbs, as mentioned previously; in her view, antipassives are not intransitive but nominative-accusative constructions. Johnson (1980), using a relational grammar approach, views the antipassive as a construction in which the direct object is no longer in a direct relation with the verb and is therefore no longer transitive. The issue has not been settled.

The existence of both structures was very early linked to pragmatic ideas of definiteness: ergative structures are used where the object is definite, and antipassive (also called intransitive, half-transitive, or accusative) structures where the object is indefinite (Kleinschmidt 1968 (1851), among others). This link has been challenged (e.g., Kalmár 1979a, Johnson 1980, Bittner 1987), as examples of definite objects in antipassive structures are common (e.g., proper names) and vice versa. The inadequacy of such an interpretation has long been recognized, and merely points to the problem inherent in assuming the existence of a category in one language that clearly exists in another: whereas there exist a definite and indefinite article in English, Danish, and French, there is no such article, independent or affixal, in the Inuit dialects. Most scholars do, however, feel that there is some pragmatic, functional difference between the two structures, whether it be degree of definiteness, givenness, focus on the object or the verb, and so on. (Bittner 1987 proposes a semantic difference based on scope.)

The description of ergative case in various non–Western European languages in the twentieth century eventually led to a reevaluation of the traditional notion of subject. In nominative-accusative languages, a category is easily established, by case marking, whereby the nominatively marked direct arguments of verbs are called subjects; this category includes the noun phrases that have the same syntactic function in both transitive and intransitive clauses. In ergative languages, however, a single case, the absolutive, includes the subject of intransitive clauses and the object of transitive clauses. A definitive definition for subject is still lacking, although the list of subject-like properties proposed by Keenan (1976) is still widely accepted. Not surprisingly, subjecthood in Inuit has also been the subject of some discussion. Nowak (1993) argues that both the absolutive object and the ergative subject of transitive clauses have subject-like properties in Inuktitut, and Inuktitut must be seen as having no single subject, although she views the instrumentally marked object of antipassive constructions as the only direct object. Others, such as Johnson (1980), assume that subject is a syntactic category independent of the relatively superficial case marking, and that ergative and absolutive are not independent categories in Inuktitut.

Ergativity is perhaps the feature of Eskimo syntax that has spawned the most discussion, but it is not the only one. The nature of incorporation has been addressed by Sadock (1980, 1991), especially in his development of autolexical syntax, and by Baker (1988) among others.[6] Switch-reference, the mechanism by which a language marks a noun phrase (usually the subject) in one clause as coreferential or not with a noun phrase (usually the subject) in another clause, has been studied by Woodbury (1982) and Fortescue (1991). Fortescue has tended to take a traditionally descriptive rather than theoretical approach to language description, but he suggests the possibility of pragmatic factors at work, such that psychological subject, or topic, determines switch-reference marking in anomalous situations. Finally, the verb moods have often been discussed, from both descriptive and theoretical approaches (for the latter, see works such as Johns 1993, 1995). Kalmár (1979a, 1982) suggests a pragmatically based distribution of the various moods, related to foregrounding and backgrounding strategies in discourse.

All the syntactic approaches described here have offered insights into the structure of the Inuit language, and some have been relatively successful in my view. For example, some structures, such as antipassives, have been widely analyzed in many languages and are, if not fully understood, at least structurally predictable, both cross-linguistically and within the language studied. The antipassive in the Inuit language can be viewed as a structure in which the direct object has been demoted, in relational terms, to the status of an oblique object. This explains the use of the instrumental in marking this object, rather than of the absolutive or ergative. It also accounts for the lack of transitive marking in the verb, the inability of some verbs in antipassive constructions to passivize, and the inability to perform dative movement in antipassive clauses. These facts argue for an antipassive rather than accusative interpretation of such structures.

Syntax alone, however, is insufficient, and all the above-mentioned theories have distinct limitations to their explanatory value. For example, most of the theoretical attempts to explain ergativity in the Inuit language are left with the problem of explaining morphologically ergative case assignment in the face of a nominative-accusative syntactic system. Neither the Chomsky-derived theories nor relational grammar can satisfactorily account for the morphological processes such as incorporation in the Inuit language. The relational explanation of antipassives does not explain the motivation for the demotion of the direct object, as opposed to the passive, in which the promotion of one argument entails the demotion of another. The psychoméchanique approach that Lowe favors does not suggest a satisfactory explanation of the difference between passive and transitive constructions, nor does it capture cross-linguistic tendencies as other theories seem to.

In studies of the various Inuit dialects, there is a consistent appeal to factors beyond the syntactic level in explanations of various syntactic phenomena (despite the theoretical aversion to such factors by the Chomskian approaches). It has been acknowledged since the early days of transformational grammar that a full description of a language must assume the interaction of more than one level of linguistic structure. Traditionally, these levels included phonology, syntax, and semantics. Sadock (1991) argues for the necessity of adding morphology to this set of linguistic levels. In view of the limitations of the theoretical explanations of the various West Greenlandic structures discussed above, there have been periodic attempts to include discourse in this set as well. For example, a pragmatic, or discourse-level, function for the distribution of ergative and antipassive structures has been suggested explicitly by Johnson (1980) and Kalmár (1979a), and suggested as possible by Fortescue (1984). P. Langgård (personal communication) has also made observations that support such an interpretation.

There are other problems besides that of a particular syntactic theory limiting one's study of grammatical structure to that of sentence structure; these lend support for the consideration of discourse in analyses of some syntactic structures. For example, by looking only at decontextualized sentences, or by focusing on simple clause combinations rather than chains in context, no one has noted the relatively rare occurrence of either ergative or antipassive structures as opposed to true intransitive constructions in discourse; yet ergative and antipassive structures are the most common topic of syntactic investigation in Inuit languages. Furthermore, their importance relative to each other has not been investigated, but as I will show in chapter 3, ergative constructions far outnumber antipassives. Such information must be accounted for in any explanation of their function, yet this information comes only from the study of connected discourse.

Other problems have their origin in the assumption that the same grammatical categories exist in West Greenlandic as do in English or other more commonly studied languages. Identifying ergative constructions with definiteness of the direct object and antipassive constructions with indefiniteness of the object is problematic in part because there is no independent morphological category of definiteness in West Greenlandic.

Alternatively, a problem may be a reflection of the different and unequal roles of syntax and discourse in the respective languages. In English, there appear to be clear sentence boundaries, strong subject properties, and so forth, which suggest a strong role for syntax in English grammar. In West Greenlandic and many other non-Indo-European languages, clause combination is qualitatively different, and Western linguists have noticed preferences for far longer "sentences" (Longacre 1985) than would be acceptable in English, for example. In morphologically ergative languages, the notion of subject as the most relevant category has sometimes been called into question, and in some cases it is information flow in texts rather than subject that is tracked through case marking. These ideas suggest that some languages may prefer to track information of various kinds in larger linguistic groupings than clause or sentence level. Thus, analyses of such languages based on clause or sentence structure alone would turn out to be misleading and inadequate. To return to the notion of definiteness, this assumes prior context, usually outside the clause, and it is this feature that recurs in explanations of the distribution of ergativity in West Greenlandic.

If definiteness is not a relevant category in Greenlandic, then some other discourse feature must be.

### 1.3 Approaches to the study of discourse

The problems associated with the study of decontextualized sentences in the Inuit dialects suggest that clause structure does not depend exclusively on syntactic factors. This is evident in the frequent appeal to pragmatics and discourse to account for exceptions to a syntactic theory. Inevitably, we must systematically investigate discourse at a structural level. The question is how to study discourse: although there are many approaches to discourse, it is a relatively new field for structuralists, and it is not clear what the elements of discourse are. In other fields of structural linguistics, there are elements that have had descriptive usefulness within those fields, such as the phoneme in phonology, the morpheme in morphology, arguments, syntactic, and semantic roles within syntax, and so forth. There is a strong tendency to describe discourse structure only in relation to other levels of linguistic structure, similar to the way in which morphology was once subordinated to syntax. For example, within studies of syntax, discourse structure is often discussed in terms of information flow, or topic-comment structure, within the clause: the relevance of context is secondary to the clause itself. This seems counterintuitive: to study the structure of discourse, we must look beyond the clause. A first task, therefore, must be to determine the structural units of contextualized language.[7]

If studies of Eskimo have shown the relevance of discourse in the analysis of syntactic structures, they have not successfully and consistently incorporated discourse in these syntactic analyses. This may be due to the lack of a delimited definition of discourse and of the relevant features to be investigated. Discourse can be defined as the study of language in context, but there are many kinds of context. For example, context can imply the cultural and social setting and expectations of a discourse, information that is generally assumed to be extralinguistic, or it can refer simply to the surrounding (linguistic) text. Discourse can be identified as any text (see de Beaugrande and Dressler 1981), regardless of size or free-standing syntactic grammaticality, but it can also be described as the study of larger-than-sentence-level units. Further, the rules for the use of language change from oral to written language, from narrative to oratory, from monologue to dialogue, and so forth.

Other aspects of discourse that are relevant to syntax, such as differences arising from culturally specific ways of using language in argumentation (Young 1994), for example, or grammatical differences between elements of a particular discourse genre, such as the narrative (Labov 1972), have also been studied. Few studies, however, show that the syntax is affected by the discourse; rather, they show that particular syntactic constructions, described in independent syntactic analyses, are expected in certain contextual environments. What studies of the Inuit language suggest, however, is that the discourse can affect the syntax, not just in the choice of constructions, but in the actual constructions. If, for example, it is true that ergative constructions in Inuktitut can be characterized as indicating the definiteness of the object, then it is a pragmatic factor that controls ergativity. (I will show in the following chapters that ergativity is dependent on the discourse, but not because of definiteness.)

In the literature, it is possible to distinguish at least four approaches to the study of discourse structure: syntactic, pragmatic, textual, and social. Some are more relevant to this study than others, and none are so well defined as to exclude the rest.

Although they differ widely in both assumptions and scope, most studies within what might be called a syntactic approach to discourse use discourse phenomena to explain syntactic structures, while never discussing structures greater than the sentence. In most cases, the discourse features are incorporated into syntactic analyses by appealing to semantics (e.g., level of agency, lexical features, etc.) or semantically based reasoning (e.g., the use of formal logic). Some, such as Kuno (1987) and Fleischman and Waugh (1991), incorporate pragmatic or discourse-level explanations, such as point of view, into the traditionally generative syntactic analyses of sentences, thereby expanding the scope of, while still maintaining a model-oriented approach to, the study of syntax. Kuno, for example, suggests a parallel between the interpretations of lexically ambiguous sentences and cognitive processes, as in visual interpretations of the Necker cube (a cube drawn in such a way that it is ambiguous as to which surface is interpreted as the front face). He proposes a series of semantic constraints on syntactic constructions to account for lexical ambiguities, particularly in the use of pronouns, which parallel generative constraints. Other scholars come from a functionalist tradition. Foley and Van Valin (1984), for example, describe syntactic systems, the components of which include case marking, predication, and clause linkage, at two levels of analysis. At one level is the actual morphosyntactic construction; at another level, semantic, or logical, structure describes the predicate and its arguments. Pragmatic notions such as illocutionary force, presupposition, topicality, and definiteness belong to the latter.

Whatever the theoretical assumptions, syntactically based studies of discourse are often unsuccessful for the very simple reason that most never study structures larger than the sentence, and most sentences used in analyses are decontextualized or invented. These studies are therefore not based in discourse. Many sentences, whether elicited or invented, are structures that may be grammatically correct but are unlikely to occur in actual speech (e.g., 'the man saw the boy'). This is particularly important in analyses of discourse-dependent concepts such as anaphora. By confining studies of anaphora to the sentence, for example, the range of acceptable structures is restricted, and exceptions to anaphoric reference within the sentence are usually dealt with in model-dependent ways. In generative approaches, exceptions are explained by proposing new features, often specific to the exceptions, a practice that lends itself to being interpreted as ad hoc. Kuno (1987), for example, proposes a feature [+reflexive] to explain the use of reflexive pronouns in English; the feature is assigned to a sentence before its interpretation. It is hard to see how this feature reflects the more general cognitive processes he describes. In Foley and Van Valin (1984) , features tend to be proposed through componential semantic analysis as needed, and descriptions of phrase-level structure tend to suffer in favor of clause-level descriptions. Again, this approach reveals little about interclausal semantics. By focusing on semantic relations as developed in the traditions of logic and formal syntax, Foley and Van Valin (1984) reveal little about communicative and social functions of language, and pragmatics plays almost no role in their linguistic descriptions.

It is nevertheless evident in the introductions of many works that there is some intuitive appeal to the notion that discourse not only affects sentence structure, but that it has structure itself. The current impasse in syntactically based studies of discourse structure is largely due to the newness of the field. It is because of a long tradition of grammatical and syntactic study that notions such as subject, object, ergativity, tense-aspect, and so on, are useful in describing sentential structure.

Explanations of the distribution patterns of various parts of sentences often fall within a pragmatic approach to discourse, for lack of a better term. Again, scholars differ widely in their assumptions and focus, but they tend to agree on the importance of such notions as focus, givenness, coreference and cohesion, topicalization, and theme, many of which originated with the Prague School of Linguistics. Early Praguian studies of syntax focused on the effect that semantic notions such as agency and discourse notions such as theme (referring to the first part of the linear sequence of a clause) have on the realization of a sentence. These studies introduced the term "theme" as a way of characterizing sentence structure based on information flow. For example, in a summary of the general approaches to linguistics by the Prague School, Vachek (1966), crediting Mathesius (1964a, 1964b), suggests the possibility that languages differ with respect to what their subjects categorize. Based on the regular use of nominalizations and passives by English, as opposed to Czech, and on the regular use of subjectless clauses by Czech, as opposed to English, he suggests the possibility that English subjects express theme and Czech subjects agent. In the 1960s the concept of theme as a factor in studies of discourse was further developed and systematized by Halliday, particularly with respect to transitivity (1967a, 1967b, 1968; see chapter 3 for a discussion of his contributions to discourse studies). Thematicity shows up in the work of later linguists, such as Kalmár (1979a), Cartier (1985), and Du Bois (1987), to explain the existence and distribution of various syntactic phenomena that are relevant to the study of West Greenlandic (e.g., ergativity, tense-aspect, case; see chapter 3). Du Bois, for example, correlates absolutive noun phrases in ergative languages with the introduction of new information in discourse and suggests that subjecthood can be determined not only by a set of characteristics that include agency, focus, and so on (cf. Keenan 1976) but also by information flow.

Another distinct subset of pragmatically based approaches includes those studies heavily influenced by Austin's lectures (1962) on expressions of illocutionary acts and the relevance of referential meaning and context. Speech act theory is an outgrowth of these kinds of considerations, although later studies of speech acts more closely resemble the formal study of logic (see Levinson 1983 for a discussion of Searle and other speech act theorists) than the study of syntax. Many European and American functionalists (including Foley and Van Valin 1984) base their syntactic work on the effect of speaker intention and presupposition on clause structure.

Finally, some scholars, such as Givón (1979a) and Garcia (1979), have sometimes rejected the existence of syntax altogether, relying on context and communicative principles as the structural bases of discourse. For example, Givón (1979a) argues that there are many facts supporting the existence of a structural level we call syntax, but that syntax has no independent existence apart from discourse structure.

Pragmatically based approaches suffer from a different set of problems than syntactically based ones, the most general one being the dependence on personal interpretation of the status of textual information, such as what is essential versus nonessential, backgrounded versus non-backgrounded, and new versus given information. The variables are many, the range of interpretations is wide, and the resulting degree of predictability and repeatability, in the scientific sense, is low. There is an intuitive appeal for discussions of information status in discourse analyses, because of its role in the choice of sentence structure in language production and interpretation. However, attempts to define precise roles for information status often have limited success, perhaps because many studies have been limited to one or two sets of pragmatic factors (e.g., focus vs. topicalization, given vs. new information, etc.), or if more are involved, they are still treated as discrete from other grammatical information. For example, Kalmár (1979b), in his study of Inuktitut case, proposes a three-way distinction for the function of the verb modes (which affect the assignment of case), involving essential versus background information, development versus elaboration, and event versus participant focus. The modes reflect particular combinations of these factors; for example, the indicative reflects essential information, development, and event focus, whereas the contemporative reflects event focus but elaboration and background information. However, his determinations of essential and nonessential information, and so on, are debatable, and they ignore the more commonly identified grammatical functions of the modes.

Another frequent problem with pragmatic approaches is the decreased ability to account for syntactic phenomena, especially in a typologically, cross-linguistically useful way. Givón (1979a), Garcia (1979), and Kalmár

(1979b) all argue for the functional determination of sentential structures in given contexts. But in rejecting theoretical assumptions of syntactic theories, they also reject information accounted for within those theories. For example, Kalmár (1979a) rejects the relational grammar notion of the antipassive as a structure in which an object is demoted to nonobject status, thereby reducing the transitivity of the clause. Whether or not one agrees with relational grammar, the theory does address the status of the object (or lack thereof) in the verbal morphology of the Inuit language. Object demotion is one way of explaining the fact that both subject and object are marked verbally in transitive clauses but only subject is in antipassive constructions, and further, the verbal inflection of antipassive and intransitive clauses is identical. In addition, object demotion appears to be useful in explaining case marking in antipassive structures cross-linguistically. For Kalmár (1979a) the antipassive retains its level of transitivity but it specifically indicates the indefinite status of the object. The morphological identity of the verbal inflection in antipassive and intransitive constructions remains unaccounted for. Explanations of sentence structure based on pragmatics alone often fail to explain systematic structural information.

Syntactic approaches tend to lack discourse-level data, and therefore discourse-level structure; pragmatic approaches tend to use texts (i.e., greater-than-sentence-level discourse) as the basis for analyses which are nevertheless still sentential in nature. Focus, topic, verbal tense-aspect, and the role of subject or object are still explained within the boundaries of the sentence, although the context is considered.

Both textual and sociological approaches to discourse analysis primarily deal with larger-than-clause-level language, and discourse is viewed as qualitatively different from syntax. In some textual approaches, the study of syntax, if sentence structure is addressed, is often undertaken not as the study of formal sentence construction as in modern syntactic theories, but as one of proposition construction. Longacre (1976) and Grimes (1975) are both concerned with the logical and semantic relationships between words and between clauses, but their approach is quite different from that of standard linguistic theories. For example, Grimes's semantic roles are based on discourse rather than syntactic factors (e.g., orientation and process roles), and Longacre's predicate calculus has more to do with notions than with the actions of verbs per se.

In a textual approach to discourse analysis, the structures of texts are often analyzed in terms of plot and notional development, event and setting information, and so forth. In this approach, structural notions that relate to syntax include semantic roles, constituent structures, predication, and theme. Textual approaches also tend to focus on the suprasentential organization of texts, such as narrative structure, thematic development, character and setting development, and argument structure (where argument refers to a method of developing ideas for the purpose of convincing or persuading, rather than to its syntactic definition as a complement of the verb). A number of textual scholars come from nonlinguistic backgrounds or approach the study of discourse from traditionally nonlinguistic points of view, as do Grimes, who brings methods of biblical exegesis and rhetoric to the study of discourse, and Toolan (1988), who discusses narrative as a literary form. Scholars have most often analyzed either written materials or traditional narratives, leaving other forms of discourse largely untouched (exceptions being Jones 1977 and McCune 1983).

The European tradition in text linguistics differs from the American in being more programmatic and closer to European functional linguistics than to rhetoric or exegesis. Here, a text is viewed as a string of well-formed sentences in sequence, for which a grammar is constructed with separate components for the speaker and the hearer. Each component of the grammar is part of an interactive system of levels of structure (including syntax, semantics, and pragmatics), and texts are analyzed with respect to operations that manipulate units and patterns of text formation. For some, the grammar is based on or modeled after formal logic; others, such as de Beaugrande and Dressler (1981), prefer a less formalized approach to capturing actual usage.

In some ways, European text linguistics is similar to the Tagmemics School, in which the emphasis is on viewing language as a composite of different levels, each indivisible from the other and each with indistinct boundaries. The unit of linguistic study is the result of a cluster of features in context; the context is heavily dependent on viewpoint. The influence of tagmemics is felt in the work of scholars such as Jones (1977), Longacre (1976), Rhodes (1992), and McCune (1983). Jones, for example, focuses on the identification of three things: (1) theme at different hierarchical levels of discourse, where theme is defined as the most important conceptual part of the text; (2) culturally defined scripts, or outlines of discourses that are conventionally structured and recognizable; and (3) syntactic phenomena that seem to be dependent on textual and contextual, rather than syntactical, factors. The identification of theme, however, is often problematic. Insofar as hearers must reconstruct the theme or topic a speaker has in mind, based on linguistic cues, the interpretation of theme is variable in any given discourse. This variability in interpretation itself becomes the focus of studies by R. Rhodes (personal communication) and McCune (1983). Rhodes, for example, suggests that themes, defined specifically as the propositional content of clauses, have different ranking and scope with respect to one another within texts. Textual ambiguities, analogous to syntactic ambiguities, arise because of the possibility of different interpretations of themes by each hearer of a text. The theme of a text is therefore determined by individual judgments of native speakers. Other scholars focus instead on questions on the cultural context of texts and on phrasing and form-content parallelisms. In a combination of textual, sociological, and linguistic (but not necessarily syntactic) approaches, Hymes (1981) shows how important is a knowledge of the culture within which the discourse is produced in order to interpret its theme, and how different speakers' beliefs about the functions of narratives is reflected in the structure.

Finally, there exists a large corpus of work on discourse based on social and cultural sociolinguistic considerations in language use, much of which will lie outside the scope of this book. Sociolinguistic approaches are often characterized by discourses elicited in the field. Sociolinguistic discourse analyses may focus on presuppositions, inferences, shared cultural information, communicative intent, levels of politeness, social stratification, turn-taking strategies, and so forth. In addition, many studies involve observations of structural differences in language across different socioeconomic strata, and such studies may lead to syntactic analyses of discourse (e.g., Labov's 1972 study of distributional patterns of sentence elements in narrative discourse). Other studies incorporate structural analyses with more sociologically based information, as does Schiffrin (1987). In a study of the role of discourse markers (e.g., 'oh', 'well', etc.) in English, she finds that markers act as boundaries "not only at different social organizational levels, but at different levels of the organization of talk" (1987:36). These markers behave differently at different levels of talk; for example, 'and'

coordinates two like constituent phrases at syntactic levels but not necessarily at discourse levels.

Neither textually nor sociologically based analyses generally address syntactic considerations in analyses of linguistic structure. Neither approach, of
course, makes any claim to answer syntactic questions, and those questions
may understandably be considered outside the scope of research. Nevertheless, the interconnection of discourse and syntactic structure is noted, and
may also be the focus of some studies. In the more structurally detailed
discussions of discourse, such as those of Longacre (1976) and Grimes
(1975), clause-level phenomena are considered, the role of subordination
in paragraphing strategies is presented, and coreference is particularly
important. Schiffrin's interpretation of 'oh' as an information management
marker, or something that shifts the discourse participants' orientation to
information by replacing one information unit with another, can easily
be restated in syntactic terms, as something that marks the boundaries
between constituents. Finally, among the scholars reviewed here, Rhodes
has a particularly strong background in purely syntactic theories, methods
of argumentation, and goals, which translates into an understanding of
the structural relationship between syntax and discourse.

In none of the approaches to discourse analysis reviewed here is there a
standardized way of relating discourse and syntax. The two are most frequently viewed as fundamentally different kinds of structures, and not merely
as different levels of linguistic structure. This difference often "explains"
exceptional syntactic structures. A mismatch between the requirements of
syntactic well-formedness and the pragmatic and social requirements in
the exchange of information may explain an instance of unusual anaphoric
agreement, for example. As long as these mismatches remain exceptional,
discourse and syntax can be viewed as different kinds of linguistic structure with no serious theoretical implications. If the relationship between
syntactic and discourse requirements is regular, however, and discourse
requirements are seen to regularly affect the outcome in the construction
of clauses, then there will have to be a predictable way of relating the two
levels of linguistic structure.

The great difference between syntax and discourse is, of course, that
whereas sentences may be studied in isolation, discourse requires linguistic context. Neighboring clauses within a text bear some relationship to

each other; usually they share one or more entity. The tracking of entities across clause boundaries is essentially the study of cohesion. In syntactic approaches to the study of discourse, a description of cohesion may focus on the constraints on (pronominal) anaphora; in pragmatic approaches, on the status of information in a clause; in textual approaches, on (thematic) continuity; and in sociological approaches, on shared sociocultural knowledge. Cohesion is what differentiates a text from a group of random sentences. Any description of discourses involving more than one sentence must in some way account for cohesive elements within these discourses.

On the other hand, both syntax and discourse share the important characteristic of needing to track entities within a structural unit. In the syntax, a tracking mechanism is required when there is more than one entity of a particular kind in a clause or across linked clauses. For example, in transitive and ditransitive sentences, there must be a way to distinguish between the two, three, or more noun phrases in a sentence. Important noun phrases, such as subjects, are often tracked in more than one way: they may be case marked, pronominally marked on the verb, given a particular slot in the ordering of words in a clause, and so forth. Within texts, the same kinds of issues are found: cohesive devices must provide various ways of tracking entities within a text. The question is, what are the analogous entities within a text, and what are the cohesive devices?

Each level of linguistic structure has components that are widely accepted as valid, although the definitions of each component may vary slightly depending on one's theoretical approach. In syntax, for example, there are arguments and predicates, syntactic roles such as subject and object, and semantic roles such as agent and patient. These components are recognized by cross-linguistically common devices for identifying and distinguishing them. For example, arguments in a clause are distinguished from each other in predictable ways, often through the tracking devices discussed above. Similar components as yet have rarely been posited for discourse, but they can be imagined. Just as there are nominal arguments within a clause, there are often recurring nominals with importance in a stretch of discourse. Just as the different nominals play different roles, or functions, in a clause, nominals in a text show up in different constructions, reflecting their relative roles within the text. Finally, just as the difference between nominal arguments in a clause is marked in some way, whether by morphological means or word order, and so forth, there are often means of identifying the important nominals within a text, including through the use of anaphoric pronouns, deixis, and so forth.

There are, therefore, good reasons for supposing that concepts primarily applied to the study of syntactic structure can be extended to the study of discourse structure. These include the notion of constituent structure within discourse, that of discourse role, and the importance of tracking particular constituents within a text. Let us consider a concrete example of the application of syntactic structural concepts to discourse. In many traditional studies of discourse, the entities with unusual prominence or importance within a text are often called topic or theme. The two terms are often used interchangeably, and they are not used with particular consistency; however, there is general consensus that they refer to prominence of some kind within a text. In other levels of linguistic structure, two opposing categories are generally identified: nouns and verbs in the lexicon, arguments and predicates in the syntax. The latter are essentially nominal and verbal in character. The same sort of opposition is readily apparent in discourse as well: nominal entities with prominence within a text, and propositional information, analogous to predication, with prominence in the same text. The terms topic and theme, therefore, can be restricted to refer to nominal and propositional units of discourse, respectively (reasons for this are given more explicitly in chapter 2). Furthermore, just as subjects and objects are considered syntactic roles, topics can be considered as discourse roles: they will have a particular function within the text. This function will be reflected in various ways, including in the ways topics are tracked within a text, as opposed to the way nontopical entities are.

## 1.4 Theoretical approach to discourse structure in West Greenlandic

A satisfactory study of discourse must consider issues central to each of the approaches to discourse discussed above, including the effect of the discourse on the syntax, the patterns of information flow, the thematic development of a text, and the sociocultural context within which a text is produced. The emphasis of one set of issues over another of course depends on the goal of a particular linguistic description, but it is unlikely that ignoring any one of these sets of issues will result in a functionally adequate description. In my analyses, I favor a functional rather than model-dependent approach to the study of linguistics. In this study, I am concerned with the effect of linguistic context on clause structure, or evidence for the influence of discourse on syntactic structures and their distribution in texts. I am interested in finding structure in discourse in the way that we have long found structure in sentences. I use syntactic terminology and structural concepts, such as subjecthood and ergativity; however, I base my study on texts rather than sentences. Where applicable, I provide pragmatic and sociocultural information, but these figure less prominently in my analysis.

The premise of this study is that certain constructions that mark textual cohesion in West Greenlandic can best be understood by assuming that discourse roles such as topic rather than syntactic roles such as subject or object are the relevant structural items. I focus on one aspect of cohesion in texts, namely topic and thematic continuity as reflected by pronominal anaphora in verbal constructions. The terms topic and theme are restricted in specific ways that are justifiable but not yet standard in the literature. The focus of chapter 2, therefore, is a discussion of the notions and definitions of topic, theme, and discourse role, and their reflection in West Greenlandic.

The syntactic structures with which I am concerned are ergative and antipassive clauses, which have a nominal referential tracking function, traditionally held to be the marking of switch-reference in nouns, but as I will show, the marking of changes of theme. As I discussed in section 1.2, the transitive constructions in West Greenlandic show ergative patterns of case marking on the nominal arguments, and they have both subject and object pronominal agreement on the verb. The intransitive and detransitivized constructions have only subject pronominal agreement on the verb. In previous studies, these patterns of agreement have been linked with the pragmatic notions of givenness or definiteness, such that absolutive objects of transitive constructions are identified as given or definite, and instrumentally marked objects of detransitivized (antipassive) constructions are identified as new or indefinite. The inadequacy of the characterization has long been recognized and was discussed briefly in section 1.2. In chapter 3, I show that instead of referencing subjects and objects, pronominal marking in West Greenlandic references topics: absolutively marked nominals are local topics, and instrumentally marked objects of antipassives are nontopics.

The subordinate moods in West Greenlandic have the means to indicate what has been identified as switch-reference, specifically as subject coreference or lack thereof with the subject of a superordinate clause. In the causative and conditional moods, this is done by pronominal inflection on the verb. In the contemporative and the participial moods, however, pronominal inflection is paradigmatically incomplete,[8] and it is assumed that the contemporative and the participial are in complementary distribution as markers of switch-reference. Exceptions to a strict interpretation of switch-reference are common, both in the pronominal inflection and in the use of the contemporative and the participial. In chapter 4, I show that switch-reference is more systematically explained by assuming topic rather than subject coreference. The verb moods, however, differ in kind from other switch-reference mechanisms, and the use of the contemporative and the participial as switch-reference mechanisms is more likely a reflection of thematic rather than topic continuity or lack thereof, a reflection of their propositional rather than nominal semantics. Further, their use as markers of thematic continuity must be seen as only one, probably secondary, function; they are more likely moods that, like the causative and the conditional, reflect a system indicating time relative to the superordinate clause.

In the final chapter, I summarize the findings and theoretical notions introduced in this work. All of the data is found in the appendix. The data were collected as texts rather than through sentence elicitation, and the speakers themselves chose the texts. I did not collect controlled texts (as in the famous pear stories collected by Chafe 1980, in which speakers are asked to tell, in their own words, a selected story after having seen a film or pictures of the story). All of the data was collected in the form of personal recollections of past experiences. Most do not qualify as narratives in the Labovian sense (Labov 1972:360), that is, as temporally ordered sequential recountings of past experiences where changes in order result in changes in interpretation of the narrative. Whereas Labov's narrators recount particular, one-time events, the Greenlandic narrators have chosen to describe life in general as it used to be in their youth, in the form of episodes only occasionally marked by particular memories of single events. Therefore, I use the term personal recollection in referring to these narrated stories.

# **2** Topic (and theme) as discourse roles

Within mainstream studies of syntax, both syntactic and semantic features are considered necessary components of a theory of linguistic structure; discourse does not generally figure in a systematic way. Discourse does figure in non-mainstream approaches, such as tagmemics (cf. Pike), works by Longacre and Grimes, and in more recent years, the functional approaches of mostly (but not exclusively) European linguists. The way discourse is included in grammatical explanation, however, has differed in kind from the inclusion of semantic or lexical features in structural analyses.

That discourse is relevant to a functional description of language is obvious from the associations made between various syntactic structures and functions in the discourse. The value of a speech act, for example, may be interpreted through the verb mood as a question (interrogative), a statement (indicative), a command (imperative), and so forth. Verb modes (dependent or independent) may indicate relative importance of information, as foregrounded or backgrounded. The sequencing of action in a narrative is indicated by the verb tenses; referential tracking by pronouns, definiteness, and so on; thematic organization by the use of particles and thematic frames (structures representing stereotyped situations and calling for a certain kind of discourse; see Brown and Yule 1983:238); and so forth. The syntax, combined with contextual knowledge, both of the real world and of the specific situation, provides signals for understanding the discourse. Each of the syntactic structures described above, however, can be interpreted in a number of ways, depending on the context, and each discourse function can be signaled in a number of ways. For this reason, one finds a fundamental difference in current studies of syntax and discourse. In syntax, the use of a particular sentence structure may depend on context and speaker choice, but the structure has predictable elements and rules of well-formedness. It is possible to explain sentence structure without reference to a sentence's function as a speech act, its status as foregrounded or backgrounded information, and so forth. In contrast, discourse structure does not appear to have predictable structural components, a fact that reinforces the longstanding impression that discourse is too unwieldy for rigorous structural analysis of the kind found in syntactic studies. There are too many things to consider in order to describe the structure of even one paragraph, let alone to propose generalized structural rules. Furthermore, aspects of discourse such as speech act and thematic organization are not only unpredictable, they are too open to personal interpretations. There is too much room for ambiguity. Explanations of discourse structure seem more descriptive in nature — not unlike early syntactic explanations (e.g., of passive transformations, in which passive clauses were seen as reorganized active clauses with appropriate modifications for voice and by-phrases). The task is therefore to move beyond description and discover predictability in discourse structure.

Viewing discourse in structural terms (rather than in terms of textual cohesiveness, pragmatics, etc.) assumes that a discourse can be analyzed as a linguistic unit composed of primitive units analogous to, for example, subjects in syntax, or to agents and patients in semantics. If we can find discourse units, or roles, we can presumably study discourse structure in a way that is comparable to the study of other levels of grammatical analysis. We can expect to find these roles acting in predictable and systematic ways, and in ways that interact with other levels of grammatical structure. If such roles exist, then the same phenomena described previously, and perhaps unsatisfactorily, in syntactic terms, should be reexamined.

Grammatical roles are intimately connected with the functions of nominals. At most levels of grammar, we recognize at least two fundamental categories or classes of things. Lexically, nouns and verbs contrast with each other, although members of one class may be transformed into members of the other. (The independent existence of other classes of words, such as adjectives, prepositions, particles, and so forth, is in no way denied by this statement.) Syntactically, the distinction between noun phrases and verb phrases, or arguments and predicates, is basic to the understanding of sentence structure. Semantically, participants and objects are opposed to states of being or actions. A more accurate statement of the semantic difference between these two classes recognizes that processes do not exist independent of their participants, objects, or otherwise affected elements;

thus the semantic equivalent of the predicate or the verb is in some sense the full clause (R. Rhodes, personal communication). Rarely, however, has this distinction been maintained in studies of discourse. Instead, distinctions of other kinds have been made, such as topic-comment or theme-rheme structure, in which topic (or theme) and comment (or rheme) are identified with segments of clauses irrespective of the nominal or verbal status of these segments. To be sure, topic or theme is often identified with nominals and discourse theme with clauses, but the definitions and uses of these terms, and assumptions on which their usage is based, relate more to their functions within a clause than to their functions as discourse elements. These terms, nevertheless, refer to discourse-level concepts: one does not generally speak of the topic or theme of a clause. The terms "topic" and "theme" are among the most widely used terms relating to discourse-level concepts, and they are the terms used for concepts that most closely resemble the nominal and verbal categories of other grammatical levels.[1] As such, they are good starting points for defining a methodology for structural analyses of discourse. First and foremost, the terms must refer to discourse-level entities, separate from (i.e., not identifiable with) lower-level entities such as subjects, objects, agents, patients, and so forth, and should represent discourse classes analogous to nominal entities such as subjects, or participants, and clausal types, such as predicates or processes.

The restriction of the terms topic and theme in this way may seem presumptuous, given the wide range of ways they have been used in the literature. There is a widespread tendency to discuss the role of topic or theme in grammatical analyses without overtly defining the terms (although notable exceptions are Givón, who defines topic but not theme, and Halliday, who defines theme but not topic). On the basis of research by Bransford and Johnson, Brown and Yule (1983:71) convincingly show that discourse topic (in their terminology) is impossible to definitively articulate or identify; by discourse topic, they refer to what I call theme. There is general agreement that either term refers to the main point of a text (or sentence), or to what the text is about, but these are vague concepts and have been criticized and dismissed as such. Despite the vagueness of these terms, however, they have been associated with the concepts that correspond to nouns and verbs at lower levels of structure. They have also been associated with what are traditionally held to be syntactic phenomena, including agreement-marking systems such as ergativity and switch-reference, whether through noted tendencies or because of examples of exceptional agreement. This association is particularly true of topicality and topic status with respect to information flow within a text.

The importance of these discourse concepts varies with the language in question. In syntactic studies of some languages, like English, topic and theme have relatively unimportant roles in the determination of grammaticality, whereas in studies of other languages, topic or theme are persistently encountered. This should come as no surprise if discourse can be viewed in structural terms rather than in terms of purely pragmatic information. Thus, just as languages differ in their structural dependence on morphology or syntax, they differ in their structural dependence on discourse. In some languages, discourse-level determinations of structure are more important than they are in other languages. Further, there are typological factors that are more likely to lead to the grammaticalization of discourse roles in some languages. A clear understanding of these terms and concepts should lead to a better understanding of structural differences between languages that favor syntactic structure and those that favor discourse structure.


## 2.1 Issues in the definition of topic

Despite the varying uses of the terms topic and theme, there is a tradition of associating them with the nominal and verbal parts of sentences. Thus, topic is often associated with a nominal, and if the term itself is not used, there is at least some concept of a nominal in a clause with textual importance. Li and Thompson (1976:484) and Givón (1976) both see subjects as grammaticalized topics (that is, topics are nominals that may be grammaticalized as subjects), albeit with some important differences, about which more below. Du Bois (1987) and Dixon (1994:208) suggest that theme (or topic, neither being fully differentiated) is generally the subject (S or A in an ergative language; see chapter 3 for an explanation of these symbols), or again, the nominal rather than verbal entity. Halliday (1967a:61) notes the general tendency in English to incorporate the main components of the message into the clauses as nominal elements, so as to maximize the contrastive possibilities of the transitivity and thematic systems (according to his definitions). Hopper and Thompson (1984:711) suggest that prototypical nouns function to introduce participants and to coincide with the referential or manipulable elements in discourse (or, in other words, with the topic). Friedman (1976), in a study of American Sign Language, equates topic with the nominal that occurs first and sets the general scene for a series of actions that are then signed. Given this tradition, it is reasonable to identify the term topic with nominal forms (although not all nominal forms are unambiguously nominal, cf. Hopper and Thompson 1984). By the same token, denominalized forms are often associated with detopicalization. Mithun (1984a:849), while not using the term topic itself, notes that lexical compounding, a simple form of noun incorporation, results in loss of specificity and definiteness of the noun, characteristics associated with the lack of topicality.

Topic is not far from being viewed as an independent discourse role in the works of some authors, although it has not actually been articulated as such. Mallinson and Blake (1981:107–8) and Givón (1984:137) suggest that topics of larger-than-sentence-level discourse can appear as either subjects or objects. Givón in fact allows any noun phrase to be a potential topic, recognizing that in practice, only those in subject or object position tend to have prominence.[2] He identifies subject as the primary clausal topic and object as the secondary clausal topic, and others for the most part as being unimportant, at least in terms of continuity in discourse, and therefore in terms of cohesion.[3] The relative importance of the different argument positions in signaling topic is generally reflected in the case-marking system, where direct and oblique arguments of the verb are semantically and morphologically differentiated. Givón sometimes confuses a description of clause-level topic with topic continuity in discourse, about which more below. Mallinson and Blake and numerous others equate topic with subject and agent, because of a general tendency for subjects, agents, and human participants to coincide.

Following Keenan's (1976) list of subjectlike characteristics, some scholars have proposed lists of topiclike characteristics of noun phrases, most notably Givón (1990), but also Li and Thompson (1976). Topics are identified as being definite and given, as well as being most likely the human participant, the agent, the nominal in subject position, and the backgrounded information of the clause. Li and Thompson grammatically distinguish topics from subjects, noting that the former are constrained to being definite, sentence-initial, not determined by the verb, and outside such grammatical processes as reflexivization, passivization, and so forth. These characteristics describe tendencies, but they still do not define the notion of topic. Definiteness, for example, has been considered a primary characteristic of topics, to such an extent that it is sometimes named as a requirement of topicality. Chafe (1976:38–43) describes definiteness as the quality a noun phrase has that allows the listener to identify what the speaker has in mind. Definiteness can be marked by a definite article, by the uniqueness of the referent, by being a proper noun, by deictic availability, or by immediate discourse context (Chafe 1976:38–43; Givón 1984:401). Li and Thompson (1976:461) write that topics must be definite based on Chafe's definition, but their conclusion does not necessarily follow: Chafe also notes that definite noun phrases are not necessarily given information, and topics being introduced are not necessarily definite. Lyons (1977:178–85) makes a further distinction, between definiteness and specificity, where specificity refers to the ability to distinguish a referent from all other possible referents: not all definite noun phrases refer to a specific noun phrase. This is especially true of predicative or attributive definite noun phrases. Further, not all specific noun phrases are definite (see especially Lyons 1977:187–88; note, for example, the specific reading of 'a heron' in Lyons's sentence 'every evening at six o'clock a heron flies over the chalet'). Definiteness by itself, therefore, is not a simplex characteristic. In my West Greenlandic texts, it is most often true that the topic is definite, either because it has been previously introduced through incorporation, or because it is unique (including unique by virtue of possession, as in 'my father'). In the following example, however, 'seals' is introduced for the first time and is signaled as topical by fronting and intonational emphasis; it is neither definite nor given.

(2.1)    (From text 1a)

127.    *Tikillaraangamik*                    *ualikkut*
         *TikiC-llaq-gaangamik*                *ualikkut*
         arrive-INTNS-whenever.3C.PL.CAUS    in.the.afternoon
         'When they came back [from hunting, to Qaqortoq] in the afternoon'

128.    *ullaakkut*         *aallarunik*
         *ullaakkut*         *aallar-gunik*
         in.the.morning    go-3C.PL.COND
         'after having gone out in the morning'

129.  *ilaanni_*          *puisit_*       *arfineq-pingasut*      *qulit*
      *ilaanni*           *puisi-t*       *arfineq-pingasut*      *qulit*
      sometimes      seal-PL       eight                      ten
      'sometimes eight, ten seals'

      *sinnerlugilluunniit*         *kalillugit.*
      *sinnerlugit-luunniit*        *kaliC-lugit*
      more.than-or.even          in.tow-3PL.OBJ.CT
      'or even more in tow [i.e., sometimes (with) eight or ten or even
      more seals in tow].'

In fact, definiteness (as well as givenness) is not a grammatically marked category in West Greenlandic, except insofar as absolutive objects have been identified with definiteness and demoted objects of antipassives with indefiniteness, an issue that I take up in chapter 3. No one has suggested a similar distinction for absolutive and ergative subjects, although Du Bois (1987) has suggested that new participants in a discourse tend to be introduced as absolutive subjects while given and therefore definite ones are continued as ergative subjects. Givón (1984:chapter 11) writes that definiteness is part of topic identification, or topic continuity, and this is more in line with my observations. Definiteness is a feature of topicality but not a prerequisite: a topic is definite once it is introduced, and not every definite noun phrase is a topic.

Another much discussed aspect of topicality is the status something has as given or new in a stretch of discourse, known as its activation status. Firbas (1964) defines something as given if it is present in the immediately preceding text; Chafe (1976:30) understands givenness as the knowledge a speaker assumes to be understood by the listener at the time of the utterance, including presuppositions based on the context and real-world knowledge. In either case, though, how does one measure the length of the preceding text, and how long can something remain given without being mentioned? Presumably, a topic that has not been mentioned in a certain span of clauses is no longer considered topical. The length of this span appears arbitrary: Firbas (1964) assumes a gap length of about seven clauses; Cooreman (1983) assumes one of twenty. The issue is of course the status of the topic with respect to a certain section of the discourse, but this may have less to do with loss of topicality and more with such factors as topic ranking, or with the organization of information in a discourse. Further, it is clear that different elements of discourse have different kinds of scope. For example, a temporal adverb or clause may have scope over an entire stretch of discourse and may be interrupted by parenthetical paragraphs, as opposed to a local topic, one that may be topical only in a given part of the discourse. In being reiterated, the temporal adverb or clause may be repeated in such a way that the listener is assumed to remember the information carried by it; that is, it is grammatically marked as previously given. Anaphoric reference in repetitions of temporal information, as I will show in chapter 4, is important in the switch-reference mechanism in West Greenlandic (although this is an example of thematic rather than topic continuity, it is presented here in connection with gap lengths). The same is true of topics: reintroduction after an interruption, usually as an overt noun phrase, is qualitatively different than a first introduction. Differences can be found in the intonational emphasis, in the use of processes such as topicalization, transitivity, or even ellipsis, in the modifiers, and so forth. All of these can be found in my texts. In text 1a, the speaker discusses 'catechists' at length; they are introduced for the first time in clauses 34 and 35 as the last in a list of professionals and taken up as an extended topic in clause 36:

(2.2)    (From text 1a)

34.      ... *kiisalu*        *atuarfitsinni*       *atuarfinni*        *ajoqit,*
         *kiisa-lu*          *atuarfik-tsinni*      *atuarfik-ni*       *ajoqi-t*
         finally-and        school-1PL.           school-1SG.        catechist-PL.ABS
                            POS.LOC               POS.LOC

'... and finally catechists in our schools, in my school'


35.      *ajoqit*           *taamani*              *ilinniartitsisutut*
                            *atorfeqarput*          *aamma.*

         *ajoqi-t*          *taamani*              *ilinniartitsisoq-tut*
                            *atorfik-qaq-vut*       *aamma*

         catechist-PL       at.that.time           teacher-EQ
                            job-have-3PL.IND       and

'and the catechists at that time had jobs as teachers.'

36. *Assorujussuarlu ajoqit, taamani pingaaruteqarput.*

*assut-rujussuaq-lu ajoqi-t taamani pingaar-ut(i)-qaq-vut*

very-very-and catechist-PL at.that.time important-means.to-have-3PL.IND

'And the catechists were very, very important in those days.'

The only substantial interruption in this discussion occurs in clauses 71 to 75; the reintroduction of 'catechists' as the topic in clause 76 involves both fronting and two deictic modifiers:

(2.3)  (From text 1a)

71. *Makkua allaapput_ palasit_ ilinniartitsisukkut_*

*Makkua allaa-vut palasi-t ilinniartitsisoq-t-kkut*

those different-3PL.IND priest-PL teacher-PL-'and.fellows'

'Those ones were different, [like] the priests, together with the teachers'

*aammalu KGH-mi taamanikkut*
*aamma-lu Kongelig Grønlandske Handeln-mi taamani-kkut*
and-and Royal Greenlandic Trade-LOC at.that.time-VIA
'and at the KGH at that time'

*sulisuusut*
*sulisut-u-soq-t*
personnel-COP-PART-PL
'the workers (i.e., and the workers at the KGH at that time)'

*imaattumi sannavinni_ aamma saffiorfinni.*

*imaaC-soq-mi sannavik-ni aamma saffiorfik-ni*

be.like.this-PART-what    about           carpentry.shop-PL.LOC
                                          and smithy-PL.LOC

'what about [those] in the carpentry shops and in the smithies.'

72.  *Taakku     nutserteqattaarneqanngillat*
     *taakku     nutser-tit-qattaaq-neqaq-nngit-lat*
     those       move-cause-again.and.again-PASS-NEG-3PL.NEG.IND
     'Those ones did not move much [they weren't moved much]'

73.  *nunaqarfimmi     illoqarfimmi     illoqarfinni     taakku*
                                                         *inuupput*

     *nunaqarfik-mi    illoqarfik-mi    illoqarfik-ni    taakku*
                                                         *inuu-vut*

     village-LOC       town-LOC         town-LOC.PL      those
                                                         live-3PL.IND

'those ones lived in the village, the town, the towns'

74.  *illoqarfiup        inuinut             ilanngullutik*
     *illoqarfik-up      inuk-inut           ilannguC-lutik*
     town-REL           person-3SG.POS./     include/join-3PL.CT
                        PL.POSM.TERM
'to become members of the town [to join the township]'

75.  *nuutsinneqassanatik.*
     nuuC-tit-neqaq-ssa-natik
     move-cause-PASS-FUT-3PL.NEG.CT
     'they were never moved.'

76.  *Kisiannili   ukua    ajoqit*
     *Kisianni-li  ukua    ajoqi-t*
     but-but              these    catechist-PL
     'But these catechists'

     *taakku_     puiorsinnaanngilakka . . .*
     *taakku_     puior-sinnaa-nngit-lakka*

those        forget-can-NEG-1SG.SUBJ/3NC.PL.OBJ.NEG.IND
'I cannot forget them . . .'

In text 2 the speaker discusses the place(s) used for setting up fishing nets; this is introduced in clauses 71 and 72 as the subject and repeated in clause 75 as the object of a transitive construction:

(2.4)    (From text 2)

71.    *Tassalu*        *Amerloq_*      *illugiillugu*
       *Tassa-lu*       *Amerloq*       *illugiig-lugu*
       that.is-and    Amerloq        be.pair-3SG.OBJ.CT
       'And Amerloq was on both'

       *saqqaa-tungaa*    *alanngualu*                    *tamanna*
       *saqqaa-tungaa*    *alanngoq-a-lu*                 *tamanna*
       sunside-toward    shadow-3SG.POS.ABS-and    this
       'the sunshine side and on the shadow side'

72.    *taamanikkut*          *piniusersorfigineqartarpoq*
       *taamani-kkut*         *piniut-lersor-fik-gi-neqaq-saq-voq*
       at.that.time-VIA      (fishing).equipment-equip.with-place-have-
                             PASS-HAB-3SG.IND
       'it was the place the hunting equipment was kept in those days/
       where one put nets'

       *saarullinnik*          *tamakkuninnga*
       *saarullik-nik*         *tamakku-ninnga*
       codfish-PL.INST      these-PL.INST
       'for codfish and others'

73.    *qassusersorfigalugu*
       qassuser-soq-fi-gi-lugu
       set.nets-PART-place-have-3SG.OBJ.CT
       'it had a place for setting nets.'

74.    *Tassalu*        *tappavannga*      *imaappoq*
       *tassa-lu*       *tappav-annga*     *imaaC-voq*
       that.is-and    up.there-ABL      be.like.this-3SG.IND
       'And so from up there, you know'

| *taamanikkut* | *siullermik* | *Akisaminngaanniit* |
|---|---|---|
| *taamani-kkut* | *siullermik* | *Akisa-minngaanniit* |
| at.that.time-VIA | at.first | Akisa-ABL |

'at that time at first from Akisa'

| *Utoqqaat* | *Saqqaanut* | | *allaat* | *taamanikkut* |
|---|---|---|---|---|
| | | | *tassa_* | *ipuinnaq* |
| *Utoqqaat* | *Saqqa-anut* | | *allaat* | *taamani-kkut* |
| | | | *tassa* | *ipu-innaq-o* |
| Utoqqaat | Saqqa-3SG.POS.TERM | others | at.that.time-VIA |
| | | that.is | oar-only-ABS |

'Utoqqaat, even to Saqqa [even to its south side], others in those
days only oars [only rowing]'

qassusersorfigalugu
qassuser-soq-fik-gi-lugu
set.nets-NOMZ-place-have-3SG.OBJ.CT
'setting nets [having a place for nets]'

75.    *piniusersorfigisarpagut.*
piniut-lersor-fik-gi-saq-vagut
[fishing/hunting].equipment-equip with-place-have-HAB-1PL.
SUBJ/3PL.OBJ.IND
'we used to have them as a place for hunting equipment [we went
hunting there].'

Likewise, important background (nontopical) information may also be
reintroduced differently. In text 2 the speaker mentions parenthetically
in clause 48 that he and his colleagues only had boats with oars (*ipu* 'oar';
*ipuinnaq* 'only oars'):

(2.5)    (From text 2)

48.    *imaak — _ (taamanikkut     ipuinnarmik*
                                          *angallateqarpugut . . .*

     *ima*         *taamani-kkut*       *ipu-innaq-mik*
                                             *angallat-qaq-vugut*

    so               at.that.time-VIA    oar-only-INST
                                                    vessel-have-1PL.IND

'so — (at that time we had only boats with oars . . .'

Some thirty clauses later, in clause 74 listed in example 2.4 above, 'oars' is repeated without overt reference to the action implied by the use of oars, 'rowing'.

Finally, the interruptions that necessitate reintroduction of a topic may involve one or more clauses, as can be seen from the examples above and from Firbas's and Cooreman's discussions of gap lengths. It is often the case that explanatory or descriptive (or "background") information intervenes without the loss of topicality, despite sometimes quite lengthy gaps. In text 3a, clauses 71–92, for example, the interviewer asks whether or not speaker 3 goes out for walks; after first explaining that she used to like her old house and doesn't much care for her new house, speaker 3 responds to the question: 'I used to go for walks'. There are seventeen intervening clauses and no indication of loss of topicality from the question to the answer. For a more detailed discussion of this, see example 4.46 in chapter 4. Grimes (1975:58–59) suggests that background information of this sort is a means for the speaker to communicate the importance of the main point of the text. The particular methods used to organize discourse, including the use of background material in the way described above, vary from one speaker to another and from one sociocultural setting to another. Attempts to define givenness in terms of gap length, therefore, are too programmatic.

Being definite and given implies preceding reference, or continuity, in the discourse. Accordingly, topics are often ranked with respect to continuity in discourse on a number of scales, including phonological size (from zero-anaphora to full noun phrases), word order (right or left dislocation, theme-rheme structure, etc.), animacy (agent being the most topical role, followed by datives/benefactives and patients), subordination, active status, and so forth. These lists, however, incorporate certain obvious and circular observations. A topic, being defined (inexplicitly) as what the discourse is about, will be more likely to be expressed with zero-anaphora or pronominals than with full noun phrases in noninitial clauses. This is especially obvious from Friedman's (1976) studies of American Sign Language, or from a language like West Greenlandic, where pronominal agreement on verbs is sufficient in noninitial clauses. It will also often (but not necessarily) be definite or given as a result of being topical, rather than the other way around (topical as a result of being definite or given). In one study of topic, Cooreman (1983) shows that affected participants (or patients) in passive clauses are more topical and more continuous than agents, which may or may not be present in any case. These lists unfortunately also do little to describe or help determine relative topicality; in a discourse about a participant, say a man, and an affected item, say a boat, is the topic the man or the boat, when both are continuous? Most scholars have assumed that the man, as agent or as subject, is the topic, or at least the primary topic. Topicality hierarchies in fact predict that the man, as agent, is the topic; whether or not this is what the discourse is about is debatable. Cooreman, supporting Givón, ranks agents as higher than affected participants (or patients) on a topicality hierarchy; in dwelling very briefly on the following, however, she downplays her own crucial observation:

> It is necessary to stress the importance of the term narratives here. The data investigated consisted of a number of legends and folk tales. . . . If one were to investigate written texts of scientific interest or even kitchen recipes different results concerning topicality and animacy of referents may be obtained. . . . I concluded that the subject is more topical than the direct object. Since it is also true that animate referents are more topical than inanimate referents in narrative discourse one should not be surprised at the fact that subject referents in general tend to be more animate than direct object. (1983:456)

What is crucial is that topic is not automatically equatable with syntactic or semantic roles such as subject or agent, despite the appeal of a topicality hierarchy, nor are they equatable with definiteness or givenness. In particular types of discourse, such as narrative, one is more likely to find a coincidence of roles, whereas in others, such as technical texts, one may be less likely to do so. In my West Greenlandic data, it is generally true that the subjects of transitive verbs are the most agentive (and therefore in most cases human; these most often coincide with the first-person form) and the objects are the next most likely topic on a topic hierarchy (second person, third-person animate, and so forth). What is more telling, however, is that the subjects of neighboring intransitive clauses are often identical with the objects of the transitives. In other words, the local topic is not constrained to being the subject of one of the few transitive clauses in a section. This is obvious in the following example from text 2, in which clauses 34 and 35 are transitive constructions, yet the subject is unspecified, although presumably 'fishermen' is more agentive than local topic 'codfish':

(2.6)    (From text 2)

32.      *Eqqaamavaralu*
         Eqqaama-vara-lu
         remember-1SG.SUBJ/3SG.OBJ-and
         'And I remember it'

33.      *taamanikkut       saarulliit       tunineqartartut*
         *taamani-kkut       saarullik-it      tuni-neqaq-saq-tut*
         at.that.time-VIA    codfish-PL        sell-PASS-HAB-3PL.PART
         'at that time the codfish used to be sold'

34.      *sumilluunniit_     niaquernagit*
         *sumik-luunniit     niaquer-nagit*
         what-or.even        take.head.off.(fish)-3PL.OBJ.NEG.CT
         'without [them] even taking their heads off'

35.      *ammarnagilluunniit*
         ammar-nagit-luunniit
         open.up-3PL.OBJ.NEG.CT-or.even
         'or even opening them up.'

36.      *Aammalu_     nalunngilara*
         *aamma-lu     nalunngi-lara*
         and-and       know-1SG.SUBJ/3SG.OBJ.NEG.IND
         'And I know [it]'

37.      *taamanikkut              kilomut      9 øremik      akeqartut,*
         *taamani-kkut             kilo-mut     9 øre-mik     akeqaq-tut*
         at.that.time-VIA          kilo-TERM    9.øre-INST    cost-3PL.PART
         'they cost nine øre a kilo at that time'

         *tunitsivileqqaaramik,                          saarullit.*
         *tunitsi-vik-leq-qqaar-gamik*                   *saarullik-t*

sell-really-begin-first.time-3C.PL.CAUS    codfish-PL
'when they first started to really sell, the codfish.'

The suggestion, therefore, that topics are subjects or agents is an overly broad generalization based on one form of discourse. As for the identification of topic with backgrounded material, the importance in discourse of a constituent or clause is often a matter of personal interpretation; I discuss this further below, with respect to theme.

The example of the man and the boat, above, points to a further dimension in this discussion: that of competing topics in a single stretch of discourse. In first-person narratives, for example, the narrator is likely to be subject more often than not, but the narration may only partially emphasize the narrator's role in the discourse, or another participant may have as important a role, as in the following example, in which the object is at least as much a focus of information as the subject is:

(2.7)    I saw a stray cat yesterday and took it home and fed it, and now
         I'm so in love with it, I want to keep it.

The narrator is the agent and the subject throughout, but can the narrator be said to be what the text is about? Undeniably, the text is about the narrator, as most texts probably are, from a strictly psychological interpretation of the purpose of the narration, but it is also about the stray cat. Givón, as mentioned above, suggests that the subject is the primary topic in a clause. I argue that clause structure alone does not allow one to make such a determination. Further, in discourses larger than one or two paragraphs, one is likely to identify a global topic and one or more local topics, each with prominence within their stretch of discourse. For example, a text about hunters may have a local topic 'hunters' and a more global topic such as the id of the speaker, reflected in the use of the first-person pronoun: 'I remember the hunters . . . I was a child then . . . the hunters used to . . . ' This is the case in my Greenlandic data (the clauses given here in English translation are from text 4). In some cases, the different levels of topicality may be grammaticalized. For example, Grimes (1975:103, 361–68) notes the use of grammatical features to mark thematic organization, including global or local topicality, in conjunction with the structure of paragraphing in some South American languages. This may be particularly relevant to discussions of activation status, as well as to identifications of competing topics and paragraph structure (see below for a discussion of topic introduction and identification, as well as chapter 4 for a more complete discussion of competing topics in relation to my data, and particularly in relation to text 3b).

With these considerations in mind, I define topic as a nominal entity with prominence across a continuous stretch of discourse. Any noun phrase is potentially a topic, but most noun phrases in nonargument positions rarely have prominence over more than a clause, and a topic is determined with reference to more than one clause. Whereas subjecthood, agency, and position within a clause are all determined by their function within the clause, the topic is not bounded by the clause. The topic role is therefore not restricted to a particular syntactic or semantic role, as in subject or agent, nor is it restricted to a particular position in a clause: it is not first, or last, necessarily. It is not identical with given information, but it is, in the traditional sense, the entity that a text is about.[4]

## 2.2  Issues in the definition of theme

Turning now to the term theme, there are at least two very different traditions concerning its use. V. Mathesius (1964a, 1964b, 1964c) and later F. Daneš and J. Vachek (1964), members of the Prague School, use theme very specifically to refer to the first of two identifiable parts of the clause as the theme, or that which is known or given from previous context, and to the second as the rheme, or the new information conveyed by the clause. The theme may be any kind of grammatical element. Halliday (1967a, 1967b, 1968, and in some respects Daneš 1964 too) sees the theme as the point of departure of a message within the information structure of a clause. He differentiates between a number of different grammatical levels, including intonational (information) unit, information (thematic) structure, and cognitive content (transitivity, by which he means predication system irrespective of word class): the roles at one level are interdependent with those at another level, but they are not identical. Thus, a theme is often also a subject and an agent and represents given information, but it is not necessarily so (Halliday 1967b:211). Within intonational units, he identifies the points of informational focus as points of prominence (see note

2), and these are most often not the points of departure and are therefore not thematic. Several important observations are captured by the Prague School linguists and Halliday: the very first part of a clause has special significance in discourse; it does not, however, generally carry the intonationally prominent information in the clause; and the role of one level of grammatical description may interact with, but does not depend on, that of another.

The notion of theme-rheme was developed for Slavic languages, which have fairly free word order. Information indicated by the choice of a particular word order in a language with free word order is necessarily of a different kind than that in languages with much more rigid word order like English. This is partially explained by the different uses the different language types make of the same syntactic constructions; for example, English makes extensive use of the passive whereas the Slavic languages do not. Other problems arise with yet other language types. Greenlandic, for example, has relatively free word order, although unmarked order is preferentially SOV. It is a highly polysynthetic language, however, and one verb form often incorporates information that in English or Czech would result in a complex clause. Theme-rheme structure thus becomes less useful for the purposes for which it was conceived. Halliday (1968:214), in discussing transitivity in English, suggests that verbs do not readily associate with any form of prominence in discourse and are rarely thematic (in his terminology, where theme is related to order in a clause). Applied to Greenlandic, this would mean entire sequences of clauses are neither prominent nor thematic, which is clearly misleading.

The introduction and organization of information in texts is reflected in the choice of word order and grammatical construction. This is, however, a categorically different type of importance from that of topic and what I propose is its propositional correlate. Furthermore, the definition of theme in this way depends on clause-level structure, and not on discourse structure. Its discourse equivalent, thematization or "staging," is discussed by Brown and Yule (1983:133–34) and Grimes (1975:323) and refers to the idea that every level of discourse is organized around a particular element that is taken as the point of departure and that has prominence in the text. Such a definition assumes, however, that all discourses are structured in the same way, main point first, elaboration following. This is an inaccurate view of discourse, both with respect to different discourse types in a single language and to differences in discourse organization cross-linguistically.

There is another tradition in which the rather vague notion of discourse theme is similar to what I will propose. Few syntacticians, typologists, or functional grammarians actually define this term. Many use it interchangeably with topic, as do Dixon (1994) and Du Bois (1987), for example; some use it in the sense in which others use topic, as do Brown and Yule (1983:135) and Longacre (1976). Grimes (1975:103, 324) uses it in a number of ways, including as the starting point of the message, as the topic, and as an element of the organization of the text, and to confuse matters, he uses the terms in ways standard to nonlinguistic fields (such as topic sentence). Most, however, including Grimes, understand theme as the main idea of a discourse, differing, if the distinction is made, from topic in being an abstraction of the entire discourse rather than an identifiable nominal entity. Despite the confusion of terminology, there is a conceptual consistency in this view of discourse theme. Jones (1977:1–2) defines the term as the most important idea of the discourse; since theme is not always overtly and concisely stated as one of the clauses, however, the theme of a discourse must be derived in a statement (by the scholar, i.e., outside the text) that generalizes enough to represent the whole discourse but still differentiate it from other discourses. This suggests a very important difference between the notions of topic and theme. The term topic refers specifically to a nonoblique nominal entity in a clause and by extension in a text; a topic is therefore present either as the subject or object of a clause, whether overtly stated or not. Unlike topics, however, themes are not clearly identifiable. Speakers rarely show thematic continuity through continued repetition of a verb or clause, and generally not in contiguous clauses. Thematic continuity as expressed through lexical identity in the following example is unusual:

(2.8)   (From text 2)

77.      ... *isersarnaartartoq,*
         isersarnaaq-saq-soq
         wind.going.into.fjord-HAB-3SG.PART
         '... there was a wind going into the fjord'

80.    *isersarnerajuttuummat)*
       isersarneq-gajug-toq-u-mmat
       wind.coming.in.the.fjord-tendency-PART-COP-3NC.SG.CAUS
       'because there was a tendency to have a wind coming in the
       fjord) . . .'

More often, the theme is developed by means of semantically closely related but etymologically unrelated terms:

(2.9)   (From text 2)

76.    *Tassali*       *kisianniuna*     *kangerluk_*     *anorlertartoq*
       *Tassa-li*      *kisianni-una*    *kangerluk-ø*    *anorler-saq-soq*
       that.is-but     but-DEIC          fjord-ABS        blow.(of.wind)-HAB-
                                                          3SG.PART

       'But so the fjord was usually windy'

77.    *isersarnaartartoq,*
       isersarnaaq-saq-soq
       wind.going.into.fjord-HAB-3SG.PART
       'there was a wind going into the fjord'

78.    *qajassuunnagu.*
       qajassuut-nagu
       be.cautious/spare-3SG.OBJ.NEG.CT
       'it was very windy [i.e., not a cautious wind, it didn't spare
       them].'

   In the next example, the speaker introduces the theme with an evaluation in clause 47 (although he more frequently introduces a theme or topic with what I call a reflection clause, a clause in which the speaker reflects, remembers, or in some way expresses cognition; an example of a reflection clause is seen in example 2.6). He then summarizes the theme in clause 50, that catechists were not well treated:

(2.10)  (From text 1a)

47.    *Taamaattumik*     *ajoqit_*        *imaannaanngitsumik*
       *Taamaattumik*     *ajoqi-t*        *imaannaanngisoq-mik*
       Therefore          catechist-PL     ones.not.without.importance-INST
       'And therefore the catechists, who are not without importance'

> *qutsavissarai*      *nunatta_*  *ullumikkut*
> *qutsavi-ssaq-gi-vai*    *nuna-tta*  *ullumikkut*
> thank-FUT-have-3SG.SUBJ/  land-1PL.POS today
> 3PL.OBJ.IND
> 'our land should thank them today'

48. *aamma* *tamakku* *sulerujussuarsimasut*
   *aamma* *tamakku* *suli-rujussuaq-sima-sut*
   and  those  work-very.much-PERF-3PL.PART
   'and they worked a lot, those ones'

49. *imaannaanngitsorujussuarmik_*   *sulisimasut*
   *imaannanngitsoq-rujussuaq-mik*  *suli-sima-sut*
   ones.not.without.importance-   work-PERF-3PL.PART
   very.much-INST
   'they worked in a very important/meaningful/able way'

50. *kisianni_* *pitsaviunngitsumik_*  *pineqartarsimasut*
   *kisianni* *pitsak-vik-u-nngit-soq-mik* *pi-neqaq-saq-sima-sut*
   but   excellent-genuine-COP-  do-pass-HAB-PERF-
       NEG-NOMZ-INST   3PL.PART
   'but they have not been paid well/well taken care of [be taken
   care of]'

   *aqutsisuninngaanniit* . . .
   aqutsisut-ninngaanniit
   management-PL.ABL
   'by the management . . .'

But how do we determine that the speaker is speaking of the mistreatment of the catechists rather than their hard work, which was the theme of the preceding discourse? Identifying clause 50 as the most concise statement of the theme is only possible from the following text. From clauses 51 to 66 of text 1a, the speaker elaborates on the theme, describing more specifically the ways in which the catechists were not taken care of:

(2.11) (From text 1a)

51. . . . *tassa* *taamani_* *Grønlands Styrelsep*
   *tassa*  *taamani*  *Grønlands Styrelse-p*

that.is        at.that.time     Greenland.Steering-REL
'. . . so at that time, Greenland Steering'

*tamaasa*                     *ingerlatarivai*
*tamaq-asa*                   *ingerlaC-saq-gi-vai*
the.whole/all-3PL.O           work.with-PASS.PART-have-3SG.SUBJ/
                              3PL.OBJ.IND
'worked with them'

52.    *provsteqarfik*         *aqqutigalugu.*
       *provsteqarfik-0*       *aqqut-gi-lugu*
       deanery-ABS            way-have-3SG.OBJ.CT
       'via the deanery.'

53.    *Ajoqillu*              *taamani*        *tassa_*    *palasillumi*
       *Ajoqi-t-lu*            *taamani*        *tassa*     *palasi-t-lu-mi*
       catechist-PL-and       at.that.time     that.is     priest-PL-and-sure
       'And the catechists at that time, and of course the priests'

       *ingattammik*     *ajoqit_*            *nuutsinneqartarput_*
       *ingattammik*     *ajoqi-t*            *nuuC-tit-neqaq-saq-vut*
       especially        catechist-PL         move-cause-PASS-HAB-3PL.IND
       'especially the catechists'

       nunaqarfinnut
       nunaqarfik-t-nut
       village-PL-PL.TERM
       'they were moved to villages'

54.    *aperinagilluunniit*
       aperi-nagit-luunniit
       ask-3PL.OBJ.NEG.CT-or
       'without even asking them'

55.    *oqarfigisarpaat*
       oqarfigi-saq-vaat
       say-HAB-3PL.SUBJ/3PL.OBJ.IND
       'they would say to them'

56. *"Uunnga      nuussuutit!"*
    *Uunnga      nuuC-ssaa-vutit*
    Over.here    move-FUT-2SG.IND
    '"Move over there!"'

57. *taavalu       piumanngikkaangata*
    *taava-lu      piuma-nngit-gaangata*
    then-and     want-NEG-when(ever).3NC.PL.CAUS
    'and if they didn't want to'

58. *soraarsittarlugit.*
    soraarsit-saq-lugit
    fire-HAB-3PL.OBJ.CT
    'they would fire them.'

59. *Nuutsikkaangamigillu                     taamani*
    *nuuC-tit-gaangamigit-lu                  taamani*
    move-cause-when(ever).3PL.SUBJ/          at.that.time
    3NC.PL.OBJ.CAUS-and
    'And when they had moved them at that time'

60. *illussaqartinneqarneq                       ajorput.*
    *illu-ssaq-qaq-tit-neqaq-neq-0              ajor-vut*
    house-FUT-have-cause-PASS-NOMZ-ABS    bad-3PL.IND
    'they were not given a house to stay in/they didn't house them.'

61. *Nuukkaangamillu,*
    NuuC-gaangamik-lu
    move-when(ever).3C.PL.CAUS-and
    'And whenever they moved'

62. *nammineq      illulioqqaarlutik*
    *nammineq      illu-lioq-qqaaq-lutik*
    self          house-build-first-3PL.CT
    'they first had to build a house themselves'

63. *ilaanni       ukiorsuaq        sinnerlugu*
    *ilaanni       ukioq-suaq       sinner-lugu*

    sometimes   winter-big-ABS   over/more.than-3SG.OBJ.CT
    'sometimes over more than a year'

64.    *illumi*      *inissisimallutik*
       *illu-mi*     *inissi-sima-lutik*
       house-LOC   live-PERF-3PL.CT
       'they had to live in a[nother] house

65.    *uffa*   *meeraqarlutik*
       *uffa*   *meeraq-qaq-lutik*
       even   child-have-3PL.CT
       'even having a child'

66.    *nuliaqarlutillu.*
       nuliaq-qaq-lutik-lu
       wife-have-3PL.CT-and
       'and having a wife.'

In this section of the text, specific themes such as 'move', 'build house', 'have child', and so on, are not of great importance, and they are not continued in later sections. They are introduced as elaborations of the idea that catechists were not well taken care of. In none of the clauses is this theme explicitly repeated. Unlike topic, therefore, the determination of theme is more open to interpretation, more likely to be seen as based on the linguist's intuition, and less easily integrated into grammatical theory. Because a great majority of clauses in my texts are intransitive structures, however, it is impossible to ignore theme as a concept in text structure.

There are distinguishing characteristics of themes, which, taken together, allow one to identify boundaries between themes, and by so doing to identify thematic units of texts; Givón (1984) discusses these at length.[5] The thematic coherence, or unity, of a text can be measured by the degree of unity in time, place, action, and participants in a segment of discourse; these are indicated by tense, location, aspect, and participants (or topics). Within a text, one can identify thematic paragraphs by the relative degree of thematic unity within each paragraph, as indicated by these grammatical features. The text is also characterized by thematic continuity between paragraphs, or in other words, by some degree of continuation of the abstract discourse theme that unifies the entire text. To take a simple example from my West Greenlandic data, the text immediately preceding example 2.6 above, from clauses 19–31 of text 2, concerns the description of a house that was used as a factory during the early years of the fishing industry. 'House', first introduced in clause 21, is the topic; the theme is a general description of the topic. The speaker uses a reflection clause to introduce the theme in clause 19. The topic and theme are developed in clauses 21–26:

(2.12)  (From text 2)

19.  *Eqqaamalluarpara*
Eqqaama-lluaq-vara
remember-well-1SG.SUBJ/3SG.OBJ.IND
'I remember it well'

20.  *meeraallunga_          taamanikkut*
*meeraq-u-lunga          taamani-kkut*
child-COP-1SG.CT     at.that.time-VIA
'I was a child, in those days'

21.  *massakkut      amutsiviup          akiani*
*massakkut      amutsivik-up      aki-ani*
now          shipyard-REL      other.side-3SG.POS.LOC
'now on the other side of the shipyard [opposite the place that is now the shipyard]'

*ilinniartut_          ilinniartut          illukuat;*
*ilinniartoq-t          ilinniartoq-t          illu-ku-at*
student-PL          student-PL          house-former-3PL.POS.ABS
'there was a former students' house [there was formerly a students' house]'

22.  *taassuma          illup          kangia          tungaani_*
*taassuma          illu-p          kangia          tungaani*
that.one-REL     house-REL     lying.east     over.there/in.that. direction
'to the east of that house over there'

*itersiumanermiikkami          qooqqiumanermi*
*itersi-juma-neq-mii-gami          qooqqi-juma-neq-mi*

    make.hole.in.ground-want-     make.furrow-want-NOMZ-LOC
    NOMZ-be.in-3C.SG.CAUS
    'because it is in a little depression in a valley'

23.     *illungaatsiapilorujussuaq*
      *illu-ngaatsiaq-pilorujussuaq-0*
      house-rather-very.big-ABS
      'a little bigger than a big house'

24.     *imaappoq*          *sanaaq,*
      *imaaC-voq*        *sanaaq-0*
      be.like.that-3SG.IND    something.one.has.done-ABS
      'that is, it has been built'

25.     *illungaatsiapilorujussuaq*       *uingasoq*
      *illu-ngaatsiaq-pilorujussuaq-0*     *uinga-soq*
      house-rather.big-very.big-NOMZ    slant-3SG.PART
      'the rather larger than big house was slanted'

26.     *taanna*     *"Eqaluit*    *inaannik"*        *taasarparput.*
      *taanna*     *eqaluk-it*    *ini-annik*        *taasar-varput*
      that.one    char-PL     place-3PL.POS.INST    call-1PL.SUBJ/
                                                   3SG.OBJ.IND
      'that one we called "char's place."'

Topic, thematic, and temporal continuity with the next paragraph are indicated in a number of ways, most strikingly by repetition. Clauses 27–31 of text 2 essentially repeat the above (see the appendix for the full text and see chapters 3 and 4 for a full analysis.) Each section (i.e., clauses 19–26 and 27–31) is introduced by a reflection clause, in each case a variation of the phrase 'I remember'; the clauses in question are 19 and 32. Each reflection clause is followed by one instance of the temporal adverb *taamanikkut* 'at that time' per section; these are found in clauses 20 and 33. There is a clear shift in theme from clause 32, starting with another reflection clause and following temporal clause. After clause 32, 'house' is no longer mentioned, and 'codfish' is introduced for the first time in clause 33. The theme has to do with how the codfish were sold. Thus, without being able to exactly and definitively articulate the themes of both sections, we see that within each section, the theme remains constant, that between the two sections, the theme changes, and that there are temporal and referential indications at section boundaries.

Both Grimes (1975) and Halliday (1976), using different terminology (e.g., setting, staging, referential coherence, and so forth), also discuss textual cohesion and thematic unity and agree that discourse theme is reflected in a discourse through continuity of the factors mentioned above. Furthermore, although many aspects of theme remain vague and intuitive, these factors are relevant in analyzing certain grammatical features; some languages regularly employ morphemes that mark theme rather than subject or even topic (see Kroeker's appendix A in Grimes 1975:367–68).

Like topics, themes can exist at different levels, and one can speak of global or local themes, the former being the overall theme of the discourse, the latter being one with prominence in a given section of the discourse (Grimes 1975:367–68; also Jones 1977:9). Jones (1977:130–68) provides a detailed description of thematic hierarchy, with themes specific to clauses, paragraphs, and discourses. She writes specifically about expository discourse, but the principles may be applied to other types of discourse. Her proposed "constituents" of discourse units in expository discourse consist of "points" (or "theorems"), "arguments," and "presuppositions" that form part of the exposition, at the level of the paragraph. The theme is the nuclear point of a level, and one of the constituents of the next lowest level: thus, in a paragraph the theme of a point is a clause. The theme of a higher level of discourse may be captured in a cluster of points, or a paraphrase thereof. Both Jones (1977) and Longacre (1976, 1996) identify themes according to logical components of scripts, or general frameworks within which a type of discourse is developed (e.g., ordering food at a restaurant, lecturing to students, etc.). The structure of the discourse is dependent on the constituents of these scripts and the relations that hold between the elements. A script involving comparison or contrast, for example, involves two or more items in a particular relation to each other. The theme is then identified according to the type of script. Such a view of theme identification is fundamentally plausible but difficult to work with and subject to different interpretations. In my analyses of West Greenlandic texts, I provide a general identification of paragraph themes based on repetition and paraphrase.

To summarize, theme can be viewed as the result of a complex of information associated with processes and actions (which includes information about participants) across more than one clause. Unlike topic, no single clause necessarily captures the theme of a stretch of discourse. Processes within single clauses may be thought of as clause-level themes, but only the highest-ranked theme is read as the theme of a continuous text, and this theme is not necessarily overtly, obviously, or unambiguously marked. This may result in differing interpretations of a discourse theme: one text may have a number of different readings, just as one sentence may be ambiguous (McCune 1983; R. Rhodes, personal communication).

Insofar as discourse theme is determined as the most important theme of a group of clauses, one might assume that some clauses more directly express this theme than others. The terms foregrounding and backgrounding have often been used to distinguish between thematically important clauses and others, and they have also figured prominently in analyses of information structure and flow. Labov (1972:361), in his analyses of narrative structure, suggests an inherent difference between narrative clauses, by which he means any sentence in a narrative that is sequentially ordered with respect to the narrative, and non-narrative clauses. He does not identify the latter as background clauses per se, but he identifies certain characteristics of non-narrative clauses that have been important in the distinction of backgrounded and foregrounded information in later studies; among these are subordination, explanation, nonpunctual mood, and so forth. Mallinson and Blake (1981:99) further associate background clauses with low transitivity, and foreground clauses, which signal the main point of discourse, with high transitivity, perfective action, and referentiality. As with topicality and theme, there is a range of associations between grammatical forms and the concepts of foregrounding and backgrounding, both with respect to the clause and to the text. However, successful identification of backgrounding and foregrounding is still a matter of individual interpretation. Grimes (1975:58) observes, for example, that what might be considered background information in a narrative actually may contain information essential to understanding the importance of the narrative. Further, most studies of backgrounded and foregrounded information have been applied to narratives, but different discourse genres differ in what is considered background, or nonessential, information: explanatory texts, for example, cannot be said to use explanation as background (Grimes 1975:56; see also Longacre 1976, 1996).

Not surprisingly, discussions of backgrounding and foregrounding suffer from some of the same problems as do the terms topic and theme, including the confusion between discourse and syntactic levels of analysis. For example, Givón (1990:845) suggests that topics, not being the main point of a clause, are backgrounded information; the foregrounded information in a clause is the locus for new information. However, although topic may be considered given and (therefore?) backgrounded information within a clause, can it be said to be backgrounded in a discourse? Further, it is easy to reduce foregrounding to independent clauses and backgrounding to all others, but it is not a very useful distinction. In my West Greenlandic texts, I see no systematic relation between discourse theme and independent clauses, and between backgrounding and dependent clauses. In fact, thematic paragraphs in West Greenlandic can consist of dependent clauses only: in spoken West Greenlandic, the causative mood can often be found in place of an indicative in the main clause of a paragraph or intonational unit. Therefore, discussions of foregrounding or backgrounding do not figure prominently in my analyses.

I have discussed theme at length to show in what way the basic opposition noun–verb, or argument–predicate, can be extended to discourse structure. Because it is inherently more difficult to uniquely identify in any given text, theme is a secondary, albeit important consideration in my analysis of West Greenlandic. It cannot be ignored, given that in many texts a majority of clauses are intransitive, and the text is consequently developed through predicate structure, not through topic changes. Nevertheless, my focus is on the role of topic in the determination of syntactic structure, as it is the topic, not the theme, that is reflected in nominal agreement patterns.


## 2.3 Introduction and identification of topics and themes

If topics and themes are real, they must be identifiable within a text. But how are topics or themes introduced, and what signals are there in larger discourses of a change in topic or theme? Second, how is their status maintained, or what signals are there of continuing topicality or thematicity within a paragraph?

The two questions have not generally been clearly differentiated, perhaps because it is not always possible to do so. For example, discussions of topic and theme often focus on the properties of thematic or topical elements in a clause or a discourse, or on status maintenance. We see this in the commonly linked notions of givenness, definiteness, topicality, and position in a clause. Thus, many studies (see the discussion in point 2.1) suggest that the topic is either the first element of a clause or the subject thereof, that it is generally a participant (and typically an agent) and that it is identified by being definite or given. Effectively, this means that a topic is recognized as such after it has already been introduced, but in ergative languages this is problematic. Du Bois (1987), for example, notes that the absolutive in ergative languages is the preferred case for introducing new participants in discourse; at the same time, he views topics as subjects. In intransitive clauses, therefore, the absolutive argument would introduce a new participant and have topic status, while in transitive clauses, the absolutive argument would not be the topic. Furthermore, the introduction of a new participant is not necessarily the same as the introduction of a new topic, and so the question remains as to how topics are identified as such. Can we assume that topics are identified by their position or syntactic or semantic function in a clause? If so, it would certainly be immediately identifiable to the listener of a discourse. However, reasons for not equating topic with either have already been discussed, and topics are not automatically first in a clause, subjects, participants, or agents.

If, instead, we focus on topic introduction, a common problem seems to be that topics are identified after their initial introduction, whether we view topic in traditional terms or as a nominal entity with prominence in a stretch of continuous discourse. Further, the characteristics that together signal a new topic or theme at paragraph boundaries will also act as the signal for thematic unity within a paragraph. Both Grimes (1975) and Longacre (1996:119), for example, discuss setting as the introductory material of a paragraph; the setting expresses temporal and locational information and is maintained throughout a "constituent part" of a text (Grimes 1975:51). At thematic boundaries, temporal or locational information may be mentioned, marking the start of a new topic or theme.

Despite these difficulties, it is important to examine the questions of topic introduction and status maintenance separately, and from this point on, I will use the term topic in the restricted meaning I have proposed here.

Techniques for introducing a topic are many and varied, and probably have a great deal to do with the speaker's level of expertise in relating events. Although a new topic may not always be clearly identified by the speaker, there may be some predictable mechanisms in the grammar. In Mundurukú, for example, a new topic is introduced as either the object or the goal of a transitive sentence (Grimes 1975:103, quoting from a manuscript on paragraphing in Mundurukú discourse by Sheffler). The immediately preceding clause is also apparently essential in the identification of the new topic and must include a particle meaning 'I am going to talk about something else'. The use of overt statements of intent is common in West Greenlandic too, and this technique for introducing topics or themes may be typologically widespread. Other techniques for topic introduction in West Greenlandic include fronting of the nominal (whether the fronting is contrastive or not), incorporation, the use of reflection clauses, the use of discourse particles to reflect different levels of paragraph structure and perhaps different levels of topicality, interactions between theme and topic, and verb form. They each contribute to signaling topicality in discourse, but their individual effects are difficult to gauge.

Information that can become topical in West Greenlandic is typically expressed in one of three ways: by means of information carried in the verb, that is, thematic information; by means of incorporation of the noun into a verbal structure; and by means of an overt noun phrase, whether in direct relationship with the verb or not. In text 1b, for example the speaker uses all three in one section:

(2.13)  incorporation (from text 1b):

136.  . . . *tamuatsivaartorluta* *tassa*
      *tamuatsivaaq-toq-luta* *tassa*
      tamuatsivaaq-eat-1PL.CT that.is
      '. . . we ate "tamuatsivaaq" (seal skin and fat chewing gum)'

(2.14)  theme (from text 1b):

139.  . . . *tassa* *taanna_* *tamuarujoortarparput*
      *tassa* *taanna* *tamua-rujoor-saq-varput*
      that.is that.one.ABS chew-casually-HAB-1PL.SUBJ/
      3SG.OBJ.IND
      '. . . we used to chew it continually'

(2.15)  overt nominal (from text 1b):

140.    . . . *tamuatsivaamik_*        *taasarparput*        *uagut*        *taqqavani.*
        *tamuatsivaaq-mik*            *taasar-varput*        *uagut*        *taqqava-ni*
        tamuatsivaaq-INST            call-1PL.SUBJ/         1PL.ABS       south-LOC
                                     3SG.OBJ.IND

        '. . . we in the south used to call it "tamuatsivaaq."'

There is a marked preponderance of intransitive structures in the texts:
about 428 of 620 clauses, or over two-thirds of all clauses, are intransitive
(the same tendency is found in Dixon's Dyirbal text samples, 1972:368–97).
Information must therefore often be introduced by means of the verb phrase.
This lends support to Givón's (1984:256) observation that new information
tends to be introduced in the verb in intransitive sentences and as either
the verb or the object in transitive sentences.[6] He suggests that intransitive
constructions are more marked than the transitive constructions, in that
the verb is included in the scope of new information in the former but not
in the latter, although I suspect this is merely a reflection of the difficulty
in defining theme as opposed to topic.

The statistical importance of intransitive clauses in a text and the possibility of incorporating a potential topic into a verbal, or thematic, structure,
highlights the necessity of considering how themes affect the introduction
of topics. This is particularly evident with respect to incorporation. An
incorporated noun that might otherwise have been an object will affect the
expression of topichood, since the topic is denominalized. Furthermore,
the choice of syntactic structure of incorporated nouns may have an effect
on topichood, as in the following, all from speaker 3:

(2.16)  (clauses 99, 112, 117 from text 3a; clause 127 from text 3b)

99.     *Tassa_*     *piniartorsuarminngooq*                *ataataqarsimavugut*
        *Tassa*      *piniartoq-suaq-mik-gooq*              *ataata-qaq-sima-vugut*
        that.is      hunter-big-inst-reported.speech        father-have-PERF-
                                                            1PL.IND

        'That is, we had a father they say [who] was a big hunter'

112.    . . . *ataataqarsimallunga.*
        ataata-qaq-sima-lunga
        father-have-PERF-1SG.CT
        '. . . I had a father.'

117. *Anaanagaara*       *Sisimiormiut.*
   *Anaana-gi-vara*      *Sisimiut-miut*
   mother-have-3SG.SUBJ/3SG.OBJ.IND Sisimiut-from
   'I have a mother from Sisimiut.' (or 'I have her as my mother
   from Sisimiut')

127. *Sooq;* *taava_* *anaana-_*      *anaanagaara B._*
                 *B.O.,*

   *sooq* *taava*          *anaana-gi-vara B.B.-0*
                  *O.-0*

   so  then  mother-have-1SG.SUBJ/ O.-ABS
           3SG.OBJ.IND    B.B.-ABS

   'So; then, I have B., B.O. as a mother, . . .' (or 'my mother
   was B.O.')

The first clause in example 2.16 is an antipassive; the second, an intransitive; the third and fourth are transitive ergative structures. All involve the incorporation of the same type of participant (speaker's father or mother). The intransitive structures can roughly be understood as 'I have a father' whereas the transitive structures can be translated as 'I have her as my mother' or 'my mother is . . .'; the transitive structures imply what others have noted, namely definiteness, givenness, or prominence.

Incorporation in West Greenlandic cannot be explained, as for example in Nahuatl (see Merlan 1976), as a way of continuing topic or as a mark of the change in status of nouns from rhematic to thematic (in the sense of order of introduction of information in a clause). Incorporated nouns in West Greenlandic often mark the first mention of the noun in the text (e.g., text 2, clause 4) and in many cases involve lexicalized constructions (as in *ukioqarpoq* 'he is X years old'). Nouns are often incorporated into intransitive structures, particularly if they are newly introduced (although they can also be found in transitive structures, as in clauses 3a.117 and 3b.127 in example 2.16 above). Information added as an afterthought to these structures will therefore be marked instrumentally, as would objects in an antipassive construction (although whether this should be interpreted as an antipassive or as a structural restriction on speech is unclear):

(2.17)  (From text 2)

52.    *Aammalu      ukiumi_        qassusiortarpugut*
       *nammineq     uagut*

       *aamma-lu     ukioq-mi       qassut-lioq-saq-vugut*
       *nammineq     uagut*

       and-and      winter-LOC     net-build-HAB-1PL.IND
                    self           1PL.ABS

       'And in the winter we ourselves used to build nets [make nets]'

       *saarullinnut        qassutissatsinnik.*
       *saarullik-nut       qassutit-ssaq-tsinnik*
       codfish-PL.TERM      net-PL-FUT-1PL.POS.INST
       'nets for the codfish.'

Finally, incorporation must affect the relationship between topic and
theme. Is an incorporated object thematic or topical? In West Greenlandic
is it a vehicle for introducing new information when there is no place for
topic? What happens when theme and topic are both important, or when
theme is new but topic is not, and vice versa? Example 2.18 illustrates some
of these issues:

(2.18)  (From text 1b)

107.   . . . *kisiannili    tassa      taamani       aamma_    piniartuuneq*
       *kisianni-li    tassa      taamani       aamma     piniartoq-u-neq*
       but-but        that.is    at.that.time  and       hunter-COP-
                                                         NOMZ.ABS

       '. . . but in those days, to be a hunter'

       *inuuneq    piniartuuneq            imaannaanngitsorujussuuvoq*
       *inuuneq    piniartoq-u-neq         imaannaanngit-soq-*
                                           *rujussuaq-u-voq*
       life        hunter-COP-NOMZ.ABS    be.amazing-PART-very.
                                          much-COP-3SG.IND

       'to live, to be a hunter it was very amazing'

108.   *nunatsinni_            inuit         amerlanersai,*
       *nuna-tsinni            inuk-it       amerla-nersaq-i*

land-1PL.POS.LOC    person-PL    be.many-NOMZ.most-3PL.
                                 POS/PL.POSM.ABS

'in our land, its many people'

ullumikkut       oqartarpugut
ullumi-kkut      oqaq-saq-vugut
today-VIA        say-HAB-1PL.IND
'today, we say'

109.    (aalisarneq       inuutissarsiutit      pingaarnersarivaat).
        aalisarneq-0      inuutissarsiut-it     pingaar-nersaq-gi-vaat
        fishing-ABS       occupation-PL         important-NOMZ.most-have-
                                                3PL.SUBJ/3OBJ.IND
        '(the most important careers/occupations are fishing).'

110.    Taamani           uagut         meeraasugut
        taamani           uagut         meeraq-u-sugut
        at.that.time      1PL.ABS       child-COP-1PL.PART
        '[but] At that time [when] we were children'

111.    piniarneq         inuutissarsiutit          annersarivaat.
        piniarneq-0       inuutissarsiut-it         annersaq-gi-vaat
        hunting-ABS       career/occupation-PL      biggest-have-3PL.
                                                    SUBJ/3SG.OBJ.IND
        'the biggest careers/occupations were hunting.'

112.    Qajaqarput,            piniartut      tamarmik
        qajaq-qaq-vut         piniartoq-t    tamaq-mik
        kayak-have-3PL.IND     hunter-PL      all-3PL.S
        'They had kayaks, all the hunters'

113.    qajaqqissorsuullutik.
        qajaqqiC-soq-suaq-u-lutik
        be.good.with.kayak-PART-very.much-COP-3PL.CT
        'they were very good with the kayaks.'

In clause 112 'kayak' is incorporated and the subject is 'hunters', but
this is the first mention of both kayaks and hunters. 'Hunting' occurs as
a topic in clause 111 and as a nominalized theme in clause 107 as in 'to be

a hunter'. Is the first actual instance of 'hunter', in clause 112, really a new topic? Furthermore, what is the relative prominence of 'they had kayaks' and 'hunters'? In the immediately following text, 'kayakers' is used as a synonym for 'hunters' (see clauses 126–130). The same sorts of considerations are present in clauses 135–141 of the same text, in which the speaker describes a form of natural chewing gum, *tamuatsivaaq*. The object being chewed is first introduced as an incorporated noun (see clauses 135 and 136 'we all used to eat the liver [incorporated] and we ate tamuatsivaaq [incorporated]'), simultaneous with the introduction of 'eat' as a theme (or 'eat liver/gum'). Future mentions of *tamuatsivaaq*, in clauses 139 and 140, are all as independent nominals. One is tempted to say that incorporation must be a regular method of introducing new information, but not all instances of incorporation introduce new information. Further, the incorporated nominal once introduced seems to be topical to some degree and often shows up in subsequent text as an independent nominal argument of the verb, that is, in a position in which topics are found, although again, not all incorporated nouns have continuity in a text. At the same time, by virtue of incorporation, the nominal becomes part of the theme: in the above example of *tamuatsivaaq*, it is not the act of eating that is thematic, but the act of eating *tamuatsivaaq*. At most, one must simply acknowledge the complexity of the information a speaker can convey in a single clause.

Incorporation in West Greenlandic has syntactic ramifications evident in such features as stranded modifiers, coordination, and so forth (see Sadock 1991:91; also my data, e.g., text 2, clauses 41–42, and text 4, clauses 37–40). Hopper and Thompson (1984:714) suggest that incorporated nouns cannot be referential and that they cannot be used in further discourse without being reintroduced as independent, overt nominals. This is contradicted by my data; in clause 50, 'meeting' is incorporated, and assumed in the following clause:

(2.19)  (From text 4)

50.    . . . *aamma*    *Landsrådimi*          *ataatsimeeqataasarpoq*
       *aamma*         *Landsråd-mi*          *ataatsimii-qat-u-saq-voq*
       and             country.council-LOC    be.in.a.meeting-
                                              companion-COP-HAB-
                                              3SG.IND

'. . . and he used to be in the country council meetings'

51. *marloriarluni*        *ataataga.*
    *marloq-giaq-luni*       *ataata-ga*
    two-do.x.times-3SG.CT    father-1SG.POS.ABS
    'going twice, my father [i.e., as vice-member, taking over when the chief was indisposed].'

Sadock (1991:86) writes that an incorporated noun introduces a new topic, and this is certainly the case sometimes (see, for example, text 2, clause 4, and text 4, clause 37) but not exclusively. Some (Merlan 1976; Mithun 1984a) write that incorporation enables topic continuity (if it serves a discourse purpose; Mithun points out that not all forms of incorporation serve the same purpose). Again, I find this to be true only some of the time (cf. text 4, clause 6, 'my growing up among only the great hunters being the reason', and clause 7, 'my father himself was a hunter', where 'hunter' in clause 6 is an oblique nominal and in clause 7 an incorporated one). Despite Mithun (1984a) and Hopper and Thompson (1984), an incorporated noun can be referential and specific (cf. examples by Sadock 1991:87), and although in most cases incorporated nouns tend to be indefinite, there are examples of incorporated possessed nouns, as in 'her home' in example 2:20:

(2.20) (From text 3a)

1.    *Tassa*     *massakkut,*    *Sisimiuni*         *D.L.-ip*
                                *angerlarsimaffianiippugut*

    *Tassa*     *massakkut*    *Sisimiut-ni*       *D.L.-ip*
                                *angerlarsimaffik-ani-u-vugut*

    That.is     now         Sisimiut-PL.LOC    D.L.-REL
                                home-3C.SG.POS-COP-1PL.IND

'So now we are in D.L.'s home in Sisimiut . . .'

Sadock (1991:94) notes that structures with incorporation can be used in the same circumstances as corresponding antipassives. If so, this would mean that incorporated nominals are not topical, an assertion that requires further research and is beyond the scope of this work. If this is the case, however, then the same types of exceptions to traditional syntactic explanations are found in constructions involving incorporation as are found with antipassives (see chapters 1 and 3). Finally, many of the most ordinary verbal constructions that are used to introduce topics are only built with denominalizing suffixes; to say 'there were hunters', for example, the normal construction would necessarily involve incorporation, regardless of topic status. In summary, there are many issues with incorporation, some of which are syntactic, other lexical, and still others pragmatic. Although both themes and incorporated topics are important in the structuring of Greenlandic texts, they will not be the focus of the analyses in subsequent chapters.

Incorporation denominalizes a potential topic; the opposite situation arises when potential themes are deverbalized. What is the topic status of deverbalized constructions? Deverbal constructions often have characteristics of both nouns and verbs (Hopper and Thompson 1984; Givón 1990). Nominalizations in my texts are able to function as topics. In example 2.21 the nominalization *isikkorinnersuara* 'my looking good' in clause 28 (with the nominalizing suffix *-neq-* and a personal possessive inflectional suffix) is acting as a prototypical noun phrase; it is indexed on the verb, it is inflected in the absolutive case, and it is coreferenced by the cataphoric deictic pronoun *taanna*:

(2.21)  (From text 3a)

28.  *Tusakataavittarpara*                                                *taanna*
      *tusakataavittaq-vara*                                            *taanna*
      be.quite.tired.of.hearing-1SG.SUBJ/3SG.OBJ.IND   that.one
      'I am really quite tired of hearing that'

      isikkorinnersuara
      isikku-rik-neq-suaq-ga
      view-have.a.good-NOMZ-big-1SG.POS.ABS
      '[that] I look good . . .'

Some deverbal forms are not so unambiguous. There are several ways of nominalizing verbs in West Greenlandic, one of which involves the use of *-neq-*, as in example 2.21. Another method involves the use of the intransitive participial morphology. The intransitive participial inflected for third person can be interpreted either as a verb mood, a relativized construction, or a nominalized form, and it is not always possible to determine in which capacity the participial is functioning (as in text 1a, clauses 23–28, *qallunaatuinnaq oqaluttoq* 'he only spoke Danish' or 'who only spoke Danish' or 'one who only spoke Danish'). These forms all imply full clausal semantics, with subject and sometimes object implicit in the construction. As verbs, they express thematic information; as relative clauses, they modify a topic; as nominals, they act as a topic.

Finally, overt noun phrases, including nominalizations, may be topics. As discussed above, there are a number of ways of introducing topics in my texts, including fronting, the use of reflection clauses, reintroduction of an oblique noun phrase as a subject or object, and incorporation. In my data, fronting of overt noun phrases is the most common method of introducing a new topic. By fronting, I refer to the placement of overt noun phrases at the beginning of a clause, being distinguished from normal word order either by intonation, by repetition, or by marked word order itself.[7] In example 2.22 the speaker separates the object, 'my being someone who is good to look at', by means of intonation, indicating special emphasis:

(2.22)  (From text 3a)

25.  . . . *tassami_*  *taanna*  *isikkorneran — _ taanna isikkuminarnersuara* . . .

*tassa-mi*  *taanna*  *isi-kkuminar-neq-suaq-ga*

that.is-INTNS  that.one  eyes-be.good.for-NOMZ-big-1SG.POS.ABS

'. . . that is, my being someone who is good to look at . . .'

*tusakataavittarpara,*  *ilaa*
*tusakataavittaq-vara*  *ilaa*
be.quite.tired.of.hearing-1SG.SUBJ/3SG.OBJ.IND  you.know
'I get really quite tired of hearing, you know . . .'

In example 2.23 both intonation and repetition are used to emphasize 'hunters' and 'kayaks':

(2.23)  (From text 1a)

17.  . . . *tassanilu_*  *piniartuinnaat_*  *-ngajaviit_ (aalisartumininnguit*

*tassani-lu*  *piniartoq-innaq-it*  *-ngajak-vik-it*
*aalisartoq-mineq-nnguaq-it*

there-and          hunter-only-PL          almost-real-PL
fisherman-kind.of-DIM-PL

'. . . and there — [were] only hunters, almost only [almost
entirely], ([there were] a few fishermen'

| 18. | *taamani* | *aalisarneq* | | *suli* | *ingerlalluannginnami).* |
|---|---|---|---|---|---|
| | *taamani* | *aalisarneq-0* | | *suli* | *ingerlaC-lluaq-nngit-gami* |
| | at.that.time | fishing.[industry]-ABS | | yet | be.underway/going-well-NEG-3C.SG.CAUS |

'at that time the fishing was not yet going well).'

| 19. | *Piniartut,* | *qajat,* | *qajaannarmik* | *inuussuteqarput.* |
|---|---|---|---|---|
| | *Piniartoq-t,* | *qajaq-t,* | *qajaq-innaq-mik* | *inuu-ssuteqaq-vut* |
| | Hunter-PL | kayak-PL | kayak-only-INST | live-by.means.of-3PL.IND |

'[The] hunters, kayaks, they only used the kayak to live by [i.e.,
hunt].'

Each of these examples involves the first mention of the topic (e.g., 'my
being someone who is good to look at', 'hunters', 'kayaks') in the respective
texts. Fronting is also common as a device for emphasizing a nominal with
already determined topic status.

The second most common method of introducing a topic involves reflection clauses, or clauses that take the speaker out of the setting of the text,
express a speaker's reflection on the events or state of the text, and in
some cases evaluate these events or states. Different speakers have distinct
preferences in the frequency of their usage of reflection clauses and in the
particular verb they use, but they all involve the introduction of the topic
(or theme) as the object of the reflection. Speaker 4 uses reflection clauses
very directly:

(2.24) (From text 4)

| 1. | *Tassa_* | *siullermik* | *oqaatigissavara* |
|---|---|---|---|
| | *Tassa* | *siullermik* | *oqaatigi-ssa-vara* |
| | that.is | at.first | talk.about-FUT-1SG.SUBJ/3SG.OBJ.IND |

'So first I am going to talk about this'

2.  *uanga      Nuummi       inunngorpunga*
    *uanga      Nuuk-mi      inunngor-vunga*
    1sg.ABS     Nuuk-LOC     be.born-1SG.IND
    'I was born in Nuuk ...'

or again,

(2.25)  (From text 4)

27.  *Taava_      oqaatigissavakkalu       taamanikkut*
                                           *piniartorsuit*

     *Taava      oqaatigi-ssa-vakka-lu      taamani-kkut*
                                            *piniartoq-suaq-it*

     then        talk.about-FUT-1SG.        at.that.time-VIA
                 SUBJ/3PL.OBJ.IND-and

                                            hunter-big-PL

'Then I can talk about the big hunters in those days'

*piniartuinnarsuit             akornanni      Saarlumi*
*piniartoq-innaq-suaq-it       akornanni      Saarloq-mi*
hunter-only-big-PL             among          Saarloq-LOC
'among only the big hunters in Saarloq ...'

Speakers 1 and 2 tend to prefer statements such as 'I remember' in similar situations, but the effect is similar. Speaker 1 also makes extensive use of reflection clauses of evaluation for didactic effect in his story about the catechists; he is also more indirect in pinpointing his topic (or theme), as we see in examples 2.10 and 2.11. The use of reflection clauses, unlike fronting, very often involves the introduction of themes rather than topics (although it need not; one might reflect on the difference in focus between 'I remember when I was young' and 'I remember my youth').

Another way of establishing a topic is by using the oblique phrase of a previous clause as subject, object, or incorporated noun; speaker 4 commonly employs this technique:

(2.26)  (From text 4)

29.  *... Qaarusumminngaanniit      nuupput           Saarlumut*
     *Qaarusuk-minngaanniit         nuuC-vut          Saarloq-mut*

Qaarusuk-ABL                    move-3PL.IND    Saarloq-TERM
'. . . they moved from Qaarusuk to Saarloq'

30.    *taamaalillunilu,*
       taamaali-luni-lu
       be.like.that-3SG.CT-and
       'and it was like this/in this way'

31.    *Saarloq           inuttusiallappoq*
       *Saarloq-0         inuttu-si-allag-voq*
       Saarloq-ABS     have/be.people-INTRANS-increase-3SG.IND
       'Saarloq became more populated . . .'

In the same text, clauses 4, 7, and 47 also involve the reintroduction of an oblique noun as a direct verbal argument. This is not a common technique in other texts.

Particles or temporal adverbs, each signaling a structural change in the paragraph hierarchy, are rarely if ever used where no other devices (e.g., fronting) are. Temporal adverbs often signal the reintroduction of information:

(2.27)  (From text 2)

86.    *Atorsaroriartuaaq*
       atorsaror-giartuaaq
       wind.died.down-gradually.more.and.more
       'The wind having gradually died down more and more'

87.    *piniutigut*              *taamaani_*        *Amerlup*
                                 *saqqaaniit*       *uagut*

       *piniut-vut*              *taamaani*         *Amerloq-p*
                                 *saqqaa-niit*      *uagut*

       equipment-1PL.POS.ABS    at.that.time       Amerloq-REL
                                 sunshine.side-ABL   1PL.ABS

'our things, then the ones from the sunny side of Amerloq —
we, uh'

       *saqqaa-tungaani*         *taamaani*
       *saqqaa-tungaa-ni*        *taamaani*

sunny.side-toward-LOC    at.that.time
'on the way toward the sunny side at that time'

88.   *piniuteqarajunnerusaratta.*
piniut-qaq-gajug-neru-saq-gatta
things-have-often-more-HAB-1PL.CAUS
'we used to have more equipment.'

89.   *Saqqaanilu*       *tassa*      *atuartarlugit,*
Saqqaa-ni-lu       tassa      atuartaq-lugit
sunny.side-LOC-and  that.is  follow-3PL.OBJ.CT
'And then on the sunny side [we] used to bring them in line [the nets]'

90.   *imaattorlugit*
imaattoq-lugit
like.this-3PL.OBJ.CT
'like this [gestures]'

91.   *amuartarlugit*
amuar-saq-lugit
haul.up-HAB-3PL.OBJ.CT
'hauling them up'

92.   *taamanikkummi*          *qassuterpaalussuarnik*
                          *piniuteqartarpugut . . .*

*taamani-kkut-mi*        *qassut-(r)pak-aluk-ssuaq-nik*
                          *piniut-qaq-saq-vugut*

at.that.time-VIA-INTNS  net-many-rather-big-PL.INST
                         equipment-have-HAB-1PL.IND

'at that time we had rather a lot of nets as equipment . . .'

*Piniuti* 'equipment' is first introduced in a previous paragraph as an incorporated noun (clause 81, not listed here); in this section, it is mentioned first as an independent noun (clause 87), and then as an incorporated noun (clause 88). After a break, it is reintroduced in clause 92, again as an incorporated noun, in a clause introduced by the temporal adverb *taamani(-kkut)* 'at that time'.

More commonly, a number of devices are used at once, such that particles, fronting, and the use of indicative clauses all co-occur to signal topic introduction. There is also a high correlation of indicative clauses to topic introduction and to overt topics. In example 2.28, *ataataga* 'my father' is first introduced in clause 7, in an indicative clause:

(2.28)  (From text 4)

7.      *Ataataga*              *nammineq_*      *piniartuuvoq*
        *Ataata-ga*            *nammineq*       *piniartoq-u-voq*
        father-1SG.POS.ABS    self             hunter-COP-3SG.IND
        'My father himself was a hunter . . .'

In the same text, indicatives and topic introduction co-occur often.[8] Not all indicatives signal topichood, however, and not all topics are introduced by indicatives.

In addition to introducing a topic or theme, a speaker must also signal the relative importance of topics and themes within a stretch of discourse. Jones (1977), while acknowledging the subjective nature of thematic identification, lists a number of grammatical devices that give prominence to a theme in a text in English, including topicalization, clefting, certain uses of conjunctions or phrases with conjunctive functions (as in 'in the first place', etc.), textual organizational methods, and repetition (including paraphrasing and ellipsis). Many of these devices are common in the West Greenlandic texts: intonation, variations in word order, including both topicalization and focus constructions, reflection clauses, and repetition can all be used to emphasize a nominal, to promote textual coherence, and so forth. The choice of verb form can indicate the relative importance of a clause within a paragraph, and therefore of thematic prominence. Interestingly, focus constructions (right-dislocation) tend to occur where the speaker has not clearly identified the topic in an ambiguous text; in example 2.29, the referents of clauses 67 and 68 are unclear:

(2.29)  (From text 4)

67.     *. . . Aggu Lyngeugaluup_*        *allaaserigamiuk*
        *Aggu Lynge-u-galuaq-up*          *allaaseri-gamiuk*
        Aggu Lynge-COP-late-REL          write.about-3C.SG.SUBJ/3SG.OBJ.CAUS
        '. . . the late Aggu Lynge, when he wrote about it/him'

68.  *ataataga*                    *pisimagaa*
     *ataata-ga*                   *pi-sima-gaa*
     father-1SG.POS.ABS       thing-PERF-3SG.SUBJ/3SG.OBJ.IND
     'he did it [about my father?]'

69.  "*Pikkorinnersaallu*              *immikkut*
                                       *akissarsisippaa.*"

     *pikkoriC-neq-saat-lu*            *immikkut*
                                       *akissarsi-tit-vaa*

     clever-SUP-means.to-and       special/individual
                                   get.prize-cause-3SG.SUBJ/3SG.OBJ.IND

     '"And the cleverest will get a special prize"/"he will give a prize to
     the cleverest."'

70.  (*Tassa*    *kunngip*     *Christiaap*        *qulingata*).
     *Tassa*     *kunngi-p*    *Christiaa-p*       *qulingat-a*
     that.is   king-REL     Christian-REL      tenth-3SG.POS/SG.POSM.ABS
     '(That is, King Christian the Tenth.)'

There are at least three possible topics, 'Aggu Lynge', 'my father', and
'King Christian the Tenth'. The speaker distinguishes the relevant topic by
naming it explicitly in a focus construction; presumably it is the king who
said that the cleverest would get a prize, and cleverest may be in reference
to the father (M. Fortescue, personal communication), but it is not clear.
Another example of disambiguation through focusing is found later the
same text. In example 2.30, clause 42, *aanaavat* 'their grandmother' refers
to the topic of previous text:

(2.30)  (From text 4)
41.  . . . *tassaavoq*              *arnaq*           *utoqqaq: H.E.*
     *tassa-u-voq*                  *arnaq-0*         *utoqqaq-0: H.E.*
     that.is-COP-3SG.IND       woman-ABS      old.person-ABS: H.E.
     '. . . it was an old lady: H.E.'

42.  *Maani,*    *naluneqanngittut,*                   *J.E.-ikkut,*
                                                       *B.E.-ikkut*

| *Maani* | *nalu-neqaq-nngit-sut* | *J.E.-kkut*-0 |
| | | *B.E.-kkut*-0 |
| here | not.know-PASS-NEG-3PL.PART | J.E.-family-ABS |
| | | B.E.-family-ABS |

'Here the well-known J.E. and B.E. [families]'

*aanaavat.*
aanaa-at
grandmother-3PL.POS/SG.POSM.ABS
'their grandmother.'

In addition to signaling the introduction and maintenance of topics and themes, there are various ways of signaling topic or thematic shift. Many have already been mentioned. The use of connecting particles, such as *tassa* 'that is', *kisianni* 'but', *taava* 'then', and so forth, can signal the continuation or change of a topic or theme, parenthetical status of a clause or clauses with respect to the main paragraph, or a change in paragraph or paragraph level (Berge 1999a, 1999b). These are often accompanied by the repetition of certain clauses throughout a text, especially of temporal and locational expressions or clauses. Expressions such as *taamani* 'at that time' or *meeraallunga* 'when I was a child', for example, are mentioned not more than once per paragraph (although they are not necessarily the first expression or clause following a topic or thematic shift). One of the clearest examples of this comes from text 1b. From the beginning of the text, *taamani* 'at that time' is used at most once per paragraph, with two or three exceptions, each of which involves a parenthetical statement (see clauses 125, 177, and 179). However, clauses such as *meeraallunga* 'when I was a child' or *ukiuulluni* 'in the wintertime' are expected to be remembered across a discourse (a number of factors contribute to the clarity of paragraph structure in this text; see chapter 4 for the full discussion).

All of the above are consistent indications of topic status, particularly when several occur together. In languages that do not grammaticalize topics, we could expect to find a similar set of indicators. If topic is grammaticalized, however, we expect a more direct indication of topic status through grammatical means, such as morphological marking or special status in syntactic constructions. In fact, absolute and ergative case marking, verbal agreement, and switch-reference in West Greenlandic all refer to topic rather than subject status. These are all methods of tracking nominals across clauses or texts and they are traditionally associated with subject and object roles. Topics are, by the definition used here, nominals; if topics can be grammaticalized, then they can be tracked using these methods.

## 2.4 Discourse roles

In the previous sections, I argued that the basic distinction between nouns and verbs, noun phrases and verb phrases, arguments and predicates, and so forth, can be extended to discourse, as topic and theme. Carrying the analogy one step further, nominals at other levels of grammatical structure are associated with functional roles, such as syntactic roles (subject, object, and oblique) or semantic roles (agent, patient, recipient, and so forth). Can we find equivalent types of discourse roles? Roles such as subject, object, agent, and patient have been applied in syntactic analyses because they have been useful in identifying and describing categories in different languages. For example, nominal arguments morphologically marked in a similar way and with similar functions in the syntax may be thought to represent a natural class. Those marked with nominative case endings in a nominative-accusative language may be called subjects and those marked accusatively may be called objects. Both nominative-marked and accusative-marked nominals can be expected to have predictable functions in clauses. A definition of subject and object that depends on case marking, however, is superficial and proves inadequate for the descriptions of many languages, including English, where case is distinguished morphologically only with pronouns. Within mainstream syntactic theories, various roles have been defined with respect to the syntactic constructions they are part of, and with respect to their relationship with the predicate. Thus, in Chomskian approaches, the subject and the object are differentiated with respect to their position in a hierarchy of structural units, the subject being on an equal level to the predicate, the object being subsumed into the predicate. The arguments are defined by their position relative to the verb phrase. In relational grammar, subjects and objects are defined as primitives, but they are ranked on a hierarchy of semantic roles. There is a strong tendency for agents to be subjects in transitive sentences, patients to be direct objects, and benefactives or recipients to be indirect objects. In many languages, semantic roles have been found to be either additionally useful or more useful in describing morphological marking or syntactic categories. Comrie (1981:59) sees the usefulness of semantic roles as arising from the functional requirements of language, because semantic relations are connected with information flow, whereas it is unclear why syntactic roles are necessary (although he concedes that attempts to do away with them have not been successful). These findings may enhance the importance of semantic roles in syntactic structures. Dixon (1994:29) cites Manipuri as a language with semantically based morphological marking, and he lists a group of languages that have syntactically based marking on transitive verbs but a semantically based marking for intransitive verbs (Dixon 1994:78). In an interesting shift in the classification of English predicates, Halliday (1968:184) suggests that English clause organization may be better viewed, in some respects, as semantically ergative. Further, it has long been recognized that syntactic roles alone have not accounted for essentially syntactic phenomena (e.g., passive or antipassive constructions, etc.). Since Fillmore's (1968) discussion of case, in which he showed how underlying semantic roles can be mapped onto surface syntactic constructions, the importance of semantic roles in syntactic descriptions has been widely accepted, and characteristics of verbal arguments are often described in both syntactic and semantic terms.

The implication of proposing distinct discourse-level roles is that there must be languages with discourse roles that motivate syntactic constructions. This is not necessarily a new claim, although I am restricting the notion of a discourse role in a novel way. Comrie (1981:56–57), for example, suggests that there are pragmatic or discourse roles, but by these he refers to something quite different. Unlike semantic roles, Comrie's pragmatic roles are not restricted to noun phrases, nor do they reflect the same types of syntactic relationships with other elements that semantic roles do. They refer to the "different ways in which essentially the same information, or the same semantic content, can be structured differently to reflect the flow of given and new information" (Comrie 1981:56–57). Like Halliday (1967a), he calls "focus" the essential piece of new information carried by the sentence, and he calls "topic" what Halliday calls "theme." Some languages have even grammaticalized these pragmatic roles, as in the Japanese topic marker *wa*, for instance, or the word order patterns used to indicate focus in Hungarian. These are all still clause-level roles, however, despite the pragmatic or discourse information they convey.

More importantly, an increasing number of studies suggest that syntactic phenomena are dependent on environments greater than the sentence. Du Bois (1987), as mentioned above, effectively shows that the grammatical argument positions (subject, object) in Sacapultec are preferentially filled not only with respect to their morphological but also to their pragmatic type. Objects of transitive clauses in Sacapultec are not only marked as absolutives but they also reflect information flow: absolutive objects tend to fill a position in which new participants are introduced in the discourse, as opposed to ergative subjects, which overwhelmingly tend to be thematic (in his terminology), that is, maintained in successive clauses, definite, and given (Du Bois 1987:829). In my texts, absolutive object position is not just the slot for the introduction of new participants in the discourse, it is the slot for local topics (see chapter 3). Since not all absolutive objects are new participants, my statement is a more general than Du Bois's. For example, in example 3.12, none of the ergative structures (clauses 58 and 59) introduce a new participant or topic, but the absolutive is the topic in all cases. Thus, topic as a role is useful in the generalization of a particular syntactic category.

Givón (1976) takes a different approach to the grammaticalization of discourse by suggesting that grammatical agreement of the subject with the verb or the object with the verb or both derives from topic–verb agreement. There is a topic hierarchy, similar to a semantically based agency hierarchy, such that humans are more topical than nonhumans, definite nouns are more topical than indefinite nouns, more involved participants are more topical than less involved ones, and first and second persons are more topical than third persons. The more topical the argument, the more likely it will be to have (overt) agreement marking. This observation would account for the tendency to have overt marking for first and second persons and zero marking for third persons, for example. It also accounts for typological tendencies in hierarchical agreement marking on the verb: if a language has indirect object agreement, then it also has direct object agreement, and if it has direct object agreement, then it also has subject agreement. Further, if languages lose agreement marking on the verbs, this marking is most likely to be lost in dependent clauses rather than in independent clauses, as the former are also most likely to reflect background, or nontopical, information. Based on such evidence, Givón sees anaphoric pronominalization and verbal agreement as results of topic shift (topicalization) and afterthought constructions. However, it is unlikely that afterthought constructions are so prevalent as to lead to grammaticalization in this way, unless he is referring to right dislocation constructions. Further, the link of topics to particular types of participants, such as humans, depends on the type of discourse. However, the reinterpretation of agreement with topic rather than subject is interesting. There is evidence from other types of agreement constructions, such as switch-reference, that agreement crosses paragraph boundaries: Stirling (1993), crediting Payne, notes that the switch-reference system in Chickasaw indicates reference relations across sentence and paragraph boundaries. Coreference beyond the sentence is also found in West Greenlandic:

(2.31)   (From text 3a)

28.   *Tusakataavittarpara*                                         *taanna*
      *tusakataavittaq-vara*                                        *taanna*
      be.quite.tired.of.hearing-1SG.SUBJ/3SG.OBJ.IND    that.one
      'I am really quite tired of hearing that'

      isikkorinnersuara
      isikku-rik-neq-suaq-ga
      view-have.a.good-NOMZ-big-1SG.POS.ABS
      '[that] I look good'

29.   *Emilliannguup*          *panimma*
      *Emillia-nnguaq-p*       *paniq-ma*
      Emilia-DIM-REL           daughter-1SG.POS.ABS
      'Emily, my daughter'

      taamaallunga
      taamaa-lunga
      be.like.that-1SG.CT
      'while I am like that'

30.   *oqarfiginikuuaanga*
      oqarfigi-nikuu-vaanga

say.to-past-3SG.SUBJ/1SG.OBJ.IND
'said to me'

31.  "*Tassamiuna*          *illit_*     *ajoquteqarnerit*
     *Tassami-una*          *illit*      *ajoqut-qaq-neq-it*
     in.any.case-DEIC     2SG       sickness-have-NOMZ-2SG.POS.ABS
     '"in any case your having a sickness'

     *upperineq*               *ajornartoq*
     *upperi-neq*-0            *ajornar-soq*
     believe-NOMZ-ABS      be.impossible-3SG.PART
     'it is impossible to believe'

32.  *isikkorinnersuarmit."*
     isikku-rik-neq-suaq-mit
     view-have.a.good-NOMZ-big-ABL
     'because you look so good."'

Clause 29 contains a contemporative clause inserted in an indicative clause, the predicate of which is in clause 30. The contemporative, however, refers back to the previous clause, to the speaker's 'looking good'. The contemporative in West Greenlandic is identified as a marker of subject coreference between two clauses in a sentence. In this example, it not only does not mark subject coreference with that of its superordinate ('Emily'), but it marks coreference to a preceding clause in a previous sentence.

Explanations of agreement marking, whether the marking has to do with case or switch-reference, often hinge on the relative transitivity of the clauses in question. Most discussions of transitivity revolve around a very limited number of verbs that are taken to be prototypically transitive, such as 'kill', 'stab', 'kick', and 'love'. The majority of verbs, however, do not clearly represent action initiated by one participant and undergone by another, a fact that is reflected in their nonprototypical marking (compare 'I stabbed him' vs. 'I sat on him'). To account for semantic differences between prototypically transitive and less transitive verbs, Hopper and Thompson (1980) propose a hierarchy of transitivity traits, including degree of action, number of participants, choice of aspect, degree of volition, and so forth. The hierarchy is also used to explain anomalous agreement marking. Taking a slightly different approach, Fortescue (1991) suggests that anomalous coreference or lack thereof in West Greenlandic can be explained by viewing the marked clause (the clause marked for coreference), generally the subordinate clause, as more transitive than the unmarked, generally superordinate clause. Such explanations depend a great deal on individual interpretations of degrees of agency to determine the coreferentiality of subjects, or syntactic roles.

In my data, examples of coreference (including anomalous coreference) are more simply explained as reflecting topic continuity, while examples of switch-reference (including anomalous switch-reference) can be explained as reflecting topic shift. One of the clearest examples of coreference is in the speech of speaker 1. According to the current understanding of the use of the participial mood, it is associated with switch-reference in nonfinal narrative clauses. Speaker 1 uses participial constructions almost exclusively in reflection clauses, and in each case, the topic or theme shifts (there is no such consistency in the use of the causative mood, despite its use in both sets of clauses in example 2.32). In example 2.32, clause 147 is a participial reflection clause, the topic of the ensuing section, 'chewing gum', is introduced in clause 148 and maintained through clause 158. Clause 159 is another participial reflection clause, and a new theme, about trips to Narsaq, is introduced in clause 160:

(2.32)   (From text 1b)

147.   *Eqqaamagiga*         *tassa*      *taamani*         *Ittu*
       *eqqaama-giga*        *tassa*      *taamani*         *Ittu-0*
       remember-1SG.         that.is     at.that.time      Grandfather-ABS
       SUBJ/3SG.OBJ.PART
       'I remember Grandfather at that time'

148.   *tyggegummimik*           *amerikamiuninngaanniit*
                                 *tunisittarsimagami.*

       *tyggegummi-mik*          *amerika-miut-ninngaanniit*
                                 *tunisit-saq-sima-gami*

       chewing.gum-INST         America-people.from-ABL
                                 get-HAB-PERF-3C.SG.CAUS

       'used to get chewing gum from the Americans.'

(Clauses 149–158 continue 'chewing gum' as a topic.)

159. *Tassa*      *eqqaamalluariga*
     *tassa*      *eqqaama-lluaq-giga*
     that.is   remember-well-1SG.SUBJ/3SG.OBJ.PART
     'I remember it very well'

160. *taamani*        *Narsamukaraangatta*        *aasakkut.*
     *taamani*        *Narsaq-mukaq-gaangatta*    *aasaq-kkut*
     at.that.time  Narsaq-go.to-whenever.     summer-VIA
                      1PL.CAUS
     'in those days, whenever we went to Narsaq during the summer.'

(Clauses 161–177 continue 'trips to Narsaq' with another memory within this section about a particular trip.)

Rather than depending on semantic roles for the interpretation of the same or different subject, switch-reference can be reanalyzed as marking topic switch in West Greenlandic. The use of a discourse role simplifies the explanation considerably.

Discourse roles are merely the extension of a previous system of classification to another level of linguistic analysis. The existence of discourse roles should not be surprising. In essence, roles are reference mechanisms; they provide a way for speakers of a language (and listeners) to track an entity across a certain amount of text, whether the text is a clause, a sentence, or a larger unit.

The notion of a discourse role such as topic may explain a clustering of seemingly unrelated features in West Greenlandic and typologically similar languages, such as clause chaining, ergativity, and switch-reference. Languages that are clause chaining, as I discuss in the chapter 4, tend to have switch-reference mechanisms with similar characteristics, for example. A possible explanation for the co-occurrence of these characteristics across different languages may lie in the choice of units of speech in the different languages, specifically in the choice of sentence versus paragraph.

The difference between sentences and paragraphs, according to Longacre (1976:281; 1996:289), is not their respective sizes: sentences may be as long as paragraphs, and paragraphs as short as short sentences. Rather, they should be considered different structural units that involve different stylistic options. Sentences, if they involve more than one clause, may be structured according to two main models. In a coranking structure (I follow his use of the term), a sentence consists of a nucleus with one or more independent clauses and may include a periphery with various modifying clauses, such as temporal or purpose clauses. In a clause-chaining structure, a sentence consists of a nucleus with no more than one independent, usually final (in SOV languages), clause and a series of (optional) dependent clauses, the first of which often recapitulates preceding discourse. The latter type is commonly found in languages in parts of South America and in the Highlands of New Guinea; it is also found in the Inuit languages. (Either type may be subordinated and embedded within another sentence, an important observation for thematic coherence and interruption.) In example 2.33 the first four clauses are dependent (causative verb mood), and the final two are independent; the last is arguably a separate sentence.

(2.33)   (From text 3a)

50.   *Pujortartorujussuugaluarama*
      Pujortaq-toq-rujussuaq-u-galuaq-gama
      smoke-consume-very.much-COP-CONSEQ-1SG.CAUS
      'I used to smoke very much but'

51.   *ullormut_*       20-*it*      *nungunngilaaginnartaraluarakkit*
      *ulloq-mut*       20-*it*      *nungu-nngit-laaq-innaq-saq-galuaq-gakkit*
      day-TERM          20-PL        finish-NEG-a.little-just-HAB-CONSEQ-
                                     1SG.SUBJ/3PL.OBJ.CAUS
      'I finished a little bit less than twenty a day . . .'

52.   1987-*arsimi*        *tassanngaannarsuaq*        *pujortarunnaarama_*
      1987 *ars-mi*        *tassannga-innaq-suaq*      *pujortaq-junnaaq-gama*
      1987 years-LOC       from.then.on-only-big       smoke-no.more-
                                                       1SG.CAUS
      'in 1987, from then on I stopped smoking [I no longer smoked]'

53.   *uanga*        *cigaritsip*        *ajuleraminga*
      *uanga*        *cigaritsi-p*       *ajoC-leq-gaminga*
      1SG.ABS        cigarette-REL       be.bad-begin-3C.SG.SUBJ/1SG.OBJ.CAUS
      'cigarettes didn't like me anymore [began to be bad for me]'

54.   *uanga*        *cigaritsi*         *ajulinngikkaluarpara*
      *uanga*        *cigaritsi-0*       *ajor-leq-nngit-galuaq-vara*

1SG.REL     cigarette-ABS     be.bad-begin-NEG-CONSEQ-1SG.SUBJ/
3SG.OBJ.IND
'but I don't like cigarettes anymore [I began not to have/like cigarettes anymore]'

55.    *taamangaasit*          *oqartarpunga.*
       *taamanga-aasiit*       *oqaq-saq-vunga*
       like.that-as.usual      say/talk-HAB-1SG.IND
       'that is what I usually say [I usually say like this].'

Some languages may make limited use of one type while being predominantly of the other type; Givón (1990:865) notes that clause chaining in English exists, although it is rarely used in English oral discourse.

Sentences are generally more tightly structured and have more closure than paragraphs do (Longacre 1985), whereas paragraphs tend to have a unifying theme or topic that individual sentences do not necessarily have. In spoken speech, however, sentences are not as clearly definable as they are in theory. In English, for example, run-on sentences in spoken discourse are common and can sometimes resemble clause chains; in my West Greenlandic texts there are often series of clauses grouped by intonation but consisting of several indicatives, or in some cases, no indicatives at all.

Although clause chaining is one method of clause combination for sentences, it is also common in paragraph building. The identification of a chain as a sentence or a paragraph depends on the degree of "closure." Further, some features that distinguish clause chaining from coranking also make the former more likely to function as a paragraph. For example, some clause chains can extend over several pages, as opposed to coranking sentences, which generally do not (Longacre 1985). According to Givón (1990:865) and Longacre (1985:238) clause chains are judged to represent thematic paragraphs, or discourse-level units, rather in the way that clauses are considered units of a sentence. The main difference between sentences and thematic paragraphs is in the criteria used to define the two: sentences are defined by reference to grammatical concepts such as constituent structure, whereas thematic paragraphs are defined by pragmatic and semantic concepts such as theme and topicality. Within a thematic paragraph, certain clusters of features are found that reflect thematic coherence across clause boundaries: referential cross-clausal continuity is indicated by anaphoric or cataphoric pronouns (among other things); temporal continuity by tense, temporal adverbs, and in some cases, verb form; continuity of action by aspect; and more general continuity of theme (foregrounding, backgrounding) by subordination and mood. These are devices for constructing clauses, but it is the combination of clauses by coordination, subordination, or clause chaining that results in the indication, whether overt or not, of coreferentiality, contemporality, sequentiality, and so forth. In combination, the lack of overt marking is as important as the presence thereof; for example, dependent clauses often tend to be unspecified for tense, aspect, and subject where these qualities are identical to those of the independent clause. The more features in common between a group of clauses, the more tightly the paragraph is defined. Clause chains all share more features of coherence than do clauses between chains. The text from which example 2.12 is drawn illustrates this feature of clause chains (for the full text, see the appendix). Clauses 19–25 form one chain; clauses 27–31 a second; and clauses 32–35 a third. The chains are internally unified by a series of subordinate clauses dependent on a final independent one, by intonation, by theme or topic continuity, by the use of the temporal particle *taamani* only once per chain, by the indication of aspect once in each chain (although aspect is not necessarily marked on the independent verb mood in West Greenlandic), and so forth. This is different in coranking structures, where two conjoined (and somewhat independent) clauses may each be marked for the features described above. This is not to suggest that coranking structures cannot be thematic paragraphs, or that they cannot share coherence features. Givón (1990:865) observes that complement clauses in equi-subject or equi-object constructions tend to be less marked for tense or aspect, for example. It does, however, suggest that clause chains are more likely to share coherence features based on paragraph-level considerations.

All of the features of thematic coherence described above may well be true for any language, whether it is clause chaining or whether it forms coranking sentences. Furthermore, languages can have either or both types of sentence formation structure, although most seem to prefer one or the other. Both coranking and clause-chaining sentences can be considered thematic paragraphs in context, and in oral discourse, sentences are generally not as clearly bounded (i.e., to have closure) as modern syntactic theories lead one to believe. In West Greenlandic, for example, final clauses are often "medial" in structure, that is, they are dependent clauses. Grimes (1975) and Longacre (1985) note that clause chains in a clause-chaining language are often roughly the same length as paragraphs in languages that are described in terms of coranking sentences. A single clause chain is a thematic paragraph and is linked by topic continuity. The same is generally (but not necessarily) said of more than one coranking sentence. Considerations like these suggest that languages with clause-chaining structure may plausibly rely on discourse roles for reference marking within a chain. Rather than subject continuity within a sentence, we can speak of topic continuity within a thematic paragraph. Furthermore, the fact that switch-reference is so often identified as a system for marking same or different subjects may have to do with the tendency for topic and subject to coincide in clause chains, especially in intransitive clauses. Example 2.34 illustrates this. The topic is 'Greenland seals'. All clauses are intransitive and all subjects are identical with the topic, with the exception of clause 83, which is the start of the chain in which 'Greenland seals' is introduced as a topic:

(2.34)  (From text 4)

83.  *. . . piniagassat*            *saqqummeriartortarput*
     *piniagassat*            *saqqummer-giartor-saq-vut*
     hunting.animals.PL    come.out-more.and.more-HAB-3PL.IND
     '. . . the hunting animals used to come out more and more'

84.  *allatuulli_*                  *taava*   *aataarpassuit*
     *allatooq-t-li*                *taava*   *aataaq-passuit*
     young.Greenland.seal-PL-INTNS   then   Greenland.seal-lots.of.PL
     'and young Greenland seals, and lots of Greenland (harp) seals'

     *Newfoundlandip*        *avataaninngaanniit*     *nunatsinnut*
     *Newfoundland-ip*       *avataa-ningaanniit*     *nuna-tsinnut*
     Newfoundland-REL        coast-PL.ABL             land-1PL.POS.TERM

     tikerallaraangamik
     tiker-gallaq-gaangamik
     arrive-INTNS-whenever.3C.PL.CAUS
     'arrived continually from the Newfoundland coast to our land'

85.  *sineriapput_*                  *kangerluillu_*        *pulaararlugit*
     *sineriak-vut*                  *kangerluk-it-lu*      *pulaar-ar-lugit*
     coast-1PL.POS/PL.POSM.ABS    fjord-PL-and         visit-for.a.while-
                                                           3PL.OBJ.CT

     'visiting our coasts and the fjords for a while'

86.  *aataarpassuanngortarput*
     aataaq-passuaq-nngor-saq-vut
     Greenland.seal-lots.of-become-HAB-3PL.IND
     'there used to be lots of Greenland seals [coming]'

     *meeraaffimma*                  *nalaani*             *Saarluni.*
     *meeraq-ffik-ma*                *nalaani*             *Saarloq-ni*
     child-place-1SG.POS.REL      time.period-3C.      Saarloq-LOC
                                     SG.POS.LOC
     'in the time of my childhood in Saarloq.'

In languages with ergative marking, ergativity can be said to reflect the fact that topic, rather than subject or object, is the cohesive link in the paragraph.[9] As ergative and switch-reference marking are both forms of agreement marking, it is reasonable to expect that if topic is grammaticalized as the relevant determiner of agreement for one (ergativity), it is also the relevant determiner for the other (switch-reference).

I do not suggest that all clause-chaining languages must have topic agreement systems, but rather that different languages grammaticalize categories at different levels, and that discourse should be considered one of those levels. If discourse is grammaticalized, then discourse roles must be relevant throughout the grammar. Just as there are languages that seem to be adequately described with reference to syntactic roles, and others with reference to semantic roles, one can expect still others to be effectively described with reference to discourse roles. In the following chapters, I will show that there are discourse roles in West Greenlandic.

# **3** Ergativity as a reflection of topic status

Ergativity refers to a system of case-marking in which the subjects of intransitive clauses and the objects of transitive clauses are marked in one way, and the subjects of transitive clauses are marked in another. It is common, in descriptions of ergativity in West Greenlandic, to focus on the existence of both ergative and antipassive structures, and to explain these as a function of the definiteness or givenness of the object. Given this tendency to include discourse factors in explanations of ergativity in the language, one might predict that discourse factors have an important role in determining its grammatical structure. The question is, are there compelling reasons to prefer explanations that make reference to topic over traditionally syntactic or semantic explanations? In order to answer this question, I first present a description of ergativity in West Greenlandic and the status of the antipassive object and the association or lack thereof between passive and ergative structures (section 3.1). I then review some of the principle issues with ergativity (section 3.2), how it has been related to subjecthood and topichood in the general literature (section 3.3), and how this applies to West Greenlandic (section 3.4). Finally, I present the data (section 3.5) and conclusions (3.6) in relation to the proposal that ergativity in Greenlandic is directly related to topic marking.

## 3.1 Ergativity in West Greenlandic

Ergative-absolutive morphology in West Greenlandic is found both on nominals, through case endings on the subject and direct object, and on verbs, through argument agreement. Of the eight case endings in West Greenlandic, five play a role in indicating the relationship between arguments and the verb. The first two are the purely syntactic cases, absolutive and relative, or ergative. The subjects of intransitive clauses and the objects of transitive clauses with transitive verbal morphology are morphologically unmarked and are in the absolute case. The subjects of transitive clauses with transitive verbal morphology receive relative case endings and are in the ergative case. The three others are oblique cases with multiple functions, including the marking of demoted agents or patients: the instrumental marks objects of antipassive constructions, and the ablative or the terminalis marks the agent in a passive construction; the ablative is the case of preference in South Greenland, and the terminalis in Central and North Greenland.

There are three active constructions, intransitives, transitives, and antipassives, as illustrated in examples 3.1–3.3. In all three, the agent is the subject; however, in antipassive constructions, verbs with transitive semantics are intransitively inflected, and they have absolute subjects and instrumentally marked objects.

(3.1)   Intransitive clause
        *Arnaq*          *sinippoq.*
        *arnaq*-0        *sinik-voq*
        woman-ABS    sleep-3SG.IND
        'The woman is sleeping.'

(3.2)   Transitive (= ergative) clause
        *Angutip*      *arnaq*              *takuvaa.*
        *angut-ip*      *arnaq*-0            *taku-vaa*
        man-REL     woman-ABS      see-3SG.SUBJ/3SG.OBJ.IND
        'The man sees the woman.'

(3.3)   Antipassive clause
        *Angut*        *arnamik*            *takuvoq.*
        *angut*-0       *arnaq-mik*          *taku-voq*
        man-ABS     woman-INST     see-3SG.IND
        'The man sees a woman.'

These examples also illustrate subject-object agreement in the verbal inflectional morphology. Intransitive clauses and antipassive clauses have subject agreement only; transitive clauses have both subject and object agreement in most moods, although the contemporative mood differs in having only object agreement in its transitive clauses.

The lack of object agreement on antipassive verbs is sometimes taken as evidence that these structures are antipassives rather than transitives and of the instrumentally marked nominals as demoted objects rather than accusatives. There are even more compelling reasons to prefer such an analysis. Johnson (1980:14–15), for example, shows that whereas transitive structures can be passivized, antipassives cannot (the following examples, from Johnson 1980:16–17, are in Inuktitut):

(3.4)   Transitive
       *Maaliup*      *Piita*         *nagligivaa.*
       *Maali-up*    *Piita-0*      *nagligi-vaa*
       Molly-REL   Peter-ABS   love-3SG.SUBJ/3SG.OBJ.IND
       'Molly loves Peter.'

(3.5)   Passive
       *Piita*         *Maalimut*      *nagligijauvuq.*
       *Piita-0*      *Maali-mut*     *nagligi-jau-vuq*
       Peter-ABS   Molly-TERM   love-PASS-3SG.IND
       'Peter is loved by Molly.'

(3.6)   Antipassive
       *Maali*        *Piitamik*      *nagligusukpuq.*
       *Maali-0*     *Piita-mik*    *nagligusuk-puq*
       Molly-ABS   Peter-INST   love.INTRANS-3SG.IND
       'Molly loves Peter.'

(3.7)   *Passive of antipassive
       **Piita*     *Maalimut*      *nagligusuktauvuq.*
       *Piita-0*    *Maali-mut*    *nagligusuk-jau-vuq*
       Peter-0    Molly-TERM   love.INTRANS-PASS-3SG.IND
       '*Peter is loved by Molly.'

Further, while transitive structures can have dative variants, and passives thereof, antipassives cannot (Johnson 1980:16–17, Inuktitut examples):

(3.8)   Transitive
       *Angutiup*   *titiraut*     *nutararmut*    *tunivaa.*
       *angut-up*   *titiraut-0*   *nutaraq-mut*   *tuni-vaa*
       man-REL    pencil-ABS   child-TERM   give-3SG.SUBJ/3SG.
                                        OBJ.IND
       'The man gave a/the pencil to the child.'

(3.9)   Dative
        *Angutiup       titirautimik      nutaraq           tunivaa.*
        *angut-up        titiraut-mik      nutaraq-0         tuni-vaa*
        man-REL         pencil-INST       child-ABS         give-3SG.SUBJ/3SG.OBJ.IND
        'The man gave the child a/the pencil.'

(3.10)  Passive based on dative (For a passive based on transitive that
        has not undergone dative movement, see example 3.5 above.)
        *Angutimit       titirautimik      nutaraq           tunijauvuq.*
        *angut-mit        titiraut-mik      nutaraq-0         tuni-jau-vuq*
        man-ABL         pencil-INST       child-ABS         give-PASS-3SG.IND
        'The child was given a pencil by the man.'

(3.11)  Antipassive
        *Angut           titirautimik      nutararmut         tunisivuq.*
        *angut-0          titiraut-mik      nutaraq-mut       tuni-si-vuq*
        man-ABS         pencil-INST       child-TERM        give-INTRANS-3SG.IND
        'The man gave the child a pencil.'

(3.12)  *Antipassive based on dative
        **Angut          titirautimik      nutararmik        tunisivuq.*
        *angut-0          titiraut-mik      nutaraq-mik       tuni-si-vuq*
        man-ABS         pencil-INST       child-INST        give-INTRANS-3SG.IND
        '*The man gave the child a pencil.'

Finally, the case marking on the object in antipassive constructions is
suggestive of an oblique rather than a direct object. The object in these
constructions is in the instrumental case, which is a default case in West
Greenlandic. Its most important function is not as a direct object marker,
but as an adverbial, whether of cause, manner, or time (example from P.
Langgård, personal communication):

(3.13)  Instrumental in adverbial of manner
        *Asannitumik       isigivaa.*
        *asannitoq-mik      isigi-vaa*
        love-INST          look-3SG.SUBJ/3SG.OBJ.IND
        'He looks at her with love.'

According to Kleinschmidt (1851:84), its essential function is as a marker for instrumental constructions (example from Fortescue 1984:214):

(3.14)  Instrumental construction
    *Nanuq    savimminik*        *kapivaa.*
    *nanoq_0  savik-ni-nik*       *kapi-vaa*
    bear-ABS knife-3C.SG.POS-INST    stab-3SG.SUBJ/3SG.OBJ.IND
    'He stabbed the polar bear with his knife.'

In addition to these primary functions, it can function as an appositive to an incorporated nominal (example from P. Langgård, personal communication),

(3.15)  Instrumental with incorporation
    *Sakkortuumik    kaffiliorpunga.*
    *sakkortoq-mik    kaffi-lioq-vunga*
    strong-INST    coffee-make-1SG.IND
    'I made strong coffee.' (where the strength is in the coffee, not in the action of making the coffee)

as the complement to the relative derivational suffix *-lik* 'provided with' (example from Bergsland 1955; spelling changed to reflect contemporary Greenlandic orthography),

(3.16)  Instrumental with relative *–lik*
    *toqungasunik*         *uppatilik*
    *toqungasut-nik*        *uppatit-lik*
    dead.one.PL-INST.PL    thigh.PL-provided.with
    'the thighs of the dead ones'

or as an indirect object (or "remote" object) with transitives (example from Bergsland 1955:77; spelling changed to reflect contemporary Greenlandic orthography):

(3.17)  Instrumental with indirect object
    *Qassuserniarnermik*        *ilinniartikkumaarpakkit.*
    *qassuser-niar-neq-mik*     *ilinniartit-jumaar-pakkit*
    set.nets-FUT-NOMZ-INST    teach-FUT-1SG.SUBJ/2SG.OBJ.IND
    'I will teach you to set nets.'

Common to all of these is the complement status of the instrumentally marked noun phrase. Semantically, this complement may be obligatory, but there is no syntactic evidence showing a direct relationship between the complement and the verb. Thus, for both morphological and syntactic reasons, and despite arguments by Kalmár (1979a) and more recently by Nowak (1993) that oblique nominals of antipassive structures are still objects, these obliques are best seen as demoted objects. In the following discussion, I use the term antipassive rather than accusative to explain the structures in question.

One of the recurring theories of the character of ergative languages is that of their passive nature, an identification made on the basis of case-marking similarities to passive structures in accusative languages: the object, or patient, is marked, as is the subject not only of basic intransitive constructions but also of passive constructions, with obvious syntactic and semantic similarities to the surface subjects of the passives. Ergativity in West Greenlandic is not to be equated with passivity. In addition to an antipassive construction, there are a number of passive constructions with various degrees of passive meaning (see Fortescue 1984:265–66 for a more complete description). Among the most common are those formed with the derivational morphemes *–neqaq-* and *–saq-* (examples from Fortescue 1984:265–66; spelling changed to reflect contemporary Greenlandic orthography):

(3.18)   Dynamic passive: passive perfective morpheme *-neqaq-*:
        *Nanoq*       *inunnit*        *takuneqarpoq.*
        *nanoq-0*    *inuk-nit*      *taku-neqaq-voq*
        bear-ABS    person-PL.ABL   see-PASS-3SG.IND
        'The bear was seen by the people.'

(3.19)   Stative passive: passive participle morpheme *-saq-*:
        *Asasaavoq.*
        asa-saq-u-voq
        love-PASS.PART-COP-3SG.IND
        'She is loved.'

Examples 3.4 and 3.5 also show that transitive (ergative) and passive constructions are semantically distinct, although the importance of the agent may be reduced in both.

West Greenlandic is not thought of as a split-ergative language. There are, however, some indications of an agency split in the pronominal marking on the transitive verbs, while in the contemporative, objects of transitively marked contemporative verbs sometimes indicate the subject of an underlying intransitive verb (see example 4.71 in chapter 4); the objects are in the absolutive case. Vaxtin (1976) finds a distributional difference between nominal and verbal ergative marking in the person and mood paradigms of Asiatic Eskimo verbs: first- and second-person pronominal inflection on verbs in the independent moods reflect an ergative case-marking pattern, whereas third person reflects a nominative pattern. At the same time, first- and second-person independent pronouns have only one case form for both the absolutive and relative functions. In other words, nominal and verbal pronominal ergative marking are in complementary distribution. Fortescue (1995) notes that the indicative third-person object has a clearly ergative pattern, and the first- and second-person objects in both subordinate and independent moods have an ergative pattern by paradigmatic extension, but the third-person object of subordinate moods has an accusative pattern. This kind of split is not analogous to splits based on a nominal hierarchy (Trask 1976:399), although Fortescue's findings fit the Silverstein hierarchy (see below for further discussion of this).

West Greenlandic is a morphologically rather than syntactically ergative language, although this is sometimes obscured by a number of West Greenlandic inflectional features that regularly disambiguate nominals in complex structures. For example, although clauses can be coordinated along the lines of Dixon's famous example "Father saw mother and returned" (Dixon 1979:63), in which the subject of returned is 'mother', the clauses would typically consist of an indicative and a subordinate form, with a switch-reference mechanism in the subordinate clause to disambiguate the subject of 'returned' (or of 'saw', depending on which verb is subordinated). If both verbs are independent, this switch-reference mechanism is generally unavailable, and the subjects would be understood to be coreferent. If the subordinate mood is in the contemporative mood, this switch-reference mechanism is not available, since only one argument is coindexed; Fortescue (1984:131) claims that it is not possible to coordinate two active sentences where the subject of one is the object of the other using the contemporative (examples from Fortescue 1984:131):

(3.20)  Coordination with contemporative and same subjects
    *Hansi*        *iserpoq*        *Kaalamillu*        *takuneqarluni.*
    *Hansi-0*      *iser-voq*       *Kaalat-mit-lu*     *taku-neqaq-luni*
    Hansi-ABS    enter-3SG.IND    Kaalat-ABL-and    see-PASS-3SG.CT
    'Hansi came in and was seen by Kaalat.'

(3.21)  Coordination with contemporative and subject/object
    **Hansi*      *iserpoq*      *Kaalallu*      *takullugu/takulluni.*
    *Hansi-0*      *iser-voq*      *Kaalat-lu*     *taku-lugu/luni*
    Hansi-ABS    enter-3SG.IND    Kaalat-and    see-3NC.SG.OBJ.CT/
                                          3C.SG.OBJ.CT
    '*Hansi came in and Kaalat saw him.'

(3.22)  Coordination with two indicatives
    *Hansi*        *iserpoq*        *Kaalallu*      *takuaa.*
    *Hansi-0*      *iser-voq*      *Kaalat-lu*     *taku-vaa*
    Hansi-ABS    enter-3SG.IND    Kaalat-and    see-3SG.SUBJ/
                                            3SG.OBJ.IND
    'Hansi came in and Kaalat saw him.'

Unfortunately, Fortescue also lists a number of ways in which this is contradicted. Two clauses sharing the same derivational affix on different
nominal bases may involve coordination with the contemporative, even
though the subjects are not coreferential (example from Fortescue 1984:134):

(3.23)  Coordination with contemporative, different subjects
    *Suuvvia*       *ataaniippoq*       *Kaalallu*
                                       *iniminiilluni.*

    *Suuvvia-0*     *ataa-niit-voq*      *Kaalat-lu*
                                       *ini-mi-niit-luni*

    Suuvvia-ABS   below-be.at-3SG.IND   Kaalat.ABS-and
                                          room-3C.SG.POS-be.
                                          at-3SG.CT

    'Suuvvia is downstairs and Kaalat is in her room.'

Furthermore, transitive contemporatives, marking only the object, may
occasionally have objects coreferent with the subject of the superordinate

(example from Fortescue 1984:148; a more detailed discussion of this is found in chapter 4, section 4.4.2.1):

(3.24)   Coordination with contemporatives and subject/object
     *igalaaq*           *urninniarlugu*               *aserorpoq*
     *igalaaq-0*        *urniC-niaq-lugu*            *aseror-voq*
     window-ABS     approach-try-3SG.OBJ.CT    break-3SG.IND
     'When one tried to approach the window, it broke.'

Example 3.24 appears to show syntactic ergativity. However, other factors may be at work: Fortescue (1984:148) notes that in most such cases, the superordinate is generally less agentive than the contemporative. Vaxtin (1976:287) also suggests the existence of some syntactic ergativity in Chaplino Eskimo, but it is unclear whether or not the example he gives (reproduced as example 3.25) reflects true syntactic ergativity or whether it is a result of the pronominals indexed in the verb which disambiguate the third persons:

(3.25)   Syntactic ergativity?
     *Laghanhwa, Ungasimun kanighata, upughataqiqangit.*
     and-so, to Ungasik when-they-come, they-meet-them
     'So, when theyᵢ come to Ungasik, theyⱼ meet themᵢ.'

West Greenlandic has many features regarded as canonical typological characteristics of ergative languages (see Trask 1976:385–86). It is an SOV language, it is morphologically ergative, the ergative case is overtly marked, transitive verbs index the object, and it is identical with the relative (possessive, genitive) case. It also has a fully developed passive voice, ergativity is not confined to certain tenses or aspects, and if it has a split based on a nominal hierarchy, this split is restricted to the indexing on verbs. It has characteristics both of languages in which ergative structures developed from passives and of those in which the ergative developed from perfectives, although the latter is more likely to have happened in West Greenlandic.

Perfectives are nominalized deverbal forms with stative semantics. Stative verbs are said to lack an agent (e.g., he fell; the vase broke) and clauses with stative verbs are therefore formally analogous ergative constructions, since the nominal most closely connected to the stative verb, either the subject of an intransitive or the object of a transitive, is unmarked. The agent of a stative verb is marked overtly in an oblique case; when such verbs are nominalized (that is, they are perfective), the agent is most often indicated by means of a possessive construction. The ergative would then result from a reinterpretation of the perfective as a part of the inflectional verbal system, and its formal identity with the possessive construction is explained as well as the lack of a verb 'to have', itself marking a possessive relationship (Trask 1976:395–97). Languages with an ergative system derived from a perfective have superficial ergativity, with overt case marking on transitive subjects only and no object indexing on the verb; a tense-aspect based split, with past tense or perfective aspect requiring ergative case structures; a semantic difference between verbs in ergative and accusative structures, such that the former have a perfective and the latter an imperfective meaning; a correlation between ergative and possessive marking; and no verb 'to have'.

West Greenlandic fits this pattern in several important ways, but not exclusively. It lacks an independent verb 'to have', having only the morphologically bound affixes *-qaq-* (for intransitive constructions) and *-gi-* (for transitive constructions); it has an ergative construction that is formally identical with the possessive construction; and there are often semantic differences between verb stems that require an intransitive or antipassive construction and related stems that require a transitive one. For example, *tusaa-* (intransitive) in Inuktitut is glossed as 'hear (a continuous sound)' by Mallon (1990:1.24), whereas *tusaq-* (intransitive and transitive) is glossed as 'hear a short burst of sound' (Mallon 1990:2.147; the glosses are not quite so different in the Greenlandic dictionary *Oqaatsit*).

However, West Greenlandic transitive verbs are typically marked for both subject and object agreement, and the inflectional paradigm is relatively complete across most moods and all persons. There is some small evidence of syntactic ergativity; noun incorporation is highly productive in all the Inuit dialects, including West Greenlandic; and there is no tense-aspect split. With the exception of a split in the nominal hierarchy, which West Greenlandic has to a limited extent, all these features are characteristic instead of passive-derived ergativity (Trask 1976:389). For such cases, Trask has suggested a later extension of the original ergative system.

The historical development of ergativity in Eskimo from the passive participle is assumed in the work of Dorais (1988), Mallon (1974, 1990), and Kalmár (1979b), among others. All sources at various times gloss transitive verbs as combinations of passive participles and possessive suffixes, as in the following:

(3.26)  Passive semantics of transitive verbs
        takuvara
        takuvaq-ga
        seen.thing-1SG.POS
        'my seen thing' (= 'I see it')

Fortescue (1995) also states that the Inuit ergative comes from a passive participle third-person object form in the indicative, which was then extended throughout the rest of the paradigm. Morphologically, this is still relatively transparent today.

Whatever its origin, ergativity in Greenlandic is more than superficial, and it does not have particularly passive semantics. This has implications for any study of topicality in West Greenlandic, since the passive construction is one way of shifting the emphasis from one verbal argument to another. If ergativity is well established and independent of passive or perfective semantics, then its role in the structuring of discourse is independent of these semantics.

## 3.2 Treatment of ergativity in modern syntactic theories of West Greenlandic

A number of formal syntactic theories have been proposed to explain the function, use, and distribution of transitive and antipassive clauses in Inuit narratives, but they have met with only varying degrees of success. Early modern syntactic descriptions are based on transformational grammar and its offshoots, with grammatical relations being structurally defined according to a constituent hierarchy, such that subjects are defined as the outside argument of the verb and objects as the dependent argument. This early work, including Mallon's (1974, 1990) descriptions of Inuktitut, fails to account for the existence of both ergative and antipassive patterns of sentence formation in Eskimo, nor are case assignment, incorporation, and the results of a highly polysynthetic morphology adequately accounted for. Bok-Bennema (1991) has specifically addressed the problem of ergativity in Inuktitut from within the framework of government-binding theory, especially with respect to case assignment. Her discussion revolves around the ability of transitive verbs in ergative languages to assign case; she treats ergative case as genitive and allows transitive clauses to assign nominative and genitive cases, intransitives to assign nominative, and antipassives to assign accusative case.[1] The proposed theory is essentially descriptive in nature, leaving the ultimate explanation of ergativity to ad hoc specifications in the lexicon.

An offshoot of generalized phrase structure grammar, autolexical syntax was developed by Sadock (1991) especially in reference to problems encountered in descriptions of West Greenlandic. Autolexical syntax involves a three-tiered grammatical system composed of syntax, morphology, and semantics (or logical form). Each of these three faces, as they are called, affects the final structure of a sentence. Each is autonomous; in no way is one to be seen as hierarchically related to another. This means, however, that a well-formed, grammatical sentence must fulfill the requirements of each of these three faces, requirements that may or may not conflict with those of another face. In their interaction, therefore, one may sometimes see mismatches, or nonalignment, between the requirements of one and the requirements of another face. For example, in West Greenlandic, noun incorporation results not only in the incorporation of a noun into the verb but also in the stranding of a noun's modifiers; this leads to a structure in which morphologically, the modifier's head is part of the verb but in which syntactically, the incorporated noun is still independent. The theory primarily addresses the questions of cliticization and incorporation. Although the applicability of this theory to case assignment is briefly discussed (but not with respect to West Greenlandic), it has not explored ergativity and accusativity in great depth. Sadock has consequently not addressed the coexistence of ergative and antipassive structures in West Greenlandic (or of passives, which are of considerable importance in Bok-Bennema 1991). Viewing sentence structure as the result of the interaction of more than one level of grammar is reminiscent of Halliday's (1967a, 1967b, 1968) functional approach, but Sadock's (1991) approach is more modular than functional, and it is not clear how to incorporate discourse considerations into his theory.

Much recent work on West Greenlandic and other Inuit dialects has been either descriptive or typological in nature, and the tendency among typologists has been to favor a relational approach, with arguments of the verb treated as hierarchically ranked primitives associated with semantic roles. Case is a reflection of the relationship of the arguments to the verb. Thus, an ergative structure consists of a subject and direct object in direct relationship with the verb, and an antipassive structure of a subject in direct relationship with the verb but a direct object demoted to peripheral object status, as reflected by the instrumental case assigned to the antipassive object. The nature of the relationship between case and argument status, however, has not always been clearly defined. In an early article on Greenlandic Eskimo and ergativity, combining elements of relational and transformational grammars, Woodbury (1977) finds that all clauses must contain an absolutive argument, and therefore the laws that apply to subjects apply to absolutives, and those that apply to direct objects apply to ergatives (Woodbury 1977:328). One of the most problematic issues in connection with ergativity has been the definition of subject and direct object; subsequent studies have not equated case and argument status, and ergativity is seen as a secondary, derived function in the grammar, as opposed to subjecthood. More objectionable to some researchers has been the theoretical equation of antipassives with intransitive structures. Kalmár (1979a) in particular has argued not only for acknowledging the transitive nature of the antipassive clause but also for viewing both ergative and antipassive clauses as equally basic, as opposed to considering one clause type, usually the active transitive clause, as basic and others as derived from it.

Kalmár's (1979a, 1979b, 1982) work represents a third major school of structural study of the Inuit dialects, distinguished by the attempt to explain syntactic structures from a functional, discourse-based perspective, much of which seems to originate in the work of Menovshchikov. Menovshchikov (1969) explains the ergative, absolute (antipassive), and passive structures in Eskimo-Aleut (with particular reference to Asiatic Eskimo) as a reflection of "logical accent," by which he means focus or topic. The logical accent of an ergative clause is its object, that of an absolute clause its subject, and that of a passive its surface subject but underlying object (he writes in terms of "real" vs. "actual" arguments). An added complication is the possibility of having the logical accent on the verb, which Menovshchikov understands to be the case with detransitivized verbs (also called half-transitives). He does not clearly justify these identifications, other than through transitive or intransitive inflection on the verb. His interest is in verbal inflection rather than case marking, which he does not view as distinctive (i.e., there is no "ergative" case per se because one and the same case, the relative, is used for possession and ergative marking). Menovshchikov's (1969) theory is in some respects similar to what I propose below.[2]

Functional interpretations of the ergative did not begin with Menovshchikov. Very early in the study of Greenlandic, scholars had identified the ergative structure with definiteness of the direct object, and the antipassive with indefiniteness thereof. Both Egede (1760) and Kleinschmidt (1851:85) make this connection. Kalmár (1979a, 1979b), Fortescue (1984), and others note that this identification is not an adequate description of the distribution of ergative and antipassive structures in Greenlandic or in any of the Inuit dialects. Kalmár (1979a) suggests that the distinction between the two structures is one of givenness rather than definiteness, and elsewhere (Kalmár 1979b), that case assignment is dependent on a number of inter-related factors, including predication, coreference, and thematic coherence. In brief, the ergative/accusative distinction reflects given/new information and rheme (theme being reflected in passive clauses), assuming Prague School definitions of theme-rheme. In his view, patient, or direct object, is ultimately more important in the determination of case marking than agent, or subject; this observation is supported by my data. Kalmár raises important issues sometimes missed by others, including the functional independence of the antipassive (accusative in his terminology) clause within the grammatical system of Inuktitut (and by extension, West Greenlandic), or the distributional differences in instances of the ergative or antipassive (e.g., in elicited materials; see Kalmár 1979a). Some of his interpretations, however, seem less likely. For example, the structural identity between patient and agent in antipassive and reflexive structures leads him to conclude that a one-argument clause in Inuktitut cannot be said to be active or passive, since the distinction agent/patient is neutralized.

Little has been done on discourse in the Inuit languages, save for a few comments in passing within articles on syntactic phenomena. Fortescue (1991) suggests the possibility of "psychological subject" (i.e., topic) as the controlling factor in West Greenlandic switch-reference (see chapter 4, section 4.3), and Per Langgård (personal communication) suggests that the focus or topic of ergative clauses is the object, and that of antipassives and intransitives is the subject. Nothing systematic has yet been done with such suggestions, however.

## 3.3 Subjecthood, agency, and topic

Ergativity and accusativity are generally defined by and related to case marking and to syntactic or semantic roles of verbal arguments. The nominal arguments of a verb can be described at several different levels of structure, each of which involves different terminology. Grammatical relationships are indicated by the terms subject and object; semantic relationships by agent and patient; pragmatic relationships by such concepts as given/new, topic/comment, or theme/rheme; and discourse relationships, as I suggest in chapter 2, by topic and theme. The identification of core elements representing such relationships has been a major focus of attention in typological discussions of case and grammatical structure; at the heart of these discussions is the question of what can be considered a structural primitive. In the syntax, subjects and objects are primitives, both traditionally and within some syntactic theories, such as relational grammar. The discovery by Western linguists of ergative languages raised issues in the identification of subjects, and the ergative was often interpreted as a passivelike structure. In an attempt to define the term subject, Keenan (1976) noted that what were identified as subjects tended to have a cluster of features, many of which were semantic in nature. This characterization of subjecthood has generally served as the point of reference for subsequent discussions of subjecthood. One apparently typologically widespread feature of subjects was that of agency.

Linking syntactic roles with semantic roles is now standard and captures the typological tendency to find certain correlations of the two in certain types of sentence structures. Thus, in basic transitive sentences, agents tend to be subjects of active predicates, patients to be direct objects, and so forth. The semantic role of the subject is different in related sentences (e.g., active and passive), and conversely, a semantic role is realized as a subject, direct object, or other object in related sentences. Languages may differ in the degree of distinction made within semantic roles; for example, some languages distinguish agents with respect to degree of control, volition, animacy, and so on. Nevertheless, the general concept of semantic roles is important in explaining differences between related sentences in a great many languages.

There have been a number of attempts to explain tendencies in discourse by means of semantic roles, based on cross-linguistic tendencies of the sort just noted. For example, Silverstein (1976) found that in split-ergative languages, ergative marking is more likely to be associated with noun phrases lower on an animacy hierarchy, namely third person and common nouns, than with elements higher on the hierarchy, such as first- or second-person pronouns. This animacy hierarchy is explained by the naturalness or markedness of a noun phrase in its function as an agent of a transitive verb. Thus, the use of an ergative or an accusative structure in a split-ergative language depends on the status of a subject or agent on the animacy hierarchy with respect to an object or patient.

One of the methods of accounting for tendencies such as these has been to redefine the entities taken to be primitives. In relational grammar, grammatical relations, including subjects and objects, are assumed to be undefined primitives (Blake 1990:1). Dixon (1994:113; see also Dixon 1979 and Comrie 1981) takes subjects of intransitive clauses (henceforth S), subjects of transitive clauses (A), and objects (O) to be universal core categories of nominal arguments, and suggests that syntactic rules in every grammar are framed around them. At a further level, S and A may be grouped together as subject and considered important to the grammar of some but not necessarily all languages. At another level, S and O may be grouped together as a natural category reflecting information flow in discourse, and especially in terms of the opposition given/new (Dixon 1994; Du Bois 1987).

It is then a small step to group together as topic noun phrases with prominence in connected text. In fact, such a category is more easily described than one reflecting information flow and givenness. The grouping of S and O as topic is not new. Dixon (1972) makes extensive reference to topic chains and topicality in reference to Dyirbal, and particularly with reference to ergative structures, in which he tries to show how topic is reflected in connected text. He identifies (1972:67) any noun phrase with absolutive (or nominative, in his terminology) case as a topic, although he does not define the term itself; this use of the term topic is what he refers to in later writings as pivot (1979, 1994). A noun phrase that has the same referent and is the topic in two or more consecutive sentences is called a common topic; the sequence of sentences with a common topic is called a topic chain. There is also a difference in emphasis between ergative and anti-passive constructions, such that in the former, the object is the topic and the actor (A) implicates the goal in the event, and in the latter, the actor, goal, and action (S and verb) make up the event (Dixon 1972:65–66). He suggests the difference is one of topic and provides examples explaining the motivation for identifying a topic in a stretch of text and for claiming that a topic has shifted, been elaborated, or been taken up again (Dixon 1972:72).[3] His stated theory is close to what I propose, the analyses of his Dyirbal texts (1972:368–97) support my analyses of West Greenlandic, and the distribution of ergative and antipassive structures in Dyirbal mirror that of West Greenlandic. He nevertheless remains within the traditional interpretive framework and does not allow for the possibility of an inanimate topic, nor does he allow more than one topic within a topic chain. These are important points: his texts for the most part show consistency with the identification of absolutively marked noun phrases with topic, but Dixon himself is sometimes inconsistent in this identification. For example, absolutively marked objects are not considered topics if they are not animate (see his treatment of 'heart' in text 1, 1972:370). He does not seem to know what to do with stray nominals, especially where they have been topics in previous stretches of text or where they are nonagentive. In some topic chains, he identifies what we might call the global topic as the common topic, despite its occurrence as the A of ergative constructions and contrary to his observations about the topic of ergative constructions. He therefore places topic continuity ahead of topic ranking in the determination of topicality. For example, in a chain of two sentences both of which are ergative, with 'child' as A and two different O's, he identifies the topic as 'child' and suggests the O's have in some way elaborated the topic:

(3.27)   'He [the child] drank from the heart without pausing for
         breath. As a result he [the child] vomited a lot; he vomited up
         breastmilk' (Dixon 1972:375)
         'child' is A, 'heart' and 'breastmilk' are O's

(Longacre [1996] might say these are sentences in a paragraph that reflects contrast. At any rate, if one holds that absolutive nominals are topics, then one must say that the emphasis in the above sentences is on what the child drank and vomited, that is, the [blood from] the heart and the breastmilk.) Thus, Dixon notes some tendencies in Dyirbal and explains them as well as possible within a semantic framework, where topic is not a category that, like subject, influences the structure of clauses, but rather as a category that more loosely reflects information flow. In later work (Dixon 1994), he sees absolutive as a category that reflects new information being introduced, but not exclusively. Syntactic grouping resulting from coordination, reflexivization, and so forth, which is based on absolutive marking rather than subject function in a language, is described by another term, pivot (Dixon 1979, 1994:168). This suggests a different form or level of categorization of absolutive nominals, having more to do with clause combination within a sentence than with discourse.

There is a certain ambiguity in the characterization of the absolutively marked noun phrase as both the bearer of new information and as the topic. As I noted above, Dixon emphasizes continuity as a means of identifying topic, and generally finds that absolutive objects of transitive constructions are topics, but this clearly conflicts with a view of the absolutive case as a means for introducing new information. Presumably, a newly introduced entity may have some topicality status, but it is not considered topical compared with the ergative noun phrase if the latter is continued from previous discourse. In his later work, Dixon modifies his concept of topicality, such that topics tend to be subjects (about which more below). I take the opposite approach, and assume that this conflict arises because not all absolutives introduce new entities, and not all new entities are introduced as absolutives.

The link between ergativity and information flow, in particular the flow of given versus new information, has been systematically explored by Du Bois (1987). Du Bois sees the distinction between given and new information as "more fundamental than, and in some sense prior to, the decision between morphological expressions" (1987:830). He notes a correlation between the distribution of lexical subjects and objects and their status as given in the discourse; for example, new participants tend to be introduced through noun phrases in the absolutive (i.e., S and O), while the ergative (A) tends to not be lexical or new. Further, in his analysis of Sacapultec texts, he generally finds not more than one lexical argument per clause and not more than one new argument per clause. If, therefore, two or more new arguments are never introduced at the same time in the same clause, there is less likelihood of needing two lexical arguments in the same clause. The importance of givenness in his explanation of ergativity has been reflected by, or is paralleled by, Dixon (1994), as discussed above; both scholars are considered influential in the field.

Du Bois (1987:816) also notes that it is easier to decide if a nominal referent is new or not, or whether there are one or two new entities in a clause, than if a verb and its modifiers represent one, two, or more pieces of new information. He therefore confines the concept of given or new information to the direct arguments of the verb, and verbally or obliquely introduced information is not taken into account, given the difficulty of analyzing information introduced in verbal entities. However, since so much information is introduced in verbal constructions or oblique arguments, the importance of givenness must surely be limited if discussion thereof is confined to the direct verbal arguments. Perhaps the most obvious effect of givenness is in the full lexical realization of a nominal entity; beyond this, it is difficult to gauge the correlation between givenness and grammatical features such as ergativity. Rather, it must be a feature that relates specifically to nominals which determines the choice of ergative or nonergative constructions. The closest correlate to givenness in this respect may be topicality. I suggest that it is the intended topicality of the newly introduced or already given noun phrase that is important.

Du Bois (1987) does address the issue of topicality and topic continuity. He assumes that nominals higher on the animacy hierarchy are more topical than those lower on the hierarchy, noting that both intransitive and transitive subjects tend to behave similarly with respect to human referents, and that human referents tend to be more continuous in stretches of discourse than other referents. In effect, he equates agent with topic[4] and correlates agency with a high likelihood of human agency. As I have pointed out (see chapter 2, section 2.1), topics are not agents, nor are topics automatically relatable to the animacy hierarchy. Topic status depends on the speaker's signal of the prominence of a participant in the discourse; it is a feature of discourse and connected text, not of the clause. Topics can be identified within a single clause, but the relative importance of topics within a clause can only be determined through the text. Therefore, although human referents, and especially first and second person, tend to be recurring verbal arguments in connected texts, they are not automatically the topic with prominence. Their treatment will depend on what features are grammaticalized in a language, and at what level. In a language in which animacy is truly a grammaticalized feature, one can expect grammatical structures to be modified depending on the status of the subject or object argument: a clause with a subject lower on the hierarchy than the object may require passive treatment, and so on. Where topichood is grammaticalized, as I argue is the case in West Greenlandic, the identification of topic with agent, or topic with human referent, and so forth, is irrelevant; instead, what is relevant is the identification of topical prominence.

If the topic is the agent, then it might as well be called the subject, which is, in fact, what Dixon (1994:211–13) suggests. He identifies the topic ("theme" in his terminology) of a clause as the noun phrase with an underlying S/A alignment or function, or in other words, as the subject, partly because it tends to be associated with control. The most likely "themes" are therefore higher on the animacy hierarchy and more prototypically agentlike. In languages with an S/O alignment, or pivot, an antipassive structure is needed because the theme (i.e., topic) is likely to be an S in one clause and an A in the next. (Dixon, incidentally, finds that antipassives are almost never used at the beginning of discourse; rather, they continue it. Kalmár [1979a] claims the opposite.) In languages with split ergativity, he finds that clauses that involve the development of the theme, the foregrounded information, are likely to have accusative grammar, while clauses that provide background information, such as setting or minor participants, are ergative. Furthermore, the introduction of a new participant, which typically links S and O structures, is a feature of intraclausal grammar, whereas the continuation of a discourse theme, in an S or A function as described above, is one of interclausal grammar. Accusativity therefore marks "thematic" continuity, whereas ergativity marks the introduction of new material (despite its being backgrounded).

Dixon's (1994) conclusions are problematic. Not all ergative structures involve new material, and therefore a stated tendency (that new material is introduced as absolutives objects) misses a generality (that absolutive objects are topical). Further, identifying topics as subjects leaves no satisfactory explanation for S/O morphological grouping: if topics are subjects, and subjects are S's and A's, what then motivates S/O grouping? The identification of topic with agency in particular, even if only a tendency, again restricts topichood to clause-level structure, since agency is determined within the clause. By depending on the animacy hierarchy to define topics, Dixon associates accusativity with discourse structure and ergativity with the demands of intraclausal thematic (or topic) development. I find instead that ergative structures reflect cross-clausal topical continuity, and in most cases, the absolutive object is not new information, whereas the antipassive object reflects indefinite and new information. Accusative structures may show topic continuity, but so do ergative ones, albeit in a different way, since continuity is not reflected through the subject. As I have already argued, the grammatical relation of subject is one that belongs to the clause. It may indeed be the case that languages with split-ergativity use one set of structures for signaling intra-clausal grammar and another for inter-clausal grammar. If so, I might predict that the accusative clauses reflect clausal grammar whereas ergative ones reflect discourse grammar. Dixon's association of thematic (topic) continuity with accusativity may be a result of the multiple meanings he associates with "theme" (topic), including foregrounding. However, as we have seen, determination of fore- or backgrounding are often subjective (see chapter 2, section 2.1). Both Du Bois (1987) and Dixon (1994) are influenced by Praguian views of "theme," although their determination of givenness is not based on word order but on grammatical hierarchies.[5]

In another study of ergativity and grammatical relations, Bechert (1976:53) incorporates discourse-level considerations by viewing noun phrases as carriers of discourse categories such as topic, comment, focus, and presuppositions. Although he firmly links subjects to agents and topics, and objects to patients and comments, he allows for the possibility of a realignment to patient-topic and agent-comment (1976:57). This aspect of his study rather than his conclusion, in which he identifies ergative languages as ones with agent rather than subject agreement, lends support to several proposals made by Mallinson and Blake (1981:99–114) concerning topicality in accusative and ergative languages. Mallinson and Blake do not actually define their use of the term topic, but they suggest that it is related to the concept of semantic prominence, or to "what the clause is about" (1981:107), and they allow for degrees of topicality within a clause, as well as for the possibility of more than one topic per clause (1981:108). Subjects and topics are considered separate concepts, but subjects in accusative languages can be seen as grammaticalized topics, based on similarities between subject position, agreement, and case-marking and topicalization strategies (1981:100). Objects are also topical, but secondary to the subject. In ergative languages, however, at least syntactically ergative ones, the absolutive is the locus of the topic (i.e., S/O or patient alignment). Among a number of supporting arguments, two directly reflect the state of the ergative in West Greenlandic: the tendency for first and second persons to be unmarked for ergativity (which is true of the independent pronouns in West Greenlandic) and the tendency for nonspecific patients to be demoted to a peripheral marked case (i.e., the antipassive construction). Topics in both ergative and accusative languages are generally associable with a grammatical category such as subject or absolutive, but in belonging to a larger discourse, they need not be automatically or uniquely identified with either. In accusative languages, the primary topic tends to be associable with the subject and the secondary topic with the object, although which will be the primary topic of a clause ultimately depends on the surrounding context. In ergative languages, the primary topic is seen as the absolutive and the secondary topic as the ergative. (This explains the incompatibility of theories identifying the ergative construction with the passive, insofar as passive constructions detopicalize the agent, whereas ergative constructions do not). It is this feature of the relative importance of topics in a clause that Du Bois (1987:840–841) has missed when he refers to S/A alignment in the continuous treatment of human referents in a text. As noted above, it is not that agents are not topics, but rather that other nominals can be the primary topics.

Mallinson and Blake's (1981) and Dixon's (1972) views of topicality and its function in ergative languages come the closest to what I propose for ergativity and accusativity in West Greenlandic.

## 3.4 Role of topic in the use and distribution of ergative structures in West Greenlandic

Thus far, I have presented some of the characteristics of ergativity in West Greenlandic, some of the issues raised through traditional syntactic explanations of ergative and antipassive structures, and some of the observations that have led to the inclusion of discourse factors in syntactic analyses of ergativity. If explanations of ergativity in West Greenlandic require reference to discourse, then what role do syntactic and semantic notions play in these explanations? They are certainly necessary categorization devices in syntactic structuring, but they are not the only ones, or even necessarily the most important ones. Syntactically, subject is problematic because a distinct and identifiable morphological category subject is absent in ergative languages. Another way of categorizing nominal entities in a clause using semantic roles seemingly allows the semantic category agent to substitute for subject, thereby accounting for the fact that most ergative languages are merely morphologically ergative, and not syntactically so. However, subject and agent, as clause-level concepts, do not account for discourse-level tendencies such as the correlations between ergative and antipassive structures and information flow.

To explain discourse-level phenomena, one must have access to concepts and terminology that are relevant at the level of discourse. By clearly separating the syntactic and semantic from discourse roles, we arrive at a notion of topicality rather like that proposed by Mallinson and Blake (1981), with topic as a purely discourse category.[6] In the following discussion of my data, I restrict my usage of the term topic to the entity or entities in direct relation to the verb that has prominence within a stretch of continuous discourse, according to the definition I presented in chapter 2.

The importance of topic in explaining syntactic structures probably varies from language to language. Many languages with clearly defined subjects also have relatively clearly defined sentences; it therefore makes sense to discuss syntactic roles in these languages. Many clause-chaining languages, however, tend to have more clearly defined paragraph structures. Longacre (1985) proposes that on a continuum of possible constituent structures, languages vary in the importance placed on each structure. For example, a language might have a tightly controlled morphology or syntax but a less tightly controlled paragraph structure, and vice versa. West Greenlandic is a clause-chaining language with many features in common with other languages of the type. If West Greenlandic has a more clearly defined paragraph structure, then sentence-level roles such as subject and object are less likely to be the defining elements than are paragraph-level roles such as topic.

Given the tendency to include discourse factors in explaining ergativity in West Greenlandic, and given the typological characteristics of the language, one might predict that topic will be an important factor in determining its grammatical structure. The question is, then, are there compelling reasons to prefer explanations that make reference to topic over traditionally syntactic or semantic explanations? In fact, there are clear advantages to incorporating the notion of topic in such explanations. Problems in the description of West Greenlandic were briefly discussed above, and include the lack of object marking on verbs in antipassive structures; the lack of subject marking on the transitive contemporative verb forms; the imperfect correlation of ergative structures with given or definite information and antipassives with new or indefinite information; and the typological difficulties in identifying West Greenlandic as a superficially ergative language. These problems are resolved at the level of discourse. If West Greenlandic verbs mark topic rather than subject/object, the lack of object marking on antipassives is the result of the lack of topic status of the object. The lack of subject marking on transitive contemporatives reflects the importance of the object as the primary topic — in other words, if the transitive construction is going to lack subject or object inflection, it is the nontopic inflection that is lacking. The tendency for objects of antipassives to be indefinite or new has to do with the peripheral nature of the object with respect to topicality; peripheral nominals tend not to be repeated in discourse. The opposite is true of the object of an ergative construction, which, being the primary topic, will have been mentioned previously and will therefore be given or definite. Thus, an explanation based on the assumption of a topic role has descriptive and explanatory value.

Topic role may identify the absolutive arguments of the verb, but as suggested by Mallinson and Blake (1981), grammatical structures need not be limited to one topic per clause. The ergatively marked noun phrase, or agent[7] of a transitive construction may be a topic: in my texts, the agent always refers to an entity that is topical, but it is most often a global topic with general importance across the text, but not with emphasis. For example, the ergative agent is often the narrator or a group of people that includes the narrator. Although a text is generally about the narrator, a section of text may emphasizes another entity (see chapter 2, section 2.1). Where an ergative subject may also be a local topic, the section has two or more local topics which change in rank across the text (see section 3.5). To summarize, absolutively marked noun phrases are local topics, or global topics where the two coincide, ergative noun phrases are likely to be global topics, and instrumentally marked demoted objects of antipassive constructions are nontopics. Case marking thus reflects a natural category, topic, rather than parts of two categories (subject and object for absolutive marking, subject for ergative marking).

## 3.5 Data analysis

I now examine whether or not the theoretically plausible suggestion that ergativity in West Greenlandic reflects topichood rather than subjecthood or agency is borne out in reality. In the analyses that follow, I compare the instances of intransitive, ergative, and antipassive clauses in their contexts. I look specifically at the continuity or lack thereof of nominals in subject and direct object positions. Nominals that are introduced as topical may be signaled as such by the speaker in any of a number of ways, as described in chapter 2; these include fronting, intonational emphasis, the use of reflective clauses, the use of particles, and so forth. Which techniques a speaker uses may vary from speaker to speaker and depend on the speaker's level of expertise in relating events; however, they may be interpreted as clues to the topicality of the nominals in question. By looking at ergative marking or lack thereof, continuity of a nominal or lack thereof, and other methods of signaling topicality, I find that ergativity is a predictable indicator of topic status. Several contextual situations are considered, including simple examples of ergative structures involving at most one topic; apparent exceptions, such as reflection clauses, in which the objects are not always obviously or unambiguously the topics, and temporal adverbial clauses, in which the continuity of the verbal arguments is questionable; and finally, parts of texts that clearly involve multiple topics, and in which the identification of primary as opposed to secondary topic is at issue. Each of these situations is discussed in turn, before looking at the distribution of antipassive structures in the texts and the relative topic status of the arguments of antipassives.

There are approximately 620 clauses in the texts I have collected and analyzed. The majority of clauses in these texts are intransitive, either through the use of incorporation or, more often, through the use intransitive lexical forms. There are, however, often transitive alternatives to these intransitive structures. Examples 3.28 and 3.29 illustrate intransitive and comparable transitive structures from the same text:

(3.28)  (From text 1a)

35.   ... *ajoqit*        *taamani*        *ilinniartitsisutut*        *atorfeqarput aamma_}*

      *ajoqi-t*        *taamani*        *ilinniartitsisoq-tut*        *atorfik-qaq-put aamma*

      catechist-PL    at.that.time    teacher-EQ        work/job-have-3PL.IND and

'... and the catechists at that time had jobs as teachers.'

38.   ... *ullut*    *tamaasa*                    *atuarfinni*        *ajoqit_*
      *ulloq-t*    *tamaq-asa*                    *atuarfik-ni*        *ajoqi-t*
      day-PL    the.whole/all-3PL.O school-PL.LOC    catechist-PL
'... every day in the schools the catechists'

      *ilinniartitsisutut*        *sulisarput_}*
      *ilinniartitsisoq-tut*        *suli-saq-put*
      teacher-EQ            work-HAB-3PL.IND
'used to work as teachers.'

In the first clause, the noun *atorfik* 'job' is incorporated; in the second, the intransitive *suli-* 'work' is used. Later in the same text, the speaker expresses the duties of the catechists using the transitive forms *tigummi-* 'to take care of' and *atuartit-* 'to teach':

(3.29)  (From text 1a)

83.   ... *ajoqip*        *atuarfik*        *tamaat*                *tigummivaa_*
      *ajoqi-p*        *atuarfik-0*        *tamaq-at*                *tigummi-vaa*
      catechist-REL    school-ABS    the.whole/all-3SG.S hold.in.hands-3SG.SUBJ/3SG.OBJ.IND
'... the catechist has the whole school to take care of'

**Table 3.1** Ergative/antipassive clause count

| | Texts | | | | | |
|---|---|---|---|---|---|---|
| | 1A | 1B | 2 | 3A | 3B | 4 |
| No. of clauses | 103 | 114 | 113 | 124 | 68 | 98 |
| No. of ergatives | 26 | 40 | 30 | 48 | 21 | 27 |
| No. of antipassives | 1 | 6 | 2 | 3 | 0 | 1 |

84. *atuartut* *tamaasa* *atuartissavai_*

   *atuartoq-t* *tamaq-asa* *atuar-tit-ssa-vai*

   student-PL the.whole/all-3PL.O learn-cause-FUT-3SG. SUBJ/3PL.OBJ.IND

   'he has to teach all of the students . . .'

In most texts, slightly less than one-third of the clauses in each text are ergative in structure, and ergative structures make up the majority of the semantically transitive structures. In all texts, a negligible number of clauses are antipassive. Where ergative structures are used, the primary topic is the absolutive argument of the clause. Where antipassive structures are used, the instrumentally marked object is of peripheral importance in the text.

### Clear examples of topichood and ergativity

When a piece of text involves a single and unambiguous topic, there is a straightforward correlation between topic and argument structure. In the following example, 'catechist' is the global topic of a stretch of text spanning about seventy clauses; here, 'knowledge' is introduced in clause 43 as an oblique nominal and reintroduced with emphasis (fronting) in clause 44, becoming a local topic in the clauses that follow. It is in all cases the object of ergative constructions, and it is overtly expressed in clause 45 and pronominally expressed in clause 46. The topic 'catechist' is overtly expressed in clause 43 and clause 47; in the latter, it is the object, it is both fronted and intonationally emphasized, and it marks the end of the small section of text in which 'knowledge' was topical, as we see from the ensuing clauses:

(3.30)  (From text 1a)                          Topic  Argument Structure

43.   {*Taakkutuaappullu*     *ajoqit*        catechists        S   INTRANS
      *tassa_*

      *taakku-tuaq-u-vut-lu*   *ajoqi-t*
      *tassa*

      those-only-COP-        catechist-PL
      3PL.IND-and
      that.is

      'And the catechists were the only ones then'

      *taamanikkut*        *ilisimasassanik_*  knowledge            NOM
      *tiguinnarisassanik_*

      *taamani-kkut*       *ilisimasat-ssaq-nik*
      *tigu-innaq-giaq-ssaq-nik*

      at.that.time-VIA    knowledge-FUT-PL.INST
      take-only-INTNS-FUT-PL.INST

      'in those days [who] could spread knowledge'

44.   *ilinniartinneqarsimasut*                 catechists      S   INTRANS
      *Ilinniarfissuarmi_/*

      *ilinniartit-neqaq-sima-sut*
      *Ilinniarfissuaq-mi*

      teach-PASS-PERF-3PL.PART
      Greenlandic.Seminary-LOC

      'they had been educated in the Greenlandic Seminary'

45.   *taakkulu*           *ilinniakkatik,*   knowledge            N
      *taakku-lu*          *ilinniagaq-tik*
      that/those-and      training-3C.PL.POS/PL.POSM.ABS
      'and this knowledge/training'

      *namminerlu*         *aamma_*          knowledge     O   ERG
      *eqqarsaatersuutisik* *atorlugit_*      catechists     S

*nammineq-lu*                    *aamma*
*eqqarsaatersuut-tik*            *ator-lugit*

self-and                    and
aphorism-3C.PL.POS/PL.POSM.ABS    use-3NC.PL.OBJ.CT

'and using their own philosophy/thought'

*qaammarsaaneq*                            knowledge    N
*annertoorujussuaq_*

*qaammarsaaneq*-0
*annertooq-rujussuaq*-0

illumination/educational.standard-ABS
voluminous/extensive-very.much-ABS

'the enormous education/knowledge'

46.  *sinerissami*        *tamarmi_*                    knowledge    O    ERG
     *ingerlatarivaat_*}                               catechists   S

*sinerissaq-mi*    *tamaq-mi*
*ingerla-uti-saq-gi-vaat*

coast-LOC        the.whole/all-3SG.O
spread-manner-PASS.PART-have-3PL.SUBJ/3PL.OBJ.IND

'they spread it all over the coast.'

47.  {*Taamaattumik  ajoqit_*                    catechists
     *imaannaanngitsumik_*

*taamaattumik*    *ajoqi-t*
*imaannaanngisoq-mik*

therefore        catechist-PL
ones.not.without.importance-INST

'And therefore the catechists, who are not without importance'

*qutsavissarai*                *nunatta_*        catechists    O    ERG
*ullumikkut_/*

*qutsavi-ssaq-gi-vai     nuna-tta
ullumikkut*

thank-FUT-have-3SG.    land-1PL.POS
SUBJ/3PL.OBJ.IND
today

'our land should thank them today'

48.  *aamma    tamakku*                    catechists    S    INTRANS
*sulerujussuarsimasut_/*

*aamma     tamakku
suli-rujussuaq-sima-sut*

and         those
work-very.much-PERF-3PL.PART

'and they worked a lot, those ones'

49.  *imaannaanngitsorujussuarmik_*           catechists    S    INTRANS
*sulisimasut*

*imaannanngitsoq-rujussuaq-mik
suli-sima-sut*

ones.not.without.importance-very
very.much-INST  work-PERF-3PL.PART

'they worked in a very important/meaningful/able way'

50.  *kisianni_     pitsaviunngitsumik_*        catechists    S    INTRANS
*pineqartarsimasut_*

*kisianni       pitsak-vik-u-nngit-soq-mik
pi-neqaq-saq-sima-sut*

but             excellent-genuine-COP-NEG-PART-INST
do-pass-HAB-PERF-3PL.PART

'but they have not been paid well/well taken care of'

*aqutsisuninngaanniit*
aqutsisut-ninngaanniit

management-PL.ABL
'by the management'

51. *tassa*    *taamani_*   ·   *Grønlands Styrelsep_*
    *tassa*    *taamani*     *Grønlands Styrelse-p*
    that.is    at.that.time    Greenland Steering-REL
    'so at that time, Greenland Steering'

    tamaasa             ingerlatarivai      catechists   O    ERG
    tamaq-asa           ingerlaC-saq-gi-vai
    the.whole/all-3PL.O    work.with-PASS.PART-
                             have-3SG.SUBJ/3PL.OBJ.IND
    'worked with them all'

52. *provsteqarfik*     *aqqutigalugu_}*          catechists   O    ERG
    *provsteqarfik-0*    *aqqut-gi-lugu*
    deanery-ABS        way-have-3SG.OBJ.CT
    'via the deanery.'

Clauses 45 and 52 involve transitive contemporatives, which coindex at most one argument. In traditional interpretations, contemporatives are said to mark subject coreference (see chapter 4); thus, subject coindexing on transitive contemporatives is redundant and therefore absent. If local topics are coindexed, however, then the coindexing pattern on contemporatives is determined by relative topicality of the argument. In transitive contemporatives, the object is the local topic. In all examples, transitive contemporatives are consistently used where the absolutive object is the topic.

In the following example, the topic 'house' is first mentioned in clause 21; it is overtly mentioned in clauses 21, 22, 23, and 28, and mentioned by means of a deictic pronoun in 27 and 31. There are no other overt noun phrases in this section of text. 'House' is the subject in all but four clauses, clauses 19, 20, 26, and 30. Clause 19, 26, and 30 are ergative; in clauses 26 and 30, 'house' is the object. Clause 19 is a reflection clause that introduces this section of text. Clause 20 is an intransitive adverbial clause of time. In other words, the topic 'house' is continually present and is the local topic in all clauses from 21 to 31. Where it is not the subject, but the object, the clause is ergative. The subjects of the ergative clauses are first-person inflectional pronouns and are not maintained in continuous text. The first-person singular tends to be used for reflection clauses and the first-person singular or plural for indicating participants within the framework of the recollections.

(3.31)  (From text 2)                              Topic    Argument    Structure
19.     {*Eqqaamalluarpara*
        eqqaama-lluaq-vara
        remember-well-1SG.SUBJ/3SG.OBJ.IND
        'I remember it well'

20.     *meeraallunga_*          *taamanikkut_*
        *meeraq-u-lunga*         *taamani-kkut*
        child-COP-1SG.CT         at.that.time-VIA
        'I was a child, in those days'

21.     *massakkut*     *amutsiviup*      *akiani_*
        *massakkut*     *amutsivik-up*    *aki-ani*
        now            shipyard-REL      other.side-3SG.POS.LOC
        'now on the other side of the shipyard'

        *ilinniartut_*     *ilinniartut*             house
        *illukuat_/*

        *ilinniartoq-t*    *ilinniartoq-t*
        *illu-ku-at*

        student-PL      student-PL
        house-former-3PL.POS.ABS

        '[there was] formerly a students' house'

22.     *taassuma*      *illup*       *kangia*       *tungaani_*
        *taassuma*      *illu-p*      *kangia*       *tungaani*
        that.one-REL    house-REL     lying.east     over.there/in.that.
                                                     direction
        'to the east of that house over there'

        *itersiumanermiikkami*                    house            S     INTRANS
        *qooqqiumanermi_*

        *itersi-juma-neq-mii-gami*
        *qooqqi-juma-neq-mi*

make.a.hole.in.ground-want-NOMZ-be.in-3C.SG.CAUS
make.a.furrow-want-NOMZ-LOC

'because it is in a little depression in a valley'

23. *illungaatsiapilorujussuaq* house
*illu-ngaatsiaq-pilorujussuaq-0*
house-rather-very.big-ABS
'a little bigger than a big house'

24. *imaappoq* *sanaaq_'* house
*imaa-voq* *sanaaq-0*
be.like.this-3SG.IND something.one.has.done-ABS
'that is it has been built'

25. *illungaatsiapilorujussuaq* house S INTRANS
*uingasoq_/*

*illu-ngaatsiaq-pilorujussuaq-0*
*uinga-soq*

house-rather.big-very.big-ABS
slant-3SG.PART

'the rather larger than big house was slanted'

26. *taanna* *"Eqaluit* house O ERG
*inaannik"* *taasarparput}*

*taanna* *eqaluk-it*
*ini-annik* *taasar-varput*

that.one char-PL
place-3PL.POS.INST call-1PL.SUBJ/3SG.OBJ.IND

'that one we called "char's place."'

27. *{Tassalu* *taanna_* house
*aalisarnermut_*

*tassa-lu* *taanna*
*aalisarneq-mut*

then-and   that.one
fishing.(industry)-TERM

'And that [house], to the fishing industry'

*saarulliornermut_*                    *Sisimiuni_*
*saarullik-lioq-neq-mut*                *Sisimiut-ni*
codfish-make-NOMZ-TERM     Sisimiut-PL.LOC
'to the codfishing industry/factory in Sisimiut'

*aallarnersaataalluni_*                  house             S      INTRANS
aallarner-saq-uti-u-luni
begin-AGENT-means.to-COP-3SG.CT
it was the means with which to begin
[i.e., 'It was the means to begin the codfishing industry in
Sisimiut.']

28.   *taanna*      *illuusarsuaq*              house          S      INTRANS
      *uingasoq_/*

      *taanna*      *illu-u-saq-suaq-abs*
      *uinga-soq*

      that.one   house-COP-FUT-big-ABS
      uneven/slant-3SG.PART

      'that shack was slanted/uneven'

29.   *uingasumik*      *qalialik_/*      house
      *uinga-soq-mik*   *qaliaq-lik*
      slant-PART-INST   roof-provided.with
      'the one with the tilted roof'

30.   (*eqaluit*       *inaannik*            house             O            ERG
      *taasartagarput*)

      *eqaluk-it*      *ini-annik*
      *taasar-saq-varput*

      char-PL.REL    place-3PL.POS.INST
      call-HAB-1PL.SUBJ/3SG.OBJ.IND

'(we used to call it the place of char)'

31.  *tassa     ima*                          house          S    INTRANS
     *tarajorterivittut*
     *atoqqaarsimavoq_/*          *taanna_}*

     *tassa     ima*
     *tarajorterivik-tut*
     *ator-qqaaq-sima-voq*          *taanna*

     that.is    you.know
     salting.place-EQ
     use-first-PERF-3SG.IND    that.one

     'like, you know, it was first used as a [cod-]salting place, that one.'

In example 3.32 the local topic 'mother' was introduced earlier and is now reintroduced as a topic in clause 127 in the form of an incorporated noun; the first overt nominal mention is in the form of a fronted subject in line 131. From lines 137 to 148, the primary topic is 'mother'; there are a few other overt nominal entities, none but the last being continuous in any way, but all linked by common semantics: 'trader', 'Danes', and 'Bro' are all Danish traders that 'mother' worked for as a maid. 'Mother' is the subject of all clauses but the following: 137 (intransitive temporal adverbial clause) and 138 (dummy subject of incorporated particle), and 138, 140, 157, 158, and 159. The last five are all ergative, with 'mother' as their object:

(3.32)  (From text 3b)                     Topic    Argument    Structure
137.   *{Tassa    anaanaga_*          (mother)
       *ataataarukkatta_*

       *tassa     anaana-ga*
       *ataata-eruC-gatta*

       that.is    mother-1SG.POS/SG.POSM.ABS
       father-be.no.more-1PL.CAUS

       'That is, my mother—we lost my father'

       *imaattoq_*                     *1918-imi_'*
       *erniinnaararsuaq_'*            *ukiuk*

*novemberip*                    2-*ni*_}

*imaat-toq*                     1918-*mi*
*erniinnaq-araq-suaq*           *ukiuk*-o
*november-ip*                   2-*ni*

be.like.this                    1918-LOC
soon-a.little-very/extremely    winter-ABS
November-REL                    2-LOC

'like that in 1918 very soon after, winter on the second of November.'

138.    {*Taava_        kiguninnguatigut*
        *anaanaga*

        *taava          kinguneq-nnguaq-tigut*
        *anaana-ga*

        then            after-little-PL.VIA
        mother-1SG.POS/SG.POSM.ABS

        'Then, a little bit after the trader'

        *niuertukkut      qaaqquaat_'*     mother      O           ERG
        *niuertoq-kkut     qaaqqu-vaat*    trader      A
        trader-family.     call.on-3PL.SUBJ/
        PL.REL             3SG.OBJ.IND

        'came to call on my mother'

139.    *imaattoq_/*
        imaaC-soq
        like.this-3SG.PART
        'it's like this'

140.    *ikiortigisarumallugu_/*          mother      O           ERG
        *ikiorti-gi-saq-juma-lugu*         trader      A
        helper-have-PASS.PART-want-3SG.OBJ.CT
        '[he] wanted to have her help'

141. *tassalu      taamanimiilli*
     *anaanaga     qallunaanut_*

     *tassa-lu     taamani-miit-li*
     *anaana-ga    qallunaaq-nut*

     that.is-and                    at.that.time-ABL-INTNS
     mother-1SG.POS/SG.POSM.ABS     Dane-PL.TERM

     'and that is right from this time, my mother'

     *kiffanngorpoq_}*              mother          S    INTRANS
     kiffaq-nngor-voq
     maid-become-3SG.IND
     'was a maid for the Danes.'

142. {*Qallunaarparujorujussuit*
     Qallunaaq-pak-ruju-ruju-ssuaq-it
     Dane-a.number-many-many-big-PL
     'Many, many Danes'

70-it *sinnerlugit*                 mother          S    INTRANS
     *70-it     sinner-lugit*
     70-PL      be.more.than-3PL.OBJ.CT
     'Not before she was more than seventy'

143. *ukioqalereerluni    aatsaat_*  mother          S    INTRANS
     *ukioq-qaq-leq-      aatsaat*
     *reer-luni*
     year-have-begin-
     already-3SG.CT       first
     'years old'

144. *kiffartorunnaarpoq_}*          mother          S    INTRANS
     kiffartor-junnaar-voq
     be.in.service-no.more-3SG.IND
     'she was no longer a maid [i.e., to the Danes].'

145. (*Taamaammat*
     taamaat-mmat

therefore-3NC.SG.CA
'Therefore'

| | | | |
|---|---|---|---|
| 146. | *toqummat_'* | mother | S | INTRANS |

toqu-mmat
die-3NC.SG.CAUS
'when she died'

| | | | |
|---|---|---|---|
| 147. | *Bro niuertuulluni_* | Bro | S | INTRANS |

Bro niuertoq-u-luni
Bro trader-COP-3C.SG.CT
'Bro being the trader'

148. *kransersuarmik*
*naasortalerpaa_/*    mother   O   ERG

*kranse-suaq-mik*
*naasorta-ler-vaa*    Bro   A

wreath-big-INST
flowers-provide.with-3SG.SUBJ/3SG.OBJ.IND

'lay a big wreath of flowers [on it] [i.e., grave]'

149. *(tassa    kiffartorsimanera*   mother   O   ERG
*pillugu)_}*

*tassa    kiffartor-sima-neq-a*   Bro   A
*pi-lugu*

that.is    be.in.service-PERF-NOMZ-
3SG.POS/SG.POSM.ABS
do-3SG.OBJ.CT
'(that is [because] she had been in his service [he had her
service]).'

The casual introduction of another participant, 'Bro', in clause 147 is also
interesting. This participant remains peripheral to the text, or in other
words, nontopical, even though it is the subject of an ergative construction
in clause 148. The subject of an ergative is not the local topic (as discussed

in chapter 2), and 'Bro' is certainly not a global topic in the same sense that 'mother' or even the narrator is in the text.

The text continues with a change in theme but with the same topic; from clause 150 to clause 161, the speaker describes the mother's industry in getting food. 'Mother' is overtly expressed in clause 150 and is the subject of all clauses except clauses 154 and 157 (dummy subjects of setting clauses) and 155 (intransitive setting clause), and 150, 160, and 161. The latter three clauses are all transitive, ergative structures, and 'mother' is the object in each case; the only overt subject is in clause 160.

| | | Topic | Argument | Structure |
|---|---|---|---|---|
| (3.33) | (From text 3b) | | | |
| 150. | {*Arnaq* | mother | S | ERG |
| | *imaannanngitsorujussuartut* | | | |
| | *taasinnaavara* | | | |

*Arnaq-0*
*imaannanngit-soq-rujussuaq-tut*
*taa-sinnaa-vara*

woman-ABS
unusual-PART-very.much-EQ
call-just-1SG.SUBJ/3SG.OBJ.IND

'I could just call her a special woman'

| | | Topic | Argument | Structure |
|---|---|---|---|---|
| | *anaanaga_}* | mother | | |

anaana-ga
mother-1SG.POS/SG.POSM.ABS
'my mother'

| | | Topic | Argument | Structure |
|---|---|---|---|---|
| 151. | *eqiasuitsorujussuaq_* | mother | | NOM |

*eqiasuiC-soq-rujussuaq-0*
be.diligent-PART-very-ABS
'she was very industrious'

| | | Topic | Argument | Structure |
|---|---|---|---|---|
| 152. | *sulinngiffimmigut_* | mother | S | INTRANS |
| | *sinissanani* | | | |

*sulinngiffik-migut*
*siniC-ssa-nani*

vacation/free.time-3SG.POS.VIA
sleep-FUT-3SG.NEG.CT

'in her free time she didn't sleep'

153.  *piliniartartoq_*                  mother          S    INTRANS
piliniaq-saq-soq
provide-HAB-3SG.PART
'she was getting/hunting for food [for the winter]'

154.  *saarulleqallarmat*                 *taamanikkut*
*saarullit-qaq-llaq-mat*            *taamani-kkut*
codfish-have-great-3NC.SG.CAUS     at.that.time-VIA
'there was a lot of codfish at that time'

155.  *1920-ikkut*    *aallartilaarneranni,*
*1920-kkut*     *aallarti-laaq-neq-anni*
1920-VIA        begin-a.bit-NOMZ-3PL.POS/SG.POSM.LOC
'at the very beginning of the 1920s'

*umiaasaarannguaqaratta_'*
umiaasaaraq-nguaq-qaq-gatta
flat-bottomed.boat-little-have-1PL.CAUS
'we had a little flat-bottomed boat'

156.  *kiffaaffini_*    *unnukkut*          mother          S    INTRANS
*suliunnaaraangami*

*kiffaaffik-ni*    *unnuk-kkut*
*suli-junnaaq-gaa-gami*

housework-3C.SG.POS.LOC     evening-VIA
work-no.more-whenever-3C.SG.CAUS

'whenever she stopped working as a maid in the evening'

157.  *unnuarsiorluni*
unnuaq-sioq-luni
night-deal.with-3SG.CT
'when it was night [i.e., she was doing nightshift]'

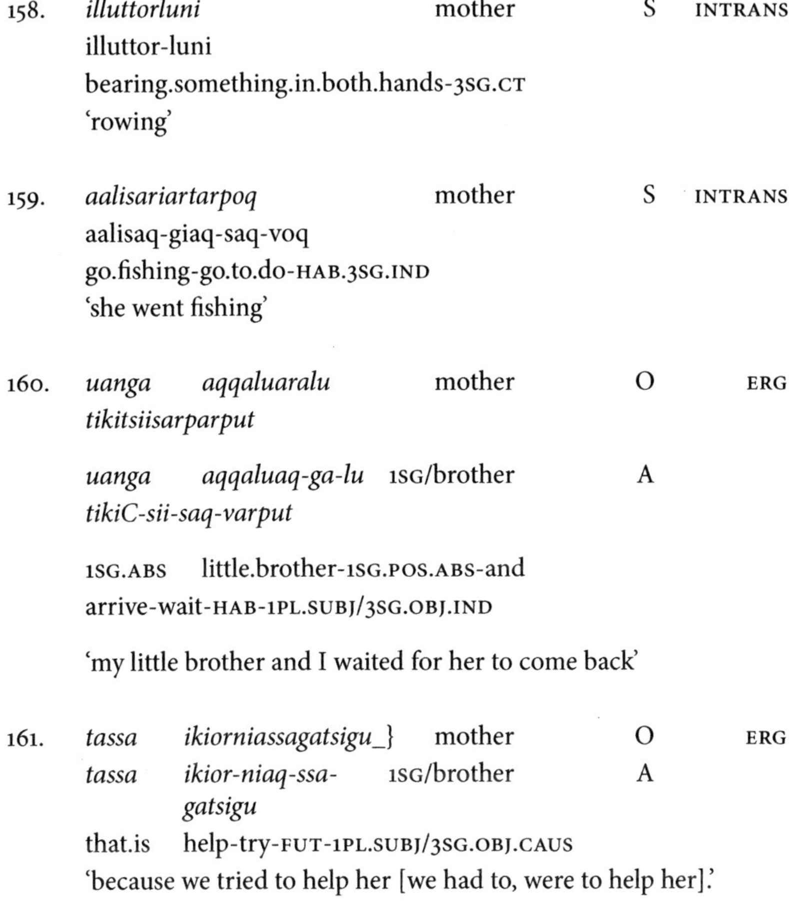

158. *illuttorluni*                    mother        S   INTRANS
illuttor-luni
bearing.something.in.both.hands-3SG.CT
'rowing'

159. *aalisariartarpoq*                mother        S   INTRANS
aalisaq-giaq-saq-voq
go.fishing-go.to.do-HAB.3SG.IND
'she went fishing'

160. *uanga    aqqaluaralu*           mother        O        ERG
*tikitsiisarparput*

*uanga    aqqaluaq-ga-lu*   1SG/brother     A
*tikiC-sii-saq-varput*

1SG.ABS    little.brother-1SG.POS.ABS-and
arrive-wait-HAB-1PL.SUBJ/3SG.OBJ.IND

'my little brother and I waited for her to come back'

161. *tassa    ikiorniassagatsigu_}*    mother        O        ERG
*tassa    ikior-niaq-ssa-*   1SG/brother     A
                *gatsigu*
that.is    help-try-FUT-1PL.SUBJ/3SG.OBJ.CAUS
'because we tried to help her [we had to, were to help her].'

(Another very clear example of topic from text 3 is given in example 3.59.)

## Reflection clauses

In addition to clear examples of topic, there are regular uses of ergative structures, especially in reflection clauses, in which the object may be ambiguously interpreted as referring cataphorically to a topic or theme. Reflection clauses are one of the common ways of introducing a topic or theme (see chapter 2, section 2.3). In example 3.34 the direct object of the reflection clause in line 7 is the cataphorically expressed topic 'old people' in line 8:

|          |                        | Topic      | Argument | Structure |
|----------|------------------------|------------|----------|-----------|
| (3.34)   | (From text 3a)         |            |          |           |
| 7.       | *. . . makku    soorlu*  | old people | O        | ERG       |
|          | *oqaluuserivagut_/*    |            |          |           |

*makku          soorlu*
*oqaluuseri-vagut*

this-PL.REL    for.example
talk.about-1PL.SUBJ/3PL.OBJ.IND

'. . . for example, we talk about these'

| 8. | *utoq— nunatsinni* | *ullutsinni* | *utoqqaat_* |
|----|----------------|-----------|----------|
|    | *nuna-tsinni*  | *ulloq-tsinni* | *utoqqaq-it* |
|    | land-1PL.POS.LOC | day-1PL.POS.LOC | old.person-PL |

'in our land, in our days, the old people'

*amerliartuaartut_*          old people          S    INTRANS
*amerliC-giartuaaq-tut* or *toq-t*
be.more.and.more-gradually.more.and.more-3PL.PART
'they are gradually increasing in number . . .'

In example 3.35, however, there are several options for interpreting the
object of clause 15: the object may refer to the development of a new theme
or more specifically to the topic 'father':

|          |                       | Topic  | Argument | Structure |
|----------|-----------------------|--------|----------|-----------|
| (3.35)   | (From text 4)         |        |          |           |
| 15.      | {*Oqaatigissavaralu*  | father | O        | ERG       |

*oqaatigi-ssa-vara-lu*
talk.about-FUT-1SG.SUBJ/3SG.OBJ.IND-and
'And I will talk about [him/it]'

| 16. | *ataataga*   | *aamma* |
|-----|-------------|---------|
|     | *ataata-ga* | *aamma* |
|     | father-1SG.POS.ABS | and |

'and my father'

*tamalaarpassuarnik*          father          S    INTRANS
*soqutigisaqarami_*'

*tamalaaq-passuaq-nik*
*soqutigisaq-qaq-gami*

a.little.of.everything-a.lot-PL.INST
interest-have-3C.SG.CAUS

'he was interested in many things . . .'

The ambiguity here is typical of many reflection clauses, although in most cases it is possible to view the clause as having undergone something like subject-to-object raising (which may not always be clear from the translation): the following clause is signaled as topically important, and it is a clausal object to the reflection clause. The subject of the following clause is the topic of the section, as in examples 3.35–3.37:

| (3.36) | (From text 2) | | Topic | Argument | Structure |
|---|---|---|---|---|---|
| 32. | {*Eqqaamavaralu* | | codfish | O | ERG |
| | eqqaama-vara-lu | | | | |
| | remember-1SG.SUBJ/3SG.OBJ-and | | | | |
| | 'And I remember it' | | | | |

| 33. | *taamanikkut* | *saarulliit* | *tunineqartartut_* |
|---|---|---|---|
| | *taamani-kkut* | *saarullik-it* | *tuni-neqaq-saq-tut* |
| | at.that.time-VIA | codfish-PL | sell-pass-HAB-3PL.PART |
| | 'at that time the codfish used to be sold . . . (i.e., I remember codfish used to be sold)' | | |

| (3.37) | (From text 1a) | | Topic | Argument | Structure |
|---|---|---|---|---|---|
| 13. | . . . *eqqaamavara_* | | Qaqortoq | O | ERG |
| | eqqaama-vara | | | | |
| | remember-1SG.SUBJ/3SG.OBJ.IND | | | | |
| | '. . . I remember it . . .' | | | | |

| 16. | . . . *Qaqortoq* | *inukitsunnguuvoq_* |
|---|---|---|
| | *Qaqortoq-0* | *inuk-kit-soq-nnguuvoq* |
| | Qaqortoq-ABS | person-have.little-PART-DIM-COP.3SG.IND |
| | '. . . Qaqortoq did not have many people . . .' | |
| | [i.e., 'I remember Qaqortoq did not have many people'; clauses 14 and 15 are parenthetical adverbial clauses of time] | |

In many cases, the clausal object of the reflection clause is an incorporated topic, as in example 3.38, or it develops a theme rather than a topic, as in example 3.39:

(3.38) (From text 1b)                    Theme    Argument    Structure
117.    {*Qaqortumi*      *uanga*              have         O          ERG
        *eqqaamavara*     *tassa*          rowboats
        *taamani*

        *Qaqortoq-mi*      *uanga*
        *eqqama-vara*      *tassa*
        *taamani*

        Qaqortoq-LOC    1SG.ABS
        remember-1SG.SUBJ/3SG.OBJ.IND        that.is
        at.that.time

        'In Qaqortoq, I remember it, that is, at that time'

118.    *umiaasaqaraluarpoq,*
        umiaasaq-qaq-galuaq-voq
        little.flat.bottomed.rowboat-have-CONSEQ-3SG.IND
        'there were little flat-bottomed rowboats . . .'

(3.39) (From text 1b)                    Theme    Argument    Structure
159.    {*Tassa*    *eqqaamalluariga*          go to        O          ERG
        *tassa*     *eqqaama-lluaq-giga*      Narsaq
        that.is    remember-well-1SG.SUBJ/3SG.OBJ.PART
        'I remember very well'

160.    *taamani*          *Narsamukaraangatta*                *aasakkut*
        *taamani*          *Narsaq-mukaq-gaangatta*            *aasaq-kkut*
        at.that.time    Narsaq-go.to-whenever.1PL.CAUS    summer-VIA
        'in those days, whenever we went to Narsaq during the
        summer . . .'

## Temporal adverbs

A second clause type that is commonly ergative but not always clearly topical is a temporal adverbial clause relating to periods in the year, as exemplified by 3.40:

(3.40) (From text 1a)
21.   . . . *ukiorlu*              *naallugu*
      *ukioq-0-lu*            *naa-llugu*
      winter-ABS-and     be.finished-3SG.OBJ.CT
      '. . . and all winter long . . .'

Here, 'winter' is the object of a transitive construction with an unspecified, or dummy, subject. There are perhaps seven such clauses in the texts, two of which show thematic continuity with the previous clauses:

(3.41) (From text 2)
76.   {*Tassali*          *kisianniuna*        *kangerluk_*
      *anorlertartoq*

      *tassa-li*          *kisianni-una*     *kangerluk-0*
      *anorler-saq-soq*

      that.is-but     but-DEIC          fjord-ABS
      blow [of.wind]-HAB-3SG.PART

      'But so the fjord was usually windy'

77.   *isersarnaartartoq,*
      isersarnaaq-saq-soq
      wind.going.into.fjord-HAB-3SG.PART
      'there was a wind going into the fjord'

78.   *qajassuunnagu}*
      qajassuut-nagu
      be.cautious/spare-NEG.3SG.OBJ.CT
      'it was very windy [i.e., not a cautious wind, it didn't spare them].'

In clause 76, the windiness is first mentioned; in both clauses 76 and 77, the concept is thematic, or verbally expressed. Clause 78 is a transitive construction with a dummy subject that is not encoded in the inflection because of the contemporative mood. The closest the text comes to expressing a nominal entity at this point is in clause 77, with *isorsarnaar-*, which is related etymologically to *isorsarneq* 'wind coming into the fjord'. If the object of clause 78 is 'wind coming into the fjord', then it does express the topic. The conceptual problem with such clauses is that the object is semantically the subject. The object status is more clear in example 3.40 above, in which *ukioq* 'winter' is absolutive, or in example 3:42:

(3.42)  (From text 2)

100.   {*Taamalu_*    *ullaassanngoriartornerani_*
       *Taama-lu*    *ullaassaq-nngor-giartor-neq-ani*
       then-and     dawn-become-almost-NOMZ-3SG.POS.LOC
       'And then when it got closer to dawn'

101.   *seqernup*    *nuiartornerani*        *tassa_*
       *seqineq-up*   *nui-giartor-neq-ani*      *tassa*
       sun-REL      [sun].rises-more.and.more-   that.is
                       NOMZ- 3SG.POS.LOC
       'in the sun's rising, that is'

102.   *uernaleriartuaaq,*
       uerna-ler-riartuaaq
       sleepy-nearly-gradually.more.and.more
       '[we] begin to be sleepy'

103.   *seqineq*   *kissakkiartuaaartillugu_/*
       *seqineq-0 kissaq-giartuaaq-tit-lugu*
       sun-ABS   warm-gradually.more.and.more-cause-3SG.OBJ.CT
       '[it] is causing the sun to get warmer . . .'
       [i.e., 'the sun is getting warmer'; perhaps 'the sun's rising is causing the sun to get warmer']

As with example 3.41, there is some thematic continuity leading up to the transitive construction in clause 103. Thematically, 'the sun's rising' is the speaker's emphasis; in this clause, however, 'sun' is the overtly expressed object (overtly expressed only once before, as the possessor in clause 101). Theme and topic continue to interact in the continuation of the text (see clause 104 'at dawn' and clause 107 'in the morning the sun rose', where 'sun' is overtly expressed). In any case, *seqineq* 'sun' is absolutive and must be syntactically the object.

    There are five cases with no such temporal continuity. Of these, three have overtly expressed absolutive objects that are semantically the subjects, as we saw in example 3.40, and in 3.43 (clause 63) and 3.44 (clause 104) below:

(3.43)　(From text 1a)

59.　{*Nuutsikkaangamigillu*　　　　　　　　*taamani_*
　　　*nuuC-tit-gaangamigit-lu*　　　　　　　*taamani*
　　　move-cause-when(ever).3PL.SUBJ/　at.that.time
　　　3NC.PL.OBJ.CAUS-and
　　　'And when they had moved them at that time'

60.　*illussaqartinneqarneq*　　　　　　　　　*ajorput_}*
　　　*illu-ssaq-qaq-tit-neqaq-neq-0*　　　　　*ajor-put*
　　　house-FUT-have-cause-PASS-NOMZ-ABS　bad-3PL.IND
　　　'they were not given a house to stay in/they didn't house them.'

61.　{*Nuukkaangamillu,*
　　　nuuC-gaangamik-lu
　　　move-when(ever).3C.PL.CAUS-and
　　　'And whenever they moved'

62.　*nammineq*　　*illulioqqaarlutik_*
　　　*nammineq*　　*illu-lioq-qqaaq-lutik*
　　　self　　　　　house-build-first-3PL.CT
　　　'they first had to build a house themselves'

63.　*ilaanni*　　　*ukiorsuaq*　　　*sinnerlugu_/*
　　　*ilaanni*　　　*ukioq-suaq*　　*sinner-lugu*
　　　sometimes　winter-big-ABS　over/more.than-3SG.OBJ.CT
　　　'sometimes over more than a year'

(3.44)　(From text 3a)

103.　. . . *ataatagooq_*　　　　　　*pingajungaarami*
　　　*ataata-0-gooq*　　　　　　　*pingajuq-ngaaq-gami*
　　　father-ABS-reported.speech　get.something/be.lucky-a.lot-3C.
　　　　　　　　　　　　　　　　　SG.CAUS
　　　'. . . my father, they say, got a lot/always got something'

104.　*qaammatit_*　　*ullui*　　　　　　　　　　*naasarpai_/*
　　　*qaammat-it*　　*ulloq-i*　　　　　　　　　*naa-saq-vai*
　　　month-PL　　　day-3SG.POS.PL.POSM.ABS　be.done-HAB-3SG.
　　　　　　　　　　　　　　　　　　　　　　　SUBJ/3PL.OBJ.IND
　　　'the days of the month used to be done/pass'

105.    *ataasiinnaanngitsunik*          *puisinik*          *tikiussuilluni_}*
        *ataasiq-innaa-nngit-soq-nik*    *puisi-nik*         *tiki-ussor-i-luni*
        one-only-NEG-PART-PL.INST        seal-PL.INST        arrive-one.after.
                                                             another-INTRANS-
                                                             3SG.CT

'he arrived with not just one seal [he got more than one seal].'

In both examples 3.43 and 3.44, the time period is being emphasized: in text 1a, clause 63, the sheer length of time the catechists had to wait before getting their own house is stressed, and in text 3a, clause 104, the number of days (all the days of the month) is stressed as the number of times the speaker's father arrived with one or more seal.

The final two examples of ergativity in temporal clauses involve a construction with the agentive suffix *-tit-*; the clauses in question are 91 and 82, respectively:

(3.45)    (From text 3a)
89.       . . . *aneersuarlunga_*
          aneer-suaq-lunga
          go.for.a.walk-a.lot-1SG.CT
          '. . . I went for walks a lot'

90.       *ullorsuaq*          *pisarpunga*
          ulloq-suaq-0         pi-saq-vunga
          day-big-ABS          thing-HAB-1SG.IND
          'I used to do this all day long'

91.       *silagitsillugu_/*
          sila-gik-tit-lugu
          weather-have.a.good-cause-3SG.OBJ.CT
          'if the weather was good'

92.       *Assorsuaq*          *maqaasivara*          *massakkut_}*
          Assut-suaq           maqaasi-vara          massakkut
          much-very.much-ABS   miss-1SG.SUBJ/        now
                               3SG.OBJ.IND
          'I miss it very much now.'

(3.46)  (From text 4)

79.     . . . *taavalu*      *aamma_*      *soorunalumi*        *puisit_'*
        *taava-lu*      *aamma*      *sooruna-lu-mi*      *puisi-t*
        then-and      and        of.course-and-      seal-PL
                                  what.about

        '. . . and then of course what about the seals'


80.     *sikukkut*      *avungalu,*                *Natsilimmut_'*
        *siku-kkut*      *avunga-lu*                *Natsilik-mut*
        ice-VIA        in.the.north-and        Natsilik-TERM

        'across the ice up north to Natsilik'


        *Saarluminngaanniit*        *ilaanni*        *sisoraaserlutik*
        *Saarloq-minngaanniit*      *ilaanni*        *sisorar-uti-ler-lutik*
        Saarloq-ABL                sometimes      ski-device-begin-3PL.CT

        'sometimes putting skis on from Saarloq'


81.     *piniariartarlutik_}*
        piniar-giaq-saq-lutik
        hunt-go.to.do-HAB-3PL.CT
        'hunting.'


82.     {*Taava_*      *upernariartortillugu*
        *taava*      *upernar-giartoq-tit-lugu*
        then        become.spring-go.to.do-cause-3SG.OBJ.CT

        'Then when spring came'


83.     *piniagassat*                *saqqummeriartortarput_'*
        *piniagassat*                *saqqummer-giartoq-saq-vut*
        hunting.animals.PL          come.out-more.and.more-HAB-
                                    3PL.IND

        'the hunting animals used to come out more and more . . .'


These kinds of clauses could also be structured intransitively; therefore, the
decision to use transitive structures is difficult to explain. Contemporatives
involving an incorporated noun and the agentive affix *-tit-* may implicate
a human agent in the action (P. Langgård, personal communication); this
would require a transitive construction for structural reasons. On the other

hand, the use of the affix in this construction frequently does not have an agentive component in the meaning and is semilexicalized in this use as 'while' (M. Fortescue, personal communication). If so, the use of the transitive is simply a syntactic requirement and does not reflect discourse or semantic considerations.

In fact, the ergative structures in all of these temporal clauses may simply be interpreted as syntactic requirements rather than forcing a discourse-based explanation.

### Sections with more than one topic or theme in interaction

All of the sections reviewed have had one identifiable primary topic; other noun phrases that could have been topics had no continuity. There are several more complicated sections in the texts, where more than one topic or theme is treated as important, as in example 3.47:

(3.47)  (From text 3b)                     Topic/Theme   Argument   Structure

163.   {*Aana*            *suli*
       *tupinnarneq_*'

       *aana*             *suli*
       *tupinnaq-neq*

       here.it.is/that.one.there      yet
       wonderful/unusual-SUP.ABS

       'And what was most wonderful of all'

164.   *aqqaluara*          *apersortittussaasoq_*'      (1930-*imi*)_'
       *aqqaluaq-ga*        *apersortit-sussaa-soq*      1930-*mi*
       little.brother-1SG.   be.confirmed-planned/        1930-LOC
       POS/SG.POSM.ABS     shall-3SG.PART
       'when my little brother was to be confirmed (in 1930)'

165.   *illutaarpugut_*'                    get house                INTRANS
       illu-taaq-vugut
       house-get.a.new-1PL.IND
       'we got a new house'

166. *takanna    suli*                    house
    *illukoq    oqaluffiup*
    *kanginnguani*

    *takanna       suli*
    *illu-koq-0    oqaluffik-up*
    *kangia-nnguaq-ni*

    this.one.down.there       yet
    house-former/old-ABS    church-REL
    east-little-3SG.POS

    'this old house, still a ruin, beside [a little east of] the church'

    *taanna*
    *qaqqajunnaasannguup*                house        S    INTRANS
    *qaaniittoq_'*

    *taanna*
    *qaqqajunnaqasag-nnguaq-up*
    *qaani-iC-soq*

    that.one
    low.hill-little-REL
    top-COP-PART or 3SG.PART

    'on the top of that little hill'

167. *tassa*                *anaana*    get house                INTRANS
    *taamanikkut*        *illutaarpoq_}*

    *tassa*                *anaana-0*    mother        S
    *taamani-kkut*        *illu-taaq-voq*
    that.is                mother-ABS
    at.that.time-VIA    house-get.a.new-3SG.IND
    'that is, my mother got the house then.'

168. *{Anaanama_*
    *tupinnartumik_*                    mother

> *anaana-ma*
> *tupinnaq-soq-mik*
>
> mother-1sg.pos.REL
> wonderful-part-inst
>
> 'It was wonderful that my mother'

| | | | | |
|---|---|---|---|---|
| *naminneq* | *tamaat* | house | O | ERG |
| *akilerlugu_'* | | | | |

| | | | |
|---|---|---|---|
| *naminneq-o* | *tamaq-at* | mother | A |
| *aki-leq-lugu* | | | |

self-REL　　the.whole/all-3SG.O
pay-provide-3SG.OBJ.CT

'paid for it all herself'

| | | | |
|---|---|---|---|
| *sanasullu* | *tamaasa_* | workers | O |
| *sanasoq-t-lu* | *tamaq-asa* | | |

worker-PL-
and　　the.whole/all-3PL.O

'and all the workers'

169. *angutitaqannginnatta_'*
　　 anguti-taq-qaq-nngit-natta
　　 man-belonging.to-have-NEG-1PL.NEG.CAUS
　　 'because we didn't have a man [in our family]'

170.
| | | | | |
|---|---|---|---|---|
| *sanasullu* | *tamaasa* | workers | O | ERG |
| *akilerlugit_* | | | | |

| | | | |
|---|---|---|---|
| *sanasoq-t-lu* | *tamaq-asa* | mother | A |
| *aki-leq-lugit* | | | |

worker-PL-and　　all-3PL.O
pay-provide-3PL.OBJ.CT

'she paid all the workers'

171.
| | | | |
|---|---|---|---|
| *assigiinngitsut* | | house | O | ERG |
| *inuit—inuit* | *sanavaat* | | | |

*assigiinngitsut*                     workers              A

*inuk-it inuk-it sana-vaat*

different-REL          person-PL

person-PL          work-3PL.SUBJ/3.OBJ.IND

'different people worked on it'

172.   *angutit_'     sanavaat_'*        house              O              ERG

      *angut-t     sana-vaat*         workers            A

      man-PL     work-3PL.SUBJ/3.OBJ.IND

      'men worked on it'

173.   *tassa        tamaasa*

      *akilerlugit,*                     workers            O              ERG

      *tassa        tamaq-asa*

      *aki-ler-lugit*                    mother             A

      that.is     the.whole/all.-3PL.O

      pay-provide-3PL.OBJ.CT

      'she paid them all'

In this section, ignoring all noncontinuous nominal entities, there are at least three topics all vying for prominence. 'Mother', the topic of the preceding section (see example 3.33) appears once overtly, in clause 168, and is only found as the subject in this section. 'House' is introduced in clause 165 as an incorporated noun, then mentioned overtly as the subject in clause 166. After this, it is only found as an object (in clauses 169, 171, and 172). Finally, 'workers' is introduced in clause 168 as an elaboration of the theme of the mother paying for the house by herself; in addition to this, itself a remarkable achievement, the mother paid for all the workers. 'Workers' is then repeated overtly as an object in clauses 170 and 173, and as a subject using synonyms in clauses 171 and 172. All clauses with two of these three topics are ergative in structure, with the exception of clause 167, which involves an incorporated noun 'house' and the reintroduction of the topic after a parenthetical break (clause 166). The prevalence of ergative structures is hardly surprising, since almost all are semantically transitive actions; therefore, this section does not by itself prove that the objects of transitive constructions are topics. However, it can serve as confirmation.

Example 3.48 illustrates another text with multiple topics. This section is particularly interesting because of the use of the instrumental in clauses with three direct arguments of the verb, in particular in clauses 149, and 153:

(3.48)  (From text 1b)                          Topic    Argument    Structure

144.    . . . *taavalu*    *anaanama*  Grandfather
        *ataataa_*

        *taava-lu*        *anaana-ma*
        *ataata-a*

        then-and        mother-1SG.POS.REL
        father-3NC.SG.POS/SG.POSM.ABS

        '. . . and then my mother's father'

        *taalliortorsuarput_/*
        *Kalaallit Nunaata*                 *taalliortorsua_*

        *taalliortoq-suaq-rput*
        *Kalaallit Nunaat-a*                *taalliortoq-suaq-0*

        poet-big-1PL.POS/SG.POSM.ABS
        Greenland-3SG.POS.REL               poet-big-ABS

        'our poet, Greenland's big poet'

        *Iinndaleeraq*                  *Indaleeraq*
        *Henrik Lund_'*             (Grandfather)

        *Iinndaleeraq-o*
        *Henrik Lund-0*

        Henry-ABS
        Henrik Lund-ABS

        'Henry, Henrik Lund'

145.    *aasat*              *tamaasa_'*
        *aasaq-t*            *tamaq-asa*

summer-PL.ABS    the whole/all_3PL.0
'every summer'

| *tikeraartaratsigu*                 | Grandfather | O   | ERG |
| *Qaqortuminngaanniit*               |             |     |     |

| *tikeraar-saq-gatsigu*              | 1PL | A |
| *Qaqortoq-minngaanniit*             |     |   |

visit-HAB-1PL.SUBJ/3SG.OBJ.CAUS
Qaqortoq-ABL

'we used to visit him from Qaqortoq'

146. | *uagut*  *aasiffigisaratsigu*  | Narsaq | O | ERG |
     | *Narsaq_/*                     |        |   |     |

| *uagut*  *aasi-ffigi-saq-gatsigu*  | 1PL | A |
| *Narsaq-0*                         |     |   |

1PL spend.the.summer-TRANS.have.as-HAB-1PL.SUBJ/3SG.OBJ.
CAUS Narsaq-ABS
'we used to spend the summer in Narsaq [have summer vacation
with him in Narsaq; have Narsaq as a summer vacation place]'

| (*meeqqat*      | *aamma*           | 1PL |
| *anaanakkut*    | *ataatakkullu*    |     |
| *meeqqat*       |                   |     |

| *meeraq-t*      | *aamma*           |
| *anaana-kkut*   | *ataata-kkut-lu*  |
| *meeraq-t*      |                   |

| child-PL            | and                     |
| mother-family.ABS   | father-family.ABS-and   |
| child-PL            |                         |

'(the children and [my] mother's family and [my] father's family
the children'

| *qatanngutigullu*    | *tamatta_)}*   |
| *qatanngut-tivut-lu* | *tamaq-tta*    |

siblings-family.PL.ABS-and     the whole/all.1PL
'and the sibling's family, all of us).'

147.    {*Eqqaamagiga*     *tassa*        Grandfather            O          ERG
         *taamani*          *Ittu_*'

         *eqqaama-giga*     *tassa*
         *taamani*          *Ittu-0*

         remember-1SG.SUBJ/3SG.OBJ.PART      that.is
         at.that.time                      Grandfather-ABS

         'I remember Grandfather at that time'

148.    *tyggegummimik*            chewing gum          O          ANT
         *amerikamiuninngaanniit*    Grandfather          A
         *tunisittarsimagami_*}

         *tyggegummi-mik*
         *amerika-miut-ninngaanniit*
         *tunisit-saq-sima-gami*

         chewing.gum-INST
         America-people.from-ABL
         get-HAB-PERF-3C.SG.CAUS

         'used to get chewing gum from the Americans.'

149.    {*Tyggegummimik*         chewing gum          IO         ERG
         *tuningaagamitigut*                 1PL         O

         *Tyggegummi-mik*         Grandfather          A
         *tuni-gaa-ngamitigut*

         chewing.gum-INST
         give-whenever-3NC.SG.SUBJ/1PL.OBJ.CAUS

         'Whenever he gave us a lot of chewing gum'

150.    *oqartarpoq_/*               Grandfather          S      INTRANS
         oqaq-saq-voq

say-HAB-3SG.IND
'he used to say'

151. *"Qallunaat tamuatsivaavat"_/*      *tamuatsivaaq*

*Qallunaaq-t tamuatsivaa-at*

Dane/white.man-PL tamuatsivaa-3PL.POS.ABS

'"[This is] white man's tamuatsivaaq"'

152. *taava nammineq*      Grandfather      S      INTRANS
*sukuloortuugami_ Iinndaleeraq_}*

*taava nammineq sukulooq-tooq-gami Iinndaleeraq*

then self chewing.tobacco-take-3C.SG.CAUS Henry

'then he would take some chewing tobacco [for] himself, Henry.'

153. *{Tyggegummimik*      chewing gum      IO      ERG
*tuneriarluta_'*

*tyggegummi-mik*      1PL      O
*tuni-riar-luta*

chewing.gum-INST
give-INTNS-1PL.OBJ.CT      Grandfather      A

'Giving us chewing gum'

154. *nammineq_ sukuluumik*      tobacco      O      ANT
*oqormersisarpoq*

*tassa_/*

*nammineq sukulooq-mik* Grandfather   A
*oqummer-si-saq-voq*
*tassa*

self    chewing.tobacco-INST
put.in.mouth-INTRANS-HAB-3SG.IND
that.is

'himself biting into chewing tobacco'

155. *ammaraangamiut*    tobacco box   O  ERG
*taanna*
*qillertuusaarannguaq*

*ammar-gaangamiut*   Grandfather   A
*taanna*
*qillertuusaq-araq-nnguaq-0*

open-whenever.3C.SG.SUBJ/3SG.OBJ.CAUS
that.one   container-little-little-ABS

'whenever he opened that little [chewing tobacco] container.'

156. *Taava  oqartarpoq*  Grandfather   S INTRANS
*tassa_/*

*taava  oqaq-saq-voq*
*tassa*

then  say-HAB-3SG.IND
that.is

'Then he would say'

157. "*Tassa  Ittup    tamuatsivaaq*
*tamuatsivaava*"_}

*tassa  Ittu-p*
*tamuatsivaaq-a*

that.is      Grandfather-REL

tamuatsivaaq-3NC.SG.POS

"'That is Grandfather's tamuatsivaaq.'"

'Grandfather' is introduced in clause 144; he is overtly mentioned in clauses 144, 148, and 157. In all but clauses 145, 146, and 147, 'Grandfather' is the subject. 'We' is variously used throughout text 1b to mean different groups in which the speaker is including himself; in this segment of the text, the speaker specifically refers to his family and relatives as a unit. The first use of 'we' in this way in this example (as opposed to 'we children' in the immediately preceding piece) is in clause 145, and the first overt mention is in clause 146, in which the speaker both uses an independent pronoun and lists the participants included. 'We' is the object in clauses 149 and 153. The previous section's topic, 'tamuatsivaaq', is continued, with the added topics 'chewing gum' and 'chewing tobacco'. These three topics are expressed overtly in all clauses in which they occur, with the exception of clause 152, in which 'chewing tobacco' is incorporated, and clause 155, in which 'chewing tobacco' is semantically subsumed in 'chewing tobacco container'. 'Tamuatsivaaq' is always marked in the absolutive case. 'Chewing gum' is always marked in the instrumental case and occurs either as an indirect object of an ergative construction (with 'us' as the direct object) or the object of an antipassive construction, as in clause 148; this marks the first time this noun phrase is introduced. 'Chewing tobacco' is variously an incorporated noun, when it is first introduced (clause 152); an instrumentally marked object of an antipassive, when it is first used as an independent noun phrase (clause 154); and finally as the absolutive object of an ergative construction (clause 155). Neither 'chewing gum' nor 'chewing tobacco' are as topical as 'tamuatsivaaq', given the topicality of 'tamuatsivaaq' in the previous section, and perhaps also as a reflection of the relative cultural value of the three. Most valued and central to the thematic development of the text is 'tamuatsivaaq'; after this is 'chewing tobacco', reserved for 'Grandfather', and finally 'chewing gum'. The choice of constructions reflects this: the former is always marked as most topical, with absolutive case marking, and 'chewing gum' is always obliquely marked. Using the standard explanation, clause 154 is difficult to explain, since 'chewing tobacco' is already given and one would therefore expect an ergative rather than absolutive structure.

The same sorts of considerations are raised in example 3.49, from the same text, 1b, in which the speaker describes the start of a typical day:

|  |  | Topic | Argument | Structure |
|---|---|---|---|---|
| (3.49) | (From text 1b) |  |  |  |
| 182. | {*Tassa* | 1PL | S | INTRANS |
|  | *Ittukkunniikkaagatta,* |  |  |  |
|  | *tassa* | Grandfather |  | INCORP |
|  | *Ittu-kkut-niit-gaan-gatta* |  |  |  |
|  | that.is |  |  |  |
|  | Grandfather-family-be.by-whenever-1PL.CAUS |  |  |  |
|  | 'Whenever we were with Grandfather' |  |  |  |

183.   *eqqaamagiga,*
*eqqama-giga*
remember-1SG.SUBJ/3SG.OBJ.PART
'I remember it'

184.   *eqqaamaqaara*     *taamani_*
*eqqaama-qi-vara*     *taamani*
remember-INTNS-1SG.     at.that.time
SUBJ/3SG.OBJ.IND
'I really remember it in those days'

185.   *Iinndaleeqqap_*   *Ittup_*   Grandfather
*Ittup_*

*Iinndaleeraq-p*   *Ittu-p*
*Ittu-p*

Henry-REL     Grandfather-REL
'Henry, Grandfather, Grandfather'

| *ullaakkut_*   *tamatta* | 1PL | S | INTRANS |
|---|---|---|---|
| *iteraangatta_* |  |  |  |

*ullaaq-kkut*   *tamaq-tta*
*iter-gaangatta*

morning-VIA   the.whole/all-1PL
wake.up-whenever.1PL.CAUS

'in the morning all of us together would wake up'

186.  *tiitoreerluta_/*                          1PL               S      INTRANS
*tii-toq-reer-luta*
tea-drink-already-1PL.CT
'when we had already drunk tea'

187.  *taava       inimut*                       1PL               S      INTRANS
*iserluta_'*

*taava       ini-mut*
*iser-luta*

then         room-TERM
enter-1PL.CT

'then [when] we entered/came into the room'

*Ittup       issia_*           Grandfather                              ELLIPSIS
*Ittu-p      issia [vik-minut]*
Grandfather-REL    chair-3C.SG.POS.TERM
'Grandfather to his chair'

188.  *pattagissaminut*
*ingikkuni_/*                   Grandfather             S      INTRANS

*pattagiaq-minut*
*igiC-guni*

piano-3C.SG.POS.TERM
sit.down-3C.SG.COND

'if he sat down at the piano'

189.  *taava_   inersimasut_*              adults          S      INTRANS
*taava    inersimasoq-t*
then      adult-PL
'then the adults'

*nalaasaarfimmut*
*issiavikuluunullu*          *issaallutik*

*nalaasaarfik-mut*
*issiavik-kulooq-nut-lu*       *isser-a-lutik*

couch-TERM
arm.chair-big-TERM.PL-and     sit-PL-3PL.CT

'when/while sitting down on the couch and in armchairs'

190.    *uagut*       *meeqqat*    1PL (children)       S    INTRANS
         *natermut*     *ingilluta_'*

         *uagut*        *meeraq-t*
         *nateq-mut*    *ingiC-luta*

         1PL            child-PL
         ground-TERM    sit.down-1PL.CT

         'we children sitting down on the ground'

191.    *taava*    *Ittup*             prayer       O        ERG
         *qinnutinnguaq*      *atuartarpaa_/*

         *taava*    *Ittu-p*           Grandfather       S
         *qinnut-nnguaq-0*    *atuar-saq-vaa*

         then      Grandfather-REL
         prayer-little-ABS    read-HAB-3SG.SUBJ/3SG.OBJ.IND

         'then Grandfather would read a little prayer'

192.    *palasiugami*      *aamma_* Grandfather       S    INTRANS
         *palasi-u-gami*    *aamma*
         priest-COP-       and
         3C.SG.CAUS
         'and [i.e., because] he was also a priest'

193.    *Taamaasereeraangamilu*    Grandfather       S    INTRANS
         *taamaat-si-reer-gaangami-lu*

the.whole/all-INTRANS-already-
whenever.3C.SG.CAUS-and
'and he was doing all this'

194. *taava*           religious song     O      ANT
*ullaarsiummik*
*tussiummik_*    *tussiartarpugut_/*

*taava*                     1PL      A
*ullaarsiut-mik*
*tussiut-mik*    *tussiar-saq-vugut*

then
morning.prayer-INST
psalm-INST    sing.psalms-HAB-1PL.IND
'then we sang a morning psalm'

195. *Ittu*                   piano      O      ANT
*pattagissamik*
*pattattoq_/*

*Ittu-0*           Grandfather      A
*pattagiaq-ssaq-mik*
*pattaC-soq*

Grandfather-ABS
piano-FUT-INST
play-3SG.PART

'Grandfather played the piano'

196. *taava*     *ilaanneeriarluta* nonreligious song O      ANT
*aamma*     *tassa,*

*taava*     *ilaanni-ir-riaq-luta*    1PL      A
*aamma*     *tassa*

then        sometimes-verb-INTNS-1PL.CT
and        that.is

'then sometimes we did'

*erinarsuummik_*
*erinarsuut-mik*
song-inst
'a [regular/normal/nonreligious] song'

197. *nalinginnaasumik* nonreligious song  O
*erinarsuummik_*

*nalinginnaq-u-soq-mik*
*erinarsuut-mik*

normal/usual-COP-PART-INST
song-INST

'a normal song'

(*ullormik* *tassunga*
*naleqqussorisaminik*

*ulloq-mik* *tassunga*
*naleqquC-sori-saq-minik*

day-INST over.there
suitable-think-PASS.PART-3SG.POS.INST

'that seemed suitable for that day'

198. *erinarsortittarpaatigut*  1PL  O  ERG
*tamatta_/*

*erinarsor-tit-saq-vaatigut* Grandfather A
*tamaq-tta*
sing-cause-HAB-3SG.SUBJ/1PL.OBJ.IND
the.whole/all-1PL

'he let us sing all together'

*tassami*  1PL  O
*inersimasullu* *meeqqallu_/*

*tassami*
*inersimasoq-t-lu* *meeraq-t-lu*

in.any.case
adult-PL-and          child-PL-and

'in any case the adults and the children'

199.  *taamaalilluta*                          day          O          ERG
      *ulloq          aallartittarparput_}*

      *taamaali-luta ulloq-0*                  1PL          A
      *aallartit-saq-varput*

like.that-1PL.CT
day-ABS          begin-HAB-1PL.SUBJ/3SG.OBJ.IND

'and that is how we began the day.'

There are several topics in this section; two are clearly continuous over the entire stretch of text, 'Grandfather' and 'we'. 'Grandfather' is overt in clauses 185, 187, 191, and 195, and it always occurs as the subject (unless it is actually the object of clause 184). 'We', which variously includes everyone including 'Grandfather', 'adults', and 'we children', is overt in clauses 185, 189, 190, and 198. Where 'Grandfather' and 'we' both occur in the same clause, 'we' is the object. Finally, there is a third potential topic, broadly 'song', more specifically 'prayer', 'morning psalm', or 'nonreligious song', which occurs overtly in all cases and as an object only. Complications arise in clauses 191, 194, 196, and 197. In clause 191 there is an ergative structure; one might assume that it ought not to be, given that the object, 'prayer', is a third topic with variable interpretation, just as 'chewing gum' was above. Clause 191 is just as problematic to the traditional theory, since it is the first introduction of 'prayer' and could be expected to be antipassive. But clauses 194, 196, and 197 are antipassives; if clause 191 is explained according to the same method used for 'chewing gum' above, then these clauses should be expected to follow the same pattern, which in any case they do not. It is fairly clear that both 'Grandfather' and 'we' are topical, and further, that 'Grandfather' is the more global topic and 'we' the more local one, as is evident by the greater continuity of 'Grandfather' in text 1b, as well as by the relative ranking of 'Grandfather' vis-à-vis 'we'. The particularly revealing clause is clause 198 'he let us sing a normal song all together', where three nominals are present: like 'chewing gum', 'song' is marked with the instrumental. I suggest that the fundamental emphasis of this section is not on the particular song, but on the relationship between 'Grandfather' and 'we', and therefore, that 'song' is not a very important topic. This explains the antipassives in clauses 194, 196, and 197; I further note that an antipassive also occurs with the use of the nominal 'piano' in clause 195, although this is more obviously a nominal peripheral to the text. The speaker summarizes the theme of the section in clauses 199 and 200 'and that is how we began the day', which suggests that the section is really more about a general procedure than about 'singing psalms'. All of this is suggestive but not conclusive, and again, sections with multiple topics are better understood in reference to a theory rather than as proof of it. In this case, if it is accepted on prior evidence that absolutives are topics, then the demoted objects of the antipassives in clauses 194, 196, and 197 can be interpreted as nontopical, and the absolutive object of clause 191 can be interpreted as the local topic (in one clause only — this is generally contrary to the idea that topics have continuity across texts, but the speaker may have had the intention of emphasizing 'psalms' and changed his mind as he continued his story). Sections with multiple topics may very easily lead to textual ambiguities of the sort commonly found in clauses with syntactically ambiguous structures: the listener may be able to interpret a text in more than one way because of textual ambiguities resulting from the interaction of more than one topic.

Theme rather than topic may be responsible for the ergative structures in example 3.50. In the immediately preceding clauses 49 to 55, the speaker is asked whether or not she has smoked; the section starts out with a clearly defined topic, 'cigarettes' or 'tobacco', introduced by the interviewer, but in the follow-up question in clause 56 — 'like how did they stop liking you?' — the focus shifts to the theme, 'to smoke'. Many of the ergative structures here reflect the abstract object 'smoke', never actually stated overtly (since it is implied by the semantics of the verbs).

| (3.50) | (From text 3a) | | Topic/Theme | Argument | Structure |
|---|---|---|---|---|---|
| 57. | {*Tassa_* | *sapilerakku* | (smoke) | O | ERG |
| | *ilaa_* | | | | |
| | | | | | |
| | *tassa* | *saper-leq-gakku* | | | |
| | *ilaa* | | | | |

that.is  cannot-begin-1SG.SUBJ/3NC.SG.OBJ.CAUS
you.know

'That is I just couldn't do it [i.e., smoke], you know'

58. *millussisaraluarpunga_*       to smoke
  *millu-ssi-saq-galuaq-vunga*
  inhale-do.like-HAB-CONSEQ-1SG.IND
  'I used to inhale, but —'

59. *iserneq*    *saperami_/*  (smoke) S INTRANS
  *iser-neq-o*   *saper-gami*
  go.in-NOMZ-ABS cannot-3C.SG.CAUS
  'it couldn't go in [i.e. smoke]'

60. *soorlu_*     *ilaa_*  (smoke) S INTRANS
  *maanga*  *piumajunnaarami*   *ilummut_}*

  *soorlu*   *ilaa*
  *maanga*  *pi-juma-junnaaq-gami*   *ilummut*

  for.example you.know
  to.here   thing-want-no.more-3C.SG.CAUS to.inside

  'for example, you know, it wouldn't come inside anymore.'

61. *{_Tassa* *paasivara*     *ilaa_'*
  *tassa*  *paasi-vara*     *ilaa*
  that.is  understand-1SG.SUBJ/3SG.OBJ.IND you.know
  'That is, I understand it, you know'

62. *(pujortaqqissinnaajunnaarlunga)/*    to smoke
  *pujortaq-qqik-sinnaa-junnaaq-lunga*
  smoke-again-can-no.more-1SG.CT
  '(I just couldn't smoke anymore)'

63. *aamma* *maqaasinngilara_*  (act of smoking) O ERG
  *aamma* *maqaasi-nngit-lara*
  and  miss-NEG-1SG.SUBJ/3SG.OBJ.NEG.IND
  'and I didn't miss it'

64.　*aamma_　ajornartorsiutiginngilara,*　(act of smoking)　O　ERG
　　*aamma　ajornartorsiut-gi-nngit-lara*
　　and　　　problem-have-NEG-1SG.SUBJ/3SG.OBJ.NEG.IND
　　'and it wasn't a problem for me [I didn't have a problem]'

65.　*pujortarunnaarama_*　　　　　　　　　　　　to smoke
　　*pujortaq-junnaaq-gama*
　　smoke-no.more-1SG.CAUS
　　'that [when] I didn't smoke anymore'

66.　(*tassa　massakkut　qujaannartarpunga*
　　*tassa　massakkut　qujaannaq-saq-vunga*
　　that.is　now　　　thankful-HAB-1SG.IND
　　'(that is, now I am thankful'

67.　*pujortarunnaarsimagama_*)}　　　　　　　to smoke
　　*pujortaq-junnaaq-sima-gama*
　　smoke-no.more-PERF-1SG.CAUS
　　'because I have stopped smoking).'

There are a number of sections throughout the texts in which themes
are expressed as abstract objects in ergative constructions. In most of these
cases, the objects are not stated overtly, as the theme is stated verbally.
In some cases, the object is a nominalized verb form, as in the following
example from text 4 (the nominalization is in clause 25):

(3.51)　(From text 4)　　　　　　Topic/Theme　Argument　Structure
24.　{*Taamaalilluni*
　　*taamaali-luni*
　　be.like.that-3SG.CT
　　'And in this way'

25.　*ajoqitut　　　sulilivinnini_'*　　　　　work as catechist　N
　　*ajoqi-tut　　　suli-leq-vig-neq-ni*
　　catechist-EQ　work-begin-really-NOMZ-3C.SG.ABS
　　'he really began to work as a catechist [i.e., his really beginning to
　　work as a catechist was authorized]'

26.     (*tassami*          *uppernarsaaserlugu_/*)}
        *tassami*          *uppernarsaat-ler-lugu*
        in.any.case    proof/certificate-provide.with-3SG.OBJ.CT
        '(in any case he got a certificate).'

## Antipassive structures

If ergative-absolutive case marking is used when the primary topic is in object position, then instances of antipassive structure should indicate the lack of topic status of the demoted object. In West Greenlandic, objects of antipassive constructions are marked with the instrumental case, in the same way that indirect objects of transitive constructions or modifiers of incorporated nouns are:

(3.52)   Antipassive (from text 1b)
194.    . . . *taava*    *ullaarsiummik*          *tussiummik*      *tussiartarpugut_/*
        *taava*          *ullaarsiut-mik*         *tussiut-mik*
        then             morning.prayer-INST      psalm-INST
        '. . . then we sang a morning psalm . . .'

3.53    Indirect object (from text 1b)
149.    {*Tyggegumminik*          *tuningaagamitigut*
        *tyggegummi-mik*          *tuni-gaa-ngamitigut*
        chewing.gum-INST     give-whenever-3NC.SG.SUBJ/1PL.OBJ.CAUS
        'Whenever he gave us a lot of chewing gum . . .'

3.54    Modifier of incorporated noun (from text 3a)
42.     . . . *immiaarartortarpunga*          *ataatsimik_/*
        *immiaq-araq-toq-saq-vunga*          *ataaseq-mik*
        beer-little.one-drink-HAB-1SG.IND     one-INST
        '. . . I would drink one little beer'

In addition, there is a common construction, formed with a nominal (often nominalization) in the absolutive case and the intransitively inflected *ajor-* 'be bad':

3.55    Nominal + *ajor-* (from text 3a)
48.     . . . *baajatorneq*          *ajorpunga_*}}
        *baaja-toq-neq*             *ajoq-vunga*

beer-drink-NOMZ     be.bad-1SG.IND
'. . . I haven't drunk beer'\

Only the first example above is an antipassive; noun incorporation is probably related in some way to topic or thematic coherence and the question of ergative or accusative marking, but it is not examined here.

There are very few antipassive constructions in the texts, and in most cases it is clear that the objects are nontopical. In example 3.49 above, clauses 182 to 199 describe the start of the day in the speaker's family; clause 195, an antipassive, has the object 'piano', an argument that has been introduced obliquely in clause 188 and not continued as a topic. Its only other occurrence is in clause 195. According to standard theory, one would expect an ergative clause, because the 'piano' is both definite and given (clause 188). In example 3.56 an antipassive occurs in a rather vague section about the power of the senses of sight and hearing (the 'Grandfather' in question was perhaps the most well-known recent Greenlandic poet and artist, and he is waxing poetic in this section). The object of the antipassive in clause 204 is 'paper and pencil'; it is first introduced in this clause and is never brought up again. (The Topic/Nontopic, or T/NT, column in the following examples refers to topic status; the object in antipassive constructions is to be understood as nontopic):

|  |  | T/NT | Argument | | Structure |
|---|---|---|---|---|---|
| (3.56) (From text 1b) | | | | | |
| 202. | . . . *Ittu* | | Grandfather | S | INTRANS |
| | *aallaraangami* | | | | |
| | *Ittu-0* | | | | |
| | *aallaq-gaangami* | | | | |
| | Grandfather-ABS | | | | |
| | walk/go-whenever.3C.SG.CAUS | | | | |
| | '. . . whenever Grandfather went walking' | | | | |
| 203. | *qaqqamut* | | Grandfather | S | INTRANS |
| | *pisuttuaraangami_/* | | | | |
| | *qaqqaq-mut* | | | | |
| | *pisuC-suaq-gaangami* | | | | |

mountain-TERM
walk-with.strength-whenever.3C.SG.CAUS

'whenever he walked to the mountains'

204.  *pappilissamik*                          paper/pencil    O
      *aqerluusamillu*        *nassartarpoq*

      *pappiala-ssa-mik*                        Grandfather    S    ANT
      *aqerluusaq-mik-lu*   *nassar-saq-voq*

      paper-FUT-INST
      pencil-INST-and    bring.with-HAB-3SG.IND
      'he used to bring along paper and pencil . . .'

Other antipassives in text 1b include clauses 148, 154, 194, 196, and 197; some of these have been discussed previously (see example 3.52).

In example 3.57 the settlement 'Qeqertalik' is described in part of a larger section describing the hunting of codfish. 'Qeqertalik' is introduced in clause 41 and there is some ellipsis of the verb in clause 42, leaving an instrumentally marked object with no overt verb. The verb in clause 41 involves an object, 'houses', which is incorporated with the intransitive verbalizing postbase –*qaq*- 'to have'; the ellipsis in clause 42 arises because of the incorporating structure. The instrumental object 'salting place' is introduced and not continued in the text; for that matter, 'houses' is not continuous either:

(3.57)  (From text 2)                    T/NT   Argument   Structure
41.    {*aamma*       *Qeqertalik_*   Qeqertalik              S    INTRANS
       *taamani_*     *illoqarpoq*

       *aamma*        *Qeqertalik*
       *taamani*      *illu-qaq-voq*

       and            Qeqertalik
       at.that.time   house-have-3SG.IND

       'and Qeqertalik at that time had houses' [i.e., was a settlement]

42.    *aamma*    *tarajorterivimmik*                  salting place    O
       *aamma*    *tarajorterivik-mik*

  and   salting.place-INST
  'and a salting place'

43. *taavalu*  *upernaakkut*  *tappavunga*  *aallaartarpugut*
  *taava-lu*  *upernaaq-kkut*  *tappav-unga*  *aallaar-saq-vugut*
  then-and  spring-VIA  up.there/to.  travel.to.hunt-
              the.east-TERM  HAB-1PL.IND

  'and then in the spring we used to travel up there to hunt'

44. *tappanna*      *saarullippassuaqartarmat_}*
  *tappa-nna*      *saarullik-passuaq-qaq-saq-mat*
  up.there/to.the.east-NOMZ  codfish-a.lot.of-have-HAB-3NC.
              SG.CAUS

  'because there used to be a lot of codfish up there.'

45. *tassa*  *meeraanitsinni_}}*
  *tassa*  *meeraaneq-tsinni*
  that.is  childhood-1PL.POS.LOC
  'that is, in our childhood.'

In example 3.58 the speaker is responding to the question 'haven't you drunk beer in your whole life?'; the actual response is 'when I was still working, when I ate some Greenlandic food, I would drink one little beer, sometimes not finishing it' and continuing from line 44, reproduced here. The antipassive is in clause 45, and the nontopic is 'beer'. The focus is on the last time the speaker drank beer, not on the drinking of beer:

(3.58) (From text 3a)       T/NT Argument Structure
44. {*Tassa* *ukioq_*  *naluaraluunniit* year    O   ERG
  *tassa* *ukioq-0* *nalu-vara-luunniit*
  that.is year-ABS not.know-1SG.SUBJ/3SG.OBJ.IND-even
  'That is, the year, I don't even know'

  *ukioq*  *massakkut* *ukioq*  *suna*    year  O
  *ukioq-0* *massakkut* *ukioq-0* *suna*
  year-ABS now   year-ABS what
  'the year, now, what year'

45. *baajamik*    *usserama*                          beer    O    ANT
    *baaja-mik*    *usser-gama*
    beer-INST    try-1SG.CAUS
    'when I tasted beer.'

46. *naluara*                                       year    O    ERG
    nalu-vara
    not.know-1SG.SUBJ/3SG.OBJ.IND
    'I don't know'

47. *eqqaamasaaruppunga_}*
    eqqaama-saq-erup-vunga
    remember-PASS-privative.(take.away)-1SG.IND
    'I don't remember [I have lost my memories].'

In example 3.59, from the same text, the speaker is discussing her old house; the 'old house' is very clearly the topic of the section from clause 74 to 86 and possibly to clause 92. The antipassive is in clause 79, the only clause to discuss the son's fishing, which is the perfect example of a "background" clause, a clause that gives information to make sense of why the speaker is no longer in her house. It is nontopical:

| (3.59) | (From text 3a) | | T/NT | Argument | Structure |
|---|---|---|---|---|---|
| 75. | . . . *ernerma,* | *uagut* | son, house | | |
| | *illutoqarput* | | | | |

    *erneq-ma*          *uagut*
    *illu-toqaq-vut*

    son-1SG.POS.REL  1PL
    house-old-1PL.POS.ABS

    '. . . my son, our old house'

| | *ernerma* | *suliarinikuugamiuk_'* | house | O | ERG |
|---|---|---|---|---|---|
| | *erneq-ma* | *suliaq-gi-nikuu-gamiuk* | son | A | |
| | son-1SG.POS.REL | work-have-PAST.PERF- | | | |
| | | 3C.SG.SUBJ/3NC.SG.OBJ.CAUS | | | |

    'my son had fixed our old house'

76.  *nutarterlugu*                                         house   O   ERG
     *nutarter-lugu*                                        son     A
     make.new-3SG.OBJ.CT
     'making it new/modernizing it'

77.  *tamaat*      *nutaanngorlugu*                         everything   O   ERG
     *tassami_*

     *tamaat*      *nutaanngor-lugu*            (i.e., in house)
     *tassami*

     everything    become.new-3SG.OBJ.CT
     in.any.case

     'making everything new/modern in any case'

78.  *atortorissaarutit*                *tamaasa* everything   O
     *tamaat_/*

     *atortorissaarutit-o*              *tamaq-asa*
     *tamaat*

     technological.appliances-ABS      the.whole/all-3PL.O
     everything-3SG.O

     'all modern things'

79.  *kisianni*   *upernaaq*     *manna_*   *siornali_*
     *kisianni*   *upernaaq-0*   *manna*    *siorna-li*
     but          spring-ABS     this       last.year-but
     'but this spring, but last year'

     *aalisarnermik*      *ajutoorami_/*                 son   S   ANT
     *aalisarneq-mik*     *ajutooq-gami*                 fishing   O
     fishing-INST         unlucky-3C.SG.SUBJ.CAUS
     'he was unlucky at fishing . . .'

Finally, there are several examples of intransitive constructions that involve incorporated nouns and stranded modifiers, superficially resembling antipassives (indicated by [ANT] in 3.60–3.61 below; see also examples 3.52–3.54 for the distinction between antipassives and stranded modifiers).

Although the effects of incorporation on topicality and thematic develop-ment are not addressed in this work, the structural resemblance of stranded modifiers with antipassives seems more a result of a syntactic requirement than a reflection of discourse needs. In example 3.60 the speaker discusses his father's becoming a catechist (clauses 10 to 14); in clause 16 he men-tions that his father was interested in many things (stranded-modifier construction), and in clauses 17 to 26 he again talks about his father's work as a catechist. The father's other interests are mentioned one by one, in succeeding paragraphs. In clause 16, therefore, the 'many things' that the father is interested in is not the topic of the paragraph; 'father' is the topic and 'work as a catechist' might be the theme

(3.60) (From text 4)            T/NT    Argument    Structure

14.     ... *meeraaffinni Saarlumi_*

*meeraq-vik-nni*
*Saarloq-mi*

child-place-1SG.POS.LOC
Saarloq-LOC

'... in the place where I was a child, in Saarloq'

*ajoqitut*       *sulivoq_*         father          S    INTRANS
*ukior-passuit_}*

*ajoqi-tut*       *suli-voq*
*ukioq-passuaq-it*

catechist-EQ    work-3SG.IND
year-a.lot-PL

'he worked as a catechist for many years.'

15.     {*Oqaatigissavaralu*
*Oqaatigi-ssa-vara-lu*
talk.about-FUT-1SG.SUBJ/3SG.OBJ.IND-and
'And I will talk about this'

16.  *ataataga*                *aamma*
     *ataata-ga*               *aamma*
     father-1SG.POS.ABS        and
     'and my father'

     *tamalaarpassuarnik*                        many things   O   (ANT)
     *soqutigisaqarami_'*

     *tamalaaq-passuaq-nik*                       father   S
     *soqutigisaq-qaq-gami*

     a.little.of.everything-a.lot-PL.INST
     interest-have-3C.SG.CAUS

     'was interested in many things'

17.  *siullermik_*    *seminariami*    *atuaqataavoq*
     *siullermik*     *seminaria-mi*   *atuaqat-u-voq*
     at.first         seminary-LOC     schoolmate-COP-3SG.IND
     'the first time he went to the seminary (teacher's school) . . .'

In example 3.61, an incorporated structure has a nominal object and involves
a topic that is prevalent throughout an extended portion of the text. The
preceding text, from clauses 50 to 59, describes the 'nets' used to catch
the codfish; from clauses 60 to 70 there is an ill-defined description of
the settlements and the hunters from those settlements; from clauses 71
to 75, a brief description of 'Amerloq' as a place for setting nets; and from
clauses 76 to 88, a loose section on the wind and the best time to look
after the fishing equipment. The text of example 3.61 is given from clause
89, which begins a description of net maintenance. Clause 92 contains the
incorporation with an instrumental object and takes up the topic of 'nets'
in a parenthetical paragraph; it then serves as a basis for the ensuing text,
once again about some aspect of the work involved with the setting of nets:

| (3.61) | (From text 2) | | T/NT | Argument | Structure |
|---|---|---|---|---|---|
| 89. | {*Saqqaanilu* | *tassa* | | | |
| | *atuartarlugit,* | | nets | O | ERG |
| | *Saqqaa-ni-lu* | *tassa* | | | |
| | *atuartaq-lugit* | | 1PL | S | |

sunny.side-LOC-and      that.is
follow-3PL.OBJ.CT

'And then on the sunny side [we] used to bring them in line [the nets]'

90.    *imaattorlugit,*                                    nets    O    ERG
       imaattoq-lugit
       like.this-3PL.OBJ.CT
       'like this' [gestures]

91.    *amuartarlugit_/*                                   nets    O    ERG
       amuar-saq-lugit
       haul.up-HAB-3PL.OBJ.CT
       'hauling them up'

92.    *taamanikkummi*                              nets    O    (ANT)
       *qassuterpaalussuarnik*          *piniuteqartarpugut . . .*

       *taamani-kkut-mi*                           1PL    S
       *qassut-(r)pak-aluk-ssuaq-nik*    *piniut-qaq-saq-vugut*

       at.that.time-VIA-INTNS
       net-many-rather-big-PL.INST    equipment-have-HAB-1PL.IND

       'at that time we had rather a lot of nets as equipment . . .'

The object *qassuterpaalussuarnik* 'a lot of nets' can be interpreted as the stranded modifying noun phrase to *piniuti* 'equipment', which is incorporated. Thus, these two last examples may be better explained with reference to incorporation.


## 3.6 Chapter conclusion

In summary, of the 620 clauses in my body of data, about 192 are ergative and perhaps thirteen are antipassive. Most of the ergative structures in the texts, about 182 of them, fit well within a theoretical framework that includes topic as a grammatical role, although many require special explanation for assigning topic to the object position. The clearest cases, those that do not merely support but demonstrate the topicality of the absolutive object and the peripherality of the instrumental object (in antipassives) are those that involve at most one topic. Most other cases, involving multiple topics or topic and theme combinations, require further explanation; they can be interpreted according to the theory but cannot independently prove the theory. The clearest examples of the nontopic status of demoted objects in antipassive constructions also are those in which the nominal has no second mention. There are, however, a number of passages in the texts that present difficulties for the analysis suggested here, including some parts of example 3.45, for example, or example 3.62. In example 3.62 the speaker presents a list of duties that the catechist was responsible for; each clause in which a duty is specified is ergative, and in each case, there is a different object. The same line of reasoning applied to the temporal adverbial clauses might be used here: in these clauses, the speaker emphasizes the objects by using an ergative construction. Alternatively, this section may reflect the importance of thematic continuity (i.e., that the catechists worked hard at many things).

(3.62)  (From text 1a)                T/NT  Argument  Structure

83.    . . . *ajoqip*    *atuarfik*

*tamaat*    *tigummivaa_*  school      O      ERG

*ajoqi-p*    *atuarfik*-0  catechist    A

*tamaq-at*    *tigummi-vaa*

catechist-REL    school-ABS

the.whole/all-3SG.O hold.in.hands-3SG.SUBJ/3SG.OBJ.IND

'the catechist has the whole school to take care of'

84.    *atuartut*    *tamaasa*          students  O  ERG

*atuartissavai_*

*atuartoq-t*    *tamaq-asa*         catechist  A

*atuar-tit-ssa-vai*

student-PL    all.of.them-3PL.O

learn-cause-FUT-3SG.SUBJ/3PL.OBJ.IND

'he has to teach all of the students'

85. 1.  *klassiminngaanniit*  grades  O  ERG
    7.  *klasse*  *tikillugu_*

    1.  *klasse-minngaanniit*
    7.  *klasse*  *tikit-lugu*

    first  class-ABL
    seventh  class  arrive-3SG.OBJ.CT

    'from the first grade [going] to the seventh grade'

86. *kisimiilluni_*  catechist  INTRANS
    *kisimi-u-luni*
    alone-COP-3SG.CT
    'being alone'

87. *ulloq  tamaat*  catechist  INTRANS
    *suleriarluni_/*

    *ulloq  tamaq-at*
    *suli-giaq-luni*

    day  the.whole/all-3SG.O
    work-go.to.do-3SG.CT

    'when he's going to [be at] work all day'

88. *sapaammi  naalagiartitsilluni_/*  catechist  INTRANS
    *sapaat-mi  naalagiartitsi-luni*
    Sunday-LOC  lead.divine.service-3SG.CT
    'leading services on Sunday'

89. *Toqusoqarpat*  dead one  INTRANS
    *toqusoq-qaq-pat*
    dead.one-have-3NC.SG.COND
    'When/if there is a dead one [when someone has died]'

90. *toqusunik  ilisilluni_/*  dead one  O  ANT
    *toqusoq-nik  ilisi-luni*  catechist  A
    dead.one-PL.INST  bury-3SG.CT
    'he buries the dead ones'

91.    *kuisittoqassappat*                christenee   INTRANS
       *kuisiC-toq-qaq-ssa-ppat*
       christen-part-have-FUT-3NC.SG.COND
       'when/if there is someone to be christened'

92.    *kuisillugit_/*                      christenee   O    ERG
       *kuisiC-lugit*                     catechist    A
       christen-3pl.obj.ct
       'he christens them . . .'

Explanations provided by the traditional theories for the structures in example 3.62 are no better, however. All the objects are indefinite and new, and one would expect antipassives. The antipassive in clause 90 is particularly perplexing in comparison with the ergative in clause 92. The two clauses are semantically parallel, and should be structurally parallel as well. Neither theory properly explains these clauses. P. Langgård (personal communication) suggests that the speaker may have had a particular christening in mind but no particular dead person in mind. This observation supports the idea that absolutive object are topics.

In another example from text 1b (not given here), the section from clauses 158 to 181 involves the speaker's recollection of 'going to Narsaq' (a theme); from clauses 164 to 177 there is a subsection concerning a particular instance of 'going to Narsaq' in which the speaker remembers seeing piked whales circling the boat. 'Motor boat' is not mentioned anywhere but in clause 173, as the absolutive object, and one might have predicted an antipassive structure for the clause. One might therefore presume that the speaker has incorporated the notion of 'motor boat' in the statements 'going to Narsaq', as going by means of a motorboat is the only feasible and regular way of getting to Narsaq from Qaqortoq on a regular basis. This is an assumption that can be made only if it is generally true that absolutive objects are topical, as there is no great difference in type of information content between this example and some of the antipassives explained above (cf. text 1b, clause 194). Again, examples such as this one may be interpreted in this way as a result of a general understanding of the nature of ergativity as an indicator of topic status, but unlike such examples as 3.30 or 3.31, they do not prove topic status.

Example 2.29 in the previous chapter is another example of some possibly unclear uses of ergative structures; however, if the topic is 'father' there is exceptional structure to explain. The passage is confusing, even to those with native speaking ability. Part of the problem in this and other problematic sections involves the identification of the primary topic, which in many cases is the local topic, but which may be the more global topic where several topics are present. Problems arise especially where three or more topics or combinations of topics and themes interact in a continuous way within a section of text. This is a reflection of the difficulty normally associated with the presentation of more than one piece of information at once. It occurs, but when it does, it can cause ambiguity or confusion to the listener.

In all, there are ten or fewer problematic cases, two or three of which involve antipassive constructions. In most cases it is possible to show that the ergative structures reflect definiteness or givenness, and antipassives the opposite. Furthermore, many of the passages of text that present difficulties for the more standard theory, which views ergativity as a reflection of givenness or definiteness, also present difficulties for an interpretation of ergativity as a reflection of topicality. There is one obvious instance of a passage in the texts that is more readily explained according to the standard theory; it is presented in example 3.61. If so, by assigning the value topic to the absolute argument of a transitive clause, are we just renaming the problem, from definite or given to topic? Does the proposed theory actually have any more explanatory power than the traditional theories?

There are several reasons for preferring the reanalysis as given. First, it is perfectly common for features such as subject or object to be coded in the verb, as inflectional endings, just as it is for features such as person and number. It is not as common to see features such as definiteness or givenness coded in the verb, rather than in the noun phrase to which the feature belongs, and it is particularly not the case in West Greenlandic. Topic is a structural feature, just as subject and object are, the difference being one of structural level; therefore, it is plausible for topic to be encoded in the verb. As such, the lack of topic marking in antipassives, or the topic marking in contemporatives, can be explained, as I show in the next chapter, whereas I have not yet come across an explanation for these marking systems within the standard theories of definiteness or givenness.

Further, the importance of considering topic over definiteness or givenness lies in the recognition that not just any random object is marked as definite, given, or topical. The topic has continuous reference in a given stretch of speech, for the most part; or, in some cases, it is the center of pragmatic emphasis (as in example 3.60 above, or as in temporal clauses) in a stretch of speech. Therefore, even though many (but not all) examples given above might be explained quite simply according to the standard theory, a theory of topical or thematic coherence has more explanatory value.

Finally, as I will show in the following chapter, topic is also the relevant category in other parts of West Greenlandic grammatical structure, and is therefore to be preferred over givenness or definiteness as a factor in West Greenlandic discourse.

# 4 Switch-reference or thematic coherence and topic continuity?

Switch-reference is a relation between two clauses in which two noun phrases are marked as coreferential or noncoreferential.[1] In Greenlandic, it is generally associated with subject coreference or lack thereof, although examples of anomalous switch-reference are common. In addition, the contemporative and the participial verb moods in West Greenlandic have been identified as switch-reference mechanisms, although each mood has a number of other functions and there are commonly identified environments for anomalous coreference. How useful is it, then, to think of the switch-reference mechanisms in West Greenlandic as indicators of switch-subject? In section 4.1 I review the various mechanisms associated with subject coreference or switch-reference in West Greenlandic, and the problems associated with a subject-based approach; in section 4.2, I present some typological information on switch-reference systems and evidence for discourse-based effects on these systems; in section 4.3, I discuss switch-reference in West Greenlandic as a topic-based system; and in section 4.4, I present the data to support this view. The conclusions are presented in 4.5.

## 4.1 Switch-reference in West Greenlandic

Switch-reference is marked both nominally and verbally in West Greenlandic. At least three mechanisms for indicating switch-reference are generally described, including nominal possessive inflection, pronominal inflection on some subordinate verbs, and the complementary distribution of contemporative and participial verb forms. The first two are typologically unexceptional and are illustrated in tables 4.1 and 4.2:

**Table 4.1** Nominal possessive inflection

| POSSESSOR | SINGULAR POSSESSUM | PLURAL POSSESSUM |
| --- | --- | --- |
| 3SG coreferential | *-ni/i* | *-ni* |
| 3SG noncoreferential | *-a* | *-i* |
| 3PL coreferential | *-(r)tik* | *-tik* |
| 3PL noncoreferential | *-at* | *-i/at* |

(4.1)    Switch-reference marking in nominal possessive inflection
*nuliani*
*nuliaq-ni*
wife-3C.SG.ABS
'his$_i$ wife' (verb$_i$)[2]

*nuliaa*
*nuliaq-a*
wife-3NC.SG.ABS
'his$_j$ wife' (verb$_i$)

(4.2)    Switch-reference marking in pronominal inflection in
subordinate moods (example from Fortescue 1984:147; spelling
changed to reflect contemporary Greenlandic orthography):
*Nuliani    qiareerami    isermat.*
*nuliaq-ni    qia-reer-gami    iser-mat*
wife-3C.SG.ABS cry-already-3C.SG.CA enter-3NC.SG.CA
'When his$_i$ wife came in because she$_j$ had finished crying.'

*oqarpoq*
*oqaq-voq*
say-3SG.IND
'he said (something)/he talked'

Fortescue (1991) also notes, in rare cases, the use of 3c forms on indicative
endings, although they are commonly held not to exist.

The third mechanism, which involves the complementary distribution
of verb moods, is unusual. Briefly, the contemporative is identified with

**Table 4.2** Subordinate pronominal mood inflection

| MOOD | INTRANSITIVE | TRANSITIVE 3NC OBJ | TRANSITIVE 3C OBJ |
| --- | --- | --- | --- |
| Causative SG coreferential | *-gami* | *-gamiuk* | — |
| Causative SG noncoreferential | *-mmat* | *-mmagu* | *-mmani* |
| Causative PL coreferential | *-gamik* | *-gamikku* | — |
| Causative PL noncoreferential | *-mmata* | *-mmassuk* | *-mmanni* |
| Conditional SG coreferential | *-guni* | *-guniuk* | — |
| Conditional SG noncoreferential | *-ppat* | *-ppagu* | *-ppani* |
| Conditional PL coreferential | *-gunik* | *-gunikku* | — |
| Conditional PL noncoreferential | *-ppata* | *-ppassuk* | *-ppanni* |

subject coreference and the participial subject with noncoreference (Fortescue 1984; P. Langgård, personal communication). The transitive form of the contemporative lacks subject pronominal agreement, and this is taken as evidence for same-subject interpretation, since marking the subject of both the contemporative and the superordinate verb form is redundant if they are coreferent. In most cases, the contemporative clause does in fact have the same subject as its superordinate clause. Except for third-person noncoreferent object, the transitive form of the contemporative is identical with that of the intransitive:

(4.3)   Identity of intransitive and transitive contemporative forms
    *takullunga*                    *takulluta*
    *taku-lunga*                    *taku-luta*
    see-1SG.CT or 1SG.OBJ.CT        see-1PL.CT or 1PL.OBJ.CT
    'I see or [subject] sees me'     'we see or [subject] sees us'

**Table 4.3a** The contemporative verb mood

| PERSON | INTRANSITIVE/SUBJECT | TRANSITIVE/OBJECT |
|---|---|---|
| 1SG | *-llunga* | *-llunga* |
| 2SG | *-llutit* | *-llutit* |
| 3C.SG | *-lluni* | *-lluni* |
| 3NC.SG | — | *-llugu* |
| 1PL | *-lluta* | *-lluta* |
| 2PL | *-llusi* | *-llusi* |
| 3C.PL | *-llutik* | *-llutik* |
| 3NC.PL | — | *-llugit* |

*takullutit*
*taku-lutit*
see-2SG.CT or 2SG.OBJ.CT
'you see or [subject] sees you'

*takullusi*
*taku-lusi*
see-2PL.CT or 2PL.OBJ.CT
'you see or [subject] sees you'

*takulluni*
*taku-luni*
see-3SG.CT
'he sees or [subject] sees him$_i$'[3]

*takullutik*
*taku-lutik*
see-3PL.CT
'they see or [subject] sees them$_i$'

*takullugu*
*taku-lugu*
see-3SG.OBJ.CT
'[subject] sees him$_j$'

*takullugit*
*taku-lugit*
see-3PL.OBJ.CT
'[subject] see(s) them$_j$'

There are both 3SG coreferent and noncoreferent forms of the contemporative: the pronominal morpheme *-ni-* is used for coreferent third-person singular in both intransitive and transitive forms, and *-gu-* is used for the third-person singular object in transitive forms.

There are a number of cases where the subject of the contemporative is not coreferent with that of the superordinate clause. Some of these exceptions result from a mismatch between structural requirements and semantics. For example, when a passive clause heads a sentence with a dependent transitive contemporative, and no other argument is named as its object, the passive subject is the object of the contemporative; that is, they have the same underlying objects (example from Kleinschmidt 1851:92; spelling changed to reflect contemporary orthographic conventions):

(4.4)   *Sinittillugu*                      *toqutaavoq.*
        *sinik-tit-lugu*                    *toqu-saq-u-voq*
        sleep-cause-3SG.OBJ     kill-PASS.PART-COP-3SG.IND
        'Letting him sleep, he was killed.'
        [i.e., 'While they let him sleep, they killed him.']
        [i.e., 'While he slept, he was killed.']

Contemporatives can also be dependent on nominals as well as clauses, in which case they show coreference with the nominal. It is not unusual, however, to find that the object of the contemporative is the subject of a superordinate, whether the latter is active or passive; this is discussed at length below.

The participial, unlike the contemporative, has full subject/object transitive inflection (from Fortescue 1984:60):

(4.5)   Participial pronominal inflection
        *Atertunga*              *Antariarsip*          *tikippaanga.*
        *ater-sunga*             *Antariarsi-p*         *tikiC-vaanga*
        go.down-1SG.PART     Antariarsi-REL     come.to-3SG.SUBJ/1SG.
                                                                     OBJ.IND
        'When I went down Antariarsi came to me.'

The transitive 3C.OBJ form of the participial has become lexicalized as 'when(ever) . . .' and can be used with either transitive or intransitive verbs (from Fortescue 1984:61):

**Table 4.3b** The participial verb mood

| PERSON | INTRANSITIVE | TRANS 3NC OBJ | TRANS 3C OBJ |
| --- | --- | --- | --- |
| 3SG | *-soq* | *-gaa* | *-gaani* |
| 3C.SG | | *-ginni* | |
| 3PL | *-sut* | *-gaat* | *-gaanni* |
| 3C.PL | | *-gitsik* | |

(4.6)  *Anigaanni*                                *qiianaqaaq.*
       *ani-gaanni*                               *qiiana-qi-voq*
       go.out-3PL.SUBJ/3C.SG.OBJ.PART    be.cold-INTNS-3SG.SUBJ.IND
       'When you go outside it's really cold.'

Despite the existence of 3C subject morphology, both Fortescue and
P. Langgård claim that the participial is used where there is no subject
coreference between the subordinate and superordinate form. Exceptions
exist, however. Bergsland (1955:49) writes that although he has found no
evidence of participials and superordinates with same subjects but different
objects, a 3C object suffix on a transitive participial can correspond to the
subject of the superordinate. Kleinschmidt (1851:74) notes the same thing,
and suggests that the principle reason for the use of the participial is to
indicate the status of the object argument. Where a participial is used, there
are three relevant arguments, the subject of the main verb, the object of the
main verb (which is either coreferential with the subject of the participial
or is different), and the object of the participial (assuming both clauses
are transitive). In addition, participials can have both nominal[4] and verbal
heads with coreferential subjects, although Kleinschmidt declares this use
to be obsolescent, being preferentially replaced by the contemporative.
If so, the modern language may have grammaticalized the coreferential/
switch-reference functions of these verb moods in the recent past, perhaps
within the past century (this is further discussed below).

   Both the contemporative and the participial forms fulfill many other
functions in the grammar. The contemporative has so many other functions
that it is considered the default mood; some of these functions have been
listed in chapter 1, section 1.3. These moods have a high functional load in
part because there are no markers of relative clauses in West Greenlandic.
Adverbial clauses are generally expressed through subordination, with
contemporatives often indicating manner. A primary function of the
contemporative is to conjoin clauses; in this capacity, it tends to reflect
a temporal relationship with the main verb, such that the action in the
subordinate clause takes place at the same time as or within the time frame
of the action in the main clause. According to Fortescue (1984:34), the
contemporative has both subordinate and coordinate senses, depending
on whether it precedes or follows the superordinate verb. Contemporatives

are also found in impersonal clauses, as objects of transitive verbs, and more.

The participial is closely related to nominalizations. The morphemes *–soq* and *–saq* can function either as active and passive participial mood endings, respectively, or as nominalizing suffixes, with *–soq* turning the verb into a present participle, and *–saq* turning it into an abstract noun reflecting patient role:

(4.7)  *Peerip*      *Anna*        *takuaa*
       *Per-p*       *Anna-0*      *taku-vaa*
       Per-REL    Anna-ABS    see-3SG.SUBJ/3SG.OBJ.IND
       'Per sees Anna'
       *takusaq* = 'the object seen' = 'Anna'

True participials often correspond to English relative or temporal clauses, particularly impersonal temporal clauses. They can also be subject or object clauses of the superordinate.

The contemporative and the participial function in many ways but are defined as markers of switch-reference, as opposed to the causative and conditional verb moods, which indicate switch-reference through pronominal inflection but are defined according to their functions. The question is whether it is useful or even accurate to think of the contemporative and participial verb moods as markers of switch-reference. Furthermore, the complementary use of verb moods to indicate switch-reference is unusual. Is there a historical basis for suggesting that the contemporative and participial moods indicate switch-reference?

The contemporative in Greenlandic is so named because it indicates cotemporaneous/simultaneous time with that of the main verb. The term used for this mood in most other Inuit dialects is appositional, because one of its functions is conjunctive. The appositional in all other Inuit dialects has two forms, distinguishing between past/present and future action (example from Dorais 1990:112; the digraph 'll' is a voiceless liquid fricative):

(4.8)  Eastern Canadian Inuktitut, Baffin Island:
       *takullunga*
       *taku-llunga*
       see-1SG.PRES.CT
       'while seeing, I . . .'

*takulunga*
*taku-lunga*
see-1SG.FUT.CT
'while seeing, I will . . .'

In addition, all other dialects appear to have a formal distinction between appositional forms with coreferent and noncoreferent subjects, based on a causative (or agentive) morpheme (from Dorais 1990:112; applicable to all other dialects except for Greenlandic):

(4.9)    Eastern Canadian Inuktitut, Baffin Island:
*takutillunga*
*taku-tit-lunga*
see-cause-1SG.CT
'while I see, you/he/she/they . . .'

Although this construction exists in West Greenlandic, it is not a formal mechanism for indicating switch-reference. Per Langgård (personal communication) suggests that it continues to indicate same-subject, showing an element of control in the actions of the main clause subject.

In the westernmost Inuit dialects, there are two verb moods where there exists only one in all other dialects: an appositional and a contemporative. The (almost identical) western dialects Inupiaq (according to Dorais 1990:56) and Uummarmiutun (according to Lowe 1985) both distinguish between the appositional, which is morphologically the same as the appositional in other dialects and the contemporative in Greenlandic, and the contemporative, which has been completely lost (recently, in some cases) in other dialects. The appositional (or conjunctive, in Lowe's terminology), expresses manner, reason, coordination in a clause chain, sequential time in a narrative, or simultaneous time, and is unmarked for subject in the transitive forms — in other words, it has most of the functions that the contemporative has in West Greenlandic. The many different functions of the appositional probably reflect the fact that there is no comparable category in English (or French, Danish, Latin, or Russian, the languages of those who have produced Eskimo grammars). Lowe suggests that the subordinate mood forms in Uummarmiutun can be understood in terms of the way they express relationship to the main verb. The causative indicates the anteriority of a real event relative to another real event (and therefore is associated with past tense) (example from Lowe 1985:202):

(4.10)　Uummarmiutun dialect, Western Canada
　　　　*Paulatuumukkama*　　　　　*apiqrukkara.*
　　　　*Paulatuk-umuk-kama*　　　　*apiqru-kkara*
　　　　Paulatuk-go.to-1SG.CAUS　　ask-1SG.SUBJ/3SG.OBJ.PAST.IND
　　　　'When I went to Paulatuk, I asked him.'

The conditional indicates the anteriority of a hypothetical event to another hypothetical event (and therefore is associated with future or irrealis) (from Lowe:1985:202):

(4.11)　Uummarmiutun dialect, Western Canada
　　　　*Paulatuumukkuma*　　　　　*apiqrurniariga.*
　　　　*Paulatuk-umuk-kuma*　　　　*apiqrur-niaq-giga*
　　　　Paulatuk-go.to-1SG.COND　　ask-FUT-1SG.SUBJ/3SG.OBJ.PRES.IND
　　　　'If I go to Paulatuk, I will ask him.'

The appositional indicates the time frame in or during which the event expressed by the main verb occurs (from Lowe 1985:203):

(4.12)　Uummarmiutun dialect, Western Canada
　　　　*Havakhuni*　　　*kiliqtuaq.*
　　　　*Havak-huni*　　　*kiliq-tuaq*
　　　　work-3SG.CT　　cut-3SG.PAST.IND
　　　　'While working, he cut himself.'

This interpretation of the subordinate moods is applicable to the other Eskimo dialects, and may make lists of functions such as "expresses manner, reason, simultaneous time," and so forth, unnecessary, leaving only the question of its role as a switch-reference marker.

The contemporative (henceforth contemporative₁, or CT₁, to distinguish it from the use of the term contemporative to refer to the Greenlandic mood) expresses what Lowe describes as a "reflexive" type of action performed at the same time as that of the main verb and involving the same persons. Among its characteristics are:

1. Lack of tense marking, its interpretation depending on that of the main verb (examples from Lowe 1985:232):

    (4.13)   *Muqpaurillarma*        *naalaktuaqtuanga.*
               *muqpauri-llarma*       *naalaktuaq-tuanga*
               make.bread-1SG.CT$_1$    listen.to.radio-1SG.PAST.IND
               'While making bread, I was listening to the radio.'

    (4.14)   *Muqpaurillarma*        *naalaktuaqtunga.*
               *muqpauri-llarma*       *naalaktuaq-tunga*
               make.bread-1SG.CT$_1$    listen.to.radio-1SG.PRES.IND
               'While making bread, I am listening to the radio.'

2. Subject coreferentiality with the main verb in the intransitive, but either subject, agent, or subject to "agent" (according to Lowe) coreferentiality in the transitive (examples from Lowe 1985:233):

    (4.15)   *Ikayullapku*              *hiñikhaqtunga.*
               *ikayuq-llapku*          *hiñikhaq-tunga*
               help-1SG.SUBJ/3SG.OBJ.CT$_1$   sleep-1SG.IND
               'While I was helping him, I fell asleep.'

    (4.16)   *Ikayullamni*              *hiñikhaqtuq.*
               *ikayuq-llamni*          *hiñikhaq-tuq*
               help-1SG.SUBJ/3C.SG.OBJ.CT$_1$   sleep-3SG.IND
               'While I was helping him, he fell asleep.'

3. An alternative set of third-person transitive verb endings that do not differentiate object person (Lowe 1985:235):

    (4.17)   *uqautillaan*
               *uqauti-llaan*
               wait-3.SUBJ/1, 2, or 3SG.OBJ.CT$_1$
               'he is waiting for me/you/him/her/it'

4. A set of coreferential and noncoreferential pronominal endings for third person (Lowe 1985:234–35):

    (4.18)   *uqautillapku*
               *uqauti-llapku*
               wait-1SG.SUBJ/3SG.OBJ.CT$_1$
               'I am waiting for him$_j$ [. . . he/him$_i$]'

> *uqautillamni*
> *uqauti-llamni*
> wait-1SG.SUBJ/3C.SG.OBJ CT$_1$
> 'I am waiting for him$_i$ [. . . he/him$_i$]'

The contemporative$_1$, therefore, has both a full set of both subject and object pronominal endings in the transitive, as well as a full set of pronominal switch-reference markers, just as the causative and the conditional do. Perhaps because of the similarity in usage between the appositional and the contemporative$_1$, and because of the resulting interchangeability in certain cases, the contemporative$_1$ has been lost in other dialects, and its functions have been associated with the appositional mood. Like the contemporative in West Greenlandic, the contemporative$_1$ can mark continuity in either subject or object.

If Lowe's description is correct, identifying the contemporative$_1$ as a mood specific to cases of coreferential subject is not only unnecessary but also fails to account for cases of subject-object or object-object coreference. In fact, this looks like an issue of topic continuation. In West Greenlandic this is supported by the morphological identity between all but third-person (Greenlandic) contemporative forms, both intransitive and transitive, or in other words, in both subject and object forms.

The same sort of complicating factors affect the participial. Historically, the participial is morphologically related to the indicative. In most other Inuit dialects, the participial form, *-j/t-*,[5] is used as a variant of the indicative mood:

(4.19)   West Greenlandic          Inuktitut
   *takuvoq*                  *takuvuq/takujuq*
   *taku-voq*                 *taku-vuq/taku-juq*
   see-3SG.IND               see-3SG.IND
   'he sees'                  'he sees'

All dialects have *-v/p-* variants, but in a number of dialects, these forms are quite restricted in their application. The Labrador dialect of Inuktitut primarily makes use of *-v/p-* forms, the *-j/t-* variant occurring only in the third person. Other Inuktitut dialects vary in their preference of forms, with Southeastern Baffin Island Inuktitut preferring *-j/t-*, and Northern

Baffin Island tending to prefer -*v/p*- as the normal form of the indicative. In these Eastern Canadian Inuit dialects, the -*j/t*- form is still morphologically identical to nominalized verbs and relative clauses. In more western dialects, such as Siglutun, Uummarmiutun, Inuinaqtun, and Natsilingmiutun, the -*j/t*- forms are the normal indicative forms; -*v/p*- are rare, in some cases found only with transitive endings, and used only in traditional narratives. Ronald Lowe (1985:135) calls these "*kiihaimma* declaratives," indicatives that are used to indicate the end of an episode in a narrative:

(4.20)   *kiihaimma, pikhaqqivaa!*
         'and finally, it landed on him!'

(4.21)   *kiihaimma, qaaqpuq*
         'finally, he exploded'

In Inupiaq, three types of indicative are distinguished, two of which involve the -*j/t*- form. These two together are the forms primarily used for declarative speech; the third, -*v/p*-, is restricted and has the same function as Lowe's *kiihaimma* declaratives (Dorais 1990:57). Thus, West Greenlandic is the only dialect with a clear distinction between the indicative and the participial. The distinction between participial and indicative has been maintained in Yup'ik, however, where the participial has a clear predicative or nominal function, but not a switch-reference function.

The relation is more than merely morphological. M. Fortescue (personal communication) finds a long history within all Inuit dialects for participials taking over as indicatives, possibly for discourse reasons. The indicative comes to be associated with completive action (cf. *kiihaimma* declaratives above), and the participial with noncompletive action of the narrative.[6]

Historically, therefore, there is little reason to suggest that either the contemporative or the participial are by themselves part of the switch-reference mechanism of Greenlandic. They are first and foremost part of the mood/tense/aspect system of West Greenlandic. There are, however, good reasons both of these verb moods might have become associated with the switch-reference system. In clause chains, most clauses are intransitive and all are linked thematically (excluding parenthetical clauses). The use of the contemporative as one of the structurally important clauses in a clause chain (as opposed to the participial, for reasons stated below) coincides with the use of at most one argument, since the contemporative lacks the means of marking more than one argument in a clause. This argument is often the subject; thus, the contemporative comes to be associated with coreference. The participial is morphologically related to nominalized forms and relative constructions, in addition to the indicative. These are constructions that often have a different relationship to the superordinate than other clauses in a clause chain. The nominalized form may not need the overt expression of information such as the subject and the object to suggest clausal semantics,[7] and the relative clause relates to a noun phrase within a clause chain and not necessarily to one that is an argument of the main clause. Thus, an interpretation of the participial as a marker of non-coreference is plausible on purely structural grounds. Finally, these moods may have become identified with the switch-reference system because of attrition of this system in West Greenlandic; but this connection is still loose, as is evident from the number of exceptions often noted.

The association of these verb moods with switch-reference is more systematic in written than in oral West Greenlandic. To what degree the written language diverges from the oral language, and for what reasons, remains unclear. Several factors may contribute to the more systematic use of contemporatives for same subject and participials for different subject in written texts. For example, there is far less parataxis in modern written texts than in the oral language, and there is thus less likelihood of finding participials in same-subject environments. The teaching of written rather than oral standards in schools may reinforce this effect.

Although the correlation between mood and switch-reference and between switch-reference and subjecthood is understandable, it is far from perfect in actual oral language. While my texts are poor in examples of nominal possessive switch-reference inflection, there are a number of examples of anomalous subordinate mood pronominal inflection, and the complementary distribution of the contemporative and participial verb moods is imperfect. Exceptions almost exclusively involve subject–to–direct object or direct object–to–subject coreference. This pattern suggests the category of topic. If topic is a relevant factor in the grammar of West Greenlandic, and if switch-reference in West Greenlandic is understood as a switch-topic mechanism, these "anomalies" are not anomalies. The contemporative and the participial moods, on the other hand, are more likely to have become identified as markers of thematic continuity or shift, rather than as switch-subject markers. In keeping with the lexical and grammatical divisions between nominal and verbal or clausal entities, one expects verb moods to indicate thematic rather than topic continuity or shift. Switch-topic is reflected in grammatical agreement patterns on nominals (i.e., ergativity, pronominal switch-reference). The assumption of discourse-based agreement accounts for a number of arbitrary exceptions to the identification of the contemporative as a marker of coreferential subjects, and the participial as one of noncoreferential subjects.

## 4.2 Switch-reference as a system of subject or topic/thematic coherence

Typologically, switch-reference seems to be largely, although not exclusively, a phenomenon of SOV languages. Characteristics of languages with switch-reference systems include verbal switch-reference marking, switch-reference marking on the subordinate verb but not the main verb, clause chaining, subordinate clause predominantly preceding the main clause, and final position of the verb, among others. Typically, overt switch-reference marking is found on the verbs; however, systems with nominal marking and independent sentence-particle marking of switch-reference are known; West Greenlandic has both verbal and nominal switch-reference.

Although switch-reference marks coreference or lack thereof between two clauses, only one clause is actually marked overtly (Comrie 1983:23–25). Switch-reference is found in both subordinate and coordinate structures; where there is clear subordination, it is the subordinate structure that is marked for switch-reference. In West Greenlandic, verbal switch-reference marking is found exclusively in subordinate structures;[8] nominal switch-reference is independent of verb mood; and coordinate switch-reference structures are presumably signaled by use of the contemporative. Coordination in West Greenlandic is indicated by enclitics, by conjunctional particles, or by the use of the contemporative mood on all but one of the coordinated clauses (Fortescue 1984:120), presumably the independent clause.

Another feature often associated with SOV languages, and therefore with most languages with switch-reference systems, is clause chaining (see also chapter 2, section 2.4). The dependent verbs in a clause chain are generally nonfinal (and are therefore referred to as medial);[9] they are often not fully inflected for tense, aspect, or mood; and they often share topic or thematic unity (Longacre 1985:238; Givón 1990:864–65). In clause chains, switch-reference marking is found on the dependent, nonfinal clauses. West Greenlandic shows all the signs of being a clause-chaining language, although it has not been formally identified as such (even Woodbury 1983, addressing switch-reference in Yup'ik, does not call it clause chaining). It is predominantly an SOV language, it is generally described as building sentences from strings of dependent clauses and one final independent clause, and it is the dependent clauses that are marked for switch-reference. The emphasis on clause order is perhaps not deserved in reference to West Greenlandic chains, at least in spoken discourse, and not all dependent clauses precede the independent clause, with various effects on the interpretation of coreference.

Languages differ in the particulars of their switch-reference systems. Some languages mark both coreference and noncoreference, while others only mark one of the two. Others can be classified by what Nichols (1983:247) calls restricted and open reference: a form is restricted if it can have only same or different subject reference, and open if it can have either. Languages differ in the way they treat overlapping reference, whether as same-subject or different-subject. In some cases, switch-reference can be shown to relate a subject and a nonsubject noun phrase, although only where a switch-reference system also regularly relates subjects. The prototypical system of switch-reference, according to Comrie (1983:36), is sensitive only to coreference or noncoreference of subjects; where other factors are involved, such as semantics, the expansion of the switch-reference system is attributable to diachronic development of the switch-reference system.

Various studies have shown that switch-reference can be related to syntactic, semantic, and discourse-level factors. Munro (1983) shows that nonstandard uses of same-subject markers in Chickasaw can be attributed to the grammaticalization of contextual factors, resulting in the acquisition of new syntactic functions of the switch-reference markers and in some cases in the loss of the switch-reference function. The use of same-subject markers, for example, has been extended to differentiate between ordinary switch-reference and relative constructions, and in some cases has become morphologized in auxiliary constructions. In these constructions, the same-subject markers have lost their switch-reference meaning. A same-subject interpretation for certain participial verb forms arises from the phonological reduction of a coordinating conjunction and from a lack of subject-person marking on the verb to which the conjunction is attached. This, along with the lack of a corresponding different-subject marker, distinguishes it from ordinary switch-reference in Chickasaw. The lack of subject marking and the coordinating function of this form bear certain surface similarities to the West Greenlandic contemporatives; it is noteworthy that in both languages, these forms are different from the common switch-reference markers.

In a study of switch-reference in Quechuan languages, Cole (1983) suggests that in addition to same- or different-subject marking, a person hierarchy is involved. Same-subject marking is used when the subordinate subject outranks the superordinate subject.[10]

Woodbury (1983) proposes the existence of two systems for organizing discourse in Yup'ik, one involving the traditional syntactic explanation for switch-reference, the other involving prosodic phrasing. Within the syntax, the appositional (i.e., contemporative) mood is a restrictive switch-reference mechanism, although because of other functions of this mood (e.g., denoting simultaneous or sequential time), there are cases in which the appositional is used even when the coreference conditions are not strictly met (1983:297). However, in discourse, rhetorical structure does not always correspond to acceptable sentence structure. At this level, switches in subjects from one appositional to another is predictable from rhetorical structural devices such as intonation; within a rhetorical group, one can expect subject coreference among appositional clauses. This is similar to Nichols's (1983) observation that while field elicitations show grammatically expected properties, texts show a different pattern, due to factors inherent in the construction of texts (1983:257).

Fortescue (1991) lists environments in which anomalous switch-reference in West Greenlandic is found; these include many of the environments I list in section 4.4.2.1, such as elliptical, impersonal, or overlapping constructions, and cases in which the antecedent of a coreferent form is found outside the sentence. He sees the use of noncoreferent forms in atypical situations as a result of the greater transitivity of the subordinate clause, where transitivity is defined as a set of features including action, telicity, the existence of more than one participant, punctual aspect, volition, and agency. The notion of transitivity is extended to include coreference with the "psychological subject" of a preceding discourse context (although he does not provide the context with his examples), in which the psychological subject is the principal participant or agent in ongoing discourse (participant being agentive and displaying high transitivity; Fortescue 1991:68). If there are regular anomalies with respect to all switch-reference marking, including marking on nominals, and if topic is shown to be the determining factor in switch-reference marking elsewhere (i.e., on verbs), then it is also relevant in explaining switch-reference marking on nominals. For lack of data, I do not address anomalous nominal switch-reference marking below, and take Fortescue's evidence as support for my own interpretation. It is also noteworthy that he assigns a pragmatic value to the use of the contemporative as a switch-reference mechanism (he does not discuss the participial).

Finally, Givón (1990:879ff.) takes thematic coherence rather than subject coreference to be the relevant notion. Givón cites evidence from Swahili, an SVO language with non-clause-chaining-type subordinate and superordinate verb forms, to show that switch-subjects in multiclause sentences can be explained as thematic rather than subject switches.

Givón's approach to switch-reference is fundamentally different from the more standard, interclausal-based understanding thereof (cf. Comrie 1983:36). Givón (1984:137ff.) assumes that switch-reference is one form of coherence, albeit the most obvious and widely spread form. Coherence is an outcome of multipropositional discourse. Between the different elements of discourse (i.e., clauses, propositions, etc.), there exist relations of meaning and signals of the continuity and recurrence of important elements in discourse. Givón calls this cohesive aspect of discourse thematic coherence, the components of which include temporal, action-event (or sequential), locational, and referential (participant) coherence. Temporal and sequential unity tend to be reflected in the tense-aspect-modality systems of a language and are especially relevant in the discussion of clause chaining and subordination below. Referential coherence denotes topic (participant) continuity, and since topic is most commonly subject or object, referential coherence is Givón's general term for what is meant by switch-reference. Textual cohesion is indicated by the use of grammatical devices whose scope crosses clause boundaries. Thus, referential cross-clausal continuity is indicated by anaphoric or cataphoric pronouns (among other things); temporal continuity by tense, temporal adverbs, and in some cases, verb form; continuity of action by aspect; and so forth. The examples below illustrate the different kinds of continuity:

(4.22)  1.  referential: 'Sally ate the wilted lettuce, but she didn't like it very much.'
        2.  temporal: 'Sally opened the door and ran out.'
        3.  action: 'Sally is jumping up and down and waving her hands.'

With respect to referential coherence, Givón proposes a topic hierarchy, as discussed in chapter 3, with subject being the primary topic and direct object being the secondary topic. It has been generally noted that subjects tend to be presupposed, old, or background information (Givón 1984:256; Chafe 1976, among others); when both direct and indirect objects are present, the direct object tends to be presupposed, old, or background information. (All languages, however, have mechanisms for reversing this hierarchy and allowing less likely parts of a proposition/clause to become the topical entity.) Therefore, the subjects and sometimes the direct objects are elements of the proposition that must reflect textual cohesion through some form of anaphora.

Temporal and sequential continuity are related to more or less predictable syntactic characteristics that different clause types have in combination with other clauses. The degree of dependency of one clause on another can be described in grammatical terms by varying levels of finiteness (Givón 1990:852–64). Syntactically, a clause is finite if it is marked for tense, aspect, modality, and in languages with pronominal agreement, for pronominal agreement. On a hierarchy of finiteness, the clauses that are most finite are indicative, followed by subjunctives, participials, infinitives, and finally nominalized verb forms. The more predictable a feature is, the less finite the verb form is likely to be, since marking for that feature becomes redundant. Therefore, dependent verbs tend to be less finite, in that one or more of these features are not marked. Subordinate clauses and medial clauses in chains tend to be more predictable and therefore less finite. In a chain, one expects tense-aspect-modality agreements and subject agreement; conversely, a break in agreement, signaled by explicit marking of any of these forms of agreement, can mark the end of a chain. In clause chains where there is no explicit switch-reference system, medial clauses tend to have the same subject as the final clause. The degree of finiteness is therefore a consequence of thematic coherence (Givón 1990:876).

These generalizations do not all hold for West Greenlandic. Tense-aspect markers are found on subordinate or coordinate clauses (contemporatives, participials, and causatives) where they are not marked on indicatives, and all but the contemporative have full pronominal agreement. A number of the dependent moods can act as the independent verb form in a clause chain. Finally, contemporatives can function as either subordinate or coordinate clauses, whereas causatives and conditionals do not. However, within a clause chain, one tends to find at most one temporal adverb, one set of aspect markers,[11] and so forth. Thus, predictability does affect marking in a clause chain, although marking is not restricted to independent forms. On the other hand, contemporatives and participials do differ in significant ways from other subordinate structures. Structurally, therefore, subordinate and coordinate verb forms in West Greenlandic are morphologically and functionally dissimilar, despite the fact that they are both dependent on the main verb.

Participials (as defined by Givón 1990) tend to be less finite and more nominal, to have the same subject as their main clause, and to reflect simultaneous, or cotemporal, action or state and progressive aspect, or sequential time and perfective aspect. Givón equates progressive aspect with backgrounding and sequentiality with foregrounding (although this is one of his less convincing proposals). Order with respect to the main clause is important. Preposed participials tend to have wider scope and be anaphoric to elements in previous sentences, whereas postposed participials tend to refer to the main clause (Givón 1990:844-47), in addition to which participial placement often affects the temporal interpretation (i.e., as sequential vs. contemporal). My data (section 4.4) strongly suggest that the placement of participials or contemporatives before or after the superordinate clause is related in much the same way to thematic coreference (see also Fortescue 1984:59). Givón's participials describe West Greenlandic contemporatives and participials both, and this suggests an interpretation of the West Greenlandic forms more in line with Lowe's description of the tense system in Western Canadian Inuit dialects than with switch-reference proper.

## 4.3 Role of topic in the use and distribution of switch-reference marking in West Greenlandic

As we have seen, there is evidence from switch-reference systems in other languages that they can be extended to other phenomena, including discourse-level phenomena such as thematic coherence. Unlike studies of ergativity, however, studies of switch-reference have not shown a clear link to topicality, and switch-reference is generally accepted as referring to subject coreference or lack thereof. However, the kinds of exceptions that have been noted for cases of switch-reference in West Greenlandic strongly suggest discourse-level phenomena. Fortescue's (1991:56) list of anomalous switch-reference environments can be restated as discourse environments; reference that lies outside the boundaries of a sentence is an obvious example. In such an environment, topic continuity is already relevant. Pronominal inflections that mark for switch-reference can just as well mark switch-topic. The contemporative and the participial forms, however, are verb moods, and in addition to their purported function as referential coherence markers, they also carry information about other kinds of thematic coherence (temporal, sequential, etc.) Unlike ergative or pronominal switch-reference inflection, which marks identifiable entities in a clause, or in other words, subject or topic, and so on, verb moods cannot be said to identify roles in the same way. In fact, to the extent that they can be said to mark switch-reference, they mark thematic, or propositional switch-reference, rather than topic switch-reference.

The importance of subject in switch-reference marking is a result of the structure of a West Greenlandic sentence. It is an artifact of clause chaining, where a thematic paragraph commonly consists of same-subject clause chains because of the continuity of the topic. Switch-reference is explained by assuming a discourse role, topic, such that switch-topic marking reflects paragraph-level organization within and across clause chains. Further, to the extent that the contemporative and the participial forms indicate referential continuity or lack thereof, they are discourse-level thematic coherence markers. This is especially noticeable when looking at the scope of coreference and the placement of the contemporative or participial clauses with respect to their superordinate, as mentioned above.

## 4.4 Data analysis

In the sections that follow, I review the textual data according to an interpretation of switch-reference that hinges on discourse-level agreement. Subject versus topic agreement is discussed in examples of pronominal switch-reference marking in subordinate clauses, and contemporative and participial clauses are examined according to thematic versus subject-based switch-reference. Because the link between verb mood and switch-reference is unusual, given the productive pronominal means of marking switch-reference, I look at the distribution of the verb moods in detail, including their relative order with respect to the superordinate clause, instances of contemporatives and participials with exceptional subject agreement or lack thereof, and the adequacy of both traditional and discourse-based explanations of their distribution.

### 4.4.1 SUBORDINATE PRONOMINAL INFLECTION

In my texts, most instances of switch-reference marking in the subordinate moods are consistent both with a traditional analysis of same or different subject and with a discourse-based analysis of same or different topic. This is unsurprising, as most examples involve intransitive forms, so that subject and topic coincide:

(4.23)   (From text 4)                 Topic   Transitivity       Mood    SR
44.     . . . *ataataga*              father    INTRANS      SUBORD    3C
        *aamma*      *soqutigisaqaqigami*

        *ataata-ga*
        *aamma*      *soqutigisaq-qaq-qi-gami*
        father-1SG.POS.ABS
        and               interest-have-INTNS-3C.SG.CAUS

        '. . . because my father had many interests'

45.     *kommunerådi*              father      INTRANS      SUPERORD
        *Nuummi*      *ilaasortaavoq_'*

        *kommuneråd-0*
        *Nuuk-mi*      *ilaasortaq-u-voq*

**Table 4.4** Anomalous subordinate mood pronominal inflections

|  | TEXT | | | | | |
|---|---|---|---|---|---|---|
|  | 1A | 1B | 2 | 3A | 3B | 4 |
| Number of switch-reference | 12 | 24 | 15 | 12 | 6 | 9 |
| Number of anomalies 3C | 3 | 6 | 9 | 7 | 0 | 1–3 |
| Number of anomalies 3NC | 0 | 1 | 0 | 0 | 0 | 0 |

community. council-ABS
Nuuk-LOC     member-COP-3SG.IND

'he was a member of the community council in Nuuk . . .'

There are, nevertheless, a number of exceptions to subject coreference or switch-reference. The following table lists the number of clauses marked for switch-reference (SR) in the respective texts, the number of anomalous coreferent forms (ANOM.3C), and the number of anomalous noncoreferent forms (ANOM.3NC).

Anomalous reference can be found approximately one-fourth of the time and is confined to coreference rather than noncoreference, although this may be related to the similarities in type of texts analyzed. P. Langgård (personal communication) suggests there is a tendency toward paradigmatic leveling of the causative, as the noncoreferential third-person form is suppletive. However, the speakers in my texts are at ease with both coreferential and noncoreferential forms. These instances of anomalous coreference can be explained by an analysis based on topic continuity or shift.

Example 4.24 below is part of a section that actually beings in clause 122 with a reflection clause, *eqqaamavara* 'I remember it . . .'; clauses 122–125 are descriptive clauses that set the stage for the text reproduced below (see appendix for full text):

| (4.24) | (From text 1b) | Topic | Mood | SR |
|---|---|---|---|---|
| 126. | . . . *amerlasoorpassuupput* | hunters | SUPERORD | 3PL |
|  | *taamani)}}* | | | |

*amerlasuut-rpassuit-uC-vut*
*taamani*

many-many-COP-3PL.IND
at.that.time

'. . . there were very many at that time.'

127.    {*Tikillaraangamik*                          hunters    SUBORD    3C
        *ualikkut_'*

        *TikiC-llaq-gaangamik*
        *ualikkut*

        arrive-INTNS-whenever.3C.PL.CAUS
        in.the.afternoon

        'When they came back [from hunting, to Qaqortoq] in the
        afternoon'

128.    *ullaakkut*           *aallarunik_'*          hunters    SUBORD    3C
        *ullaakkut*           *aallar-gunik*
        in.the.morning     go-3C.PL.COND
        'after having gone out in the morning'

129.    *ilaanni_*        *puisit_*     *arfineq-pingasut*     *qulit_*
*ilaanni puisi-t*              *arfineq-pingasut*             *qulit*
        sometimes      seal-PL     eight                 ten
        'sometimes eight, ten seals'

        *sinnerlugilluunniit*                seals (O)   SUBORD   3NC(O)
        *kalillugit_}*

        *sinnerlugit-luunniit*                hunters (S)
        *kaliC-lugit*

        more.than-or.even
        in.tow-3NC.PL.OBJ.CT

        'or even more in tow' [i.e., 'sometimes (with) eight or ten or even
        more seals in tow'].

130.    {*Tikileraangata_'*                   hunters (S)   SUBORD   3NC
        *tikiC-leq-gaangata*

arrive-begin-whenever.3NC.PL.CAUS
'Whenever they began to arrive'

131.   *meerarpassuulluta*     children   SUBORD   1PL
*meeraq-passuit-u-luta*
child-many-COP-1PL.CT
'we were a lot of children [there were a lot of us children]'

132.   *sissamukaasaratta_*     children   SUBORD   1PL
*sissaq-mukar-a-saq-gatta*
beach-go.to.do-many.do-HAB-1PL.CAUS
'we used to go as a group to the beach'

133.   *tassani*   *pilattaramikkit*     seals (O)   SUBORD   3C
     *tassa*    *taamani_*

     *tassani*   *pilaC-saq-gamikkit*     hunters (S)
     *tassa*     *taamani*

     there     cut.up/carve-HAB-3C.PL.SUBJ/3PL.OBJ.CAUS
     that.is    at.that.time

'and there they used to cut them up, that is, in those days'

134.   *pilannerini_'*
pilaC-neq-ini
cut.up/carve-NOMZ-3PL.POS.LOC
'in its being cut up [and then they cut it up]'

135.   *uagut_*     *tinguttuuttarpugut_/*   children   SUPERORD   1PL
     *uagut*      *tinguk-toq-uti-saq-vugut*
     1PL       liver-eat-many.of.us-HAB-1PL.IND
'we all used to eat the liver'

136.   *aammalu_*     children   SUBORD   1PL
     *tamuatsivaartorluta*     *tassa_/*

     *aamma-lu*
     *tamuatsivaaq-toq-luta*     *tassa*

and-and

tamuatsivaaq-eat-1PL.CT          that.is

'and we ate tamuatsivaaq . . .'

There are several competing topics in this text, namely 'hunters,' 'children,' 'seals,' and 'tamuatsivaaq.' There is, consequently, frequent alternation between topics, and this is evident in the marking of coreferentiality or lack thereof. All clauses morphologically marked for subject coreference or noncoreference are causative or conditional. Clause 126 is the last clause of the preceding intonation group, the subject is a pronominal reference to 'hunters,' and it is indicative; the next indicative is in clause 135 and the subject is 'we' (in reference to either 'children' or to all people present, including unspecified adults). In either case, the subordinately marked clauses in this section have anomalous reference marking. The subordinate clauses 127 and 128 have coreferential marking and clearly refer back to the subject clauses 127 and 128 have coreferential marking and clearly refer back to the subject of the preceding clause 126 (and hence to the preceding sentence). Clause 130 is marked for noncoreference, and 133 for coreference. If 'hunter' is assumed to be the superordinate reference (from clauses 126, 127, and 128), then clause 130 is anomalous. If 'child' is assumed to be the superordinate reference (cataphorically, from clause 135), then clause 133 is anomalous. In context, however, it can be seen that the topic changes, briefly, in clause 129, with the fronting and intonational isolation of 'seals' (this is more than a brief, passing local topic; it is taken up again in the clauses that follow); immediately thereafter, in clause 130, 'hunters' is marked as noncoreferential. The coreferential marking in clause 133 reestablishes 'hunters' as topical, but the clause is ergative, and the object is 'seals.' In fact, both 'hunters' and 'seals' are topics, and coreferential marking on the verb here signals degree of topicality. Explanations that depend on the degree of transitivity of the subjects fail, given that 'hunters' is clearly more agentive than 'seals' and that 'hunters' is the subject in both the coreferent and noncoreferent cases.

In the same text, there are several examples of coreference that can only be explained as thematic, as in example 4.25, although they involve incorporated nouns (or topics indicated as such by parentheses under the "theme" column in the following example):

(4.25)   (From text 1b)           Theme     Mood     SR

164.   {*Qaqortuminngaanniit*
      *Narsamukartarpugut_'*         go to N.    SUPERORD    1PL

      *Qaqortoq-minngaanniit*
      *Narsaq-mukaq-saq-vugut*

      Qaqortoq-ABL
      Narsaq-go.to-HAB-1PL.IND

      'We used to go from Qaqortoq to Narsaq'

165.   *Ataasiarlunga*                         SUBORD    1SG
      *ataasiar-lunga*
      do.once-1SG.CT
      'I did once [one time]'

166.   *eqqaamagiga*             (whales)    SUBORD    1SG
      *eqqaama-giga*
      remember-1SG.SUBJ/3SG.OBJ.PART
      'I remember it'

167.   *taamanikkut*     *aamma_*      (whales)    SUBORD    1SG
      *eqqaamalluariga_*

      *taamani-kkut*     *aamma*
      *eqqaama-lluaq-giga*

      at.that.time-VIA    and
      remember-well-1SG.SUBJ/3SG.OBJ.PART

      'and at that time I remember it well'

168.   *assorujussuaq*     *taamani_*
      *tikaagulleqartarami_}*          whales    SUBORD    3C

      *assut-rujussuaq-0*    *taamani*
      *tikaagullik-qaq-saq-gami*

      many-many-ABS    at.that.time
      piked.whale-have-HAB-3C.SG.CAUS

      'at that time there were many, many lesser rorquals.'

Technically, there should be no coreference here, although the superordinate clause in 164 has a 1PL subject and clause 168 has a 3C.SG subject. Clause 168 can, however, be seen as the object of the participials in clauses 166 and 167 (see section 4.4.2.2), which explains not only the transitivity of the participials but also the coreference marking on what is overtly identified as topical (i.e., the presence of the whales, or their presence at a particular time). The previous section, through the superordinate clause of this section, clause 164, is thematically about going to Narsaq by boat. From clause 165 through 177, there is a diversion in the narrative to a particular episode in the speaker's life regarding whales. The use of the participial by this speaker tends to signal a change in topic or theme (see example 4.80). For other clear examples from this text, see clauses 119 and 179 in the appendix. Noun incorporation results in the incorporation of the topic into the theme in this and the following examples.

In example 4.26 most of the potential subjects are incorporated into the verb form, and the clauses are translatable in English only through the use of dummy subjects; in West Greenlandic, the subject is either 3SG or 3PL and refers to the incorporated noun:

(4.26) (From text 2)                                        Topic        Mood      SR

65.    {*Taavalu_        taamanikkut*

       *angallaterpassuusaramik,*                           ships       SUBORD     3C

       *Taava-lu        taamani-kkut*
       *angallat-(r)passuit-u-saq-gamik*

       then-and         at.that.time-VIA
       vessel-a.lot.of-COP-HAB-3C.PL.CAUS

       'And then at that time there were a lot of ships'

       (*aammalu         piniarniat,*                       hunters, settlements
        *maanilu          nunaqarfiit,*

        *aamma-lu         piniarniaq-t*
        *maani-lu         nunaqarfik-it*

        and-and          hunter-PL
        here-and         settlement/village-PL

       'and hunters and settlements here'

66.  *taamanikkut*        *Sisimiut_*
     *taamani-kkut*       *Sisimiut*
     at.that.time-VIA     Sisimiut
     'and at that time Sisimiut'

     *nunaqarfippaalussuaqarami*       settlements    SUBORD    3C
     *aamma)_/*

     *nunaqarfik-pak-aluk-ssuaq-qaq-gami*
     *aamma*

     village-many-rather-big-have-3C.SG.CAUS
     and

     'had rather many settlements' [i.e., within the governing district
     of Sisimiut]

67.  *Ikerasakkut*        *Uummannaarsukkut*        *Saqqakkut*
     *tamakkua*           *Itillikkut_*

     *Ikerasak-kkut*      *Uummannaarsuaq-kkut*     *Saqqa-kkut*
     *tamakkua*           *Itilleq-kkut*

     Ikerasak-group       Uummannaarsuaq-group      Saqqa-group
     those                Itilleq-group

     'Ikersak Uummannaarsuaq Saqqa and this one Itilleq'

     *tamakkua*    *inuit*       *Assaquttakkut_/*    people
     *tamakkua*    *inuk-it*     *Assaquttaq-kkut*
     those         person-PL     Assaqutta-people
     'and those people, the people from Assaqutaq'

68.  *aamma*       *taamanikkut*        *tappavunga*
     *ilummut*     *kangerlummut*       *tassa_*

     *aamma*       *taamani-kkut*       *tappav-unga*
     *ilummut*     *kangerluk-mut*      *tassa*

     and           at.that.time-VIA     up.there/to.the.east-TERM
     inwards       fjord-TERM           that.is

'and at that time [they took] to the fjord up there (eastward), you know'

69.  *upernaakkut       tappanna*            codfish   SUBORD   3NC
     *saarulleqarnerusarmat_/*

     *upernaaq-kkut     tappa-nna*
     *saarullik-qaq-neru-saq-mat*

     spring-VIA          up.there/to.the.east-ABS
     codfish-have-more-HAB-3NC.SG.CAUS

     'because in the spring up there there used to be more codfish'

70.  *tappavunga*                              people   SUBORD   3C
     *aallaarrattartorsuugamik_}*

     *tappav-unga*
     *aallaar-CCati-saq-soq-u-gamik*

     up.there.(to.the.east)-TERM
     go.hunting-a.lot.of people.do-HAB-PART-COP-3C.PL.CAUS

     'they were a lot of people who used to camp up there.'

It would be inaccurate to say that the subjects of clauses 65, 66, and 70 are the same despite coreferential marking on the verbs. In the first place, the end of clause 65 and all of clause 66 are parenthetical to the clause chain. In clause 65 the subject is 3PL and refers to the incorporated noun and the following coordinated nouns. In the next clause, the subject is clearly 'Sisimiut'. In clause 70 it is again 3PL, referring this time to the incorporated nominalized form 'ones who go hunting/camping a lot'. Assuming topic or thematic reference, however, we see that there is thematic continuity throughout: 'settlements' is repeated (lexically) from the end of clause 65 to clause 66, and it is in the semantics of clause 70. 'Ships', 'hunters', and 'settlements' in this section refer to the theme of previous sections, namely the activity surrounding the codfishing industry at the time. The noncoreferent 3SG form in clause 69 refers to the incorporated noun 'codfish'; the only mention of 'codfish' in this section is in this clause. While clause 69 is not anomalous according to traditional interpretation, it supports one in which topic or theme replaces subject as the relevant factor in determining coreference.

In the same text is a clear example of a nonincorporated topic determining coreference:

|  |  | Topic | Mood | SR |
|---|---|---|---|---|
| (4.27) | (From text 2) |  |  |  |
| 92. | . . . *qassuterpaalussuarnik* | nets | SUPERORD | 1PL |
|  | *piniuteqartarpugut*     tassa_} |  |  |  |

*qassut-(r)pak-aluk-ssuaq-nik*
*piniut-qaq-saq-vugut*        *tassa*

net-many-rather-big-PL.INST
equipment-have-HAB-1PL.IND     that.is

'. . . at that time we had rather a lot of nets as equipment, you know.'

| 93. | {*Taavalu_*       *arlalip* — | nets | subord | 3C |
|---|---|---|---|---|
|  | *soorunami*     *arlalippasuusaramik* |  |  |  |

*taava-lu*       *soorunami*
*arlallit-passuit-u-saq-gamik*

then-and       naturally/of.course
several/more.than.one-many-COP-HAB-3C.PL.CAUS

'Because of course there were a lot of'

*tamakkua*     *qassutit_/*
tamakkua       qassutit
those          net.PL
'those nets'

94.  *aammalu     ipuinnaq     tassa     imaak*
     *angalasuugatta_/*
     *aamma-lu     iput-innaq-0     tassa     imaak*
     *angala-soq-u-gatta*
     and-and       oar-only-ABS     that.is     like.this
     be.on.the.road-PART-COP-1PL.CAUS
     'and by rowing [with oars] only you know since we moved like this'

95. *unnuaq      ilaanni      tamangajaat        tamaat*
    *tassami_*

    *unnuaq-0    ilaanni      tamangajaat        tamaq-at*
    *tassami*

    night-ABS   sometimes    almost.the.whole    the.whole/3SG.O
    in.any.case

    'sometimes almost the whole night, the whole in any case'

96. *piniuserisarpugut_/*                        nets   SUPERORD   1PL
    *piniut-leri-saq-vugut*
    equipment-deal.with-HAB-1PL.IND
    'we had to deal with the equipment' [i.e., make it ready
    to use]

97. *aammami     imak*                           nets   SUBORD    3C
    *ilarussimasartorsuugamik*

    *aamma-mi    imak*
    *ilaguC-sima-saq-soq-suaq-u-gamik*

    and-INTNS    like.this
    tangled-PERF-HAB-PART-big-COP-3C.PL.CAUS
    'and they were usually very tangled [it could be they might have
    to be untangled]'

98. *imaalitsiaannarlugit*                       *aamma_/*
    *imaali-tsiaq-innaq-lugit*                    *aamma*
    be.like.this-a.little-only-3PL.OBJ.CT        and
    'and in a short period of time/soon/fast'

99. *naammassineq*                               nets   SUBORD    3C
    *ajornartaramik_}*

    *naammassi-neq-0*
    *ajornar-saq-gamik*

    accomplish/finish-NOMZ-ABS
    be.impossible-HAB-3C.PL.CAUS

    'they were usually impossible to finish.'

The local topic is 'nets'; it is also the subject of clauses 93, 97, and 99, all of which are marked for coreference. The subjects of all independent and superordinate clauses, however, is 1pl ('we'). Where traditional interpretations fail, the problem is resolved by assuming topic rather than subject coreference.

Example 4.28 provides another example of topic coreference:

(4.28)  (From text 3a)                                    Topic    Mood    SR

49.    {*Makkuami*
       *pujortagassat*          *cigaritsit?*}        cigarettes

       *Makkua-mi*
       *pujortagaq-ssaq-t*      *cigaritsi-t*

       These-INTNS
       stuff.that.is.smoked-    cigarette-PL
       FUT-PL

       'What about these, tobacco and cigarettes?'

50.    {*Pujortartorujussuugaluarama_*              cigarettes  SUBORD  1SG
       Pujortaq-toq-rujussuaq-u-galuaq-gama
       smoke-consume-very.much-COP-CONSEQ-1SG.CA
       'I used to smoke very much but'

51.    *ullormut_*    20-*it*                       cigarettes  SUBORD  1SG
       *nungunngilaaginnartaraluarakkit*

       *ulloq-mut*    20-*it*
       *nungu-nngit-laaq-innaq-saq-galuaq-gakkit*

       day-TERM    20-PL
       finish-NEG-little-just-HAB-CONSEQ-1SG.SUBJ/3NC.PL.OBJ.CAUS

       'I finished a little bit less than twenty a day'

52.    1987-*arsimi*        *tassanngaannarsuaq*     *pujortarunnaarama_*
       1987 *ars-mi*        *tassannga-innaq-suaq*   *pujortaq-junnaaq-*
                                                     *gama*

       1987 years-LOC      from.then.on-only-big     smoke-no.more-1SG.
                                                     CAUS

'in 1987 from then on I stopped smoking [I no longer smoked]'

53.   *uanga*      *cigaritsip*                    cigarettes   SUBORD   3C
      *ajuleraminga_/*

      *uanga*       *cigaritsi-p*
      *ajor-leq-gaminga*

      1SG          cigarette-REL
      be.bad-begin-3C.SG.SUBJ/1SG.OBJ.CAUS

      'cigarettes didn't like me anymore [began to be bad for me]'

54.   *uanga*      *cigaritsi*                    cigarettes   SUPERORD   1SG
      *ajulinngikkaluarpara_/*
      *uanga*          *cigaritsi-0*
      *ajor-leq-nngit-galuaq-vara*

      1SG          cigarette-ABS
      be.bad-begin-NEG-CONSEQ-1SG.SUBJ/3SG.OBJ.IND

      'but I don't like cigarettes anymore [I began not to have/like
      cigarettes anymore]'

55.   *taamangaasit*      *oqartarpunga}*              SUPERORD   1SG
      *taamanga-aasiit*   *oqaq-saq-vunga*
      like.that-as.usual   say/talk-HAB-1SG.IND
      'that is what I usually say [I usually say like this].'

56.   *Qanutut*      *ajuleramitit?*            cigarettes SUPERORD   3C
      *Qanoq-tut*    *ajor-leq-gamitit*
      how-EQ        be.bad-begin-3C.PL.SUBJ/2SG.OBJ.CAUS
      'Like how did they stop liking you [how did they begin to be bad
      to you/for you]?'

In all clauses with coreferent marking, the subject is 'cigarettes', yet the
subject of the superordinate clauses (clauses 50–52 are all causative, clauses
54 and 55 are both indicative) is the narrator (1SG). 'Cigarettes' is established
as topical by the interviewer in clause 49 and is maintained as the topic
throughout this stretch of text. In the same text, the narrator establishes
a theme, 'to smoke/inhale', and coreference can be seen to pertain to this

theme (see clauses 59 and 60). Other clear examples of topic or thematic coreference can be found in text 3a, clauses 75, 83, and 103, and in text 4, clause 12 (see appendix).

On the surface, an interpretation of switch-reference as switch-topic in West Greenlandic works well. There is a complicating factor in the form of object coreferent morphology. If the object of a subordinate construction is the topic, which it must be according to the interpretation of transitive marking that was suggested in chapter 2, then this object should be marked for coreference. This is not the case in my data. In example 4.28 'cigarettes' is the topic; yet in clause 51, the verb is marked with 1SG.SUBJ/3NC.OBJ causative agreement (*-gakkit*). The expected form would have been *-gatsik* '1SG.SUBJ/3C.OBJ.C'. Throughout my texts, where topic is in object position in a subordinate clause, the object is consistently marked for noncoreference. This is true in text 1b, clauses 133, 176, 213; in text 2, clause 11; in text 3a, clauses 2, 6, 51, 75, and 81; and in text 3b, clause 160. In most cases the subject is first person. In two cases, text 1b, clause 133 (example 4.29), and text 3a, clause 75, the object cannot be marked for coreference since the subject is:

(4.29)   (From text 1b)

133.   . . . *tassani*    *pilattaramikkit*         *tassa*    *taamani_*
          *tassani*       *pilaC-saq-gamikkit*               *taamani*
          there           cut.up-HAB-3C.PL.                  at.that.time
                          SUBJ/3PL.OBJ.CAUS
       '. . . and there they [hunters] used to cut them [seals] up, that is, in those days'

In this clause (for the context, see example 4.24) 'hunters' is vying for topic status with 'seals'. Many of the clauses listed above occur in sections with multiple local topics. In all cases, they are not coreferent with the subject of the superordinate; and the traditional interpretation of subject noncoreference has more explanatory value than one of topic noncoreference. The traditional interpretation fails when verb mood is taken into account, however. In most cases, the subjects of contemporatives are noncoreferent with those of causatives and indicatives in these sections.

Noncoreferent object marking is also consistently found in contemporative clauses. Thus, when the contemporative indexes the object, the noncoreferent form is used (*-lugu* rather than *-luni*). In text 2, for example, the speaker often uses transitive contemporative constructions, all of which involve the noncoreferent form (clauses 71, 73, 74, 89, 90, 91, 98, 103, and 110), with the topic in object position, as in example 4.30:

(4.30)  (From text 2)

103.     *. . . seqineq       kissakkiartuaartillugu_/*
         *seqineq-0          kissaq-giartuaaq-tit-lugu*
         sun-ABS            warm-gradually.more.and.more-cause-3SG.OBJ.CT
         '. . . [it] is causing the sun to get warmer [the sun is getting
         warmer] . . .'

The sun is an absolutive object, and the subject is unspecified.

In at least one example, there is a difference in transitivity between two contemporatives in the same sentence:

(4.31)  (From text 3b)

142.     *. . . 70-it       sinnerlugit*
         *70-it            sinner-lugit*
         70-PL            be.more.than-3PL.OBJ.CT
         '. . . not before she was more than seventy'

143.     *ukioqaleerluni*                    *aatsaat_*
         *ukioq-qaq-leq-reer-luni*           *aatsaat*
         year-have-begin-already-3SG.CT      first
         'years old . . .'

There are no examples of morphologically intransitive noncoreferent forms or of transitive coreferent forms in the contemporative in my texts. This leads to an apparent distributional difference: intransitive coreferent forms of the contemporative are consistently used where either the theme is expressed intransitively or the topic is in the subject position (a distinction only made when there are dummy subjects as a result of incorporation), and transitive noncoreferent forms where there is topic in object position. To adequately determine the value of coreferential marking on verb forms, therefore, examples of third-person coreferent objects in context are needed. This problem is a strong argument in favor of a traditional explanation of switch-reference as subject coreference or noncoreference. (Traditional arguments have also been based on the lack of subject coindexing on the transitive contemporative verb, but this is not problematic. If only one argument is coindexed on the verb, it is the topic.)

There is one instance of a transitive participial form with coreferent object:

(4.32)   (From text 1a)

67.      {*nersunartarsimaqaat*
         *taamani*          *ajoqit_/*

         *nersunaq-saq-sima-qi-vut*
         *taamani*          *ajoqi-t*

         admire.someone.because.he.can.last-HAB-PERF-INTNS-3PL.IND
         at.that.time      catechist-PL

         'they were impressive, the catechists'

68.      *eqqarsaatigissagaanni_*}
         eqqarsaatigi-ssa-gaanni
         think.about-FUT-when.3PL.SUBJ/3C.SG.OBJ.PART
         'when they think about it'

In this example the speaker uses the only form left of a paradigm with *-gaa-* 'whenever' and the participial endings, and it is fossilized and lexicalized in meaning. Thus, in neither case is it possible to determine the function of the object coreferent or noncoreferent inflection from the data at hand.

Unfortunately, there is no example in my texts of a third-person noncoreferent subject and third-person coreferent object, which is the combination necessary to draw a conclusion about topic versus object coreference (regardless of verb mood). Other than the lexicalized participial in example 4.32, there is no example of the use of coreferent object marking, regardless of subject (first, second, or third person). One speaker mistake was made which may or may not be suggestive:

(4.33)   (From text 3a)

2.       ...D.L.ip_       *imaa_*        *siuliatigut_*
         *D.L.-ip*         *imaa*          *siuleq-a-tigut*
         D.L.-REL          like            one.that.goes.before-3NC.SG.POS-SG.VIA
         '...D.L., you know, before'

| *innuttaasut* | *illuanni* | *utoqqaat* |
| *innuttaasoq-t* | *illu-anni* | *utoqqaq-it* |
| community.member-PL | house-3PL.POS.LOC | old.person-PL |

'in the community [members'] house [for] old people'

| *naapisimaranni —* | *naapisimaaratsigit_/* |
| *naapi-sima-ranni —* | *naapi-sima-uti-gatsigik* |
| meet-PERF-1SG.SUBJ/ | meet-PERF-for/with-1PL.SUBJ/ |
| 3C.SG.OBJ.CAUS | 3PL.OBJ.CAUS |

'I have met her — we have met them . . .'

[i.e., 'D.L., you know, when I met her —, when we met the old people before in the community house . . .']

The interviewer was going to use the third-person coreferent form to refer to the speaker of text 3a. Having misspoken, the interviewer corrected himself and used a third plural noncoreferent form to refer to 'old people'. On the other hand, speaker 3 later uses the third singular noncoreferent form *-gakku* in the same circumstances (see text 3a, clauses 81-82). Thus, without further evidence, one might suppose that object coreferent forms are much less frequently used, and that topics in object position, already identified by the use of the transitive construction, need not be redundantly marked with coreferent pronominal agreement on the verb. The question is, then, what does object coreference refer to? Lacking examples of real use, I cannot answer this at present.

Although the switch-reference system is not as easily or clearly reinterpretable as topic-based as the ergative-absolutive case marking, as presented in the preceding chapter, there are, nevertheless, advantages to explaining switch-reference with reference to the coindexing of topic rather than subject. Reinterpreting coreferential marking in clauses with the same subject as their superordinate as same topic rather than subject creates no new exceptions. In addition, it also explains many of the anomalous instances of coreference.

### 4.4.2 CONTEMPORATIVES AND PARTICIPIALS

As with subordinate pronominal marking, it is less straightforward to demonstrate that topic and theme are relevant notions in explaining the distribution of the contemporative and participial verb moods than it is to demonstrate the same for ergative structures. This is so in part because the contemporative and participial moods are associated with so many other functions. This is precisely what makes the identification of these verb moods with switch-reference of any kind tenuous. There are also complications in the determination of clause hierarchy, which will have an effect on the determination of relative order of the clauses in a chain, and in the determination of theme in a section of text. Nevertheless, it is obvious from tables 4.5a and 4.5b below that traditional explanations of the contemporative and participial verb moods are unsatisfactory, and some other explanation must be found. In at least one-third of the contemporative clauses, the subjects are noncoreferent with the superordinate clause; the proportions are smaller for participials with anomalous coreference. As contemporatives and participials together account for one-third to slightly less than one-half of all clauses (others being indicatives, causatives, conditionals, and interrogatives, with occasional nominalized and relative forms), the number of anomalies is even more significant. In this section, I will briefly discuss clause order and thematic identification, and then the distribution of the contemporative and participial verb moods, respectively.

The determination of clause hierarchy depends on a number of factors, including intonation, thematic continuation, and conjunctions. Clauses are determined to be subordinate to another clause within the same intonational group (indicated by roman numerals in the transcriptions) if they modify that clause in some way (e.g., an adverbial clause such as clause 21 in text 1a, *ukiorlu naallugu* (CT) 'and all winter long', modifies clause 22, *qajaq atorluarneqaqaaq* (P) 'the kayak is very much used'). Modification may involve a clause with subordinate mood inflection modifying a clause with independent mood inflection (see text 1a, clauses 58-59, 'and when they had moved them in those days (CA) they [were] given houses not yet built [I]') or two subordinate moods (two contemporatives as in text 1a, clauses 62-63, 'sometimes over more than a year [CT] they had to live in another house [CT]', a contemporative and a causative, as in clause 60 and clause 61, 'and whenever they moved [CAUS] they first had to build houses themselves [CT]', and so forth). Parenthetical clauses, indicated by parentheses in the data, are outside the scope of the immediate hierarchy of a group of clauses (unless contemporative or participial clauses occur within the parentheses). For the purposes of the tables below, clauses are considered subordinate to the immediately superordinate clause rather than to the highest clause in the intonational group; problems and questions that arise as a result are discussed below. Contemporative or participial clauses that begin or end an intonational group are counted as clauses that precede or follow, respectively, a superordinate clause. Medial clauses sometimes present problems in determining the hierarchy; in these cases, both intonational clues and clues from the clausal semantics and thematic continuity are used.

The number of contemporative or participial clauses with noncoreferent or coreferent subjects, respectively, is based on the hierarchies of clause order. Differences that arise from considering different hierarchical levels are discussed below.

In the following tables, the columns represent the six texts used for this analysis. The rows indicate an approximate number of clauses in the texts, the number of contemporative or participial clauses in each text, the number that precede or follow the clause to which they are subordinated, the number of clauses for which such a determination could not be made without reasonable doubt, and the number of clauses with unexpected subject coreference or noncoreference (for participials and contemporatives, respectively).

It is obvious that clause order does not conform to that of prototypical switch-reference systems, as reported in the literature. In addition, both contemporatives and participials show semantic differences based on their distribution in a clause. Fortescue writes that contemporatives can be used

**Table 4.5a** Contemporative clause count

| | | | TEXT | | | |
|---|---|---|---|---|---|---|
| Number of clauses | 1A | 1B | 2 | 3A | 3B | 4 |
| Total | 104 | 116 | 113 | 125 | 68 | 100 |
| Contemparatives | 30 | 25 | 26 | 27 | 18 | 23 |
| Before | 8 | 10 | 7 | 9 | 7 | 10 |
| After | 22 | 14 | 14 | 15 | 10 | 12 |
| Unsure | 0 | 1 | 2 | 3 or 4 | 1 | 1 |
| Different subject | 9 | 7 | 7 | 5 | 6 | 12 |

**Table 4.5b** Participial clause count

| | | | TEXT | | | |
|---|---|---|---|---|---|---|
| Number of clauses | 1A | 1B | 2 | 3A | 3B | 4 |
| Total | 104 | 116 | 113 | 125 | 68 | 100 |
| Participial | 14 | 10 | 8 | 9 | 9 | 4 |
| Before | 3 | 5 | 5 | 3 | 3 | 3 |
| After | 8 | 4 | 3 | 5 | 6 | 1 |
| Unsure | 3 | 1 | 0 | 1 (P? N?) | 0 | |
| Same subject | 10 | 3 | 1 | 0 | 1 | 0 |

in adverbial clauses of time, manner, and cause (among others), and that in these functions, the contemporatives generally precede the main verb (1984:62), and that participials usually have a temporal sense preceding the main verb and usually represent an object clause when following (1984:59). Although the pattern of participial use is confirmed, my data show notable differences in the distribution of contemporative clauses. In text after text, the majority of contemporative clauses follow the superordinate verb and have functions different from those that precede, although there is some overlap. In general, contemporative clauses that precede the independent verb tend to be temporal, causative, or locative in function, whereas those that follow tend to be adverbial clauses of manner, object clauses, or generally descriptive. These tendencies are illustrated in examples 4.34-4.36:

|        |                                         | Mood | Function |
|--------|-----------------------------------------|------|----------|
| (4.34) | (From text 1b)                          |      |          |
| 217.   | {*Aamma_*    *peroreerlunga* | CT | temporal adv |
|        | *aamma*    *peror-reer-lunga* | | |
|        | and    become.adult-already-1SG.CT | | |
|        | 'and when I was already an adult' | | |

| 218. | *tassa*    *paasivara_/* | IND |
|------|-----------------------------------|-----|
|      | *tassa*    *paasi-vara* | |
|      | that.is    understand-1SG.SUBJ/3SG.OBJ.IND | |
|      | 'I understood it' | |

| 219. | *ilumoortoq*    *taanna_}* |
|------|--------------------------------------|
|      | *ilumoortoq*    *taanna* |

true that
'that was true [it was true, that]'

(4.35)  (From text 1a)                                    Mood        Function
96.     {*pissaqarniarlutik_*                              CT          causative adv
        *pissaq-qaq-niaq-lutik*
        something.one.will.have-have-FUT-3PL.CT
        'To have food'

97.     *qajartorneq*            *ilinniartarpaat*   IND
        *qajartoq-neq*           *ilinniaq-saq-vaat*
        row.a.kayak-NOMZ.ABS     learn-HAB-3PL.SUBJ/3PL.OBJ.IND
        'they had to learn to be kayak rowers [learn kayak skills]'

98.     *ilikkavillugu_}*                                  CT          manner adv
        *ilikkaq-vig-lugu*
        learn.something-completely-3SG.OBJ.CT
        'learning it completely.'

(4.36)  (From text 3a)                                     Mood        Function
        33.  {*Naluara*                                    IND
        *Nalu-vara*
        not.know-1SG.SUBJ/3SG.OBJ.IND
        'I don't know'

34.     *sooq*    *taamaannerlunga}*                       CT          object
        *sooq*    *taamaa-ner-lunga*
        why       be.like.this-wonder-1SG.CT
        'why I am like that.'

These tendencies may explain ambiguities or lack of structural clarity
in the texts. Ellipsis of the superordinate clause is obvious in example 4.37,
in which the intonational group consists of clauses 74–81, and in which
the two overt indicatives cannot be considered the relevant superordinate
form to the contemporatives below:

(4.37)  (From text 4)                                      Mood        Function
74-78.  but then just to mention these a bit_
        I will talk a little about my childhood_/         IND

at that time in the time of my childhood_'
there were animals that were hunted_'          IND
I can give the list of the hunted animals_'
In the winter_ [there were] foxes_' ptarmigans_' and hares_'

79.   *taavalu      aamma_     soorunalumi              puisit_'*
      *taava-lu     aamma      sooruna-lu-mi            puisi-t*
      then-and     and        of.course-and-what.about  seal-PL
      'and then of course what about the seals'

80.   *sikukkut     avungalu,            Natsilimmut_'*
      *siku-kkut    avunga-lu            Natsilik-mut*
      ice-VIA      in.the.north-and     Natsilik-TERM
      'across the ice up north to Natsilik'

      *Saarluminngaanniit      ilaanni*                    CT     manner
      *sisoraaserlutik*

      *Saarloq-minngaanniit    ilaanni*
      *sisorar-uti-ler-lutik*

      Saarloq-ABL             sometimes
      ski-device-begin-3PL.CT

      'sometimes putting skis on from Saarloq'

81.   *piniariartarlutik_}*                              CT     manner
      *piniar-giaq-saq-lutik*
      hunt-go.to.do-HAB-3PL.CT
      'hunting'

In example 4.38 the intonation and the semantics clash. Clause 186, a temporal adverbial clause, should belong semantically to the following clauses rather than the preceding (it being impossible to have already drunk tea before waking up). The contemporatives in clauses 189–190 can be read as either adverbials of time or manner; given the tendencies noted above, they should probably be interpreted as temporal adverbs.

(4.38)  (From text 1b)                                   Mood     Function
185.    *Iinndaleeqqap_     Ittup_              Ittup_*

*Iinndaleeraq-p*       *Ittu-p*                  *Ittu-p*
Henry-REL              Grandfather-REL
'Henry, Grandfather, Grandfather'

*ullaakkut_*       *tamatta*              *iteraangatta_*   CAUS
*ullaaq-kkut*      *tamaq-tta*            *iter-gaangatta*
morning-VIA        the.whole/all-1PL     wake.up-whenever.
                                         1PL.CAUS

'in the morning whenever all of us together had woken up'

186.   *tiitoreerluta_/*                          CT     temporal adv
       *tii-toq-reer-luta*
       tea-drink-already-1PL.CT
       'when we had already drunk tea'

187.   *taava*    *inimut*        *iserluta_'*         CT     temporal adv
       *taava*    *ini-mut*       *iser-luta*
       then       room-term       enter-1pl.CT
       'then [when] we entered/came into the room'

       *Ittup*                   *issia_*
       *Ittu-p*                  *issia[vik-minut]*
       Grandfather-REL     chair-3C.SG.POS.TERM
       'Grandfather to his chair'

188.   *pattagissaminut*           *ingikkuni_/*     COND
       *pattagiaq-minut*           *igiC-guni*
       piano-3C.SG.POS.TERM    sit.down-3C.SG.COND
       'if he sat down at the piano'

189.   *taava_*    *inersimasut_*
       *taava*     *inersimasoq-t*
       then        adult-PL
       'then the adults'

       *nalaasaarfimmut     issiavikuluunullu          CT     temp/manner
       issaallutik*

       *nalaasaarfik-mut     issiavik-kulooq-nut-lu
       isser-a-lutik*

couch-TERM        arm.chair-big-TERM.PL-and
sit-PL-3PL.CT

'when/while sitting down on the couch and in armchairs'

190.    *uagut*        *meeqqat*    *natermut*        CT    temp/manner
*ingilluta_'*

*uagut*        *meeraq-t*    *nateq-mut*
*ingiC-luta*

1PL        child-PL    ground-TERM
sit.down-1PL.CT

'we children sitting down on the ground'

191.    *Taava*    *Ittup*        *qinnutinnguaq*    IND
*atuartarpaa_/*

*taava*    *Ittu-p*        *qinnut-nnguaq-0*
*atuar-saq-vaa*

then    Grandfather-REL prayer-little-ABS
read-HAB-3SG.SUBJ/3SG.OBJ.IND

'then Grandfather would read a little prayer'

192.    *palasiugami*        *aamma_*        CAUS
*palasi-u-gami*        *aamma*
priest-COP-3C.SG.CAUS    and
'and [i.e., because] he was also a priest'

More importantly, the semantic differences due to the different ordering of the various kinds of modifying clauses affect the scope of coreference. In all my texts, there is a clear functional difference in the scope of thematic continuity between contemporatives and participials that precede or follow the superordinate clause. Contemporative clauses that precede the superordinate refer to information from a previous paragraph or intonational group (see example 4.24, clause 131, 'when we were children', which repeats the preceding clauses 109 and 122). Those that follow the superordinate continue the theme of the immediately preceding superordinate (see example

4.38). Participials that precede their superordinates signal paragraph-level thematic shifts, and participials that follow their superordinates signal very local shifts in theme (with some variation in the meaning of local/paragraph-level between speakers). Thus, in example 4.39, speaker 1, by far the most prolific user of participials, uses the participial in clause 44 as a local shift from the theme of clauses 43 to 46:

| | | | Mood | Function |
|---|---|---|---|---|
| (4.39) | (From text 1a) | | | |
| 43. | {*Taakkutuaappullu* | | | |
| | *ajoqit* | *tassa_* | IND | |

*Taakku-tuaq-u-uut-lu*
*ajoqi-t        tassa*

Those-only-COP-3PL.IND-and
catechist-PL    that.is

'And the catechists were the only ones then [those only were the catechists that is]'

*taamanikkut        ilisimasassanik_*
*tiguinnarisassanik_*

*taamani-kkut        ilisimasat-ssaq-nik*
*tigu-innaq-giaq-ssaq-nik*

at.that.time-VIA    knowledge-FUT-PL.INST
take-only-INTNS-FUT-PL.INST

'in those days [who] could spread knowledge'

| 44. | *ilinniartinneqarsimasut* | | PART | local theme shift |
| | *Ilinniarfissuarmi_/* | | | |

*ilinniartit-neqaq-sima-sut*
*Ilinniarfissuaq-mi*

teach-PASS-PERF-3PL.PART
Greenlandic.Seminary-LOC

'they had been educated in the Greenlandic Seminary'

45. *taakkulu*          *ilinniakkatik,*
    *taakku-lu*         *ilinniagaq-tik*
    that/those-and      training-3C.PL.POS/PL.POSM.ABS
    'and this knowledge/training'

    *namminerlu*     *aamma_*                                    CT   manner
    *eqqarsaatersuutisik*                      *atorlugit_*

    *nammineq-lu*    *aamma*
    *eqqarsaatersuut-tik*                      *ator-lugit*

    self-and          and
    aphorism-3C.PL.POS/PL.POSM.ABS    use-3NC.PL.OBJ.CT

    'and using their own philosophy/thought'

    *qaammarsaaneq*              *annertoorujussuaq_*
    *qaammarsaaneq-0*            *annertooq-rujussuaq-0*
    illumination/educational.    voluminous/extensive-very-ABS
    standard-ABS
    'the enormous education/knowledge'
    (i.e., combining what they learned at the Greenland Seminary
    and their own ideas about life)

46. *sinerissami*    *tamarmi_*        *ingerlatarivaat_}*        IND
    *sineriak-mi*    *tamaq-mi*        *ingerla-uti-saq-gi-vaat*
    coast-LOC        the.whole/all-3SG.O    spread-manner-pass.part-
                                             have-3PL.SUBJ/3PL.OBJ.IND
    'they spread it all over the coast'

(Compare this to the paragraph-level shifts in theme by the same speaker,
discussed at length in connection with anomalous coreference in example 4.80.)

Unlike systems of pronominal inflection, the contemporative and the
participial are verb moods; if they indicate switch-reference, they indicate
thematic rather than topic continuity or shift. Because of the propositional
rather than nominal nature of themes, they are less likely to be uniquely
identified, and there is more room for ambiguity in and therefore disagree-
ment on the reading of a text, since themes are more likely to be expressed

via synonyms and paraphrases than topics are. It is therefore necessary to have some idea of how the theme of a section of text is introduced (see chapter 2, section 2.3, and chapter 3, section 3.4). In my texts several means of establishing the theme are apparent. These include intonational emphasis, varying word order (both of which were discussed previously), the (lexical) repetition of phrases, clauses, or other constituent parts of the text, and the appeal to contextual knowledge by the use of particular lexical items. In three of the texts, the format of the text itself, the interview, permits the general identification of local themes. Themes are established by the questions and generally expanded upon in the answers.

If, as is generally accepted, most clauses in discourse have little new information and much old information, we expect a great deal of repetition in discourse. Repetition of information encourages thematic continuity, or coherence. In extreme instances, as noted by Grimes (1975) and Longacre (1976), entire paragraphs are routinely repeated in narration. Although this level of repetition is not an inherent part of Greenlandic discourse, the speaker of text 2 does favor repetition of this sort, as we see in example 4.40, where clauses 18–26 are conceptually repeated in clauses 27–31:

(4.40)  (From text 2)                                                        Mood

18.      {*Taamanikkullu_*          1920-*ip*
         *aallartisimalernerani,*

         *Taamani-kkut-lu*          1920-*ip*
         *aallartit-sima-ler-neq-ani*

         at.that.time-VIA-and    1920-REL
         begin-PERF-begin-NOMZ-3SG.POS.LOC

         'At that time, at the beginning of the 1920s'

         *aalisarneq_*
         *aalisarneq*-0
         fishing-abs
         'fishing'

         *saarullinnik*      *aalisarneq*      *aatsaat*                      IND
         *aallarnersalerpoq_*}

         *saarullik-nik*      *aalisarneq*-0      *aatsaat*

*aallarner-saq-ler-voq*
cod-PL.INST    fishing-ABS    at.first
begin-AGENT-begin-3SG.IND

'codfish fishing was first going to start.'

19.    {*Eqqaamalluarpara*                  IND
      *Eqqaama-lluaq-vara*
      remember-well-1SG.SUBJ/3SG.OBJ.IND
      'I remember it well'

20.    *meeraallunga_*        *taamanikkut_*           CT
      *meeraq-u-lunga*       *taamani-kkut*
      child-COP-1SG.CT      at.that.time-VIA
      'I was a child then'

21.    *massakkut*    *amutsiviup*    *akiani_*
      *massakkut*    *amutsivik-up*    *aki-ani*
      now         shipyard-REL    other.side-3SG.POS.LOC
      'now on the other side of the shipyard [opposite the place that is
      now the shipyard]'

      *ilinniartut_*    *ilinniartut*    *illukuat_/*
      *ilinniartoq-t*    *ilinniartoq-t*    *illu-ku-at*
      student-PL      student-PL      house-former-3PL.POS.ABS
      'there was a former students' house [there was formerly a
      students' house]'

22.    *taassuma*    *illup*    *kangia*    *tungaani_*
      *taassuma*    *illu-p*    *kangia*    *tungaani*
      that.one-REL    house-REL    lying.east    over.there/in.that.
                                               direction
      'to the east of that house over there'

      *itersiumanermiikkami*           *qooqqiumanermi_*     CAUS
      *itersi-juma-neq-mii-gami*       *qooqqi-juma-neq-mi*
      make.a.hole.in.ground-want-      make.a.furrow-want-
      NOMZ-be.in-3C.SG.CAUS        NOMZ-LOC
      'because it is in a little depression in a valley'

23.    *illungaatsiapilorujussuaq*
    *illu-ngaatsiaq-pilorujussuaq-0*
    house-rather-very.big-ABS
    'a little bigger than a big house'

24.    *imaappoq sana —      sanaaq_'*
    *imaaC-voq sanaaq-0*
    be.like.this-3SG.IND     something.one.has.done-ABS
    'that is it has been built'

25.    *illungaatsiapilorujussuaq*       *uingasoq_/*
    *illu-ngaatsiaq-pilorujussuaq-0*    *uinga-soq*
    house-rather.big-very.big-ABS    slant-3SG.PART
    'the rather larger than big house was slanted'

26.    *taanna     "Eqaluit    inaannik"*            IND
    *taasarparput}*

    *taanna     eqaluk-it    ini-annik*
    *taasar-varput*

    that.one    char-PL    place-3PL.POS.INST
    call-1PL.SUBJ/3SG.OBJ.IND

    'that one we called "char's place"'

             Repetition                   Mood
27.    *{Tassalu    taanna_    aalisarnermut_*
    *saarulliornermut_*

    *Tassa-lu    taanna    aalisarneq-mut*
    *saarullik-lioq-neq-mut*

    then-and    that.one    fishing.(industry)-TERM
    codfish-make-NOMZ-TERM

    'And that [house], to the fishing industry to the codfishing
    industry/factory'

    *Sisimiuni_         aallarnersaataalluni_*           CT
    *Sisimiut-ni        aallarner-saq-uti-u-luni*

Sisimiut-PL-LOC     begin-AGENT-means.to-COP-3SG.CT
'in Sisimiut it was the means with which to begin,'
(i.e., 'It was the means to begin the fishing industry, the
codfishing industry, in Sisimiut')

28.  *taanna*       *illuusarsuaq*                   *uingasoq_/*
     *taanna*       *illu-u-saq-suaq-0*              *uinga-soq*
     that.one       house-COP-FUT-big-ABS     uneven/slant-3SG.PART
     'that shack [poor house, about to fall apart] was slanted/uneven'

29.  *uingasumik*          *qalialik_/*
     *uinga-soq-mik*       *qaliaq-lik*
     slant-PART-INST     roof-provided.with
     'the one with the tilted roof'

30.  (*eqaluit*    *inaannik*                   *taasartagarput*          IND
     *eqaluk-it*   *ini-annik*                  *taasar-saq-varput*
     char-PL       place-3PL.POS.INST     call-HAB-1PL.SUBJ/3SG.OBJ.IND
     '(we used to call it the place of char)'

31.  *tassa*     *ima*        *tarajorterivittut*     *atoqqaarsimavoq_/*
     *taanna_}*                                                          IND

     *tassa*     *ima*        *tarajorterivik-tut*     *ator-qqaaq-sima-voq*
     *taanna*

     that.is   you.know   salting.place-EQ     use-first-PERF-3SG.IND
     that.one

     'like, you know, it was first used as a [cod]salting place, that one.'

In most cases, however, clause-by-clause repetition of information for whole
paragraphs is not the norm in my texts. A clause that repeats information
either repeats the immediately preceding clause(s) or clauses from preceding paragraphs. The following illustrates repetition of an immediately
preceding clause:

(4.41)  (From text 1b)                                              Mood
105.  {*Taava*   *ajoqit*        *eqqartullatsiaratsigit*          CAUS
       *Taava*   *ajoqi-t*       *eqqartor-llar-tsiar-gatsigit*

so          catechist-PL      talk/tell.about-with.intensity-little-1PL.
                             SUBJ/3PL.OBJ.CAUS

'So we mentioned the catechists'

106.   *aatsaaginnaq*      *eqqartullatsiarpakka_*                     IND
       *aatsaat-innaq*     *eqqartor-llar-tsiar-vakka*
       now-just           talk.about-with.intensity-little-1SG.SUBJ/
                          3PL.OBJ.IND

'just now I talked about/mentioned them . . .'

In the second case, the clauses tend to reestablish a previously mentioned
setting (temporal, spatial, etc.). In example 4.42 the speaker focuses on
the time of his childhood; 'when we were children', or variations thereof,
is repeated throughout the text, in clauses 123 and 131:

(4.42)  (From text 1b)                                              Mood
110.   *Taamani*      *uagut*      *meeraasugut_/*                  PART
       *taamani*      *uagut*      *meeraq-u-sugut*
       at.that.time   1PL          child-COP-1PL.PART

'[But] at that time when we were children . . .'

       Repetition                                                  Mood
123.   . . . *meeraalluta*        *upernaakkut_*                    CT
       *meeraq-u-luta*            *upernaaq-kkut*
       child-COP-1PL.CT           spring-VIA

'. . . when we were children in the spring . . .'

131.   . . . *meerarpassuulluta*                                   CT
       meeraq-passuit-u-luta
       child-many-COP-1PL.CT

'. . . we were a lot of children . . .'

Clauses that establish a general setting, whether temporal or situational,
present information that is assumed to be relevant throughout the following text, unless specifically changed. Thus, the speaker in texts 1a and 1b
often alternates between the recollections, all occurring 'when we were
children', and recollection clauses such as 'today the occupations are . . .'
or 'I think this (i.e., now that I am an adult)'. Clauses that establish a
temporal or spatial setting may be repeated for emphasis, contrast, or as

a way to gain time during gaps in the narration, but these repetitions are often different in structure and content when repeated. Thus, in example 4.43, the speaker, in discussing the hardships of earlier days, says that he and his coworkers only had boats with oars at the time; in later clauses, he reminds the listener of this through elliptical constructions:

(4.43)  (From text 2)                                                                      Mood

48.    . . . (*taamanikkut      ipuinnarmik       angallateqarpugut*          IND
       *taamani-kkut        ipu-innaq-mik        angallat-qaq-vugut*
       at.that.time-VIA     oar-only-INST        vessel-have-1PL.IND
       '. . . (at that time we had only boats with oars . . .'

                           Repetition                                          Mood

74.    {*tassalu          tappavannga       imaappoq_*
       *tassa-lu          tappav-annga      imaaC-voq*
       that.is-and    up.there-ABL     be.like.this-3SG.IND
       'And so from up there, you know'

       *taamanikkut        siullermik      Akisaminngaanniit_'*
       *taamani-kkut        siullermik      Akisa-minngaanniit*
       at.that.time-VIA    at.first        Akisa-ABL
       'at that time at first from Akisa'

       *Utoqqaat_  Utoqqaat   Saqqaanut                       allaat*
       *taamanikkut tassa_*

       *Utoqqaat                           Saqqa-anut                     allaat*
       *taamani-kkuttassa*

       Utoqqaat                           Saqqa-3SG.POS.TERM    others
       at.that.time-VIA                   that.is
       'Utoqqaat, even to Saqqa [even to its south side], others in those days'

       *ipuinnaq_/*                                                             (NP)
       *ipu-innaq-0*
       oar-only-ABS
       'only oars [only rowing]'

*qassusersorfigalugu,*
*qassuser-soq-fik-gi-lugu*
set.nets-PART-place-have-3SG.OBJ.CT
'setting nets [had a place for nets] . . .'

84.     . . . *tappavanngaanniit     silammut_'*          (NP)
        *ipuinnaq_'*

        *tappavannga-anniit      silammut*
        *ipu-innaq-0*

        up.there.(ABL)-from       outside
        oar-only-ABS

        '. . . [we go] out from there, only oars . . .'

94.     . . . *aammalu     ipuinnaq        tassa      imaak*   (NP) and CAUS
        *angalasuugatta_/*

        *aamma-lu      iput-innaq-0    tassa      imaak*
        *angala-soq-u-gatta*

        and-and        oar-only-ABS   that.is    like.this
        be.on.the.road-PART-COP-1PL.CAUS

        '. . . and only oars [i.e., by only rowing], you know, since we
        moved like this . . .'

110.    {*Taamanikkut_     ipuataarluni*                       CT
        *Taamani-kkut      ipuataar-luni*
        at.that.time-VIA    row/pull.oars.through-3SG.CT
        'in those days, rowing'

Repetition may come after an extended gap, but despite the gap, the
hearer is expected to remember the preceding discourse (see chapter 2,
section 2.1). In the following example, the repetition comes after forty-two
clauses of intervening text:[12]

(4.44)  (From text 3a)                                        Mood
26.     . . . *pingaartumik     peqqippallaarneq*              CAUS
        *ajorama              massakkut*

*pingaartumik        peqqiC-vallaar-neq-o*
*ajor-gama           massakkut*

especially            healthy-so.much-NOMZ-ABS
be.bad-1SG.CAUS    now

'. . . especially as I am not so very healthy now'

*angalaniarnikkut_/*                                    NOMZ
*angala-niaq-neq-kkut*
walk-FUT-NOMZ-VIA
'when walking . . .'

27.    *(imaa        soorlu        uummaatinnik*                    NOMZ
       *patsiseqartumik)_}*

       *imaa        soorlu        uummat-nnik*
       *patsiseqaq-soq-mik*

       like.this    for.example    heart-1SG.POS.INST
       use.for.excuse-PART-INST

       'like, for example, because of my heart).'

                          Repetition                    Mood
66.    . . . *(tassa    massakkut    qujaannartarpunga*    IND
       *tassa        massakkut    qujaannaq-saq-vunga*
       that.is       now          thankful-HAB-1SG.IND
       '. . . that is, now I am thankful'

67.    *pujortarunnaarsimagama_)}*                              CAUS
       *pujortaq-junnaaq-sima-gama*
       smoke-no.more-PERF-1SG.CA
       'because I have stopped smoking).'

68.    *Sunaaffa,            uumallulerlunga_*                    CT
       *Sunaaffa            uummat-luk-leq-lunga*
       think.about.it      heart-bad-begin-1SG.CT
       'Think about it, it was because my heart was getting bad'

Reviewing the data in terms of thematic continuity or lack thereof, contemporatives and participials consistently occur with same-theme and different-topic/theme clauses, respectively. In the examples listed above, where contemporatives are used (as opposed to causatives or indicatives), they are used not to introduce but to continue or repeat a theme (e.g., example 4.42, clauses 123 and 131; example 4.43, clause 110; and example 4.44, clause 68 above).

In some cases, neither lexical repetition nor synonymy signals thematic development; rather, the hearer is assumed to have the proper cultural contextual knowledge. For example, in example 4.45, the speaker assumes a common knowledge of the local area in which the discourse is situated:

(4.45)  (From text 4)                                                    Mood

17.      . . . *siullermik_*          *seminariami*        *atuaqataavoq*              IND
         *siullermik*                *seminaria-mi*       *atuaqat-u-voq*
         at.first                    seminary-LOC      schoolmate-COP-3SG.IND
         '. . . the first time he went to the seminary (teacher's school)'

18.      *ima*      *kursuserpoq*                                               IND
         *ima*      *kursus-er-voq*
         like      course-have.a.course-3SG.IND
         'like to take courses'

19.      *maannakkutoorlugu_'*                                               CT
         *maanna-kkut-tooq-lugu*
         now-VIA-like-3SG.OBJ.CT
         'it would be called now'

20.      1929-*imi_*}
         1929-*mi*
         1929-LOC
         '[was] in 1929.'

                         Repetition                                      Mood

21.      {*Taava_*     *tamatuma*
         *kinguningaatsiarsuagut*                 1942-*imi_*

         *Taava*          *tamatuma*
         *kinguneq-ngaatsiaq-suaq-agut*    1942-*mi*

so          this-REL
result/succession-very.much-big-3SG.POS.VIA          1942-LOC

So then much later in 1942

22.    *aamma    kingumut    ukiivoq*                *Nuummi_*    IND
       *aamma    kingumut    ukii-voq*                *Nuuk-mi*
       and       again       winter.over-3SG.IND    Nuuk-LOC
       'and he again was one year [wintered over] in Nuuk'

23.    *aamma    seminariami_    atuaqataalluni_}*                CT
       *aamma    seminaria-mi    atuaqat-u-luni*
       and       seminary-LOC    schoolmate-COP-3SG.CT
       'and he learned in the seminary.'

The seminary in Nuuk is a religiously based teacher's training seminary, and until very recently it was the only one in Greenland. When the speaker says, in clause 22, that his father again spent one year in Nuuk, the speaker is assuming that the first extended period in Nuuk occurred during 1929 (see clause 17). Clause 22, therefore, is not new information, and the contemporative in clause 23 does continue a common theme. (Furthermore, going to the seminary implied an education as a catechist, whose job it was not only to provide religious education but also elementary education, among other things. The contemporatives in clauses 23, 24, and 26 of this text, therefore, all refer to information implied through clauses 11, 14, and 15-22; see the appendix for the full text.) For other examples of contextually based information and thematic development, see text 2 and the notes to text 2 in the appendix.

In addition to lexical or phrasal repetition and cultural context, a speaker may develop a theme by means of descriptive phrases. In example 4.47, clauses 47–60 (presented below in more detail in connection with individual speakers' methods of introducing themes), the speaker describes the hardships that the catechists were made to suffer at the hands of the management (cf. clause 50, 'they have not been paid well by the management') by listing a variety of hardships, such as having no say in a move, having to build their own houses, and living in another's house.

In the texts that are interviews, it possible to examine the effect of the interviewer's questions on the thematic development of the text. A question establishes a theme (even if it is only asking for elaboration of a theme introduced by the speaker) and the speaker has this in mind as he or she answers. For example, in text 3a the interviewer suggests that the speaker looks young in clause 21; in clauses 22 to 37, the speaker talks about the fact that she looks good (but does not necessarily feel good). In clause 35 the speaker suggests that perhaps the fact that she does not drink beer might affect her looks. In clause 38 she is asked about drinking beer; in clauses 39 to 48 she discusses drinking beer. In clause 49 she is asked about cigarettes; in clauses 50 to 55 she discusses cigarettes, and so forth. Although she may diverge for one or more paragraphs, her answer is shaped by the interviewer's question, as in example 4.46:

(4.46)  (From text 3a)                                                    Mood

71.        . . . *aneertarpiit?_}*                                         INT
           *aneer-saq-viit?*
           go.for.walk-HAB-2SG.INT
           '. . . do you go out for walks?'

From clauses 72 to 87 the speaker discusses her old house and her feelings about moving to a new house.

           Repetition                                                     Mood

88, 89. . . . *aneersuarlunga_*                                            CT
           *aneer-suaq-lunga*
           go.for.a.walk-a.lot-1SG.CT
           '. . . I went for walks a lot'

90.        *ullorsuaq*        *pisarpunga*                                 IND
           *ulloq-suaq-0*     *pi-saq-vunga*
           day-big-ABS        thing-HAB-1SG.IND
           'I used to do this all day long'

91.        *silagitsillugu_/*                                             CT
           *sila-gik-tit-lugu*
           weather-have.a.good-cause-3SG.OBJ.CT
           'if the weather was good'

92.        *Assorsuaq*                *maqaasivara*                        IND
           *massakkut_}*

*Assut-suaq*                    *maqaasi-vara*
*massakkut*

much-very.much-ABS        miss-1SG.SUBJ/3SG.OBJ.IND
now

'I miss it very much now.'

The speaker's digression was in fact a long introduction to the actual answer, that she used to go for walks when she still lived in her old house. The theme was never lost, the stage was merely being set; the contemporatives in clauses 89 and 90 thus do not refer to reintroduced material but to continued material, the seventeen intervening clauses notwithstanding.[13]

This form of thematic identification is of course not available in the narrative texts. Other speakers have their own, regularly preferred methods of signaling theme; however, the use of reflection clauses (see example 2.10 in chapter 2) seems to be one of the most commonly used devices. Speaker 1 tends to introduce a theme in the clauses following a reflection clause, and to elaborate on this theme in following clause chains. For example, in clause 47, the speaker makes a reflection; in clauses 48 to 50, he introduces the theme; and in clauses 51 to 66, he elaborates on this theme:

(4.47)  (From text 1a)                                                  Mood

47.   {*Taamaattumik*      *ajoqit_*           *imaannaanngitsumik_*
      *taamaattumik*       *ajoqi-t*           *imaannaanngitsoq-mik*
      therefore            catechist-PL        ones.not.without.importance-
                                               INST

'And therefore the catechists who are not without importance'

      *qutsavissarai*              *nunatta_*                          IND
      *ullumikkut_/*

      *qutsavi-ssaq-gi-vai*        *nuna-tta*
      *ullumikkut*

      thank-FUT-have-3SG      SUBJ/3PL.OBJ.IND
      land-1PL.POS today

'our land should thank them today'

48. *aamma*    *tamakku*    *sulerujussuarsimasut_/*                    PART
    *aamma*    *tamakku*    *suli-rujussuaq-sima-sut*
    and        those        work-very much-PERF-3PL.PART
    'and they worked a lot, those ones'

49. *imaannaanngitsorujussuarmik_*         *sulisimasut_'*              PART
    *imaannanngitsoq-rujussuaq-mik*         *suli-sima-sut*
    ones.not.without.importance-           work-PERF-3PL.PART
    very.much-INST
    'they worked in a very important/meaningful/able way'

50. *kisianni_*    *pitsaviunngitsumik_*                                PART
    *pineqartarsimasut_*

    *kisianni*       *pitsak-vik-u-nngit-soq-mik*
    *pi-neqaq-saq-sima-sut*

    but             excellent-genuine-COP-NEG-PART-INST
    do-PASS-HAB-PERF-3PL.PART

    'but they have not been paid well/well taken care of'

    *aqutsisuninngaanniit*
    *aqutsisut-ninngaanniit*
    management-PL.ABL
    'by the management . . .'

51–66. they were moved on a whim
       they were given houses not yet built
       they had to build the houses themselves
       etc.

This segment of text is interesting for a number of reasons. In addition to clauses introducing the theme of this section, participials are used precisely where a new theme is introduced. The next use of a participial is after a reflection clause, in clause 68, with the introduction of a new theme. Within this thematic section (clauses 51–66), however, it is the contemporatives that predominate.

Speaker 4 also regularly uses reflection clauses (see clauses 1, 15, 27, 44, and 60; they are not repeated here); he also makes use of incorporated particles to repeat a theme:

(4.48) (From text 4)          Mood

29. . . . *Qaarusumminngaanniit*  *nuupput*

   *Saarlumut_*'          IND

   *Qaarusuk-minngaanniit*  *nuuC-vut*
   *Saarloq-mut*

   Qaarusuk-ABL     move-3PL.IND
   Saarloq-term

   '. . . they moved from Qaarusuk to Saarloq'

30. *taamaalillunilu,*         CT
   *taamaali-luni-lu*
   be.like.that-3SG.CT-and
   'and it was like this/in this way'

31. *Saarloq*   *inuttusiallappoq_*'   IND
   *Saarloq-o*  *inuttu-si-allag-voq*
   Saarloq-ABS have/be.people-INTRANS-increase-3SG.IND
   'Saarloq became more populated . . .'

Examples of this are found in clauses 4, 13, 24, etc., and in most cases are in the contemporative mood; they are never in the participial mood.

### 4.4.2.1 *The contemporative*

There are a number of systematic exceptions to regular switch-reference patterns in the use of the contemporative in West Greenlandic. These exceptions are noted by Fortescue (1991), Bergsland (1955), and others, and include most of the environments discussed separately below. Questions in the determination of same versus different subject may affect the identification of a contemporative clause as one with exceptional switch-referent marking. Some arise because of structural ambiguities, others from inclusive or overlapping subjects between the contemporative and the superordinate clauses, and still others from problems in interpreting clausal hierarchy.

Structural ambiguity arises with the contemporative because the transitive and intransitive forms of the contemporative are almost identical, the only exception being the third-person noncoreferent object. Other forms are structurally ambiguous, and depend on the context for interpretation (see table 4.3a). Example 4.49 illustrates this:

(4.49)  (From text 1a)                                        Mood
89.     . . . *toqusoqarpat*                                  COND
        *toqusoq-qaq-pat*
        dead.one-have-3NC.SG.COND
        '. . . when/if there is a dead one [When someone has died]'

90.     *toqusunik*          *ilisilluni_/*                   CT
        *toqusoq-nik*        *ilisi-luni*
        dead.one-PL.INST     bury-3SG.CT
        'he buries the dead ones'

91.     *kuisittoqassappat*                                   COND
        *kuisiC-toq-qaq-ssa-ppat*
        christen-NOMZ-have-FUT-3NC.SG.COND
        'when/if there is someone to be christened'

92.     *kuisillugit_/*                                       CT
        *kuisiC-lugit*
        christen-TRANS 3PL.OBJ.CT
        'he christens them . . .'

Clause 90 can be interpreted as marking either 3SG subject or 3SG coreferential object, especially since preceding clauses, all with *-luni* or *-lugu*, alternate between transitive and intransitive, but it is clear that the form must be interpreted as intransitive here, both from the context, especially given clause 92, and from the instrumental marking on its argument. The identity of form for coreferential subject or object, however, can be confusing in conversational speech and is a source of 'exceptional' subject noncoreference in contemporatives. This example also illustrates the question of clausal hierarchy (about which more below): the contemporatives have coreferent objects but not coreferent subjects with the immediately superordinate verb form, the conditional. The subjects of the contemporatives are, however, coreferential with those of the indicative of the intonational group (the boundaries of which are unclear).

Whether or not these are examples of subject coreference, they do not conflict with an interpretation based on thematic continuity. The clauses in example 4.49 list the duties of the catechists, a theme introduced by clause 79, 'it is true those ones have worked amazingly'. Thus, although the contemporatives in this part of the text do not repeat each other, they all support the same theme.

Of the contemporative clauses identified as clauses with subjects different than the clause to which they are subordinate, a number of them in fact involve inclusive subject forms (referential overlap, discussed below). West Greenlandic treats these as same subject forms. For example, of the eight object clauses with contemporative mood, the only three that are not same subject in fact show referential overlap (illustrated in examples 4.50–4.52):

| | | | Subject | Mood |
|---|---|---|---|---|
| (4.50) | (From text 1b) | | | |
| 122. | . . .qajat_ tassa_ | qajartortut | taamani | |
| | qajaq-t tassa | qajartoq-toq-t | taamani | |
| | kayak-PL that.is | row.kayak-PART.PART-PL | at.that.time | |

'. . . the kayaks, the kayak rowers, at that time, that is,'

| | | Subject | Mood |
|---|---|---|---|
| *eqqaamavara* | | 1SG | IND |
| *eqqaama-vara* | | | |
| remember.1SG.SUBJ/3SG.OBJ.IND | | | |
| 'I remember it' | | | |

| | | | Subject | Mood |
|---|---|---|---|---|
| 123. | *meeraalluta* | *upernaakkut_* | 1PL | CT |
| | *meeraq-u-luta* | *upernaaq-kkut* | | |
| | child-COP-1PL.CT | spring-VIA | | |

'when we were children in the spring . . .'

| | | Subject | Mood |
|---|---|---|---|
| (4.51) | (From text 1b) | Subject | Mood |
| 170. | . . . *eqqaamagiga* | 1SG | PART |
| | *eqqaama-giga* | | |

remember-1SG.SUBJ/3SG.OBJ.PART
'. . . I remember it'

171.   *Qaqortuminngaanniit*      *Narsamukarluta*          1PL       CT
       *Qaqortoq-minngaanniit*    *Narsaq-mukaq-luta*
       Qaqortoq-ABL              Narsaq-go.to-1PL.CT
       'we were going from Qaqortoq to Narsaq . . .'

(4.52)   (From text 4)                              Subject    Mood
88.    *. . . eqqaamasaqanngilanga,*                  1SG       IND
       *eqqaamasat-qaq-nngit-langa*
       memories-have-NEG-1SG.NEG.IND
       '. . . I don't have any memories'

89.    *ajorsa*              *pilluta*                  1PL       CT
       *ukiorsiorlunnitsinnit_}*

       *ajor-saq-0*          *pi-luta*
       *ukioq-sioq-lug-neq-tsinnit*

       be.bad-NOMZ-ABS     thing-1SG.PL.CT
       winter-be.out.in-bad-NOMZ-1PL.POS.ABL

       '[that] we had bad luck in our bad winters.'
       [i.e., 'I don't remember that we had actual hardship because of
       bad winters']

This inclusive interpretation of switch-reference in West Greenlandic is
also found in nonobject constructions:

(4.53)   (From text 4)                              Subject    Mood
13.    *{Taamaalillutalu_'*                            1PL       CT
       *taamaali-luta-lu*
       be.like.that-1PL.CT-and
       'And we were like that [it was like that for us]'

14.    *meeraaffinni*           *Saarlumi_*
       *meeraq-vik-nni*         *Saarloq-mi*
       child-place-1SG.POS.LOC   Saarloq-loc
       'in the place where I was a child, in Saarloq'

| *ajoqitut* | *sulivoq_* | *ukiorpassuit_}* | 3SG | IND |
|---|---|---|---|---|
| *ajoqi-tut* | *suli-voq* | *ukioq-passuaq-it* | | |
| catechist-EQ | work-3SG.IND | year-a lot-PL | | |

'he worked as a catechist for many years.'

These examples also show thematic continuity. The information in example 4.50 above is a repetition of clause 109 in the same text, 'when we were children'. Clause 171 in example 4.51 repeats the information from clause 163, 'we used to go from Qaqortoq to Narsaq'. Clause 13 in example 4.53 repeats, using an incorporated particle, the information in clause 11, 'he began to have to work as a catechist' (the speaker's use of incorporated particles and the contemporative mood generally entails a following clause, in this case in the indicative, which repeats previous information with semantically full lexical items). Finally, clause 89 in example 4.52 refers to clause 86, 'there used to be lots of Greenland seals', since clause 89 refers to the plenty to be had even in bad times.

Finally, speaker production issues, such as inarticulation, redefinition, change of thought in mid-sentence, run-on sentences, and so forth, may lead to atypical chains that affect the determination of same or different subject in contemporative clauses. In example 4.54 a particle, *ima*, is incorporated and the verb is technically an indicative but is semantically empty compared to the surrounding clauses; it is a filler that allows the speaker to further define, or redefine, his thought. The following contemporative should not be seen as dependent on the semantically empty indicative but as a temporal adverb clause clarifying the preceding causative clause and modifying the following one:

| (4.54) (From text 2) | Subject | | Mood | |
|---|---|---|---|---|
| 4. | {*Tassa* | *inersimasunngorama_* | 1SG | CAUS |
| | *tassa* | *inersimasoq-nngoq-gama* | | |
| | that.is | adult-become-1SG.CA | | |

'That is, when I became an adult'

| 5. | *imaappoq_* | 3SG | IND |
|---|---|---|---|
| | *imaaC-voq* | | |
| | be.like.this-3SG.IND | | |

'that means'

6.    18-19-*inik*            *ukioqarlunga_/*                    1SG        CT
      18-19-*nik*            *ukioq-qaq-lunga*
      18-19-PL.INST         year-have-1SG.CT
      'when I was eighteen or nineteen years old'

7.    *amutsivimmi*          *ilinniartunngornikuugama_}*        1SG        CAUS
      *amutsivik-mi*         *ilinniartoq-nngoq-nikuu-gama*
      shipyard-LOC          apprentice/student-become-PAST-1SG.CAUS
      'I became an apprentice in a shipyard.'

Although the contemporative in clause 6 modifies the following causative, it also repeats and continues the thematic information of clause 4.

In example 4.55 the speaker moves rapidly from one subject to another without overtly expressing the changes. If the contemporative in clause 58 is immediately dependent on the causative in clause 57 (which is marked for noncoreferential subject), then the two clauses have different subjects. If it is dependent on the indicative in clause 55, then the two clauses have same subjects. From a syntactic point of view, this piece of text is perfectly explainable within the traditional framework for understanding the contemporative. From a semantic point of view, however, the situation is less clear:

(4.55)   (From text 1a)                          Subject      Object      Mood
53.    {*Ajoqillu*            *taamani*
       *tassa_*              *palasillumi_*

       *ajoqi-t-lu*          *taamani*
       *tassa*               *palasi-t-lu-mi*

       catechist-PL.ABS-and   at.that.time
       that.is               priest-PL-and-sure
       'And the catechists at that time and of course the priests'

       *ingattammik*                  *ajoqit_*                  catechists     IND
       *nuutsinneqartarput_*          *nunaqarfinnut_*

       *ingattammik*                  *ajoqi-t*
       *nuuC-tit-neqaq-saq-put*       *nunaqarfik-t-nut*

especially                      catechist-PL
move-cause-PASS-HAB-     village-PL-PL.TERM
3PL.IND

'especially the catechists, they were moved to villages'

54.    *aperinagilluunniit*                      catechists    CT
       *aperi-nagit-luunniit*
       ask-3PL.OBJ.NEG.CT-or
       'without even asking them'

55.    *oqarfigisarpaat_*                 G.S.    catechists    IND
       *oqarfigi-saq-paat*
       say-HAB-3PL.SUBJ/3PL.OBJ.IND
       they (Greenland Steering) would say to them (catechists)

56.    "*Uunnga     nuussuutit!*"_                      2sg    IND
       *Uunnga     nuuC-ssaa-vutit*
       Over.here    move-FUT-2SG.IND
       '"Move over there!"'

57.    *taavalu     piumanngikkaangata*          catechists (3nc)    CAUS
       *taava-lu     piuma-nngit-gaangata*
       then-and    want-NEG-when(ever).3NC.PL.CAUS
       'and if/when they (catechists) didn't want to'

58.    *soraarsittarlugit_}*                      catechists    CT
       *soraarsit-saq-lugit*
       fire-HAB-3PL.OBJ.CT
       'they (Greenland Steering) would fire them (catechists).'

This section of text has already been discussed with respect to thematic continuity (see example 4.47) within its greater context. An interpretation of thematic rather than subject continuity for the contemporatives here is more than plausible.

These possibly same-subject cases aside, however, there are a clear different-subject contemporative forms that can be loosely grouped by some common characteristics; most share a number of these characteristics. Anomalous reference in contemporary constructions is found in clauses where the noncoreferent subject of a contemporative is possessed by or is the possessor of the subject of the superordinate; in cases with ellipsis in (or of) the superordinate clause; where one of the clauses is a reflection clause; where one of the clauses involves an incorporated particle or a dummy subject; or in cases where the subject of the contemporative is coreferent with the object of the superordinate. Many of these are comparable to Fortescue's list of environments in which anomalous reference is found (1991:56), which includes ellipsis, differing levels of passivity between the clauses, impersonal subjects of contemporative constructions, part/whole relationship between the subjects of the superordinate and the contemporative, an antecedent outside of the boundaries of the sentence, and contemporative object clauses with the affix *-sori* 'think'. I differ from Fortescue primarily with regard to the consideration of relative transitivity or passivity.

### Referential overlap

Cases in which the subject of one clause is the possessor of the subject of another clause, or the subjects of both clauses are possessed by the same person, are sometimes viewed as referential overlap.

| | | Subject | Object | Mood |
|---|---|---|---|---|
| (4.56) | (From text 1a) | | | |
| 3. | {*Uanga isikka* *isigilluaqqaalermata,* | my eyes | | CAUS |

*Uanga        isi-kka*
*isigi-lluaq-qqaaq-ler-mmata*

1SG        eye-1SG.POS.ABS/PL.POSM
see-well-first-begin-3NC.PL.CAUS

'When my eyes could see well [When my eyes first began to see well],'

| | | | | |
|---|---|---|---|---|
| 4. | *siutikkalu* | *tusaalluaqqaalerlutik__*} | | |
| | | my ears | | CT |

*siuti-kka-lu        tusaa-lluaq-qqaaq-ler-lutik*
ear-1SG.POS.ABS/    hear-well-first-begin-3PL.CT
PL.POSM-and

'and my ears could hear well [When my ears first began to hear well].'

(4.57)  (From text 1a)                          Subject    Object   Mood
94.     {*Imalu         akissarsiai*   3SG (catechists)              IND
        *suunngitsigaat_*

        *ima-lu          akissarsiaq-i*
        *su-nngit-tigi-vut*

        so-and          pay-3SG.POS.ABS
        what-COP-NEG-so(equative)-3PL.IND

        'and so his pay is very little'

95.     *uffa        ilinniartitsisutullu*
        *uffa        ilinniartitsisoq-tut-lu*
        even.if    teacher-EQ-and

        *aammalu    palasitut*                   3PL (catechists)     CT
        *suligaluarlutik_*}

        *aamma-lu          palasi-tut*
        *suli-galuaq-lutik*

        and-and   priest-EQ
        work-CONSEQ-3PL.CT

        'even if they are working as a teacher and as a priest'

In example 4.56 the speaker is using metaphoric language to refer to a
time in his childhood when he first began to remember things. He is the
possessor, not the subject, in both clauses. Both clauses are structurally
parallel, and the contemporative in clause 4 continues the theme of clause
3. In example 4.57 the singular possessor of the first clause is contrasted
with the plural subject of the second, although both the possessor of the
first and the subject of the second refer to the same entity, the 'catechists'.
The contemporative clause in clause 95 repeats information which has been
thematic in the previous groups of clauses (see example 4.49).

### Subject noncoreference and ellipsis

Noncoreference between a contemporative and a superordinate clause may
occur either because of the ellipsis of a clause overtly introducing the subject

of the following clauses, or because of the lack of overt introduction of this subject, as in example 4.58 (involving ellipsis of the ergative argument):

| (4.58) | (From text 2) | | Subject | Object | Mood |
|---|---|---|---|---|---|
| 32. | {*Eqqaamavaralu* | | 1SG | it | IND |
| | *eqqaama-vara-lu* | | | | |
| | remember-1SG.SUBJ/3SG.OBJ-and | | | | |
| | 'And I remember it' | | | | |

33.     *taamanikkut*     *saarulliit*     codfish     PART
*tunineqartartut_*

*taamani-kkut*     *saarullik-it*
*tuni-neqaq-saq-tut*

at.that.time-VIA     codfish-PL
sell-PASS-HAB-3PL.PART

'at that time the codfish used to be sold'

34.     *sumilluunniit_*     *niaquernagit}*     codfish     CT
*sumik-luunniit*     *niaquer-nagit*
what-or.even     take.head.off.(fish)-3PL.OBJ.NEG.CT
'without [them] even taking their heads off'

35.     *ammarnagilluunniit}}*     codfish     CT
*ammar-nagit-luunniit*
open.up-3PL.OBJ.NEG.CT-or.even
'or even opening them up.'

In example 4.58 the subject of the indicative clause is the speaker. It could be argued that because of the participial construction, the speaker has assumed, and not expressed, a superordinate construction in which the fishermen are the subject. The participial form would then indicate switch-subject, with 'codfish' as subject, while the following contemporatives would indicate same-subject, with 'fishermen' as subject. This involves some manipulation of the syntax, and does not recognize a dependency of the contemporatives in clauses 34 and 35 on the participial in clause 33. There is, however, very obvious thematic continuity as well as topic continuity across the clauses, however. (The assumption, rather than overt expression, of more than one subject is also clearly seen in example 4.55 above, although this is not due to ellipsis of a syntactic construction.)

In example 4.59 from the beginning of a text, the speaker has not yet decided how to say what he wishes to say. After some false starts, he produces a contemporative clause, followed by an indicative, but they are not directly related to each other. The contemporative takes up the topic of the preceding nominalization. This is a problem of speaker organization and production and not ellipsis, but the effect is similar:

|  |  | Subject | Object | Mood |
|---|---|---|---|---|
| (4.59) | (From text 1a) |  |  |  |

1. *Ullumi_*        *nunatsinni_*
   *pissusiusut_*

   *Ulloq-mi*        *nuna-tsinni*
   *pissuseq-u-soq-t*

   day-LOC        country-1PL.POS.LOC
   culture-COP-PART-PL

   {*uagut*        *meeraanitsinnut*
   *naleqqiullugu,*                                1PL                        CT

   *uagut*        *meeraaneq-tsinnut*
   *naleqqiup-lugu*
   1PL        childhood-1PL.POS.TERM
   compare-3SG.OBJ.CT

   'If (we) compare our way of life today in our country with our childhood'

2. *taamani*        *inuunermik*                it                        IND
   *allarujussuuvoq__}*

   *taamani*        *inuuneq-mik*
   *alla-rujussuuvoq*

   at.that.time        life-INST
   different-very.3SG.IND

   'at that time it was a very different life.'

If fronting can establish a topic or theme, then the fronting of 'our culture' here entails the use of the contemporative in clause 1. In general, however, the use of a contemporative as the first full clause is not expected at the beginning of a text.

Many instances in which a contemporative is not subordinate to an overt superordinate structure involve the contemporative apparently functioning as the indicative, or in the same way as the indicative; this is often explained as ellipsis, as in example 4.60:

|  |  |  | Subject | Object | Mood |
|---|---|---|---|---|---|
| (4.60) | (From text 3a) |  |  |  |  |

21.  {*Sulimi          soorlu          soorluluunniit_*

*suli-mi          soorlu          soorlu-luunniit*

yet-what.about   for.example   for.example-even

'Yet for example, for example it seems like'

| *70-it* | *inoritit* | 2SG | 70 | PART |
|---|---|---|---|---|
| *70-it* | *inor-gitit* |  |  |  |
| 70-PL | under-2SG.SUBJ/3NC.PL.OBJ.PART |  |  |  |

'you are just under seventy'

| 22. | *isikkut* | *isigalugu_}* | (1SG) | (it) | CT |
|---|---|---|---|---|---|
|  | *isi-kkut* | *isigi-lugu* |  |  |  |
|  | eye-VIA | see.well-3PL.OBJ.CT |  |  |  |

'seeing well through my eyes'

## Reflection clauses

In general, the speakers uses the indicative mood for reflection clauses in the texts. In text 1b the speaker makes repeated use of the participial in this function (see below for a more detailed discussion of this). There are, nevertheless, several examples of this in the contemporative:

|  |  | Mood |
|---|---|---|
| (4.61) | (From text 1b) |  |

210-212. therefore Grandfather used to say

"bid your eyes and ears to try to do well/use them well
'from those we can get something'

213.    *iluamik*                          *atorluarutsigit_*                    COND
*iluamik*                                 *ator-luaq-gutsigit*
   the.right.way/correct/well    use-well-1PL.SUBJ/3PL.OBJ.COND
   'if we use them well'

214.    *angeqimmata,*                                                          CAUS
   *ange-qi-mmata*
   big-INTNS-3NC.PL.CAUS
   'they are incredible'

215.    *annertoqimmata,*                                                       CAUS
   *annertu-qi-mmata*
   enormous-INTNS-3NC.PL.CAUS
   'they are incredible'

216.    *taama    oqarluaannarlunga"_}*                                         CT
   *taama    oqaq-luaq-innaq-lunga*
   this        say-well-just-1SG.CT
   'let me just say it in this way.'"

(4.62)  (From text 4)    Mood

90.    *{aamakku         avatinnguatsinni*
*aalisagarpassuit_'*

   *aamakku          avati-nnguaq-tsinni*
   *aalisagaq-passuit*

   [exclamation]        outside-little-1PL.POS.LOC
   fish-lots.of.PL

   'And all this fish right outside!'

91.    *suluppaakkat_'      eqqarsaatigalugit* CT
   *suluppaagaq-t       eqqarsaat-gi-lugit*
   redfish-PL               thought-have-3PL.OBJ.CT
   'redfish, [I] have thoughts about them'

92.  *suluppaakkat        taakku*                          IND
     *piniagaanerpaapput*

     *suluppaagaq-t        taakku*
     *pinia-gaq-a-nerpaa-vut*

     redfish-PL           those.ABS
     hunt-PASS.PART-3SG.POS-SUP-3PL.IND

     'those redfish were most hunted . . .'

In both examples the contemporatives very simply comment on the theme of the preceding text. Thus, in example 4.62, clause 91 refers to clause 90, and in example 4.61, clause 216 shows wide referential scope over the preceding clauses, as discussed in Rhodes (1995:8).

### Incorporated particles

There are a number of incorporated particles with various verb moods, including the contemporative; clause 30 in example 4.48 above was one such. Example 4.63 illustrates the use of an incorporated particle, *taamaa-* 'to be like that', in clause 29, with a subject different from the superordinate clause:

(4.63)  (From text 3a)                          Subject     Mood

29.  *Emilliannguup        panimma*
     *Emillia-nnguaq-p    paniq-ma*
     Emilia-DIM-REL       daughter-1SG.POS.ABS
     'Emily my daughter'

     *taamaallunga*                              1SG         CT
     *taamaa-lunga*
     be.like.that-1SG.CT
     'while I am like that'

30.  *oqarfiginikuuaanga_/*                      3SG         IND
     *oqarfigi-nikuu-vaanga*
     say.to-PAST-3SG.SUBJ/1SG.OBJ.IND
     'said to me'

'While I am like that' in clause 29 refers to the immediately preceding clause, in which the speaker says, 'I am really quite tired of hearing that,

that I look good'; the theme of the section of text from clauses 22 to 34 is indeed that the speaker is tired of being told that she looks good.

### Subject noncoreference and general, unspecified, and dummy subjects

In example 4.64 the subject of the contemporative clauses is an unspecified human, a fisherman in general, whereas the subject of the stative indicatives is a dummy 3SG:

| (4.64) | (From text 2) | | Subject | Mood |
|---|---|---|---|---|
| 110. | {*Taamanikkut_* | *ipuataarluni* | 3SG | CT |
| | *Taamani-kkut* | *ipuataar-luni* | | |
| | at.that.time-VIA | row/pull.oars.through-3SG.CT | | |
| | 'In those days, rowing' | | | |
| 111. | *uernataarluni* | | 3SG | CT |
| | *uernga-ataaq-luni* | | | |
| | sleepy-entirely-3SG.CT | | | |
| | 'when one is really sleepy' | | | |
| 112. | *sussaanngitsorsuuvoq_'* | | 3sg | IND |
| | *sussaanngit-soq-suaq-u-voq* | | | |
| | a.bit.rotten/bad-PART-big-COP-3SG.IND | | | |
| | 'it was really bad' | | | |
| 113. | *ajorluinnarpoq_}* | | 3SG | IND |
| | *ajor-luinnaq-voq* | | | |
| | not.good-complete-3SG.IND | | | |
| | 'it was absolutely awful.' | | | |

Fortescue (1984:148; 1991:66) explains this in terms of level of transitivity. In sentences in which the superordinate clause is more passive or less agentive than the subordinate, third-person coreferential marking is used, as is the contemporative. He notes that one of the functions of the contemporative is the depersonalization or despecifization of the subject, especially in the transitive, where only the object is marked pronominally on the verb. One might argue that this is also one of the functions of the passive, and therefore also a sign of lower transitivity. Fortescue (1991:67) also notes that impersonal (contemporative) clauses are not obviously high in transitivity, but he nevertheless views them as still more transitive than their superordinate verb. This explanation can also be applied to example 4.58, in which the contemporatives are more active than the participial. The explanation seems contradictory: why should coreferentiality be associated with a verb form that specifically depersonalizes subjects? Furthermore, there are a number of systematic exceptions, including the contemporatives expressing temporal setting (see below).

In example 4.65 the verb in clause 98 is formed by incorporating the empty particle ima and adding a number of modifying affixes indicating speed. The clause was variously translated as 'it was not that easy' by the transcriber and as 'in a short period of time' by P. Langgård (personal communication). The implication is that the nets had to be untangled quickly and this was not an easy task; there are connotations missed in the English translation:

| (4.65) | (From text 2) | | Subject | Mood |
|---|---|---|---|---|
| 96. | . . . *piniuserisarpugut_/* | | 1PL | IND |
| | *piniut-leri-saq-vugut* | | | |

equipment-deal.with-HAB-1PL.IND
'. . . we had to deal with the equipment [i.e., make it ready to use]'

| 97. | *aammami_* | *imak_* | 3C.PL | CAUS |
|---|---|---|---|---|
| | *ilarussimasartorsuugamik* | | | |

*aamma-mi*                     *imak*
*ilaguC-sima-saq-soq-suaq-u-gamik*

and-INTNS                     like.this
be.tangled-PERF-HAB-PART-big-COP-3C.PL.CAUS

'and they were usually very tangled [it could be they might have to be untangled]'

| 98. | *imaalitsiaannarlugit* | *aamma_/* | (3SG) | CT |
|---|---|---|---|---|
| | *imaali-tsiaq-innaq-lugit* | *aamma* | | |
| | be.like.this-a.little-only- | and | | |
| | 3PL.OBJ.CT | | | |

'and in a short period of time/soon/fast'

99.  *naammassineq*           *ajornartaramik_}*        3C.PL      CAUS
     *naammassi-neq-0*         *ajornar-saq-gamik*
     accomplish/finish-        impossible-HAB-3C.PL.CAUS
     NOMZ-ABS
     'they were usually impossible to finish'

The subject of the indicative clause 96 is 'we'. The subject of the causative clauses is 'nets'. That of the contemporative is unspecified, and its object is 'nets'. The contemporative may be interpreted as the same subject as the superordinate, the indicative. However, both causatives are marked for coreferentiality, and neither is coreferential with the indicative; and the contemporative in clause 98 directly modifies clause 99. Thus, subject coreferentiality is already compromised in this clause chain, whether or not the subject of the contemporative is 'we' or a more general one.

Both examples above are easily explainable as instances of thematic continuity. In example 4.64, clause 111 is almost a direct repetition of clause 102, 'we begin to get sleepy'; in fact, clauses 103 to 113 are an expanded repetition of the text in clauses 100 to 102. In example 4.65, clause 98 is a further explanation of the work involved in dealing with nets, already brought up in clauses 89–97.

Example 4.66 illustrates thematic continuity despite the use of a dummy subject:

(4.66)  (From text 3a)                                     Subject    Mood
93.  {*uani_*                *allaanermit_'*           (NOM)
     *uani*                  *alla-u-neq-mit*
     here                    different-COP-NOMZ-ABL
     'Here it is different'

94.  *aneerfeqaranilu_/*                                   dummy      CT
     *aneer-vik-qaq-nani-lu*
     go.for.walk-place-have-3SG.NEG.CT-and
     'there is no place to walk . . .'

As mentioned above, the lack of subject marking on transitive contemporatives despecifies subjects. Transitive (object) inflection on verbs with essentially intransitive meaning refers to the subject (see the following section for more details); formally, the subject is a dummy subject. The semantic subject (marked inflectionally as the object) should then be coreferent with the superordinate subject. This is not the case in my data (see examples 4.46 and 4.72). The part of text that 4.66 is taken from was explained at length in example 4.46 above. Based on the previous text, one might expect a participial rather than a contemporative here, depending on what constitutes thematic continuity or shift. If the speaker is contrasting her ability to take walks in her old and new homes, then one might expect a participial; if instead this continues her answer to the interviewer's question in clause 71, 'do you go out for walks?', then the contemporative is indicating thematic continuity. Such an argument supports but does not demonstrate that thematic continuity is a relevant factor in the distribution of the contemporative and participial moods.

### Subject-object coreference

Within the literature, it is acknowledged that the contemporative can be used in cases of coreference of subordinate object and superordinate subject, as in example 4.67:

| (4.67) (From text 3b) | | Subject | Object | Mood |
|---|---|---|---|---|
| 172. | . . . *angutit_'*     *sanavaat'* | men | | IND |
| | *angut-t*   *sana-vaat* | | | |
| | man-PL   work-3PL.SUBJ/3.OBJ.IND | | | |
| | '. . . men worked on it' | | | |
| 173. | *tassa*     *tamaasa* | | | |
| | *akilerlugit,* | mother | men | CT |
| | *tassa*     *tamaq-asa* | | | |
| | *aki-ler-lugit* | | | |
| | that.is    the.whole/all-3PL.O | | | |
| | pay-provide-3PL.OBJ.CT | | | |
| | 'that is she paid them all . . .' | | | |

In some cases, however, it appears as if there is also object-to-object coreference. In example 4.68, this is complicated by the use of object incorporation into the verb:

(4.68)  (From text 3b)                              Subject    Object    Mood

178.    . . . *Ikannga*           *akitsinniit*
        *siorarsuarnit*

        *ikannga*                 *akitsi-nniit*
        *sioraq-suaq-nit*

        from.over.there    high.up-from.ABL
        piece.of.sand-big-PL.AB

        *taasartakkatsinnik*                          1PL       (sand)    CAUS
        *taa-saq-saq-gatsinnik*
        call-HAB-HAB-1PL.SUBJ/3SG.OBJ.CAUS
        'from the place we used to call "old sand" [big sand]'

179.    *sioqqiartitsilluni*                          mother    (sand)    CT
        *sioqqiar-tit-si-luni*
        fetch.sand-cause-INTRANS-3SG.CT
        'she made some people get sand' or 'she made sand
        be fetched'

The contemporative in examples 4.67 and 4.68 straightforwardly continue
the themes of preceding clauses. In example 4.67, clause 172 has its antecedent in clauses 167 'it was wonderful that my mother was able to pay for it
all herself, and all the workers' and clause 169 'she paid all the workers'. In
example 4.68, clause 177 has its antecedent in clause 176 'sand could not
be used for cement, the sand of our land').

## The contemporative and simultaneous time

Finally, there is at least one environment that produces systematic exceptions
to both the traditional explanation of switch-reference and an explanation
based on thematic continuity, where the contemporative indicates simultaneous time. In fact, it should not be viewed as an exception, since the
primary function of the contemporative is to indicate contemporaneous
time with the indicative, regardless of subject coreference or lack thereof.
This is not fulfilled by the participial, and thematic shift can be indicated
in other ways. Examples 4.69 and 4.70 illustrate this:

| (4.69) (From text 1a) | | Subject | Object | Mood |
|---|---|---|---|---|
| 20. | {*umiaasat*   *aalisariutigisarpaat_/* | 3PL | boats | IND |
| | *umiaq-asaq-t*   *aalisariuti-gi-saq-vaat* | | | |
| | *umiaq-*   fishing.vessel-have-HAB-3PL. | | | |
| | resemble-PL   SUBJ/3PL.OBJ.IND | | | |
| | 'They used to use small boats as fishing vessels' | | | |

| 21. | *ukiorlu naallugu* | dummy | winter | CT |
|---|---|---|---|---|
| | *ukioq-0-lu*   *naa-llugu* | | | |
| | winter-ABS-and   be.finished-3SG.OBJ.CT | | | |
| | 'and all winter long' | | | |

| 22. | *qajaq*   *atorluarneqaqaaq_}* | kayak | | IND |
|---|---|---|---|---|
| | *qajaq-0*   *ator-lluaq-neqaq-qi-voq* | | | |
| | kayak-ABS   use-well-PASS-INTNS-3SG.IND | | | |
| | the kayak is very much used [i.e., well used]. | | | |
| | 'the kayak is very much used.' | | | |

| (4.70) (From text 4) | | Subject | Object | Mood |
|---|---|---|---|---|
| 17. | *... siullermik_   seminariami* | | | |
| | *atuaqataavoq* | 3SG | | IND |
| | *siullermik*   *seminaria-mi* | | | |
| | *atuaqat-u-voq* | | | |
| | at.first seminary-LOC | | | |
| | schoolmate-COP-3SG.IND | | | |
| | '... the first time he went to the seminary (teacher's school)' | | | |

| 18. | *ima*   *kursuserpoq* | 3SG | | IND |
|---|---|---|---|---|
| | *ima*   *kursus-er-voq* | | | |
| | like   course-have.a.course-3SG.IND | | | |
| | 'like to take courses' | | | |

| 19. | *maannakkutoorlugu_'* | dummy | | CT |
|---|---|---|---|---|
| | *maanna-kkut-tooq-lugu* | | | |
| | now-VIA-like-3SG.OBJ.CT | | | |
| | 'it would be called now ...' | | | |

This is even more obvious in example 4.71, in which the contemporative is either immediately dependent on the preceding conditional, which itself is the temporal clause, or is codependent with it. The contemporative does have the same subject, 'father', as the superordinate indicative, but not with the conditional:

|  |  |  | Subject | Mood |
|---|---|---|---|---|
| (4.71) | (From text 4) |  |  |  |
| 71. | {*taamanikkut* | *tassa,* | father | IND |

*nersusaasorujorujoruuussuuvoq*

*taamani-kkut     tassa*

*nersor-saq-u-soq-ruju-ruju-rujussuaq-u-voq*

at.that.time          that.is

praise-PASS.PART-COP-PART-very-very-very.much-COP-3SG.IND

'At that time he was very, very, very much praised'

*ataataga,*
*ataata-ga*
father-1SG.ABS
'my father'

| 72. | *maannakkuusuuppat* | it | COND |
|---|---|---|---|

*maanna-kkut-u-soq-u-ppat*

now-VIA-COP-PART-COP-3NC.SG.COND

'if it were today/now'

| 73. | *tusaamasanngorsimagaluarluni_}* | father | CT |
|---|---|---|---|

*tusaamasaq-nngor-sima-galuaq-luni*

famous-become-PERF-CONSEQ-3SG.CT

'he would have been very popular.'

One of the ways of expressing temporal relations with the contemporative involves the use of the causative/agentive affix *-tit-* with the transitive inflections (this affix indeed requires transitive inflection). In this case, 'the formal object marked on the contemporative inflection indicates the subject of the underlying verb if intransitive or its object if transitive . . .' (Fortescue 1984:57), the underlying verb being the verb without the affix:

| (4.72) | (From text 4) | | Subject | Object | Mood |
|---|---|---|---|---|---|
| 82. | {*Taava_* | *upernariartortillugu,* | 3SG | | CT |
| | *taava* | *upernar-giartor-tit-lugu* | | | |
| | then | become.spring-go.to.do-CAUS-3SG.OBJ.CT | | | |
| | 'Then when spring came' | | | | |

| 83. | *piniagassat* | *saqqummeriartortarput_'* | animals | | IND |
|---|---|---|---|---|---|
| | *piniagassat* | *saqqummer-giartor-saq-vut* | | | |
| | hunting.animals.PL.ABS | | | | |
| | | come.out-more.and.more-HAB-3PL.IND | | | |
| | 'the hunting animals used to come out more and more . . .' | | | | |

Another example of this is found in example 4.46, clause 91. Per Langgård (personal communication) believes that such expressions show some form of subject control, so that in the above example, the hunting animals would have had something to do with the arrival of spring. These constructions have been semilexicalized with the meaning 'while', reflecting the temporal function of the verb mood.

Many of the examples above have involved dummy subjects in contemporative expressions of simultaneous time. There are also examples in the texts involving simultaneous or sequential time with semantically full subjects. In example 4.73 the speaker uses contemporatives before he has satisfactorily established the theme:

| (4.73) | (From text 1b) | Subject | Mood |
|---|---|---|---|
| 182-185. | whenever we were with Grandfather | | |
| | I remember it | | |
| | I really remember it in those days | | |
| | 'Henry, Grandfather, Grandfather' | | |

| 185. | *ullaakkut_* | *tamatta* | 1PL | CAUS |
|---|---|---|---|---|
| | *iteraangatta_* | | | |
| | *ullaaq-kkut* | *tamaq-tta* | | |
| | *iter-gaangatta* | | | |
| | morning-VIA | the.whole/all-1PL | | |
| | wake.up-whenever.1PL.CAUS | | | |
| | 'in the morning all of us together would wake up' | | | |

186.    *tiitoreerluta_/*                              1PL      CT
           *tii-toq-reer-luta*
           tea-drink-already-1PL.CT
           'when we had already drunk tea'

187.    *taava*            *inimut*                     1PL      CT
           *iserluta_'*

           *taava*            *ini-mut*
           *iser-luta*

           then              room-TERM
           enter-1PL.CT

           'then [when] we entered/came into the room'

           *Ittup*            *issia_*
           *Ittu-p*          *issia [vik-minut]*
           Grandfather-REL     chair-3C.SG.POS.TERM
           'Grandfather to his chair'

188.    *pattagissaminut*   *ingikkuni_/*         Grandfather    COND
           *pattagiaq-minut*   *igiC-guni*
           piano-3C.SG.       sit.down-3C.SG.COND
           POS.TERM
           'if he sat down at the piano'

189.    *taava_*             *inersimasut_*
           *taava*              *inersimasoq-t*
           then              adult-PL
           'then the adults'

           *nalaasaarfimmut issiavikuluunullu*      3PL adults    CT
           *issaallutik*

           *nalaasaarfik-mut issiavik-kulooq-nut-lu*
           *isser-a-lutik*

           couch-TERM       arm.chair-big-PL.TERM-and
           sit-PL-3PL.CT

           'when/while sitting down on the couch and in armchairs'

190.   *uagut*            *meeqqat*          1PL children        CT
       *natermut*         *ingilluta_'*

       *uagut*            *meeraq-t*
       *nateq-mut*        *ingiC-luta*

       1PL                child-PL
       ground-TERM        sit.down-1PL.CT

       'we children sitting down on the ground'

191.   *Taava*            *Ittup*            Grandfather         IND
       *qinnutinnguaq*    *atuartarpaa_/*

       *taava*            *Ittu-p*
       *qinnut-nnguaq-0*  *atuar-saq-vaa*

       then               Grandfather-REL
       prayer-little-ABS   read-HAB-3SG.SUBJ/3SG.OBJ.IND

       'then Grandfather would read a little prayer . . .'
       (see also clauses 189–198)

199.   *. . . Taamaalilluta ulloq*                    1PL       IND
       *aallartittarparput_}*

       *taamaali-luta*    *ulloq-0*
       *aallartit-saq-varput*

       like.that-1PL.CT   day-ABS
       begin-HAB-1PL.SUBJ/3SG.OBJ.IND

       '. . . and that is how we began the day.'

Note especially the switch from all-inclusive 1pl subjects of the contemporatives from clauses 186 to 187, to the 3pl subject 'adults' and 1pl subject 'we children' in the contemporative clauses 189 and 190. The latter two are dependent on the following indicative in clause 191, whose subject is the 3sg 'Grandfather'. Other examples with semantically full subjects and illustrative of contemporaneous or sequential time are found in text 1b, clauses 191–192, 200–219, and text 4, clauses 78–83. In general, an interpretation of thematic continuity should not be forced on these instances of the contemporative. It may be that the theme is in some way indicated in example 4.73 by both the temporal adverb 'in the morning' and the causative phrase 'when we would all wake up' in clause 185. Clauses 186 and 187 are certainly thematic within the clause chain. However, the use of the contemporative here is really an instance of its primary purpose, to indicate contemporal or sequential action.

### 4.4.2.2 *The participial*

Whereas contemporatives account for roughly one-fourth of all the clauses in a text, participials never account for more than one-seventh, with considerable variation in frequency across the texts. This variation includes both frequency in actual use of the participial and frequency in number of anomalous cases of coreference. Of all the speakers, for example, the speaker of texts 1a and 1b deviates the most from the canonical use of the participial, as described in the standard grammars. Text 1a is noteworthy because of the high proportion of participials that are interpretable as same-subject constructions. As with contemporatives, questions of structural ambiguity, partial overlap, and clausal hierarchy affect the interpretation of same or different subject between two clauses.

One of the most frequent sources of confusion with the use of participials is the morphological identity between third-person participials and nominalizations with the participially based nominalizing suffix *-soq*. The speaker of texts 3a and 3b uses many nominalized forms including nominalizations with the suffixes *-soq* and *-neq*, far more frequently than do other speakers; these nominalizers are illustrated in example 4.74:

(4.74)  (From text 3a)                                           Mood/NOMZ

25.    . . . *tassami_*              *taanna*                        NOMZ
       *isikkuminarnersuara_'*
       *tassa-mi*                    *taanna*
       *isi-kkuminar-neq-suaq-ga*

       that.is-INTNS                 that.one
       eyes-be.good.for-NOMZ-big-1SG.POS.ABS

       '. . . that is, my being someone who is good to look at'

|  |  |  |
|---|---|---|
| *tusakataavittarpara,* | *ilaa_/* | IND |
| *tusakataavittaq-vara* | *ilaa* | |
| be.quite.tired.of.hearing- | you.know | |
| 3SG.SUBJ/3SG.OBJ.IND | | |
| 'I get really quite tired of hearing, you know' | | |

26.   *pingaartumik*      *peqqippallaarneq*        NOMZ

        *ajorama*            *massakkut*             CAUS

        *pingaartumik*      *peqqiC-vallaar-neq-0*

        *ajoq-gama*          *massakkut*

        especially          healthy-so.much-NOMZ-ABS

        be.bad-1SG.CAUS     now

        'especially as I am not so very healthy now'

        *angalaniarnikkut_/*                 NOMZ

        angala-niaq-neq-kkut

        walk-FUT-NOMZ-VIA

        'when walking . . .'

The use of *-neq* nominalizations, which are unambiguously nominal, suggests the possibility that many of her *-soq* forms are nominal rather than verbal as well. This is further complicated by an additional function of the participial morpheme as a marker of relativization. In example 4.75 the form is multiply ambiguous:

(4.75)   (From text 3a)

108.    {*Taanna*     *eqqaamavara,*

       *taanna*      *eqqaama-vara*

       that         remember-1SG.SUBJ/3SG.OBJ.IND

       'I remember that one'

109.    *qajaasoq_*           *ulloq*      *taanna_/*

       *qajaa-soq*           *ulloq-0*    *taanna*

       die.in.kayak-3SG.PART    day-ABS    that.one

       or PART.ABS

       'he died by kayak that day . . .'

*or* 'who died by kayak that day . . .'
*or* 'the one who died by kayak that day . . .'

The ambiguity that arises from several possible ways of interpreting a text is particularly important in oral texts, where data do not necessarily conform to well-formed, completed clause structures, as in example 4.76:

(4.76)  (From text 1a)

23.    {*Tassalu        illoqarfimmi_      palasi_            qallunaaq_*
       *tassa-lu        illoqarfik-mi      palasi-0          qallunaaq-0*
       then-and        town-LOC          priest-ABS        Dane-ABS
       'and in the town the priest a Dane'

24.    (*kisianni       kalaallisut       oqaluttoq*)
       *kisianni       kalaallisut       oqaluk-soq*
       but            Greenlandic      speak-3SG.PART
       '(but he spoke Greenlandic)' or '(but who spoke Greenlandic)'

25.    *taavalu        niuertoq                          qallunaaq*
       *taava-lu       niuertoq-0                        qallunaaq-0*
       then-and       trader/colonial.chief-ABS        Dane-ABS
       'and then the trader, a Dane'

26.    (*qallunaatuinnaq        oqaluttoq*),
       *qallunaatut-innaq       oqaluk-soq*
       Danish-only             speak-3SG.PART
       '(he only spoke Danish)' or '(who only spoke Danish)'

27.    *niuertussat_          napparsimavimmi       nakorsaq_*
       *niviarsiat_*

       *niuertoq-ssaq-t       napparsimavik-mi      nakorsaq-0*
       *niviarsiaq-t*

       trader-FUT-PL         hospital-LOC          doctor-ABS
       nurse-PL

       'the traders in training, the doctor in the hospital, the nurses'

| *atuarfimmi* | *ilinniartitsisoq* | *qallunaaq_/* |
|---|---|---|
| *atuarfik-mi* | *ilinniartitsisoq-0* | *qallunaaq-0* |
| school-LOC | teacher-ABS | Dane-ABS |

'the teacher in the school, a Dane'

28.
| *(qallunaatuinnaq* | *oqaluttut)}* |
|---|---|
| *qallunaatut-innaq* | *oqaluk-sut* |
| Danish-only | speak-3PL.PART |

'(they only spoke Danish)' or '(who only spoke Danish).'

29.
| *{Tassa* | *taamani* | *qallunaat* | *taama* | *ikitsigipput_}* |
|---|---|---|---|---|
| *tassa* | *taamani* | *qallunaaq-t* | *taama* | *ikit-tigi-vut* |
| that.is | at.that.time | Dane-PL | just | |

few/not.many-so(equative)-3PL.IND

'That is, in those days there were not so many Danes.'

This example illustrates the not unusual feature of oral discourse of a series of clauses very loosely related as a list; in this case, the final summary in clause 29 is intonationally separate. The participial clauses 24, 26, and 28 are all intonationally parenthetical in an intonational group that has no independent verb form, unless the noun *qallunaaq* 'Dane' is understood as a predicate noun in a zero-copula construction. M. Fortescue (personal communication) states that zero-copulas are not a feature of Greenlandic; the noun *qallunaaq* would therefore have to be explained as an apposition. This section of text can be understood as a list of the types of Danes in towns, and the participials are best interpreted as locally dependent on the preceding predicate or appositional noun, in which case they clearly have the same subject as their head. If they are locally dependent, and they follow their superordinate, they show very local thematic shifts, as I showed in section 4.4.2.

The immediately following clauses 30 and 31 also form an intonational group without an independent clause:

| (4.77) (From text 1a) | | Subject | Mood |
|---|---|---|---|
| 30. | *{Taavalu atorfillit* | Greenlanders | (PART) |
| | *kalaallit_* | | |

*Taava-lu     atorfik-lik-t*
*kalaalleq-t*

then-and    position-provided.with-PL
Greenlander-PL

'And then the Greenlanders who had a job'

31.     *saffiorfimmi_*          *allaffimmi*     Greenlanders     PART
        *ikittunnguit*           *sulisut_}*

        *saffiorfik-mi*          *allaffik-mi*
        *ikit-toq-nnguaq-it*     *suli-soq-t*

        smithy-LOC               office-LOC
        few-NOMZ-DIM-PL          work-3PL.PART or PART-PL

'in the smithy, in the office they were few workers.'

Finally, as with the contemporatives, questions of sentence structure, hierarchy, and dependence have implications for the interpretation of the participials as same- or different-subject constructions. In example 4.78 the question is whether clause 183 is dependent on clause 184, or whether 184 is merely a repetition of 183 and 183 is the clause for which 182 is the object. If the former, then the participial has the same subject as its superordinate; if the latter, then it does not:

(4.78)  (From text 1b)                                          Subject     Mood
182.    {*Tassa     Ittukkunniikkaagatta,*                      Grandfather  CAUS
        *tassa      Ittu-kkut-niit-gaan-gatta*
        that.is     Grandfather-family-be.by-whenever-1PL.CAUS
        'Whenever we were with Grandfather'

183.    *eqqaamagiga,*                                          1SG          PART
        *eqqaama-giga*
        remember-1SG.SUBJ/3SG.OBJ.PART
        'I remember it'

184.    *eqqaamaqaara          taamani_*                        1SG          IND
        *eqqaama-qi-vara       taamani*

remember-INTNS-        at.that.time
1SG.SUBJ/3SG.OBJ.IND

'I really remember it in those days . . .'

These complications notwithstanding, there are examples of anomalous reference in different environments, including those with differences in levels of passivity, those with reflection clauses, and subject-object coreference. There are some important differences between the contemporatives and the participials, however. For example, whereas incorporated particles are readily declined in the contemporative mood, there are no examples of incorporated particles in the participial in anything but third-person form (singular or plural), as in clause 39 of text 3a, *imaattooq*. There are therefore no clear instances of incorporated particles with participial mood and subject coreference. Furthermore, while a dummy subject in the contemporative might be expected to require explanation, because of the implication of subject coreference with the use of the contemporative, the same is not true of a participial form with a dummy subject. Whereas one of the most important functions of the contemporative is specifically to denote an action or state contemporaneous with that of a superordinate verb, the analogously important function of the participial is to serve as a relativizer or nominalizer. There are also secondary functions of the participial that will affect the opacity of the link between participials and switch-reference, such as its required use as complements in certain constructions, regardless of same or different subject, notably with verbs of elocution (Fortescue 1984:42). Examples of this are rare in modern Greenlandic, but they are still found (a possible example is in text 3a, clauses 7–8; however, the indicative and the participial in this example have different subjects and therefore do not conclusively show the motivation for the use of the participial).

### Subject coreference

In example 4.79 all but the three middle clauses (172–174) have coreferent subjects; clause 171 involves partial overlap. Clause 170 shows anomalous coreference:

|  |  | Subject | Mood |
|---|---|---|---|
| (4.79) | (From text 1b) |  |  |
| 169. | {(*Ataasiarlunga* | 1SG | CT |

*ataasiar-lunga*
do.once-1SG.CT
'(I did it once [i.e., one time]'

170. *eqqaamagiga*                                                1SG      PART
     *eqqaama-giga*
     remember-1SG.SUBJ/3SG.OBJ.PART
     'I remember it'

171. *Qaqortuminngaanniit*     *Narsamukarluta*        1PL      CT
     *Qaqortoq-minngaanniit*   *Narsaq-mukaq-luta*
     Qaqortoq-ABL           Narsaq-go.to-1PL.CT
     'we were going from Qaqortoq to Narsaq'

172. *tikaagulliit*         *marluk_/*
     *tikaagullik-it*     *marluk*
     lesser.rorqual-PL   two
     '[there were] two lesser rorquals'

173. *pujortuleeraq*        *kaajallallugu_'*        (3PL)     CT
     *pujortuleeraq-0*    *kaajallaC-lugu*
     motor.boat-ABS     circle-3SG.OBJ.CT
     'they were circling the motor boat'

174. *pisseqattaartut_/*  3PL                         PART
     *pissiC-qattaar-sut*
     jump-again.and.again-3PL.PART
     'jumping again and again/the whole time'

175. *assut*    *alutornartut_/*                 3PL     PART
     *assut*    *alutor-naq-sut*
     very    breathtaking/moving-PL/beautiful-be.such.that-3PL.PART
     '[they were] very breathtaking/beautiful'

176. *eqqaamagaarakku*                        1SG     CAUS
     *eqqaama-ngaar-gakku*
     remember-well-1SG.SUBJ/3NC.SG.OBJ.CAUS
     'I remember it well'

177.   *taamani*        *puiorneq*        *ajorpara_)}*              1SG        IND
       *taamani*        *puior-neq*       *ajor-vara*
       at.that.time     forget-NOMZ       not.able.to-1SG.
                                          SUBJ/3SG.OBJ.IND

       'I can't forget that time.)'

*Ataasiarlunga* in clause 169 refers back to previous text, in which the speaker says he used to go from Qaqortoq to Narsaq; this is repeated in clause 171. The indicative and the causative in clauses 177 and 176, respectively, are both first-person singular subject forms, as is the participial in line 170. (The contemporative in line 173 refers to the whales, not the speaker, circling the boat, and is therefore not coreferential with the indicative clauses but rather with the phrase in line 172.) The forms in lines 174 and 175 are ambiguous and can be interpreted as participials or as nominal forms. Of interest is the participial in clause 170, whose subject is coreferential with the superordinate clause 169, and also with the causative and the indicative in clauses 175 and 176, lest it be argued that a contemporative (clause 169) is not superordinate to a participial (clause 170).

Example 4.80 illustrates not only anomalous coreference but also thematic shift, regardless of the coreference or lack thereof of the subject:

(4.80)   (From text 1b)                        Topic/Theme     Mood
141-146.   visits to Grandfather in the summer           visits

147.   {*Eqqaamagiga*     *tassa*     *taamani*     *Ittu_'*              PART
       *eqqaama-giga*     *tassa*     *taamani*     *Ittu-0*
       remember-1SG.      that.is     at.that.time  Grandfather-ABS
       SUBJ/3SG.OBJ.PART
       'I remember Grandfather at that time'

147-158.   Grandfather giving out chewing gum to the kids chewing gum

159.   {*Tassa*     *eqqaamalluariga*                               PART
       *tassa*      *eqqaama-lluaq-giga*
       that.is      remember-well-1SG.SUBJ/3SG.OBJ.PART
       'I remember it very well'

159-181.   trips to Narsaq                               Narsaq trips

182.     {*tassa     Ittukkunniikkaagatta,*
         *tassa     Ittu-kkut-niit-gaan-gatta*
         that.is    Grandfather-family-be.by-whenever-1PL.CAUS
         'whenever we were with Grandfather'

183.     *eqqaamagiga,*                                          PART
         *eqqaama-giga*
         remember-1SG.SUBJ/3SG.OBJ.PART
         'I remember it'

184-199.   how we began the day                          morning ritual

The participials clearly occur at topical and thematic boundaries. In fact, speaker 1's texts show an interesting development in his use of the participial, from frequent to rather infrequent use, and from a more specific, almost clause-level, to a more general, paragraph-level marker of switch-topic/ theme.

Other very clear examples of the use of participials at topic or thematic boundaries include example 3.31 from the previous chapter and the immediately following text; for brevity, I repeat only the last clauses of 3.31:

(4.81)   (From text 2)                              Topic/Theme     Mood
30.      ...(*eqaluit       inaannik*                    house        IND
         *taasartagarput*),

         *eqaluk-it         ini-annik*
         *taasar-saq-varput*

         char-PL            place-3PL.POS.INST
         call-HAB-1PL.SUBJ/3SG.OBJ.IND

         '... (we used to call it the place of char)'

31.      *tassa      ima         tarajorterivittut*        house        IND
         *atoqqaarsimavoq_/        taanna_*}

         *tassa      ima         tarajorterivik-tut*
         *ator-qqaaq-sima-voq      taanna*

         that.is     you.know      salting.place-EQ
         use-first-PERF-3SG.IND     that.one

'like, you know, it was first used as a [cod]salting place, that one.'

32.    {*Eqqaamavaralu*                      IND
        *eqqaama-vara-lu*
        remember-1SG.SUBJ/3SG.OBJ-and
        'And I remember it'

33.    *taamanikkut*       *saarulliit*          selling codfish   PART
        *tunineqartartut_*

        *taamani-kkut*      *saarullik-it*
        *tuni-neqaq-saq-tut*

        at.that.time-VIA    codfish-PL
        sell-PASS-HAB-3PL.PART

        'at that time the codfish used to be sold . . .'

The participial is used when the speaker begins to talk about 'cod'; he was previously discussing the 'house' used for the codfishing industry.

In example 4.82 the speaker talks in clauses 37 to 42 about the midwife his family used; clause 43 marks a shift in topic, from 'midwife' to 'father':

(4.82)  (From text 4)                      Topic/Theme   Mood
37.    {*Taava_*    *juumooqarpugut_*'          midwife     IND
        *taava*       *juumooq-qaq-vugut*
        then        midwife-have-1PL.IND
        'Then we had a midwife'

38.    *aamma,*    *ilinniarsimanngitsumik,*       midwife (NOMZ)
        *aamma*     *ilinniaq-sima-nngit-soq-mik*
        and       learn-PERF-NEG-PART-INST
        'and [she was] without learning [i.e., (she was) someone without learning]'

39.    *imaappoq*        *tiguinnakkamik_/*      midwife    IND
        *imaaC-voq*        *tigu-innaq-saq-mik*
        be.like.this-3SG.IND   take-just/only-PASS.PART-INST
        'let me say this, she was just taken' [i.e., 'that is, she was just taken']

40.    *kisianni    juumootut,*                    midwife    (NOMZ)
       *atorluartorujussuarmik,*

       *kisianni    juumooq-tut*
       *atorluaq-soq-rujussuaq-mik*

       but         midwife-EQ
       use.in.a.reasonable.way-PART-very.big-INST

       'but as a midwife, [she was] a very good one'

41.    *tassaavoq          arnaq*                   midwife    IND
       *utoqqaq: H.E._}*

       *tassa-u-voq          arnaq-0*
       *utoqqaq-0: H.E.*

       that.is-COP-3SG.IND    woman-ABS
       old.person-ABS: H.E.

       'it was an old lady: H.E.'

42.    {*Maani,    naluneqanngittut        J.E.-ikkut,    B.E.-ikkut,*
       *Maani     nalu-neqaq-nngit-sut      J.E.-kkut-0    B.E.-kkut-0*
       here        not.know-PASS-NEG-        B.E.-family-ABS
                   3PL.PART or PART.PL.ABS    J.E.-family-ABS
       'Here the well-known J.E. and B.E. [families]'

       *aanaavat_}*
       aanaa-at
       grandmother-3PL.POS/SG.POSM.ABS
       'their grandmother.'

43.    {*Taava     soorlu             oqareersunga*              PART
       *taava      soorlu             oqaq-reer-sunga*
       then        for.example/like    say-already-1SG.PART
       'Then, like I said before'

44.    *ataataga,              aamma*               father    CAUS
       *soqutigisaqaqigami*

*ataata-ga             aamma*
*soqutigisaq-qaq-qi-gami*

father-1SG.POS.ABS    and
interest-have-INTNS-3C.SG.CAUS

'because my father had many interests . . .'

For other clear examples, see text 2, clause 51, and text 3b, clause 163.

### The participial and the passive

In two cases, the use of the participial in same-subject constructions coincides with a passive construction. Although this is superficially reminiscent
of the use of third-person coreferent marking as mentioned in connection
with the use of the contemporative, the level of passivity is irrelevant. In
example 4.83 the participial is passive in clause 44, and active in clause
42. In fact, clause 42 is even more active than the preceding indicative,
in clause 41:

(4.83)  (From text 1a)                          Subject        Voice    Mood

41.    {*Tassaappullu*          *taakku*    catechists     ACTIVE     IND
       *ajoqit_*

       *tassa-u-vut-lu*          *taakku*
       *ajoqi-t*

       that.is-COP-3PL.IND-and   those
       catechist-PL

       'That is they are those catechists'

       *Kalaallit Nunaata*                      catechists                CT
       *ilinniarfissuaninngaanniit*
       *ilinniariarlutik_/*

       *Kalaallit Nunaata*
       *ilinniarfissuaq-a-ninnganniit*
       *ilinniaq-riaq-lutik*

       Greenland.3NC.SG

seminary-3NC.SG.POS-ABL
.POS.REL
learn-right.after-3PL.CT

'right after having learned in Greenland's seminary'

42.  *nunatsinnut*       *illoqarfinnut*      catechists   ACTIVE   PART
     *nunaqarfinnut*      *siaruarsimasut_}*

     *nuna-tsinnut*       *illoqarfik-nnut*
     *nunaqarfik-nnut*   *siaruaq-sima-sut*

     land-1PL.POS.TERM                town-PL.TERM
     village-PL.TERM   spread.out-PERF-3PL.PART

     'they spread out to our land to towns and villages.'

43.  *{Taakkutuaappullu*       *ajoqit*        catechists   ACTIVE   IND
     *tassa_*

     *Taakku-tuaq-u-uut-lu*    *ajoqi-t*
     *tassa*

     Those-only-COP-3PL.    catechist-PL
     IND-and
     that.is

     And the catechists were the only ones then

     *taamanikkut*            *ilisimasassanik_*
     *tiguinnarisassanik_*                     (nomz)

     *taamani-kkut*           *ilisimasat-ssaq-nik*
     *tigu-innaq-giaq-ssaq-nik*

     at.that.time-VIA        knowledge-FUT-PL.INST
     take-only-INTNS-FUT-PL.INST

     'in those days [who] could spread knowledge'

44.  *ilinniartinneqarsimasut*                catechists   PASSIVE   PART
     *Ilinniarfissuarmi_/*

*ilinniartit-neqaq-sima-sut*
*Ilinniarfissuaq-mi*

teach-PASS-PERF-3PL.PART
Greenlandic.Seminary-LOC

'they had been educated in the Greenlandic Seminary . . .'

Thus, passive or active meaning or morphology does not explain the use of the participial with same-subject constructions. This can be seen as a question of local thematic shift, as indicated by clause order (from their education to their spreading knowledge to others, and back again).

### Subject-object coreference

As with the contemporatives, it is generally recognized that occasionally a participial shows subject coreference with the object of its superordinate. Example 4.84 illustrates several issues: clause hierarchy and dependence, and coreference. If the participial refers to its preceding contemporative or nominal (clauses 152 and 151, respectively), then it is coreferent with them; if it refers back to the preceding indicative (clause 150), then it is coreferent with the object of its superordinate, and therefore overlaps in function with the contemporative:

| | | | Subject | Mood |
|---|---|---|---|---|
| 4.84) | (From text 3b) | | | |
| 150. | {*Arnaq* | *imaannanngitsorujussuartut* | | |
| | *taasinnaavara* | | 1SG | IND |

*arnaq-0*      *imaannanngit-soq-rujussuaq-tut*
*taa-sinnaa-vara*

woman-ABS     unusual-3SG.PART-very.much-EQ
call-just-1SG.SUBJ/3SG.OBJ.IND

'I could just call her a special woman'

*anaanaga_/*
anaana-ga
mother-1SG.POS/SG.POSM.ABS
'my mother'

151.    *eqiasuitsorujussuaq_*                     mother (NOMZ)
        *eqiasuiC-soq-rujussuaq-0*
        be.diligent-PART-very-ABS
        'she was very industrious'

152.    *sulinngiffimmigut_*    *sinissanani*            mother        CT
        *sulinngiffik-migut*    *siniC-ssa-nani*
        vacation/free.time-     sleep-FUT-3SG.NEG.CT
        3SG.POS.VIA
        'in her free time, she didn't sleep'

153.    *piliniartartoq_*                          mother      PART
        *piliniaq-saq-soq*
        provide-HAB-3SG.PART
        'she was getting/hunting for food [for the winter] . . .'

Clause 153 marks a shift from the mother working as a maid to the mother as provider for her children.


## 4.5 Chapter conclusion

Given the possibilities for speaker production problems, such as afterthoughts, production mistakes, changes in train of thought, sidetracks, and so forth, the level of consistency in the above analysis is remarkable. Of 620 clauses in the body of my data, about seventy-eight have switch-reference pronominal marking, and twenty-eight are anomalously marked for coreference and one for noncoreference according to the traditional interpretation of switch-reference. The use of the coreferent pronominal inflection occurs where the topic is continued, and the use of the noncoreferent inflection occurs where the topic is changed. With the exception of object coreferent morphology, the reinterpretation of switch-reference as topic reference can be successfully applied to all exceptions noted above. As I have shown, however, there is an avoidance of object coreferent forms in general and a distributional difference between the use of subject coreferent and object noncoreferent forms in the contemporative. This may reflect a grammatical development independent of switch-reference marking itself.

With respect to the verb moods, of the 620 clauses, there are about 149 contemporative clauses, of which about forty-five involve anomalous non-coreference according to traditional explanations of contemporative and participial distribution; and there are about fifty-five participials, of which fifteen show anomalous coreference according to these traditional explanations. The contemporative in my texts consistently appears where theme is continued, and the participial where the theme shifts. The number of exceptions is small, certainly smaller than the number of exceptions to the traditional explanation of switch-reference in most cases, although the exact identification of exceptions depends on the interpretation of theme made by each hearer (or reader). Most exceptions have to do with the use of the contemporative in its primary function as a marker of simultaneous time. These should not be surprising, nor should they be classified as problematic in the same sense that other clauses with exceptional switch-reference are. There are around ten problematic clauses, contemporative or participial, and most of these involve a noncoreferent object on the contemporative. I have addressed this as an issue of subordinate mood pronominal marking. The one or two remaining problems have to do with the difficulty in identifying the theme. Perhaps most problematic is an example such as the following, in which a participial should have been expected in clause 74:

(4.85)   (From text 4)                                         Topic/Theme    Mood
66-73.   Aggu Lynge wrote about speaker's father and the king

74.      {Kisianni    taava    taallatsiaannarlugit_                          CT
         kisianni     taava    taa-llatsiaq-innaq-lugit
         but          then     mention-little-just-3PL.OBJ.CT
         'But then just to mention these a bit'

75.      meeraanera_          eqqartulaassavara_/       childhood      IND
         meeraaneq-ga         eqqartor-laaq-ssa-vara
         childhood-1SG.       talk.about-a.little-FUT-1SG.
         POS.ABS              SUBJ/3SG.OBJ.IND
         'I will talk a little about my childhood'

76.      taamanikkut          meeraanerma               childhood (NOMZ)
         nalaani_'

*taamani-kkut*　　　*meeraaneq-ma*
*nalaani*

at.that.time-VIA　　　childhood-1SG.POS.REL
time.period-3C.SG.POS.LOC

'at that time in the time of my childhood'

*piniagassaapput_'*　　　　　　animals　　IND
*piniagassat-u-vut*
hunted.animal-COP-3PL.IND
'there were animals that were hunted'

77.　　*piniagassatigut*　　　　*taasinnaasakka*　　animals　　PART
　　*tassa_'*

　　*piniagassat-tigut*　　　*taa-sinnaa-sakka*
　　*tassa*

　　hunted.animals-PL.VIA　　give.provenance.
　　of-can-1SG.SUBJ/3PL.　　that.is
　　OBJ.PART

　　'I can give the list of the hunted animals . . .'

The contemporative in clause 74 is a transitive construction, and the object is plural, thus possibly referring to the animals in clause 76. If so, one cannot argue that the contemporative somehow continues the temporal setting of 'speaker's childhood', repeated numerous times in the text. On the other hand, if the antecedents of 'these' in clause 74 are the speaker's father and the king, from the preceding text, and the speaker is finishing the previous discussion, then there is no problem with the proposed theory.

It is interesting to note that speaker 4 makes very little use of participials, there being only about four in the text, and his style differs from those of the first three speakers in that his participials mark shifts in topic or theme, but not necessarily as the first clause marking the shift. His participials consistently mark global rather than local topic or thematic shifts. For example, clause 77 essentially repeats clause 76 (a related theme has already been introduced previously (cf. 'we can talk about the big hunters in those days', but this marks the first time the animals hunted are described). The contemporative in clause 74, therefore, conflicts with the expectations of a participial, which in fact is found in clause 77.

The fact that the contemporative and the participial can be identified with thematic continuity or thematic shift is not surprising; this has been discussed in section 4.1 as an artifact of clause chaining and morphological identity with various other verb moods with particular structural functions. It is also not surprising that the degree to which these moods mark thematic continuity or shift varies from speaker to speaker. This reflects the problem inherent in assigning multiple functions to a single structural form, especially where gaps in one system create a structural need, and the reinterpretation of one form does not produce constructions that conflict with the old use of that form. Thus, in most cases, the reinterpretation of the contemporative as a marker of thematic continuity does not conflict with the function of the contemporative as a marker of simultaneous or sequential time. Which function prevails may sometimes be hard to determine. In my texts, the speaker who shows the most variation in the canonical use of the verb moods in question (i.e., switch-reference with respect to subject) is speaker 1; the one who shows the least variation is speaker 4.[14] The problematic use of the contemporative in example 4.85 may therefore simply reflect some of these issues.

An explanation based on switch-topic/theme seems to be more comprehensive than one based on subject coreference in West Greenlandic. Whereas proponents of the latter have generally had to resort to lists of environments in which the contemporative or the participial is used, the number of exceptions in the former has not so much to do with different environments and different structures but rather with problems in interpreting the theme. The single regular exception appears to be contemporatives of time, which indicate time contemporaneous with that of the superordinate verb (as in 'in the wintertime', etc.). Assuming that the switch-reference mechanisms mark topic or thematic continuity or lack thereof therefore allows for a more inclusive and consistent explanation of their use than does the traditional explanation of switch-reference. It also complements the findings on case marking and topicality, and thus has wider relevance in the general grammatical description of West Greenlandic.

This having been said, the identification of the contemporative and participial verb moods as markers primarily of switch-reference is not uncontroversial. Given a choice between the following three structures, examples 4.86a and 4.86b are preferred in the written language, where the contemporative in 4.86b would be interpreted as a transitive. Nevertheless, some speakers have preferred examples 4.86b and 4.86c to example 4.86a, and have seen nothing wrong, in fact, with 4.86c. To these speakers, the contemporative still primarily indicates a temporal relation rather than a grammatical relationship:

(4.86)   a. *sinittunga,*          *atuarputit*
              *siniC-sunga*          *atuar-vutit*
              sleep-1SG.PART    read-2SG.IND
              '(while) I was sleeping, you were reading'

         b. *sinittillunga,*        *atuarputit*
              *siniC-tit-lunga*      *atuar-vutit*
              sleep-while-1SG.CT    read-2SG.IND
              'while I was sleeping, you were reading'

         c. *sinillunga,*       *atuarputit*
              *siniC-lunga*      *atuar-vutit*
              sleep-1SG.CT    read-2SG.IND
              'while I was sleeping, you were reading'

Other speakers have characterized the structure in example 4.86c as "Nuuk-speech," or in other words, as simplified language and not strictly acceptable.

The question is therefore whether these verb moods really form part of the switch-reference system in oral West Greenlandic, or whether their identification as such is really a function of the method of clause combination. A definitive answer would require a much larger study than that undertaken here, but my impression is that further research would probably show less of a relationship between the moods and the switch-reference system than is currently believed to be the case.[15]

# 5 Conclusion

## 5.1 Findings

In this study, I have been concerned with two of the syntactic systems of agreement marking in West Greenlandic, and with anomalies in the assignment of agreement arising from the traditional interpretations of the circumstances of this assignment. Specifically, I have looked at the assignment of absolutive case in a study of ergativity, and at the assignment of coreference or noncoreference in a study of switch-reference in subordinate clauses. The resolution of the problems posed by anomalous agreement patterns has required a detailed look at certain aspects of discourse and discourse theory. I have argued that these agreement patterns are better explained by assuming agreement with the discourse role *topic* rather than with the syntactic roles subject or object, and by assuming the existence of a dichotomy between topic and theme analogous to the syntactic dichotomy between noun phrases and verb phrases.

Although the assignment of absolutive case is typically not explained in traditional interpretations of West Greenlandic sentence structure, the difference between the absolutive object of a transitive construction and the demoted instrumentally marked object of an antipassive construction is generally linked to the definiteness or givenness of the absolutive object, and the indefiniteness or newness of the demoted object. Not all absolutive objects are definite or given, however, and not all demoted objects are indefinite. By reviewing ergative and antipassive clauses in context, I have shown that the absolutive objects are not random, definite noun phrases; they are ones with continuity and prominence throughout a part of text, or in other words, they are topics. Further, the demoted objects are not random indefinite noun phrases; they are specifically those noun phrases with no continuity or prominence within a part of text, or in other words, they are nontopics. I have not dwelt much on the topicality of ergative subjects, but they appear to be global topics: in most cases they have prominence throughout a greater stretch of discourse than absolutive objects, but they are less prominent locally than a local topic. Support for such an interpretation is found in the pattern of pronominal inflection on the verbs: transitive verbs coindex both subject and object arguments, and intransitive verbs coindex only the subject; neither construction involves the coindexing of definiteness. If the verbs coindex topical items, then not indexing a nontopic, such as a demoted object, is an obvious corollary.

The assignment of coreference or noncoreference marking in West Greenlandic is traditionally associated with the identity or lack thereof between the two subjects of a pair of clauses, one of which is subordinate to the other; switch-reference is shown on the subordinate verb (and subject, if possessed). However, the subject of a superordinate clause is not always the anaphor of the subject of the subordinate, and the object of one can sometimes be coreferent with the subject of another. I have shown that in context, coreferent pronominal inflection on the verb is consistently found in cases where the topic of a previous clause or piece of text is continued, and noncoreferent inflection is found where the topic is not continued; and this accounts for most cases of anomalous switch-reference. In an interesting complication, the coindexed object does not show a pattern of coreference, although the coindexed object is the local topic.

The contemporative and the participial have been identified as switch-reference mechanisms in West Greenlandic, despite the fact that they differ in kind from other methods of switch-reference marking. Further, there are as many examples of anomalous switch-reference with respect to these verb moods as there are of pronominal switch-reference anomalies, if not more. Some of these exceptions involve environments in which coreference crosses sentential boundaries. I have shown that, to the extent that contemporative and the participial are markers of switch-reference, they must be considered markers of thematic, rather than topic, continuity. As verb moods, they imply verbal, and therefore propositional, semantics. This accounts nicely for the difference in switch-reference systems based on pronominal inflection and on verb mood. I have also suggested, however, that the indication of thematic continuity or shift must be considered a secondary function of the contemporative and participial moods. For one, both the contemporative and the participial also have the means to indicate switch-reference through the inflectional system, although the inflectional paradigm is restricted in the contemporative to only one argument: the subject for intransitives, the object for transitives. Although all languages have a high level of redundancy in the grammar, it is unlikely that two verb moods exist solely, or even primarily, to indicate switch-reference when at least two other, paradigmatically complete systems to indicate it exist. Further, West Greenlandic has a system, primarily signaled by the verb moods, for indicating time relative to the superordinate. The causative tends to indicate events that occurred prior to the events of the superordinate; the conditional, events that have not yet happened with respect to those of the superordinate; and the contemporative, events that occur contemporaneously with the superordinate. If the contemporative and the participial have come to be used as markers of thematic continuity or shift, it is likely a result of sentence or discourse structure in West Greenlandic, ambiguities in certain constructions, and gaps in the inflectional paradigm. West Greenlandic is a clause-chaining language, and clauses in a clause chain tend to have topical or thematic continuity. As most clauses are intransitive, there is therefore also a tendency for subject and topic to coincide. Participial constructions are structurally ambiguous with relative and nominalized constructions, either of which tend to involve nontopical information. The gap in the contemporative's inflectional system for marking switch-reference and for marking more than one argument, the association of the participial with constructions that involve nontopical material, and the tendency of clause chains to signal topical or thematic unity, and incidentally to coincide with subject continuity, have resulted in the association of the contemporative and the participial with switch-reference mechanisms. Switch-reference, however, must be seen as their secondary function.

These interpretations of West Greenlandic constructions are not without problems. There are examples of the use of absolutive objects that cannot readily be explained by assuming the local topic to be the absolutive object. Nor can all examples of coreference or noncoreference be readily explained as instances of topic or thematic continuity or shift, especially with the contemporative or participial. However, the notions of topic and theme do consistently explain most otherwise problematic cases. The existence of less-than-obvious cases may reflect the lack of clarity or ambiguity normally found in much of oral language. Not all speakers are equally able to express themselves, nor do all speakers manipulate language in the same way. There are certainly differences in language use between the texts I have collected. Speaker 1 tends to use more participials than the others, whereas speaker 4 tends not to use them. Speaker 3 tends to use nominalizations far more than the others. Speaker 4 shows a preference for incorporated particles in structuring paragraphs, whereas others more often use independent particles. All speakers use the particles for organizing paragraphs in different ways, and so forth. Finally, especially where more than one topic is prominent, the ranks of the respective topics may be continually changing, requiring continual reassessment of topicality, both by the speaker and the hearer.

## 5.2 Some comments on the role of discourse in linguistic descriptions

All these conclusions of course depend on the soundness of the theoretical assumptions and proposals I have made regarding the nature of discourse and the effect that certain aspects of discourse have on the syntactic structures I have studied. I have shown that discourse has structure and that this structure can be systematically analyzed. In this study I have limited myself to structure as reflected by the discourse-level equivalents of nouns and verbs or arguments and predicates, namely topic and theme. There is no reason to see discourse as something necessarily and entirely different from other levels of linguistic structure. Just as the syntax has readily identifiable classes of constituents, such as noun phrases and verb phrases, or arguments and predicates, so does discourse have similarly identifiable classes, both nominal and propositional. This difference is clearly seen in the different characterizations of switch-reference in West Greenlandic, for example, where pronominal inflection marking switch-reference can be characterized as marking continuity and shift, and verb mood distribution can be characterized as marking thematic continuity and shift. The parallels extend further. Just as there are both clearly and less clearly defined noun phrases and verb phrases in the syntax, there are both clear and ambiguous topics and themes in the discourse. Hopper and Thompson (1984:707–9) suggest that the most prototypical members of the different grammatical categories (such as noun and verb) form a small set, other items having to a greater or lesser degree characteristics typically identified as belonging to a number of categories. The dearth of clear examples of transitivity is called to mind. In West Greenlandic, this is particularly evident in the use of the participial, the third-person intransitive form of which is ambiguously a verb form (the participial), a relative construction, and a nominalized form. In discourse-level interpretation, this leads to some ambiguity in determining the topic or thematic status of a particular form and consequently in determining the role of topic with respect to theme. Although the scope is wider and the variables more numerous, the issues in a structural description of discourse are similar in kind to those raised in discussions of syntax.

Further, just as we can identify roles that characterize the grammaticalization of a syntactic category, and others that do the same for a semantic category, we can also identify discourse roles that characterize the grammaticalization of a category of discourse. Insofar as roles provide a means to keep track of noun phrases in clauses and sentences, there is no necessary difference in kind between the means to keep track of noun phrases in texts. Comrie (1981) writes that the differences in case-marking systems reflect the different options available for keeping track of a noun phrase where there is more than one noun phrase in a clause. Thus, we find nominative-accusative and ergative-absolutive case marking, and in rarer instances, three-way case marking, in which S, O, and A are all inflected differently. There is no necessary difference between keeping track of more than one noun phrase in a clause and doing the same for more than one noun phrase in a text; there are simply more noun phrases to keep track of. Thus, the question of topic ranking in texts with more than one local topic is raised. In West Greenlandic, the most prominent local topic is marked (as the absolutive), and others are not. Switch-reference systems, as traditionally described, provide a way for keeping track of a noun phrase across clauses. Again, there is no necessary difference between switch-reference systems that mark the coreference or lack thereof of subjects and those that mark the coreference or lack thereof of topics. Systems that mark topic switches provide a way of keeping track of a noun phrase across a larger piece of text. In a system that marks topic switches, the coreferenced entity need not be the subject, since topics can occur in either subject or object position. Rather than speaking of exceptional examples of coreference (or lack thereof) as arising from differences in transitivity between clauses or differences in the agency of the respective subjects, differences that are not always clearly demonstrated, we can continue to speak in terms of coreferentiality. In this case, it is coreferentiality of the topic.

The terms and the methods used to describe syntactic structures can therefore be extended to describe discourse-level structures. Consequently, categories that have traditionally been described in terms of the syntax can also be described in terms of the discourse, and in some cases, such as West Greenlandic, this seems to be more useful. Thus, both ergativity and switch-reference in West Greenlandic are more clearly explained as constructions that reflect discourse roles rather than definiteness (in the former case) and subjecthood (in the latter). There is also a clear advantage of using discourse roles to explain features of the syntax of West Greenlandic: the assumption of a discourse role *topic* not only explains one aspect of West Greenlandic grammar, for example, ergativity, but also another, that is, switch-reference. The two are seemingly unrelated aspects of grammar, and traditional grammatical descriptions have assigned different explanations to the two. The explanation of switch-reference is straightforwardly based on the morphology, if one excludes the contemporative and the participial from the discussion. Ergativity, however, has been said to reflect definiteness or givenness, yet it does not have overt morphology that specifically identifies something as definite or given (cf. subjects, which are not differentiated for givenness). The assumption of a topic role, however, allows both these grammatical forms to be covered by a single explanation, and one with functional merit. Another clear advantage of discourse roles lies in the explicit differentiation between topic and theme; the two have different effects on the syntax. For example, the difference between the pronominal switch-reference inflectional systems in West Greenlandic and the use of the contemporative and the participial as part of the switch-reference system is one of topic and theme. The contemporative and the participial are verb moods, not substitutions for noun phrases.

In proposing discourse roles, I am not suggesting that categories such as subject or object are irrelevant in general, nor that they are necessarily irrelevant in West Greenlandic in particular. Nor am I suggesting that all languages have grammaticalized ways to mark discourse roles. Subjecthood, for example, has worked well as a category in the description of English. As the literature concerning subjecthood suggests, however, it has not worked well as a descriptive category for all languages. In the same way, topic may work well as a descriptive category for West Greenlandic, but it may not for other languages.

The possibility of marking noun phrases according to topichood brings up one more way in which languages can vary. Languages vary greatly within each of a number of broad subcategories of their grammars: for example, with respect to phonology, languages can differ not only in the use of particular phonemes but also in the use of suprasegmentals such as tone, intonational patterns, and so forth. Similarly, languages can vary in the particulars of their morphology, the levels of organization in their respective syntaxes, in semantics, and so on. Where some languages categorize nouns according to subjecthood, others according to agency, still others according to animacy or some other syntactic or semantic hierarchy, it is reasonable to suggest that some languages categorize nouns according to relative importance in a text. There is no a priori reason that a language should not have the means to formally distinguish the topic, regardless of the syntactic or semantic character of this topic (i.e., regardless of its status as subject or object, agent or patient, animate or inanimate entity, etc.).

Concepts such as theme-rheme structure, givenness, definiteness, and so forth may very well be useful in characterizing discourse in a language, but they reflect a different kind of information about discourse. This information is not as structurally predictable as it has often been made out to be. It reflects tendencies in language but not necessarily grammatical usage, and perhaps it also reflects questions of style. Furthermore, concepts such as definiteness and givenness tend to reflect something else (e.g., topic) rather than grammaticalized categories in and of themselves. The likelihood, therefore, that they determine a particular syntactic structure must be small (this is not to say that they cannot; in fact, if they are grammaticalized, one might assume they do affect the syntax). Their use in studies of syntax may reflect a confusion in the kinds of information being described. It is for this reason that many syntactic descriptions that make reference to the discourse concept *theme* (as in theme-rheme), for example, have no more than sentence-level applicability. Whereas syntactic structures have to do with the relationships between different clausal elements, the theme-rheme structure has to do with the linear organization of information. Thus, the first clause in a text says something about the linear organization of that text, and the first element in a sentence says something about the linear organization of that sentence, but the former is not related to the latter in the way that a noun is related to an anaphoric or cataphoric pronoun, for example.

This naturally suggests the importance of studying discourse within the setting of discourse. A study of discourse cannot be based on the study of decontextualized clauses. If discourse can affect the syntax, this also has ramifications for the study of syntax. If a language has grammaticalized discourse roles, then studying clauses and sentences in isolation will only result in inadequate and perhaps faulty descriptions. Furthermore, the study of aspects of discourse other than discourse roles that affect sentence formation must be undertaken in context. Short of the formal study of logic and the philosophy of language, the true intent of the speaker, as reflected in the choice of clausal organization (e.g., *theme* and *rheme*) and presentation (e.g., speech act) is only meaningful in context. Out of context, the native speaker's judgments about both the grammaticality and meaning of a clause is compromised. This is not to suggest that studies of syntax cannot be functional. On the contrary, the study of syntax has resulted in tremendously useful analyses of clause structures, and they have cross-linguistic value. Rather, if discourse is considered in studies of syntax, then the studies must include context with clausal analysis.

Finally, it is important to consider the flexibility inherent in language. Halliday, in reference to the order of the presentation of information in discourse, notes that slots in the sentence are generally filled according to the type of information that is expressed; he is mainly referring to givenness, but his statements are valid in all areas of the study of discourse: "These are options on the part of the speaker, not determined by the textual or situational environment; what is new is in the last resort what the speaker chooses to present as new, and predictions from the discourse have only a high probability of being fulfilled. Nevertheless the structure of the information unit does contribute in large measure to the organization of discourse, by providing a framework within which these options are exercised" (1967b:211). This suggests that the speaker ultimately decides what he or she is speaking about, and how he or she will express this. Linguistic rules are guidelines that can be broken for the purpose of the moment, within reason, communication being the deciding factor. Many syntactic theorists speak of constraints in the grammar, of disallowed structures, or of violations of rules. In a functional approach to linguistic description, these are not very useful concepts. Rather than speaking of constraints on language, we can speak of the choices that a speaker has in indicating information status in discourse. Rather than being constrained to introduce no more than one piece of salient information per unit, for example, the speaker consciously chooses to focus on one for effect. I claim that this is encoded grammatically in West Greenlandic in the choice of clause structure and referential marking, among other things. This grammaticalization gives the linguist (not to mention the hearer) some predictability in determining the meaning of a construction. Indeed, one expects predictability in a majority of cases. Ultimately, however, the structure will depend on the choices made by the speaker, and these choices vary from speaker to speaker.

# Appendix

## A1 Notes on data collection

The texts were collected from four speakers, one of whom was in her late eighties; the three others were all about twenty years younger. Two speakers were interviewed, and two recounted their recollections without intruding questions. All speakers are native speakers of West Greenlandic, although one originally came from and speaks South Greenlandic dialect in addition to West Greenlandic.

The data were originally transcribed and translated by a native Greenlander who spoke Greenlandic, Danish, and English. Each line of transcription is followed by lines of morphological analysis in Greenlandic, morphological analysis in English, and English translation. Stems listed in the dictionary *Oqaatsit* are treated as lexicalized and are not subjected to further morphological analysis. Morphemes are given in the most common allomorphic form. When the English translation is too clumsy, a less exact but better English translation is provided below the relevant selection. In some cases, the translator's translation was inadequate or inaccurate because of language barriers; the translation provided is the more accurate one, although when the original is informative, it is provided in square brackets. Square brackets are also used to indicate an alternative translation. Further, in some cases the transcriber's dialect is different than the West Greenlandic generally described in the literature. The transcriber's spellings are retained where there is no typographical mistake (through consultation with P. Langgård), and explanations are made in occasional footnotes. P. Langgård provided much of the necessary contextual knowledge (cf. text 2 with respect to nautical, climatological, and geographical information).

Texts 1 and 3 are divided into two sections each, because of the length in respect to other texts. In text 1, the speaker paused naturally for a fifteen-minute break after the end of text 1a; this formed a natural division. The division of text 3 is largely arbitrary, and text 3b follows immediately on the tape.

The data are numbered in such a way as to reflect several levels of text. Arabic numerals generally signal clauses; there is no more than one predicate text for each arabic numeral. Capital letters are used at the beginning of a line to signal the beginning of a sentence as identified by the translator. Roman numerals are used to signal sentences based on intonational cues. In the three interviews, the interviewer and speaker are identified after the roman numerals. Intonational groups are identified by the use of the symbols listed below. In some cases, the text is too long to fit on one line of transcription; where no intonational break is signaled at the end of a line of transcription, the line is to be read with the following line(s) as a single unit.

## A2 Notes on transcription and intonation

| | | |
|---|---|---|
| Brackets | {...} | Sentence |
| Underscore | _ | Pause |
| Underscore and apostrophe | _' | Rising intonation at pause |
| Underscore and slash | _/ | Substantial break, not end of sentence |
| Comma | , | Constituent-type break |
| Parentheses | (...) | Parenthetical word, phrase, clause, etc., signified by increased speed, lower and/or softer voice, usually no break in speech |
| No marker at end or beginning of line | | No break in intonation, two consecutive lines read as one |
| Underline | | Stressed, or emphasized, word |

The transcription is accurate and includes the false starts of the narrators. False starts that result in incomplete words are signaled by a dash [ — ] to distinguish them from morpheme boundaries in the morphemic analysis. In some cases, the speaker uses special intonational features (speeding up, lowering his or her voice, etc.) which may lead to unclear parsing.

**Speaker 1, text 1a**

**Recorded August 17, 1995, in Nuuk**

I

1.  *Ullumi_*    *nunatsinni_*                  *pissusiusut_*
    *ulloq-mi*    *nuna-tsinni*                *pissuseq-u-soq-t*

    day-LOC    country-1PL.POS[1].LOC      culture-COP-PART-PL
    *{Uagut*    *meeraanitsinnut*          *naleqqiullugu,*

    *uagut*    *meeraaneq-tsinnut*       *naleqqiup-lugu*
    1PL    childhood-1PL.POS.TERM    compare-3SG.OBJ.CT[2]

    'If (we) compare our way of life today in our country with our childhood
    [i.e., Today, in our country, our culture, (if) we compare it to our childhood]'

2.  *allaruju* —
    *alla-ruju* —
    different/another-very —
    'was very differ — '

    *taamani*       *inuunermik*      *allarujussuuvoq_}*
    *taamani*       *inuuneq-mik*      *alla-rujussuuvoq[3]*
    at.that.time    life-INST    different-very.3SG.IND
    'at that time it was a very different life.'

II

3.  *{Uanga*    *isikka*       *isigilluaqqaalermata,*
    *uanga*    *isi-kka*      *isigi-lluaq-qqaaq-ler-mmata*
    1SG    eye-1SG.POS.    see-well-first-begin-3NC.PL.CAUS
              ABS/PL.POSM

    'When my eyes could see well [When my eyes first began to see well]'

4.  *siutikkalu*                *tusaalluaqqaalerlutik_}*
    *siuti-kka-lu*              *tusaa-lluaq-qqaaq-ler-lutik*
    ear-1SG.POS.ABS/PL.POSM-and    hear-well-first-begin-3PL.CT

'and my ears could hear well [When my ears first began to hear well].'

III

5.      {*Kalaallit*                *nunatsinni_*
        *kalaalleq-t*               *nuna-tsinni*
        kalaalleq-PL               land-1PL.POS.LOC
        'In Greenland [the land of the Greenlanders]'

        *nunarput*                 *allarujussuuvoq*
        *nuna-rput*                *alla-rujussuuvoq*
        land-1PL.POS.ABS    different/another-very-3SG.IND
        'our land was very different'

6.      (*nunarput*                *allaanngikkaluarpoq*
        *nuna-rput*                *allaa-nngit-galuaq-voq*
        land-1PL.POS.ABS    different-NEG-CONSEQ⁴_3SG.IND
        '(our *land* was just the same [was not different]'

7.      *kisianni*   *illoqarfiit*            *allarujussuupput)_}*
        *kisianni*   *illoqarfik-it*          *alla-rujussuu vut*
        but        settlement-PL    different/another-very.3PL.IND
        'but the settlements were very different).'

IV

8.      {*Inuit*          (*inooriaassiat*)               *ullumikkumut*
        *naleqqilullugu_*

        *inuk-it*          *inooriassiat*⁵               *ullumi-kkut*⁶*-mut*
        *naleqqiup-lugu*

        person-PL    way.of.life/lifestyle.ABS    today-VIA-TERM
        compare-3SG.OBJ.CT

        'Comparing the people's way of life to today'

9.      *inuusuttunut*        *meeqqanullu*               *oqaluttuarissagutsigu*
        *inuusuttoq-t-nut*   *meeraq-t-nut-lu*          *oqaluttuaq-gi-ssa-*
                                                                    *gutsigu*

youth-PL-TERM    child-PL-TERM-and    history/story-have-
                                      FUT-1PL.SUBJ/3SG.
                                      OBJ.COND
'to the youth and the children, if you should tell the story [to
them]'

10.    *upperinavianngilaat,*
       *upperi-navianngit-laat*
       believe-most.likely.not.[INTNS.NEG]-3PL.SUBJ/3SG.OBJ.
       NEG.IND
       'they will most likely not not believe it'

11.    *uppernanngingaarmat_}*
       *uppernar-nngit-ngaar-mmat*
       be.believable-NEG-very.much-3NC.SG.CAUS
       'because it is really unbelievable.'


V

12.    {*Taamani        uagut     meeraalluta,*
       *taamani         uagut     meeraq-u-lluta*
       at.that.time     1PL       child-COP-1PL.CT
       'At that time we were children'

13.    *eqqaamavara_*
       *eqqaama-vara*
       remember-1SG.SUBJ/3SG.OBJ.IND
       'I remember it'

14.    (*tassa      Qaqortumi           meeraavunga_*
       *tassa       Qaqortoq-mi         meeraq-u-vunga*
       that.is      Qaqortoq-LOC        child-COP-1SG.IND
       '(that is, I was a child in Qaqortoq'

15.    *taamani_         silattorama_)*
       *taamani          silattoq⁷-gama*
       at.that.time      acquire.wisdom-1SG.CAUS
       'then, I got wiser) [i.e., when I acquired knowledge/wisdom/
       ability to reason]'

16. *Qaqortoq*        *inukitsunnguuvoq_*
     *Qaqortoq-0*      *inuk-kit-soq-nnguaq-u-voq*
     Qaqortoq-ABS    person-have.little-PART-DIM-COP-
     3SG.IND

     'there were not many people in Qaqortoq [i.e., Qaqortoq didn't have many people]'

17. *tassanilu_*    *piniartuinnaat_*      *-ngajaviit_*
     *tassani-lu*    *piniartoq-innaq-it*    *-ngajak-vik-it*
     there-and      hunter-only-PL      almost-real-PL

     'and there — [were] only hunters, almost only [almost entirely]'

     (*aalisartumininnguit*
     *aalisartoq-mineq-nnguaq-it*
     fisherman-kind.of-DIM-PL
     '([there were] a few fishermen'

18. *taamani*      *aalisarneq*           *suli*
     *ingerlalluannginnami_*)}

     *taamani*      *aalisarneq-0*        *suli*
     *ingerlaC-lluaq-nngit-gami*

     at.that.time    fishing.[industry]-ABS    yet
     be.underway/going-well-NEG-3C.SG.CAUS

     'at that time the fishing was not yet going well).'

VI

19. {*Piniartut,*      *qajat*
     *piniartoq-t,*      *qajaq-t*
     hunter-PL      kayak-PL
     '[The] hunters, kayaks'

     *qajaannarmik*      *inuussuteqarput_}*
     *qajaq-innaq-mik*    *inuu-ssuteqaq-vut*
     kayak-only-INST    live-by.means.of-3PL.IND
     'they only used the kayak to live by [i.e., hunt].'

VII

20.  {*Umiaasat*                           *aalisariutigisarpaat_/*
     *umiaq-asaq-t*                         *aalisariuti-gi-saq-paat*
     umiaq-resemble-PL                      fishing.vessel-have-HAB-3PL.
                                            SUBJ/3PL.OBJ.IND
     'They used to use small boats as fishing vessels'

21.  *ukiorlu*                 *naallugu*
     *ukioq-0-lu*              *naa-llugu*
     winter-ABS-and            be.finished-3SG.OBJ.CT
     'and all winter long'

22.  *qajaq*           *atorluarneqaqaaq_}*
     *qajaq-0*         *ator-lluaq-neqaq-qi-voq*
     kayak-ABS         use-well-PASS-INTNS-3SG.IND
     'the kayak is very much used [i.e., well used].'

VIII

23.  {*Tassalu*      *illoqarfimmi_*    *palasi_*       *qallunaaq_*
     *tassa-lu*      *illoqarfik-mi*    *palasi-0*      *qallunaaq-0*
     then-and        town-LOC           priest-ABS      Dane-ABS
     'And in the town, the priest, a Dane'

24.  (*kisianni*     *kalaallisut*      *oqaluttoq*)
     *kisianni*      *kalaallisut*      *oqaluk-soq*
     but             Greenlandic        speak-3SG.PART
     '(but he spoke Greenlandic)'

25.  *taavalu_*      *niuertoq*                         *qallunaaq*
     *taava-lu*      *niuertoq-0*                       *qallunaaq-0*
     then-and        trader/colonial.chief-ABS          Dane-ABS
     'and then, the trader[,] a Dane'

26.  (*qallunaatuinnaq*        *oqaluttoq*[8]),
     *qallunaatut-innaq*       *oqaluk-soq*
     Danish-only               speak-3SG.PART
     '(he only spoke Danish)'

27. *niuertussat_*
*niuertoq-ssaq⁹-t*
trader-FUT-PL
'the future traders [i.e., traders in training]'

*napparsimavimmi*    *nakorsaq_*    *niviarsiat_*
*napparsimavik-mi*    *nakorsaq-0*    *niviarsiaq-t*
hospital-LOC    doctor-ABS    nurse-PL
'the doctor in the hospital, the nurses'

*atuarfimmi*    *ilinniartitsisoq*    *qallunaaq_/*
*atuarfik-mi*    *ilinniartitsisoq-0*    *qallunaaq-0*
school-LOC    teacher-ABS    Dane-ABS
'the teacher in the school, a Dane'

28. *(qallunaatuinnaq*    *oqaluttut)}*
*qallunaatut-innaq*    *oqaluk-sut*
Danish-only    speak-3PL.PART
'(they only spoke Danish).'

IX

29. *{Tassa*  *taamani*  *qallunaat*  *taama*  *ikitsigipput_}*
*tassa*  *taamani*  *qallunaaq-t*  *taama*  *ikit-tigi-vut*
that.is  at.that.time  Dane-PL  just  few/not.many-so(equative)-3PL.IND
'That is, in those days there were not so many Danes.'

X

30. *{Taavalu*  *atorfillit*    *kalaallit_*
*taava-lu*  *atorfik-lik-t*    *kalaalleq-t*
then-and  position-provided.with-PL  Greenlander-PL
'And the Greenlanders who had a job'

31. *saffiorfimmi_*  *allaffimmi*  *ikittunnguit*
*sulisut_}*

*saffiorfik-mi*  *allaffik-mi*  *ikit-soq-nnguaq-it*
*suli-soq-t*

smithy-LOC	office-LOC	few-PART-DIM-PL
work-PART-PL or 3PL.PART

'in the smithy, in the office they were few workers.'


## XI

32.	{*Taamani	allaffillua* —	*allaffippassuaqannginnami_*}
	*taamani*		*allaffik-passuaq-qaq-nngit-gami*
	at.that.time		office-many-have-NEG-3C.SG.CAUS
	'At that time [in those days] there were not so many offices [as today].'


## XII

33.	{*taavalu	napparsimavimmi_*
	*taava-lu	napparsimavik-mi*
	then-and	hospital-LOC
	'And then in the hospital'

	*juumuut_	juumuussat_*
	*juumooq-t	juumooq-ssaq-t*
	midwife-PL	midwife-FUT-PL
	'midwives, future midwives [i.e., midwives in training]'

34.	*kiisalu	atuarfitsinni	atuarfinni	ajoqit,*
	*kiisa-lu	atuarfik-tsinni	atuarfik-ni	ajoqi-t*
	finally-and	school-1PL.POS.LOC	school-1SG.POS.LOC	catechist-PL
	'and finally catechists in our schools, in my school'

35.	*ajoqit	taamani	ilinniartitsisutut*
	*atorfeqarput	aamma_*}

	*ajoqi-t	taamani	ilinniartitsisoq-tut*
	*atorfik-qaq-vut	aamma*

	catechist-PL	at.that.time	teacher-EQ[10]
	work/job-have-3PL.IND	and

	'and the catechists at that time had jobs as teachers.'

XIII

36. {*Assorujussuarlu*       *ajoqit*
    *assut-rujussuaq-lu*      *ajoqi-t*
    very-very.much-and   catechist-PL
    And the catechists were very

    *taamani*         *pingaaruteqarput_*}
    *taamani*         *pingaar-ut(i)-qaq-vut*
    at.that.time    important-means.to-have-3PL.IND
    'very important in those days.'

XIV

37. {*Tassami_*        *oqaluffiinnaanngitsumi_*
    *tassami*        *oqaluffik-innaq-u-nngit-soq-mi*
    in.any.case    church-only-COP-NEG-PART-DEIC
    [translated as 'In any case they weren't (working) just in
    churches,' but literally 'In any case in something that wasn't just
    a church']

38. *ullut*      *tamaasa*           *atuarfinni*       *ajoqit_*
    *ulloq-t*    *tamaq*[11]*-asa*        *atuarfik-ni*      *ajoqi-t*
    day-PL     the.whole/all-3PL.O   school-PL.LOC   catechist-PL
    'every day in the schools the catechists'

    *ilinniartitsisutut*         *sulisarput_*}
    *ilinniartitsisoq-tut*      *suli-saq-vut*
    teacher-EQ            work-HAB-3PL.IND
    'used to work as teachers.'

XV

39. {*Ajoqeqarsimanngitsuuppat*
    *ajoqi-qaq-sima-nngit-soq-u-ppat*
    catechist-have-PERF-NEG-PART-COP-3NC.PL.COND
    'If there hadn't been catechists'

40. *ullumikkut_*     *ineriartorsimanerput*                *immaqa_/*
    *ullumi-kkut*      *ineriartorneq*[12]*-sima-put*           *immaqa*

today-VIA  development-PERF-1PL.POS.ABS  maybe
'today our way of life/development/evolution maybe'

*allaassagaluarpoq_}*
*allaa-ssagaluar-voq*
different-should-3SG.IND
'would be different.'

XVI

41.  *{Tassaappullu  taakku  ajoqit_*
*tassa-u-vut-lu  taakku  ajoqi-t*
that.is-COP-3PL.IND-and  those  catechist-PL
'That is, they are those catechists'

*Kalaallit  Nunaata  seminariata —*
*ilinniarfissuaninngaanniit*[13]

*Kalaallit  Nunaata  seminaria-ta —*
*ilinniarfissuaq*[14]*-a-ninnganniit*

Greenland.3NC.SG.POS.REL  seminary-3NC.SG.POS.REL
seminary-3NC.SG.POS-ABL

*ilinniariarlutik_/*
*ilinniaq-riaq-lutik*
learn-right.after-3PL.CT
'right after having learned in Greenland's seminary'

42.  *nunatsinnut  illoqarfinnut  nunaqarfinnut*
*siaruarsimasut_}*

*nuna-tsinnut  illoqarfik-nnut  nunaqarfik-nnut*
*siaruaq-sima-sut*

land-1PL.POS.TERM  town-PL.TERM  village-PL.TERM
spread.out-PERF-3PL.PART

'they spread out to our land to towns and villages.'

XVII

43.   {*Taakkutuaappullu*              *ajoqit*              *tassa_*
      *taakku-tuaq-u-vut-lu*           *ajoqi-t*             *tassa*
      those-only-COP-3PL.IND-and    catechist-PL    that.is
      'And the catechists were the only ones then'

      *taamanikkut*          *ilisimasassanik_*              *tiguinnarisassanik_*[15]
      *taamani-kkut*         *ilisimasat-ssaq-nik*           *tigu-innaq-giaq-*
                                                             *ssaq-nik*
      at.that.time-VIA    knowledge-FUT-PL.INST    take-only-INTNS-
                                                             FUT-PL.INST
      'in those days [who] could spread knowledge'

44.   *ilinniartinneqarsimasut*           *Ilinniarfissuarmi_/*
      *ilinniartit-neqaq-sima-sut*        *Ilinniarfissuaq-mi*
      teach-PASS-PERF-3PL.PART       Greenlandic.Seminary-LOC
      'they had been educated in the Greenlandic Seminary'

45.   *taakkulu*               *ilinniakkatik*
      *taakku-lu*              *ilinniagaq-tik*
      that/those-and      training-3C.PL.POS/PL.POSM.ABS
      'and this knowledge/training'

      *namminerlu*      *aamma_*     *eqqarsaatersuutisik*     *atorlugit_*
      *nammineq-lu*     *aamma*      *eqqarsaatersuut-tik*     *ator-lugit*
      self-and          and         aphorism[16]-3C.PL.        use-3NC.
                                     POS/PL.POSM.ABS          PL.OBJ.CT
      'and using their own philosophy/thought'

      *qaammarsaaneq*                   *annertoorujussuaq_*
      *qaammarsaaneq-0*                 *annertooq-rujussuaq-0*
      illumination/educational.     voluminous/extensive-very.much-
      standard-ABS                  ABS
      'the enormous education/knowledge [i.e., combining what they
      learned at the Greenland Seminary and their own ideas about
      life]'

46.  *sinerissami*[17]      *tamarmi_*            *ingerlatarivaat_}*
     *sineriak-mi*       *tamaq-mi*            *ingerla-uti-saq-gi-vaat*
     coast-LOC          the.whole/all-3SG.O    spread-manner-PASS.
                                               PART-have-3PL.SUBJ/3PL.
                                               OBJ.IND

'they spread it all over the coast.'

XVIII

47.  {*Taamaattumik*     *ajoqit_*           *imaannaanngitsumik_*
     *taamaattumik*      *ajoqi-t*           *imaannaanngitsoq-mik*
     therefore          catechist-PL        ones.not.without.
                                            importance-INST

'And therefore the catechists, who are not without importance'

     *qutsavissarai*              *nunatta_*          *ullumikkut_/*
     *qutsavi-ssaq-gi-vai*        *nuna-tta*          *ullumikkut*
     thank-FUT-have-3SG.         land-1PL.POS        today
     SUBJ/3PL.OBJ.IND

'our land should thank them today'

48.  *aamma*     *tamakku*     *sulerujussuarsimasut_/*
     *aamma*     *tamakku*     *suli-rujussuaq-sima-sut*
     and         those         work-very.much-PERF-3PL.PART

'and they worked a lot, those ones'

49.  *imaannaanngitsorujussuarmik_*      *sulerujusima —*
     *sulisimasut_'*

     *imaannanngitsoq-rujussuaq-mik*
     *suli-sima-sut*

     ones.not.without.importance-very.much-INST
     work-PERF-3PL.PART

'they worked in a very important/meaningful/able way'

50.  *kisianni_*      *pitsaviunngitsumik_*           *pineqartarsimasut_*
     *kisianni*       *pitsak-vik-u-nngit-soq-mik*    *pi-neqaq-saq-sima-sut*

but              excellent-genuine-COP-       do-PASS-HAB-PERF-
                 NEG-PART-INST                 3PL.PART
'but they have not been paid well/well taken care of' [*pi-neqaq*
'be taken care of']

*aqutsisuninngaanniit*
*aqutsisut-ninngaanniit*
management-PL.ABL
'by the management'

51.   *tassa        taamani_        Grønlands Styrelsep_*
      *tassa        taamani         Grønlands Styrelse-p*
      that.is       at.that.time    Greenland Steering-REL
      'so at that time Greenland Steering'

      *tamaasa                    ingerlatarivai*
      *tamaq-asa                  ingerlaC-saq-gi-vai*
      the.whole/all-3PL.O         work.with-PASS.PART-have-3SG.SUBJ/
                                  3PL.OBJ.IND
      'worked with them'

52.   *provsteqarfik        aqqutigalugu_}*
      *provsteqarfik-0      aqqut-gi-lugu*
      deanery-ABS          way-have-3SG.OBJ.CT
      'via the deanery.'

## XIX

53.   {*Ajoqillu           taamani       tassa_     palasillumi_*
      *ajoqi-t-lu          taamani       tassa      palasi-t-lu-mi*
      catechist-PL-and     at.that.time  that.is    priest-PL-and-sure
      'And the catechists at that time, and of course the priests'

      *ingattammik ajoqit_*
      *ingattammik ajoqi-t*
      especially catechist-PL
      'especially the catechists;'

*nuutsinneqartarput_*                    *nunaqarfinnut_*
*nuuC-tit-neqaq-saq-vut*                 *nunaqarfik-t-nut*
move-cause-PASS-HAB-3PL.IND              village-PL-PL.TERM
'they were moved to villages'

54.  *aperinagilluunniit*
     *aperi-nagit-luunniit*
     ask-3PL.OBJ.NEG.CT-or
     'without even asking them'

55.  *oqarfigisarpaat_*
     *oqarfigi-saq-vaat*
     say-HAB-3PL.SUBJ/3PL.OBJ.IND
     'they would say to them'

56.  "*Uunnga     nuussuutit!*"_
     *uunnga     nuuC-ssaa*[18]*-vutit*
     over.here    move-FUT-2SG.IND
     '"Move over there!"'

57.  *taavalu       piumanngikkaangata*
     *taava-lu       piuma-nngit-gaangata*
     then-and     want-NEG-when(ever).3NC.PL.CAUS
     'and if they didn't want to'

58.  *soraarsittarlugit_*}
     *soraarsit-saq-lugit*
     fire-HAB-3PL.OBJ.CT
     'they would fire them.'

XX

59.  {*Nuutsikkaangamigillu*                  *taamani_*
     *nuuC-tit-gaangamigit-lu*                *taamani*
     move-cause-when(ever).3PL.SUBJ/          at.that.time
     3NC.PL.OBJ.CAUS-and
     'And when they had moved them at that time'

60.    *illussaqartinneqarneq*                           *ajorput_}*
        *illu-ssaq*[19]*-qaq-tit-neqaq-neq-0*        *ajor-vut*
        house-FUT-have-cause-PASS-NOMZ-ABS    bad-3PL.IND
        'they were not given a house to stay in/they didn't house them.'

**XXI**

61.    *{Nuukkaangamillu*
        *nuuC-gaangamik-lu*
        move-when(ever).3C.PL.CAUS-and
        'And whenever they moved'

62.    *nammineq*    *illulioqqaarlutik_*
        *nammineq*    *illu-lioq-qqaaq-lutik*
        self          house-build-first-3PL.CT
        'they first had to build a house themselves'

63.    *ilaanni*      *ukiorsuaq*        *sinnerlugu_/*
        *ilaanni*      *ukioq-suaq*       *sinner-lugu*[20]
        sometimes    winter-big-ABS    over/more.than-3SG.OBJ.CT
        'sometimes over more than a year'

64.    *illumi*        *inissisimallutik_*
        *illu-mi*       *inissi-sima-lutik*
        house-LOC    live-PERF-3PL.CT
        'they had to live in a[nother] house'

65.    *uffa*    *meeraqarlutik*
        *uffa*    *meeraq-qaq-lutik*
        even    child-have-3PL.CT
        'even having a child'

66.    *nuliaqarlutillu_}*
        *nuliaq-qaq-lutik-lu*
        wife-have-3PL.CT-and
        'and having a wife.'

**XXII**

67. {*Nersunartarsimaqaat*[21]  *taamani_*
*nersunaq-saq-sima-qi-vut*  *taamani*
admire.someone.because.he.can.  at.that.time
last-HAB-PERF-INTNS.3PL.IND
'They lasted admirably/they are admired because they lasted/
they were impressive'

*ajoqit*
*ajoqi-t*
catechist-PL
'the catechists'

68. *eqqarsaatigissagaanni_}*
*eqqarsaatigi-ssa-gaanni*[22]
think.about-FUT-when.3PL.SUBJ/3C.SG.OBJ.PART
'when one thinks about [it].'

**XXIII**

69. {*Nersortariaqartut_*
*nersor-tariaqaq-sut*
thank-should/must[23]-3PL.PART
'They should be thanked'

— *torujorujorujussuartut*  *taakku*
— *soq-ruju-ruju-rujussuaq-tut*  *taakku*
part-very-very-very.much-3PL.PART  those
'very very much'

70. *uanga*  *isumaqarfigivakka}*
*uanga*  *isumaqaq-vigi-vakka*
1SG  think/believe-TRANSR-1SG.SUBJ/3PL.OBJ.IND
'I think [this].'

**XXIV**

71. {*Makkua*  *allaapput_*  *palasit_'*  *ilinniartitsisukkut_*
*makkua*  *allaa-vut*  *palasi-t*  *ilinniartitsisoq-t-kkut*

these          different-3PL.IND          priest-PL          teacher-PL-and.
                                                             fellows'[24]

'These were different, [like] the priests, together with the
teachers'

| | |
|---|---|
| *aammalu* | *KGH-mi* |
| *taamanikkut* | *sulisuusut_* |
| *aamma-lu* | *Kongelig Grønlandske Handeln-mi* |
| *taamani-kkut* | *sulisut-u-soq-t* |
| and-and | Royal Greenlandic Trade-LOC |
| at.that.time-VIA[25] | personnel-COP-PART-PL |

'and the workers at the KGH at that time, what about these?'

| | |
|---|---|
| (*imaattumi*) | *sannavinni_'* |
| *aamma* | *saffiorfinni_}* |
| *imaaC-soq-mi* | *sannavik-ni* |
| *aamma* | *saffiorfik-ni* |
| be.like.this-PART-what.about | carpentry.shop-LOC.PL |
| and | smithy-LOC.PL |

'(like) in the carpentry shops and in the smithies.'

## XXV

72.   {*Taakku*      *nutserteqattaarneqanngillat_*
      *taakku*        *nutser-tit-qattaaq-neqaq-nngit-lat*
      those           move-cause-again.and.again-PASS-NEG-3PL.NEG.IND
      'Those ones did not move much [they weren't moved much]'

73.   *nunaqarfimmi*   *illoqarfimmi*   *illoqarfinni*   *taakku*
                                                          *inuupput_'*

      *nunaqarfik-mi*   *illoqarfik-mi*   *illoqarfik-ni*   *taakku*
                                                            *inuu-vut*

      village-LOC       town-LOC          town-LOC.PL       those
                                                            live-3PL.IND

'those ones lived in the village, the town, the towns'

74.   *illoqarfiup*          *inuinut*              *ilanngullutik*
      *illoqarfik-up*        *inuk-inut*            *ilannguC-lutik*
      town-REL              person-3SG.POS./       include/join-3PL.CT
                            PL.POSM.TERM
      'to become members of the town [to join the township]'

75.   *nuutsinneqassanatik_}*
      *nuuC-tit-neqaq-ssa-natik*
      move-cause-PASS-FUT[26]-3PL.NEG.CT
      'they were never moved.'

## XXVI

76.   {*Kisiannili*    *ukua*    *ajoqit*        *taakku_*
      *kisianni-li*    *ukua*    *ajoqi-t*       *taakku_*
      but-but          these     catechist-PL    those
      'But these catechists'

      *puiorsinnaanngilakka_/*
      *puior-sinnaa-nngit-lakka*
      forget-can-NEG-1SG.SUBJ/3NC.PL.OBJ.NEG.IND
      'I cannot forget them'

77.   *isumaqarpunga*
      *isuma-qaq-vunga*
      thought-have-1SG.IND
      'I think'

78.   *oqaluttuarisariaqartut*              *assorujussuaq_*
      *oqaluttuaq-gi-sariaqaq-sut*          *assut-rujussuaq_o*
      story-have-should/must-3PL.PART       much-very.much-ABS
      'they should be talked about very much'

      *annertunerusumik_/*
      *anneq-tu-neru-soq-mik*
      big-big-more-PART-INST
      'much more.'

79. *Ilumut      taakkua_*
    *Ilumut      taakkua*
    It.is.true    those
    'It is true those ones'

    *tupinnaannamik          sulisimapput_/*
    *tupinnar-innaq-mik       suli-sima-vut*
    amazing-only-INST        work-PERF-3PL.IND
    'have worked just amazingly'

80. *qasusuissimaqaat_}*
    *qasusuiC-sima-qi-vut*
    tireless-PERF-INTNS-3PL.IND
    'they were very tireless.'

## XXVII

81. *{Nunaqarfinni*
    *nunaqarfik-ni*
    village-LOC.PL
    'In the villages'

    *(taamani        asimioqarfinnik                taaneqartartuni)_/*
    *taamani        asi[27]-miut-qaq-fik-nik       taaneqartartoq-ni*
    at.that.time    out.of.the.way.place-           so.called-LOC.PL
                 from-have-place-PL.INST
    '(in those days [they were] called "asimiuqarfinnik" [the place
    with people in an out-of-the-way place or in nature])'

    *ajoqi           tassaavoq            niuertoruserlu_'*
    *ajoqi-0         tassa-a-voq          niuertoruseq-0-lu*
    catechist-ABS   like.that-COP-3SG.IND  trade.manager-
                               ABS-and
    'the catechist was like that and the trade manager [too]'

82. *tassa_        qaammarsaasussat_}*
    *tassa        qaammar-sar-i-soq-ssaq-t*
    like.that    be.light-AGENT-INTRANS-PART-FUT-PL
    'that is, the ones to spread light [i.e., they teach].'

XXVIII

83. {*Juumooq_   ajoqip        atuarfik      tamaat
    tigummivaa_*

    *juumooq      ajoqi-p       atuarfik-0     tamaq-at
    tigummivaa*

    midwife       catechist-REL   school-ABS    the.whole/all-3SG.O
    hold.in.hands-3SG.SUBJ/3SG.OBJ.IND

    'The midwife, the catechist has the whole school to take
    care of'

84. *atuartut        tamaasa
    atuartissavai_*

    *atuartoq-t       tamaq-asa
    atuar-tit-ssa-vai*

    student-PL         the.whole/all-3PL.O
    learn-cause-FUT-3SG.SUBJ/3PL.OBJ.IND

    'he has to teach all of the students'

85. 1.   *klassiminngaanniit*   7.   *klasse   tikillugu_*
    1.   *klasse-minngaanniit*  7.   *klasse   tikit-lugu*
    first  class-ABL                seventh  class   arrive-3SG.
                                                     OBJ.CT

    'from the first grade [going] to the seventh grade'

86. *kisimiilluni_*
    kisimi-u-luni
    alone-COP-3SG.CT
    'being alone'

87. *ulloq   tamaat                    suleriarluni_/*
    ulloq   tamaq-at                  suli-giaq-luni
    day     the.whole/all-3SG.O        work-go.to.do-3SG.CT
    'when he's going to [be at] work all day'

88.  *sapaammi*          *naalagiartitsilluni_/*
     *sapaat-mi*         *naalagiartitsi-luni*
     Sunday-LOC     lead.divine.service-3SG.CT
     'leading services on Sunday'

89.  *toqusoqarpat*
     *toqusoq-qaq-ppat*
     dead.one-have-3NC.SG.COND
     'when/if there is a dead one [when someone has died]'

90.  *toqusunik*             *ilisilluni_/*
     *toqusoq-nik*           *ilisi-luni*
     dead.one-PL.INST     bury-3SG.CT
     'he buries the dead ones'

91.  *kuisittoqassappat*
     *kuisiC-soq-qaq-ssa-ppat*
     christen-PART-have-FUT-3NC.SG.COND
     'when/if there is someone to be christened'

92.  *kuisillugit_/*
     *kuisiC-lugit*
     christen-3PL.OBJ.CT
     'he christens them'

93.  *allagassarpassuillu*                          *oqaluffimmut*
     *ilagiinnut*

     *allaC-saq-ssaq-passuit-lu*                     *oqaluffik-mut*
     *ilagiit-nut*

     write-PASS.PART-FUT-many/a.lot-and     Church-TERM
     Christian.society-PL.TERM[28]

     *tunngasut*            *allallugit_}*
     *tunnga-soq-t*     ·   *allaC-lugit*
     be.about-PART-PL     write-3PL.OBJ.CT
     'he had to write a lot of things about the Church and Christian
     society.'

**XXIX**

94. {*Imalu     akissarsiai           suunngitsigaat_*
    *ima-lu    akissarsiaq-i         su-u-nngit-tigi*[29]*-vut*
    so-and    pay-3SG.POS.ABS    what-COP-NEG-so(equative)-3PL.IND
    'And so his pay is very little'

95. *uffa            ilinniartitsisutullu        aammalu*
    *palasitut      suligaluarlutik_*}

    *uffa             ilinniartitsisoq-tut-lu     aamma-lu*
    *palasi-tut      suli-galuaq-lutik*

    even.if         teacher-EQ-and           and-and
    priest-EQ      work-CONSEQ-3PL.CT

    'even if they are working as a teacher and as a priest.'

**XXX**

96. {*Pissaqarniarlutik_*
    *pissaq-qaq-niaq-lutik*
    something.one.will.have-have-FUT-3PL.CT
    'To have food'

97. *qajartorneq               ilinniartarpaat*
    *qajartoq-neq             ilinniaq-saq-vaat*
    row.a.kayak-NOMZ.ABS     learn-HAB-3PL.SUBJ/3PL.OBJ.IND
    'they had to learn to be kayak rowers [learn kayak skills]'

98. *ilikkavillugu_*}
    *ilikkaq-vig-lugu*
    learn.something-completely-3SG.OBJ.CT
    'learning it completely.'

**XXXI**

99. {*Taassuma      saniatigut       ilinniartitsereeraangamik*
    *taassuma      saniatigut       ilinniartitsi-reer-gaangamik*
    this [latter]    moreover/         teach-PAST.PERF-when[ever].3C.
               in.addition    PL.CAUS
    'Moreover, when they had taught'

100.    *atuartitsereeraangamik_}*
        *atuartitsi-reer-gaangamik*
        teach.to.read-PAST.PERF-when[ever].3C.PL.CAUS
        'when they had taught.'


## XXXII

101.    *{Piniarniartarput_*
        *piniaq-niaq-saq-vut*
        hunt-FUT-HAB-3PL.IND
        'They went hunting [would go hunting]'

102.    *iisassaqarumallutik*
        *iisassaq-qaq-juma-lutik*
        something.to.eat-have-want-3PL.CT
        'wanting to have something to eat'

103.    *nerisassaqarumallutik_}*
        *nerisassaq-qaq-juma-lutik*
        food-have-want-3PL.CT
        'wanting to have some food.'


## XXXIII

104.    *{Tassunga       unilaariarlunga. . . ._}*
        *tassunga        uni-laaq-giaq-lunga*
        there            stop-a.little-go.to.do-1SG.CT
        'I am going to stop a little there. . . .'



Speaker 1, text 1b

Recorded August 17, 1995, in Nuuk


## XXXIV

105.    *{Taava      ajoqit          eqqartullatsiaratsigit*
        *taava       ajoqi-t         eqqartor-llar-tsiar-gatsigit*
        so          catechist-PL    talk/tell.about-with.intensity-little-1PL.
                                    SUBJ/3PL.OBJ.CAUS

'So we mentioned the catechists'

106.　aatsaaginnaq　　　eqqartullatsiarpakka_
　　　aatsaat-innaq　　　eqqartor-llar-tsiar-vakka
　　　now-just　　　　　talk.about-with.intensity-little-1SG.SUBJ/3PL.
　　　　　　　　　　　OBJ.IND
　　　'just now I talked about/mentioned them'

107.　kisiannili　　tassa　　taamani　　　aamma_　　*piniartuuneq*
　　　kisianni-li　　tassa　　taamani　　　aamma　　piniartoq-u-neq
　　　but-but　　　that.is　at.that.time　and　　　hunter-COP-
　　　　　　　　　　　　　　　　　　　　　　　NOMZ.ABS
　　　'but in those days to be a hunter'

　　　inuuneq　　piniartuuneq　　　imaannaanngitsorujussuuvoq_/
　　　inuuneq　　piniartoq-u-neq　　imaannaanngit-soq-rujussuaq-
　　　　　　　　　　　　　　　　　u-voq
　　　life　　　　hunter-COP-　　　be.amazing-PART-very much-COP-
　　　　　　　　NOMZ.ABS　　　　3SG.IND
　　　'to live, to be a hunter it was very amazing'

108.　nunatsinni_　　　　inuit　　　amerlanersai,[30]
　　　nuna-tsinni　　　　inuk-it　　amerla-nersaq-i
　　　land-1PL.POS.LOC　person-PL　be.many-NOMZ.most-3PL.
　　　　　　　　　　　　　　　　　POS/PL.POSM.ABS
　　　'in our land, its many people'

　　　ullumikkut　　　oqartarpugut_
　　　ullumi-kkut　　　oqaq-saq-vugut
　　　today-VIA　　　say-HAB-1PL.IND
　　　'today, we say'

109.　(aalisarneq　　　inuutissarsiutit　　　pingaarnersarivaat)}
　　　aalisarneq-0　　inuutissarsiut-it　　pingaar-nersaq-gi-vaat
　　　fishing-ABS　　occupation-PL　　　important-NOMZ.most-have-
　　　　　　　　　　　　　　　　　　　3PL.SUBJ/3SG.OBJ.IND
　　　'(the most important careers/occupations are fishing).'

## XXXV

110.    {*Taamani*       *uagut*       *meeraasugut_/*
         *taamani*       *uagut*       *meeraq-u-sugut*
         at-that-time      1PL        child-COP-1PL.PART
         '[But] at that time [when] we were children'

111.    <u>*piniarneq*</u>       *inuutissarsiutit*       *annersarivaat_}*
         *piniarneq-0*       *inuutissarsiut-it*       *annersaq-gi-vaat*
         hunting-ABS      career/occupation-PL      biggest-have-3PL.SUBJ/
                                                                  3SG.OBJ.IND
         'the biggest careers/occupations were hunting.'

## XXXVI

112.    {*Qajaqarput,*       *piniartut*       *tamarmik_'*
         *qajaq-qaq-vut*       *piniartoq-t*       *tamaq-mik*
         kayak-have-3PL.IND      hunter-PL      the.whole/all-3PL.S
         'They had kayaks, all the hunters'

113.    *qajaqqissorsuullutik_}*
         *qajaqqiC-soq-suaq-u-lutik*
         be.good.with.kayak-PART-very.much-COP-3PL.CT
         'they were very good with the kayaks.'

## XXXVII

114.    {*Amerlanertigullu*           *sila*          *qanoq*
         *ikkaluaraangalluunniit*

         *amerla-neq-tigut-lu*           *sila-0*         *qanoq*
         *iC-kkaluaq-gaangat-luunnit*

         be.many-NOMZ-PL.VIA-and      weather-ABS      how
         be-CONSEQ-whenever.3NC.SG.CAUS-or

         'and through however many [kinds of] weather there might be'

         *ilaanni,*
         ilaanni
         sometimes
         'sometimes'

115.  *aallartarput_/*
      *aallar-saq-vut*
      go-HAB-3PL.IND
      'they went'

116.  *inuutissaqarusullutik_'*
      *inuutissaq-qaq-rusug-lutik*
      food-have-want-3PL.CT
      'wanting to have food'

      *ullut        tamaasa_}*
      *ulloq-t      tamaq-asa*[31]
      day-PL        the.whole/all-3PL.O
      'every day.'


## XXXVIII

117.  {*Qaqortumi      uanga      eqqamavara      tassa      taamani_*
      *Qaqortoq-mi     uanga      eqqama-vara     tassa      taamani*
      Qaqortoq-LOC   1SG      remember-1SG.   that.is   at.that.time
                              SUBJ/3SG.OBJ.IND
      'In Qaqortoq I remember it, that is, at that time'

118.  *umiaasaqaraluarpoq*
      *umiaasaq-qaq-galuaq-voq*
      little.flat.bottomed.rowboat-have-CONSEQ-3SG.IND
      'there were little flat-bottomed rowboats'

119.  *aasaanerusukkullu*            *umiaq ator— umiaasaq*
                                      *atorneqartarput_/*

      *aasaq-u-neru-soq-kkut-lu*      *umiaq-0 umiaasaq-0*
                                      *ator-neqaq-saq-vut*

      summer-COP-COMPAR-             umiaq-ABS rowboat-ABS
      PART-VIA-and

                                      use-PASS-HAB-3PL.IND

      'and umiaks— rowboats were used more in the summertime'

120. *aalisaatigalugit_}*
     *aalisaq-utigi-lugit*
     fish-in.order.to-3PL.OBJ.CT
     'in order to fish [i.e., in order to use them to fish].'

## XXXIX

121. *{Qajatut     aamma_'*
     *qajaq-tut     aamma*
     kayak-EQ     and
     'And as kayaks'

     *sukkatiginnginnamik_'*
     *sukka-tigi-nngit-namik*
     fast-as.much.as-NEG-3C.PL.NEG.CAUS
     'they were not as fast'

122. *qajat_*[32]
     *qajaq-t*
     kayak-PL
     'the kayaks'

     *qajartortut*                *taamani*        *tassa_*
     *qajartoq-soq-t*             *taamani*        *tassa*
     row.kayak-PART-PL     at.that.time     that.is
     'the kayak rowers, at that time, that is'

     *eqqaamavara*
     *eqqaama-vara*
     remember-1SG.SUBJ/3SG.OBJ.IND
     'I remember it'

123. *meeraalluta*             *upernaakkut_*
     *meeraq-u-luta*           *upernaaq-kkut*
     child-COP-1PL.CT     spring-VIA
     'when we were children in the spring'

124. *sikorsuit     tikillaraangata_}*
     *sikorsuit     tikiC-llar-gaangata*

big.ice.ABS      arrive-with.force-whenever.3NC.PL.CAUS
'whenever the drift ice arrived.'[33]

## XL

125.   {*Qaannamik_*'
       *qaannat-mik*
       kayaks-SG.INST
       'By kayaks'

       *Qaqortormiut*                    *qajartai,*
       *Qaqortoq-miut*                   *qajartaq-it*
       Qaqortoq-people.from.REL          kayaker-PL.POSM.ABS
       'the inhabitants of Qaqortoq, the kayakers'

       *Iindalissuasikkut,*     *Iisaakkut,*       *Jaakukkut_*}
       *Iindalissuasi-kkut*     *Iisaa-kkut*       *Jaaku-kkut*
       Big.Henry-family     Isaac-family     Jacob-family
       'Big Henry, Isaac, Jacob.'

       (*atii*           *eqqaamanngilakka*
       *ati-i*           *eqqaama-nngit-lakka*
       name-PL      remember-NEG-1SG.SUBJ/3PL.OBJ.NEG.IND
       '(I don't remember the [other] names'

126.   *amerlasoorpassuupput*              *taamani*)}}
       *amerlasuut-rpassuit-uC-vut*       *taamani*
       many-many-COP-3PL.IND       at.that.time
       'there were very many at that time).'

## XLI

127.   {*Tikillaraangamik*                        *ualikkut_*'
       *tikiC-llaq-gaangamik*                     *ualikkut*
       arrive-INTNS-whenever.3C.PL.CAUS      in.the.afternoon
       'When they came back [from hunting, to Qaqortoq] in the
       afternoon'

128.   *ullaakkut*              *aallarunik_*'
       *ullaakkut*              *aallar-gunik*[34]

in.the.morning go-3C.PL.COND
'after having gone out in the morning'

129. *ilaanni_* *puisit_* *arfineq-pingasut* *qulit_*
   *ilaanni* *puisi-t* *arfineq-pingasut* *qulit*
   sometimes seal-PL eight  ten
   'sometimes eight, ten seals'

   *sinnerlugilluunniit*[35] *kalillugit_}*
   *sinnerlugit-luunniit* *kaliC-lugit*
   more.than-or.even in.tow-3PL.OBJ.CT
   'or even more in tow [i.e., sometimes (with) eight or ten or even more seals in tow].'


## XLII

130. *{Tikileraangata_'*
   *tikiC-leq-gaangata*
   arrive-begin-whenever.3NC.PL.CAUS
   'Whenever they began to arrive'

131. *meerarpassuulluta*
   *meeraq-passuit-u-luta*
   child-many-COP-1PL.CT
   'we were a lot of children [there were a lot of us children]'

132. *sissamukaasaratta_*
   *sissaq-mukar-a-saq-gatta*
   beach-go.to.do-many.do-HAB-1PL.CAUS
   'we used to go as a group to the beach'

133. *tassani* *pilattaramikkit* *tassa* *taamani_*
   *tassani* *pilaC-saq-gamikkit*[36] *tassa* *taamani*
   there cut.up/carve-HAB- that.is at.that.time
     3C.PL.SUBJ/3PL.OBJ.CAUS
   'and there they used to cut them up, that is, in those days'

134. *pilannerini_'*
   *pilaC-neq-ini*

cut.up/carve-NOMZ-3PL.POS.LOC
'in its being cut up [and then they cut it up]'

135.  *uagut_*        *tinguttuuttarpugut_/*
      *uagut*         *tinguk-toq-uti-saq-vugut*
      1PL             liver-eat-many.of.us-HAB-1PL.IND
      'we, we all used to eat the liver'

136.  aammalu_        tamuatsivaartorluta            tassa_/
      *aamma-lu*      *tamuatsivaaq-toq-luta*        *tassa*
      and-and         tamuatsivaaq-eat-1PL.CT        that.is
      'and we ate tamuatsivaaq'

137.  *puisip*        *amia*                 *orsutalerlugu_}*
      *puisi-p*       *ameq-a*               *orsoq*[37]*-saq-leq-lugu*
      seal-REL        skin-3SG.POS.ABS       fat/grease-belong.to.one-add.
                                             to-3SG.OBJ.CT
      'adding the fat to the seal skin [i.e., eating the seal skin with the
      fat to which it was attached]'

138.  (*amimininnguaq*              *orsutalerlugu*)}}
      *ameq-mineq-nnguaq-0*         *orsoq-saq-leq-lugu*
      skin-piece.of-little-ABS      fat-belong.to.one-provide.with-3SG.
                                    OBJ.CT
      '(a little piece of skin with the fat [we chewed]).'

139.  *Tassa*    *taanna_*            *tamuarujoortarparput_'*
      *tassa*    *taanna*             *tamua-rujoor-saq-varput*
      that.is    that.one.ABS         chew-casually-HAB-1PL.SUBJ/3SG.OBJ.IND
      'We used to chew it continually'

140.  *tamuatsivaamik_*          *taasarparput*       *uagut*      *taqqavani_}}}*
      *tamuatsivaaq-mik*         *taasar-varput*      *uagut*      *taqqava-ni*
      tamuatsivaaq-INST          call-1PL.SUBJ/       1PL          south-LOC
                                 3SG.OBJ.IND
      'we called it "tamuatsivaaq," we in the south [i.e., we in South
      Greenland].'

141.      *(qanoq*        *avannaamiut*
             *qanoq*-0      *avannaa-miut*
             how-ABS     what.lies.in.the.north-people.from.PL.ABS

             *taasarnerpaat*                   *taakku?)}}}}*
             *taasar-ner-vaat*                 *taakku*
             call-wonder-3PL.SUBJ/3SG.OBJ.IND   those-ABS
             '(I wonder what the people from the north call it, those ones?)'

XLIII

142.      *{Tassa*    *eqqaamagigaana*        *taamani_*
             *tassa*      *eqqaama-giga-una*      *taamani*
             that.is    remember-1SG.SUBJ/    at.that.time
                        3SG.OBJ.PART-DEIC
             'That is, I remember'

             *sorsunnersuup*       *nalaani_/*
             *sorsunnersuaq-up*   *nalaani*
             World.War.II-REL     period.3SG.POS/SG.POSM.LOC
             'the period of World War II;'

143.      *Qaqortuminngaanniit*       *ataataga*
             *ilinniartitsisuugami*       *efterskolemi_/*

             *Qaqortoq-minngaanniit*     *ataata-ga*
             *ilinniartitsisoq-u-gami*      *efterskole-mi*

             Qaqortoq-ABL              father-1SG.POS.ABS
             teacher-COP-3C.SG.CAUS   high.school-LOC

             'when from Qaqortoq my father was a teacher in high school [for older students]'

144.      *taavalu*     *anaanama*          *ataataa_*
             *taava-lu*    *anaana-ma*       *ataata-a*
             then-and   mother-1SG.POS.REL   father-3NC.SG.POS/
                                        SG.POSM.ABS
             'and then my mother's father'

*taalliortorsuarput_/*
*taalliortoq-suaq-rput*
poet-big-1PL.POS/SG.POSM.ABS
'our poet'

| *Kalaallit Nunaata* | *taalliortorsua_* | *Iinndaleeraq* |
| *Henrik Lund_'* | | |

| *Kalaallit Nunaat-a* | *taalliortoq-suaq-0* | *Iinndaleeraq-0* |
| *Henrik Lund-0* | | |

| Greenland-3SG.POS.REL | poet-big-ABS | Henry-ABS |
| Henrik Lund-ABS | | |

'Greenland's big poet Henry, Henrik Lund'


145.　*aasat*　　　*tamaasa_'*
　　　*aasaq-t*　　*tamaq-asa*
　　　summer-PL　the.whole/all-3PL.O
　　　'every summer'

| *tikeraartaratsigu* | *Qaqortuminngaanniit* |
| *tikeraar-saq-gatsigu* | *Qaqortoq-minngaanniit* |
| visit-HAB-1PL.SUBJ/3SG.OBJ.CAUS | Qaqortoq-ABL |

'we used to visit him from Qaqortoq'


146.　*uagut*　*aasiffigisaratsigu*　　*Narsaq_/*
　　　*uagut*　*aasi-ffigi-saq-gatsigu*　*Narsaq-0*
　　　1PL　　spend.the.summer-TRANS.　Narsaq-ABS
　　　　　　have.as-HAB-1PL.SUBJ/
　　　　　　3SG.OBJ.CAUS

'we used to spend the summer in Narsaq [have summer vacation
with him in Narsaq; have Narsaq as a summer vacation place]'

| (*meeqqat aamma* | *anaanakkut* | *ataatakkullu* |
| *meeqqat* | | |

| *meeraq-t aamma* | *anaana-kkut* | *ataata-kkut-lu* |
| *meeraq-t* | | |

child-PL                and                    mother-family.ABS
father-familyABS-and                           child-PL

'(the children and [my] mother's family and [my] father's family
the children'

*qatanngutigullu*                    *tamatta_)}*
*qatanngut-tiqut-lu*                  *tamaq-tta*
siblings-family.PL-and                the.whole/all-1PL
'and the sibling's family, all of us).'

## XLIV

147.    {*Eqqaamagiga*          *tassa*      *taamani*       <u>*Ittu*</u> '
        *eqqaama-giga*          *tassa*      *taamani*       *Ittu*-0
        remember-1SG.SUBJ/   that.is    at.that.time    Grandfather-ABS
        3SG.OBJ.PART
        'I remember Grandfather at that time'

148.    *tyggegummimik*          *amerikamiuninngaanniit*
        *tunisittarsimagami_}*

        *tyggegummi-mik*          *amerika-miut-ninngaanniit*
        *tunisit*[38]*-saq-sima-gami*

        chewing.gum-INST    America-people.from-ABL
        get-HAB-PERF-3C.SG.CAUS

        'he used to get chewing gum from the Americans.'[39]

## XLV

149.    {*Tyggegummimik*          *tunigaagamitigut*[40]
        *tyggegummi-mik*          *tuni-gaa-ngamitigut*
        chewing.gum-INST       give-whenever-3NC.SG.SUBJ/1PL.OBJ.CAUS
        'Whenever he gave us a lot of chewing gum'

150.    *oqartarpoq_/*
        *oqaq-saq-voq*
        say-HAB-3SG.IND
        'he used to say'

151. "*Qallunaat*          *tamuatsuvaavat*"_/
    *qallunaaq-t*          *tamuatsivaa-at*[41]
    Dane/white.man-PL    tamuatsivaa-3PL.POS.ABS
    '"[This is] white man's tamuatsivaaq"'

152. *taava*   *nammineq*   *sukuloortuugami_*     *Iinndaleeraq_}*
    *taava*   *nammineq*   *sukulooq-tooq-gami*   *Iinndaleeraq*
    then     self       chewing.tobacco-     Henry
                              take-3C.SG.CAUS
    'then he would take some chewing tobacco [for] himself, Henry.'

## XLVI

153. *{Tyggegummimik*       *tuneriarluta_'*
    *tyggegummi-mik*      *tuni-riar-luta*
    chewing.gum-INST     give-INTNS-1PL.OBJ.CT
    'Giving us chewing gum'

154. *nammineq_*   *sukuluumik*           *oqummersisarpoq*
    *tassa_/*

    *nammineq*   *sukulooq-mik*        *oqummer-si-saq-voq*
    *tassa*

    self          chewing.tobacco-INST   put.in.mouth-INTRANS-
                                    HAB-3SG.IND
    that.is

    'himself biting into chewing tobacco'

155. *ammaraangamiut*[42]     *taanna*   *qillertuusaarannguaq}*
    *ammar-gaangamiut*     *taanna*   *qillertuusaq-araq-nnguaq-0*
    open-whenever.3C.      that.one  container-little-little-ABS
    SG.SUBJ/3SG.OBJ.CAUS
    'whenever he opened that little [chewing tobacco] container.'

156. *Taava*   *oqartarpoq*       *tassa_/*
    *taava*   *oqaq-saq-voq*     *tassa*
    then     say-HAB-3SG.IND   that.is
    'Then he would say'

157. *"Tassa* *Ittup* *tamuatsivaava"_}}*
   *tassa* *Ittu-p* *tamuatsivaaq-a*
   that.is Grandfather-REL tamuatsivaaq-3NC.SG.POS
   '"That is Grandfather's tamuatsivaaq."'

## XLVII

158. {*Iinndaleeraq* *taamatut* *oqaluttuugami_*}
   *Iinndaleeraq-0* *taama-tut* *oqaloq-soq-u-gami*
   Henry-ABS like.that-EQ tell/speak-PART-COP-3C.
             SG.CAUS
   'Henry said it like this [this is the way Henry spoke].'

## XLVIII

159. {*Tassa* *eqqaamalluariga*
   *tassa* *eqqaama-lluaq-giga*
   that.is remember-well-1SG.SUBJ/3SG.OBJ.PART
   'I remember it very well'

160. *taamani* *Narsamini — Narsamukaraangatta* *aasakkut_}*
   *taamani* *Narsaq-mukaq-gaangatta* *aasaq-kkut*
   at.that.time Narsaq-go.to-whenever.1PL.CAUS summer-VIA
   'in those days, whenever we went to Narsaq during the summer.'

## XLIX

161. {*Angallatit_* *amerlasoorsuunngillat* *taamani_*
   *angallat-it* *amerlasooq-suaq-u-nngit-lat* *taamani*
   vessel-PL.ABS be.many-big-COP-NEG-3PL. at.that.time
           NEG.IND
   'There weren't many vessels in those days,'

162. *tassa_* *uagut* *ilaagajuttarpugut*
   *tassa* *uagut* *ilaa-gajug-saq-vugut*
   that.is 1PL be.passenger-often-HAB-1PL.IND
   'we were often passengers [i.e., we often went by boat]'

   *savaateqarfiup* *pujortuleeraanut* *Hvalsømut*
   *savaateqarfik-up* *pujortuleeraq-a-nut* *Hvalsø-mut*

sheep.farm-REL       motor.boat-3SG.        Hvalsey-term
                     POS-PL.TERM
'on the sheep-farm's boat "Hvalsey"'


163.    *ilaalluta_}*
        *ilaa-luta*
        be.passenger-1PL.SUBJ.CT
        'we were passengers.'


L

164.    *{Qaqortuminngaanniit        Narsamukartarpugut_'*
        *Qaqortoq-minngaanniit       Narsaq-mukaq-saq-vugut*
        Qaqortoq-ABL                 Narsaq-go.to-HAB-1PL.IND
        'We used to go from Qaqortoq to Narsaq,'


165.    *Ataasiarlunga*
        *ataasiar-lunga*
        do.once-1SG.CT
        'I did once [one time]'


166.    *eqqaamagiga,*
        *eqqaama-giga*
        remember-1SG.SUBJ/3SG.OBJ.PART
        'I remember it'


167.    *taamanikkut*      *aamma_*     *eqqaamalluariga_*
        *taamani-kkut*     *aamma*      *eqqaama-lluaq-giga*
        at.that.time-VIA   and          remember-well-1SG.SUBJ/3SG.
                                        OBJ.PART
        'and at that time I remember it well,'


168.    *assorujussuaq*        *taamani_*     *tikaagulleqartarami_}*
        *assut-rujussuaq-0*    *taamani*      *tikaagullik-qaq-saq-gami*
        many-many-ABS         at.that.time    piked.whale-have-HAB-3C.
                                              SG.CAUS
        'at that time there were many, many lesser rorquals.'

LI

169. {(*Ataasiarlunga*
*ataasiar-lunga*
do.once-1SG.CT
'(I did it once [i.e., one time]'

170. *eqqaamagiga*
*eqqaama-giga*
remember-1SG.SUBJ/3SG.OBJ.PART
'I remember it'

171. *Qaqortuminngaanniit*   *Narsamukarluta*
*Qaqortoq-minngaanniit*   *Narsaq-mukaq-luta*
Qaqortoq-ABL   Narsaq-go.to-1PL.CT
'we were going from Qaqortoq to Narsaq'

172. *tikaagulliit*   *marluk_/*
*tikaagullik-it*   *marluk*
lesser.rorqual-PL   two
'[there were] two lesser rorquals;'

173. *pujortuleeraq*   *kaajallallugu_'*
*pujortuleeraq-0*   *kaajallaC-lugu*
motor.boat-ABS   circle-3SG.OBJ.CT
'they were circling the motor boat;'

174. *pisseqattaartut_/*
*pissiC-qattaar-sut*
jump-again.and.again-3PL.PART
'jumping again and again/the whole time;'

175. *assut*   *alutornartut_/*
*assut*   *alutor-naq-sut*
very   breathtaking/moving-PL/beautiful-be.such.that-3PL.PART
'[they were] very breathtaking/beautiful;'

176. *eqqaamagaarakku*
*eqqaama-ngaar-gakku*

remember-well-1SG.SUBJ/3NC.SG.OBJ.CAUS
'I remember it well'

177. | *taamani* | *puiorneq* | *ajorpara_)}* |
| *taamani* | *puior-neq*[43] | *ajor-vara* |
| at.that.time | forget-NOMZ | not.able.to-1SG.SUBJ/3SG.OBJ.IND |

'I can't forget that time.)'

LII

178. | *{Tassa* | *Narsamut* | *pigaagatta* | *taamani_/* |
| *tassa* | *Narsaq-mut* | *pi-gaan-gatta* | *taamani* |
| that.is | Narsaq-TERM | do-whenever-1PL.CAUS | at.that.time |

'Then when we got to Narsaq at that time;'

179. | *Narsaq* | *aamma* | *taamani* | *mikisuarakasiugami* |
| *Narsaq-0* | *aamma* | *taamani* | *miki-soq-araq-kasik-u-gami* |
| Narsaq-ABS | and | at.that.time | small-PART-small-dear-COP-3C.SG.CAUS |

'and Narsaq was very small and dear at that time'

180. *inukitsuarakasiullunilu,*
*inuk-kit-suaraq-kasik-u-luni-lu*
person-have.little-very.small.dear-COP-3C.SG.CT-and
'and there were not so many people;'

181. | *ullumikkutut* | *inngivikkami_}* |
| *ullumi-kkut-tut* | *iC-nngit-vig-gami* |
| today-VIA-EQ | COP-NEG-completely-3C.SG.CAUS |

'it is extremely different from today.'

LIII

182. | *{Tassa* | *Ittukkunniikkaagatta,* |
| *tassa* | *Ittu-kkut-niit-gaan-gatta* |
| that.is | Grandfather-family-be.by-whenever-1PL.CAUS |

'Then whenever we were with Grandfather'

183. *eqqaamagiga,*
    *eqqaama-giga*
    remember-1SG.SUBJ/3SG.OBJ.PART
    'I remember it'

184. *eqqaamaqaara*                  *taamani_*
    *eqqaama-qi-vara*                *taamani*
    remember-INTNS-1SG.SUBJ/3SG.OBJ.IND    at.that.time
    'I really remember it in those days'

185. *Iinndaleeqqap_*    *Ittup_*    *Ittup_*
    *Iinndaleeraq-p*    *Ittu-p*    *Ittu-p*
    Henry-REL        Grandfather-REL   Grandfather-REL
    'Henry, Grandfather, Grandfather'

    *ullaakkut_*       *tamatta*              *iteraangatta_*
    *ullaaq-kkut*      *tamaq-tta*           *iter-gaangatta*
    morning-VIA     the.whole/all-1PL    wake.up-whenever.1PL.
                                                CAUS
    'in the morning, all of us together would wake up'

186. *tiitoreerluta_/*
    *tii-toq-reer-luta*
    tea-drink-already-1PL.CT
    'when we had already drunk tea'

187. *taava*     *inimut*          *iserluta_'*
    *taava*     *ini-mut*        *iser-luta*
    then        room-TERM    enter-1PL.CT
    'then [when] we entered/came into the room'

    *Ittup*                *issia_*[44]
    *Ittu-p*              *issia* [*vik-minut*]
    Grandfather-REL    chair-3C.SG.POS.TERM
    'Grandfather to his chair'

188. *pattagissaminut*          *ingikkuni_/*
    *pattagiaq*[45]*-minut*       *igiC-guni*

piano-3C.SG.POS.TERM    sit.down-3C.SG.COND
'if he sat down at the piano'[46]

189.    *taava_*        *inersimasut_*
        *taava*         *inersimasoq-t*
        then            adult-PL
        'then the adults'

        *nalaasaarfimmut*        *issiavikuluunullu*              *issaallutik*
        *nalaasaarfik-mut*       *issiavik-kulooq*[47]*-nut-lu*      *isser-a-lutik*
        couch-TERM               arm.chair-big-PL.TERM-and       sit-PL-3PL.CT
        'when/while sitting down on the couch and in armchairs'

190.    *uagut*        *meeqqat*      *natermut*        *ingilluta_'*
        *uagut*        *meeraq-t*     *nateq-mut*       *ingiC-luta*
        1PL            child-PL       ground-TERM       sit.down-1PL.CT
        'we children sitting down on the ground'

191.    *taava*    *Ittup*                   *qinnutinnguaq*        *atuartarpaa_/*
        *taava*    *Ittu-p*                  *qinnut-nnguaq-0*      *atuar-saq-vaa*
        then       Grandfather-REL           prayer-little-ABS     read-HAB-3SG.
                                                                   SUBJ/3SG.OBJ.
                                                                   IND

        'then Grandfather would read a little prayer'

192.    *palasiugami*               *aamma_*
        *palasi-u-gami*             *aamma*
        priest-COP-3C.SG.CAUS       and
        'and [i.e., because] he was also a priest'

193.    *taamaasereeraangamilu*
        *taamaat-si-reer-gaangami-lu*
        the.whole/all-INTRANS-already-whenever.3C.SG.CAUS-and
        'and he was doing all this,'

194.    *taava*    *ullaarsiummik*            *tussiummik_*[48]
        *taava*    *ullaarsiut-mik*           *tussiut-mik*
        then       morning.prayer-INST        psalm-INST
        'then a morning psalm'

*tussiartarpugut_/*
*tussiar-saq-vugut*
sing.psalms-HAB-1PL.IND
'we sang [i.e., then we sang a morning psalm]'

195.   *Ittu*          *pattagissamik*      *pattattoq_/*
      *Ittu-0*        *pattagiaq-ssaq-mik*   *pattaC-soq*
      Grandfather-ABS   piano-FUT-INST   play-3SG.PART
      'Grandfather played the piano;'

196.   *taava*   *ilaanneeriarluta*               *aamma*   *tassa,*
      *taava*   *ilaanni-ir-riaq-luta*          *aamma*   *tassa*
      then    sometimes-VERB-INTNS-1PL.CT  and    that.is
      'then sometimes we did'

      *erinarsuummik_*
      *erinarsuut-mik*
      song-INST
      'a [regular/normal/nonreligious] song'

197.   *nalinginnaasumik*            *erinarsuummik_*
      *nalinginnaq-u-soq-mik*       *erinarsuut-mik*
      normal/usual-COP-PART-INST   song-INST
      'a normal song'

      (*ullormik*   *tassunga*   *naleqqussorisaminik*)
      *ulloq-mik*   *tassunga*   *naleqquC-sori-saq-minik*
      day-INST   over.there   suitable-think-PASS.PART-3SG.POS.INST
      '(that seemed suitable for that day)'

198.   *erinarsortittarpaatigut*            *tamatta_/*
      *erinarsor-tit-saq-vaatigut*        *tamaq-tta*
      sing-cause-HAB-3SG.SUBJ/1PL.OBJ.IND   the.whole/all-1PL
      'he let us sing all together'

      *tassami*   *inersimasullu*   *meeqqallu_/*
      *tassami*   *inersimasoq-t-lu*   *meeraq-t-lu*
      in.any.case   adult-PL-and   child-PL-and

'in any case the adults and the children'

199.   *taamaalilluta*       *ulloq*       *aallartittarparput_}*
*taamaali-luta*      *ulloq-0*     *aallartit-saq-varput*
like.that-1PL.CT    day-ABS   begin-HAB-1PL.SUBJ/3SG.OBJ.IND
'and that is how we began the day.'

LIV

200.   *{Tassalu*      *Ittup_*         *eqqaamavara*
*tassa-lu*     *Ittu-p*         *eqqaama-vara*
that.is-and   Grandfather-REL   remember-1SG.SUBJ/3SG.
OBJ.IND
'And then Grandfather, I remember'

201.   *Ittup*         *uagut*   *oqaluttuukkaatigut*
*Ittu-p*       *uagut*   *oqaluttuuC-gaatigut*
Grandfather-REL   1PL   tell-3SG.SUBJ/1PL.OBJ.PART
'Grandfather telling us'

*Niels Henrik-lu*        *illora_'*
*Niels Henrik-0-lu*     *illoq-ga*
Niels Henrik-ABS-and   cousin-1SG.POS.ABS
'[me] and my cousin Niels Henrik'

202.   *Ittu*         *aallaraangami_/*
*Ittu-0*        *aallaq-gaangami*
Grandfather-ABS   walk/go-whenever.3C.SG.CAUS
'whenever Grandfather went walking'

203.   *qaqqamut*      *pisuttuaraangami_/*
*qaqqaq-mut*    *pisuC-suaq-gaangami*
mountain-term   walk-with.strength-whenever.3C.SG.CAUS
'whenever he walked to the mountains'

204.   *pappilissamik*      *aqerluusamillu*     *nassartarpoq_}*
*pappiala[49]-ssa-mik*   *aqerluusaq-mik-lu*   *nassar-saq-voq*
paper-FUT-INST    pencil-INST-and   bring.with-HAB-3SG.IND
'he used to bring along paper and pencil.'

LV

205. {"*Tassa*   *isima*          *isigisai_/*
*tassa*      *isi-ma*         *isigi-saq-i*
that.is    eye-1SG.POS.REL   see-PASS.PART-3PL.POS.ABS
'"That is what my eye can see'

206. *siutimalu*          *tusaasai_/*
*siuti-ma-lu*        *tusaa-saq-i*
ear-1SG.POS.REL   hear-PASS.PART-3PL.POS.ABS
'and my ear can hear'

207. *allallugit*
*allaC-lugit*
write-3.OBJ.CT
'I am writing them'

208. *titartarniassagakkit"_/*
*titartar-niaq-ssa-gakkit*
draw-try-FUT-1SG.SUBJ/3PL.OBJ.CAUS
'I will try to draw them" [i.e., I am writing what my eye can see and my ear can hear,' i.e., 'my visual and aural impressions, I will try to draw them]'

209. *aamma*     *qalipaasarami}*
*aamma*     *qalipaa-saq-gami*
and        paint-HAB-3SG.CAUS
'and he painted [i.e., he was also a painter].'

LVI

210. {*Taamaattumik*   *tassa*   *Ittu*         *oqartarpoq_*
*taamaattumik*    *tassa*   *Ittu-0*       *oqaq-saq-voq*
therefore         that.is   Grandfather-ABS   say-HAB-3SG.IND
'Therefore Grandfather used to say'

211. "*Isigut*             *siutigullu*
*isi-vut*            *siuti-vut-lu*
eye-1PL.POS.PL.POSM.ABS   ear-1PL.POS.PL.POSM.ABS-and
'"Your eyes and your ears'

atorluarniartaqqullugit_'
ator-luaq-niaq-saq-qqu-lugit
use-well-try-HAB-bid/command-3PL.OBJ.CT
'bid them to try to do well [use them well]'

212. taakkuninngaaninngaanniit      pissarsiassagut_/
taakku-ninngaa-ninngaanniit      pissarsia-ssaq-vut
those-from-PL.ABL                get.something/purchase-FUT-
                                 1PL.POS/PL.POSM

'from those we can get something [i.e., make sure your ears and eyes really exploit their impressions since it is our purchase/what we're going to get via them]'

213. iluamik                  atorluarutsigit_
iluamik                       ator-luaq-gutsigit
the.right.way/correct/well    use-well-1PL.SUBJ/3PL.OBJ.COND
'if we use them well'

214. angeqimmata,
ange-qi-mmata
big-INTNS-3NC.PL.CAUS
'they are incredible'

215. annertoqimmata,
annertu-qi-mmata
enormous-INTNS-3NC.PL.CAUS
'they are incredible'

216. taama     oqarluaannarlunga"_}
taama     oqaq-luaq-innaq-lunga
this      say-well-just-1SG.CT
'let me just say it in this way.'"


LVII

217. {Aamma_      peroreerlunga
aamma         peror-reer-lunga
and           become.adult-already-1SG.CT
'And when I was already an adult'

218. *tassa*    *paasivara_/*
     *tassa*    *paasi-vara*
     that.is    understand-1SG.SUBJ/3SG.OBJ.IND
     'I understood it'

219. *ilumoortoq*    *taanna_}*
     *ilumoortoq*    *taanna*
     true     that
     'that was true [it was true, that].'


### Speaker 2, text 2

Recorded August 1993 in Sisimiut
Interviewed by Kêrte Jeremiassen


**I INTERVIEWER**

1.    *{Massakkut*    *_Sisimiuni_*
     *massakkut*    *Sisimiut-ni*
     now     Sisimiut-LOC
     'Now, in Sisimiut'

     *pulaarpagut*    *S.O.-kkut_*    *angerlarsimaffiannut_*
     *pulaar-vagut*[50]    *S.O.-kkut*    *angerlarsimaffik-annut*
     visit-1PL.IND    S.O.-family.ABS    home-3PL.POS.TERM
     'we are visiting the S.O. family to their home'

2.    *assigiinngitsunik*    *oqaloqatigilaarniarlugit_}*
     *assigiinngitsut-nik*    *oqaloqatigi-laaq-niaq-lugit*
     different/various-PL.INST[51]    talk.with-a.little-FUT-3PL.OBJ.CT
     'talking with them about various things.'


**II INTERVIEWER**

3.    *{S.laaqsulerisuunikuuvimmaa?}*
     *S. su-leri-soq-u-nikuu-vit-maa[nna]*
     S. what-deal.with-part-COP-PAST-2SG.INT-now/wonder
     'S., what have you been doing?'

**III Speaker**

4.     {*Tassa_*     *inersimasunngorama_*
       *tassa*     *inersimasoq-nngoq-gama*
       that is     adult-become-1SG.CAUS
       'That is, when I became an adult'

5.     *imaappoq_*[52]
       *imaaC-voq*
       be.like.this-3SG.IND
       'that means'

6.     *18-19-inik ukioqarlunga_/*
       *18-19-nik*     *ukioq-qaq-lunga*
       18-19-PL.INST     year-have-1SG.CT
       'when I was eighteen or nineteen years old'

7.     *amutsivimmi*     *ilinniartunngornikuugama_}*
       *amutsivik-mi*     *ilinniartoq-nngoq-nikuu-gama*
       shipyard-LOC     apprentice/student-become-past-1SG.CAUS
       'I became an apprentice in a shipyard.'

**IV Speaker**

8.     {*Taannalu_*
       *taanna-lu*
       that one-and
       'And that'

       *aamma*     *radiokkut*     *aallakaatitassiarilaarnikuugakku*
       *aamma*     *radio-kkut*     *aallakaatitassat-liaq*[53]*-gi-laaq-nikuu-gakku*
       and     radio-VIA     program-something.made-have-a.little-PAST-1SG.SUBJ/3NC.SG.OBJ.CAUS
       'I have also told before on the radio'

       *ilaatigut_*
       *ilaatigut*
       sometimes
       'sometimes'

9.    *imaappoq_*
      *imaa-voq*
      be.like.this-3SG.IND
      'that means'

10.   *meeraaninninngaanniit*          *amutsiviup_*
      *meeraaneq-m-ninngaanniit*       *amutsivik-up*
      childhood-1SG.POS-POS.ABL  shipyard-REL
      'from my childhood'

      *aallarteqqaarnerani*                      *amutsiviliornermi,*
      *aallartit-qqaaq-neq-ani*                  *amutsivik-lioq-neq-mi*
      begin-INTNS-NOMZ-3C.SG.POS.LOC       shipyard-build-NOMZ-
                                                          LOC
      'in the very beginning of the building of a shipyard'

11.   *suleqataarnera*                       *eqqartoreersimagakku*
      *suleqat-u-neq-ga*                     *eqqartor-reer-sima-gakku*
      partner-COP-NOMZ-1SG.POS.ABS    talk.of-already-PERF-
                                                       1SUBJ/3NC.SG.OBJ.CAUS
      'I have already talked about my partaking in the forming/
      building of the shipyard [i.e., I was a partner/my being a partner
      in the . . . ]'

12.   *aamma*      *ilaatigut_*
      *aamma*      *ilaatigut*
      and            in.some.way/sometimes
      'and in some way'

      *amutsivimmi*      *sulinera*        *eqqaalaareerlugu*        *taanna_/*
      *amutsivik-mi*     *sulineq-ga*      *eqqaa-laaq-reer-lugu*    *taanna*
      shipyard-LOC    work-1SG.      mention-a.little-        that
                            POS.ABS       already-3SG.OBJ.CT
      'I have already mentioned my work in the shipyard'

13.   *imatut_*         *massakkut_*      *eqqaaqqinngikkallassavara_}*
      *ima-tut*         *massakkut*       *eqqaa-qqi-nngit-gallaq-ssa-vara*
      like.this-EQ    now                 mention-again-NEG-continuing/
                                                 finally-FUT-1SG/3SG.IND

'so now I don't want to mention it again in this [story].'

**V Speaker**

14. {*Kisianni_*  *eqqartulaarsinnaavara*  *taamanikkut_*
    *kisianni*  *eqqartor-laaq-sinnaa-vara*  *taamani-kkut*
    but  talk.about-a.little-can-1SG.  at.that.time-VIA
    SUBJ/3SG.OBJ
    'But, I can talk a little bit about it at that time'

15. *tassa_*  *1920-kkut*  *aallartinneranni,*
    *tassa*  *1920-kkut*  *aallartit-neq-anni*
    that.is  1920-VIA  begin-NOMZ-3NC.PL.POS.LOC
    'that is, at the beginning of the 1920s'

**VI Speaker**

16. (*1918-imi*  *inuugama,*
    *1918-imi*  *inuu-gama*
    1918-LOC  be.born-1SG.CAUS
    '(I was born in 1918'

17. *taava*  *1920-kkunni*  *tassa*  *meeraasimavunga*
    *taamanikkut)_*}

    *taava*  *1920-kkut-ni*  *tassa*  *meeraq-u-sima-vunga*
    *taamani-kkut*

    so  1920-VIA-PL.LOC  you.know  child-COP-PERF-1SG.IND
    at.that.time-VIA

    'so I was a child you know then in the 1920s).'

**VII Speaker**

18. {*Taamanikkullu_*
    *taamani-kkut-lu*
    at.that.time-VIA-and
    'And at that time'

    *1920-ip*  *aallartisimalernerani,*
    *1920-ip*  *aallartit-sima-ler-neq-ani*

1920-REL    begin-PERF-begin-NOMZ-3SG.POS.LOC
'at the beginning of the 1920s'

*aalisarneq_*
*aalisarneq*-0
fishing-ABS
'fishing'

| *saarullinnik* | *aalisarneq* | *aatsaat* | *aallarnersalerpoq_*} |
|---|---|---|---|
| *saarullik-nik* | *aalisarneq*-0 | *aatsaat* | *aallarner-saq-ler-voq* |
| cod-PL.INST | fishing-ABS | at.first | begin-AGENT[54]-begin-3SG.IND |

'codfish fishing was first going to start.'

## VIII SPEAKER

19.    {*Eqqaamalluarpara*
*eqqaama-lluaq-vara*
remember-well-1SG.SUBJ/3SG.OBJ.IND
'I remember it well'

20.    
| *meeraallunga_* | *taamanikkut_* |
|---|---|
| *meeraq-u-lunga* | *taamani-kkut* |
| child-COP-1SG.CT | at.that.time-VIA |

'I was a child in those days'

21.    
| *massakkut* | *amutsiviup* | *akiani_* |
|---|---|---|
| *massakkut* | *amutsivik-up* | *aki-ani* |
| now | shipyard-REL | other.side-3SG.POS.LOC |

'now on the other side of the shipyard [opposite the place that is now the shipyard]'

| *ilinniartut_* | *ilinniartut* | *illukuat_/* |
|---|---|---|
| *ilinniartoq-t* | *ilinniartoq-t* | *illu-ku-at* |
| student-PL | student-PL | house-former-3PL.POS.ABS |

'there was a former students' house [there was formerly a students' house]'

22.    
| *taassuma* | *illup* | *kangia* | *tungaani_* |
|---|---|---|---|
| *taassuma* | *illu-p* | *kangia* | *tungaani* |

that.one-REL    house-REL    lying.east    over.there/in.that.
                                           direction

'to the east of that house over there'

| | |
|---|---|
| *itersiumanermiikkami* | *qooqqiumanermi_* |
| *itersi-juma-neq-mii-gami* | *qooqqi-juma-neq-mi* |
| make.a.hole.in.ground-want-NOMZ-be.in-3C.SG.CAUS | make.a.furrow-want-NOMZ-LOC |

'because it is in a little depression in a valley'

23. *illungaatsiapilorujussuaq*
    *illu-ngaatsiaq[55]-pilorujussuaq-0*
    house-rather-very.big-ABS
    'a little bigger than a big house'

24. *imaappoq*              *sana — sanaaq_'*
    *imaaC-voq*             *sanaaq-0*
    be.like.this-3SG.IND    something.one.has.done-ABS
    'that is it has been built'

25. *illungaatsiapilorujussuaq*              *uingasoq_/*
    *illu-ngaatsiaq-pilorujussuaq-0*         *uinga-soq*
    house-rather.big-very.big-ABS            slant-3SG.PART
    'the rather larger than big house was slanted'

26. *taanna*    *"Eqaluit*    *inaannik"*    *taasarparput}*
    *taanna*    *eqaluk-it*   *ini-annik*    *taasar-varput*
    that.one    char-PL       place-3PL.POS.INST    call-1PL.SUBJ/3SG.OBJ.IND

    'that one we called "char's place."'

## IX SPEAKER

27. *{Tassalu*    *taanna_*    *aalisarnermut_*
    *tassa-lu*    *taanna*     *aalisarneq-mut*
    then-and     that.one     fishing.(industry)-TERM
    'And that [house], to the fishing industry'

    *saarulliornermut_*              *Sisimiuni_*
    *saarullik-lioq-neq-mut*         *Sisimiut-ni*

codfish-make-NOMZ-TERM    Sisimiut-PL-LOC
'to the codfishing industry/factory, in Sisimiut'

*aallarnersaataalluni_*
aallarner-saq-uti-u-luni
begin-AGENT-means.to-COP-3SG.CT
it was the means with which to begin' [i.e., 'It was the means to
begin the fishing industry, the codfishing industry, in Sisimiut.']

28.  *taanna      illuusarsuaq                    uingasoq_/*
     *taanna      illu-u-saq-suaq-0               uinga-soq*
     that.one     house-COP-FUT-big-ABS           uneven/slant-3SG.PART
     'that shack [poor house, about to fall apart] was slanted/uneven'

29.  *uingasumik            qalialik_/*
     *uinga-soq-mik          qaliaq-lik*
     slant-PART-INST        roof-provided.with
     'the one with the tilted roof'

30.  (*eqaluit     inaannik                    taasartagarput*),
     *eqaluk-it    ini-annik                   taasar-saq-varput*
     char-PL       place-3PL.POS.INST          call-HAB-1PL.SUBJ/3SG.OBJ.
                                               IND
     '(we used to call it the place of char)'

31.  *tassa      ima         tarajorterivittut         atoqqaarsimavoq_/*
     *tassa      ima         tarajorterivik-tut        ator-qqaaq-sima-voq*
     that.is     you.know    salting.place-EQ          use-first-PERF-3SG.
                                                       IND
     'like, you know, it was first used as a [cod]salting place'

     *taanna_}*
     *taanna*
     that.one
     'that one.'


## X Speaker

32.  {*Eqqaamavaralu*
     eqqaama-vara-lu

remember-1SG.SUBJ/3SG.OBJ.IND-and
'And I remember it'

33.  *taamanikkut*      *saarulliit*      *tunineqartartut_*
     *taamani-kkut*      *saarullik-it*      *tuni-neqaq-saq-tut*
     at.that.time-VIA      codfish-PL      sell-PASS-HAB-3PL.PART
     'at that time the codfish used to be sold'

34.  *sumilluunniit_*      *niaquernagit}*
     *sumik-luunniit*      *niaquer-nagit*
     what-or.even      take.head.off.(fish)-3PL.OBJ.NEG.CT
     'without [them] even taking their heads off'

35.  <u>*ammar*</u>*nagilluunniit}}*
     *ammar-nagit-luunniit*
     open.up-3PL.OBJ.NEG.CT-or.even
     'or even opening them up.'

## XI SPEAKER

36.  *{Aammalu_*      *nalunngilara*
     *aamma-lu*      *nalunngi-lara*
     and-and      know-NEG[56].1SG.SUBJ/3SG.OBJ.IND
     'And I know [it]'

37.  *taamanikkut*      *kilomut*      *9 øremik*      *akeqartut,*
     *taamani-kkut*      *kilo-mut*      *9 øre-mik*      *akeqaq-tut*
     at.that.time-VIA      kilo-TERM      9.øre-INST      cost-3PL.PART
     'they cost nine øre a kilo at that time'

     *tunitsivileqqaaramik,*                  *saarullit}*
     *tunitsi-vik-leq-qqaar-gamik*                  *saarullik-t*
     sell-really-begin-first.time-3C.PL.CAUS      codfish-PL
     'when they first started to really sell, the codfish.'

## XII SPEAKER

38.  *{Taava_*      *tassa*      *meeraanitsinnilli*            *uagut_*
     *taava*      *tassa*      *meeraaneq-tsinnit-li*            *uagut*

then        that.is    childhood-1PL.POS.ABL-INTNS        1PL.ABS
'Then that is right from our childhood'

*aallaartuartuuvugut_*
aallaar-tuaq-soq-u-vugut
travel.to.hunt-continuous-PART-COP-1PL.IND
'we were ones who always traveled [on hunting trips]'

39.    *imaappoq_/*
       *imaa-voq*
       be.like.this-3SG.IND
       'it was like this'

40.    *saarullinniartarpugut_*              *taamanikkut_}*
       *saarullik-niaq-saq-vugut*            *taamani-kkut*
       codfish-hunt-HAB-1PL.IND              at.that.time-VIA
       'we used to hunt codfish at that time.'


## XIII SPEAKER

41.    *{aamma     Qeqertalik_     taamani_      illoqarpoq*
       *aamma      Qeqertalik      taamani       illo-qaq-voq*
       and        Qeqertalik      at.that.time   house-have-3SG.IND
       'and Qeqertalik at that time had houses [i.e., was a settlement]'

42.    *aamma      tarajorterivimmik*
       *aamma      tarajorterivik-mik*
       and        salting.place-INST
       'and [it was] a salting place [a place to salt fish]'

43.    *taavalu    upernaakkut     tappavunga       aallaartarpugut*
       *taava-lu   upernaaq-kkut   tappav-unga*[57]  *aallaar-saq-vugut*
       then-and    spring-VIA      up.there/to.      travel.to.hunt-
                                   the.east-term     HAB-1PL.IND
       'and then in the spring we used to travel up there to hunt'

44.    *tappanna*                      *saarullippassuaqartarmat_}*
       *tappa-nna*                     *saarullik-passuaq-qaq-saq-mat*

up.there/to.the.east-ABS          codfish-a.lot.of-have-HAB-3NC.
                                  SG.CAUS

'because the one in there [i.e., the fjord] used to be full of cod
[i.e., because there used to be a lot of codfish up there].'

45.    *Tassa      meeraanitsinni_}}*
       *tassa      meeraaneq-tsinni*
       that.is     childhood-1PL.POS.LOC
       'That is, in our childhood'

XIV SPEAKER

       *{taava     kisianni_     apersortereerlunga_*
       *taava      kisianni      apersortit-reer-lunga*
       then        but           confirm-already-1SG.CT
       'then when I was confirmed however'

46.    *nammineerlunga_*
       *nammineer-lunga*
       do.by.oneself/be.independent-1SG.CT
       'when I myself did [this]'

47.    *aalisarsinnaanngorama          tassami_/*
       *aalisaq-sinnaa-nngor-gama      tassami*
       fish-can-become-1SG.CAUS        in.any.case
       'when I learned to fish [i.e., became able to fish] in any case'

48.    *imaak—_     (taamanikkut       ipuinnarmik*
                                       *angallateqarpugut*

       *ima         taamani-kkut       ipu-innaq-mik*
                                       *angallat-qaq-vugut*

       so          at.that.time-VIA    oar-only-INST
                                       vessel-have-1PL.IND

       'at that time we had only boats with oars'

49.    *umiaasat_/                     umiatsiaallu*
       *taamani                        angallatigineqarput)_}*

*umiaasaq-t*          *umiatsiaaq-t-lu*
*taamani*          *angallat-gi-neqaq-vut*

flat-bottomed.rowboat-PL      rowboat-PL-and
at.that.time-VIA      vessel-have-PASS-3PL.IND

'flat-bottomed rowboats, and rowboats in those days were used.'

## XV SPEAKER

50.    {*Tassalu*          *taamanikkut_*
      *Tassa-lu*          *taamani-kkut*
      that.is-and          at.that.time-VIA
      'That is at that time'

      *eqqaamalluarpara*          *qassutit_*
      *eqqaama-lluaq-vara*          *qassutit*[58]
      remember-well-1SG.SUBJ/3SG.OBJ.IND    net.PL
      'I well remember it, the nets'

51.    *pi* — *siullermik*      *piniutigineqartut_}*
      *siullermik*          *piniuti-gi-neqaq-tut*
      at.first          equipment-have-PASS-3PL.PART
      'were used at first.'

## XVI SPEAKER

52.    {*aammalu*    *ukiumi_*      *qassusiortarpugut*
      *nammineq*    *uagut_/*

      *aamma-lu*    *ukioq-mi*      *qassut-lioq-saq-vugut*
      *nammineq*    *uagut*

      and-and    winter-LOC    net-build-HAB-1PL.IND
      self          1PL

      'and in the winter we ourselves used to build nets [make nets]'

      *saarullinnut*          *qassutissatsinnik*[59]*_}*
      *saarullik-nut*          *qassutit-ssaq-tsinnik*
      codfish-PL.TERM    net.PL-FUT-1PL.POS.INST
      'nets for the codfish.'

**XVII SPEAKER**

53.     {*Allunaasaaqqat_*
        *Allunaasaq-qat*-0
        rope/string-companion-ABS
        'The string'

        (*taamanikkut*       *imusat*)_
        *taamani-kkut*       *imusaq-t*
        at.that.time-VIA     roll/something.rolled-PL
        'at that time [they were] rolled'

        *nioqqutaapput_/*
        nioqqut-u-vut
        wares-COP-3PL.IND
        'were in the store'

54.     *taavalu*      *tamakku*      *allunaasaaqqut_*
        *taava-lu*      *tamakku*      *allunaasaq-qat*-0
        then-and     these        rope/string-companion-ABS
        'and then this string'

        *tassa_*     *qassussiarisarpagut,*
        *tassa*      *qassut-liaq-gi-saq-vagut*
        that.is     net-make-have-HAB-1PL.SUBJ/3PL.OBJ.IND
        'we used to make into nets'

55.     *nammineerlugit,*
        *nammineer-lugit*
        do.by.oneself/be.independent-3PL.OBJ.CT
        '[we] made [them] ourselves'

56.     (*qassutit*      *sanallugit*),
        *qassutit*      *sana-lugit*
        net.PL       make-3PL.OBJ.CT
        '[we] made nets'

57.     (*qimissersorlugit*),
        *qimiaq-lersor-lugit*

fishing.line-provide.with-3PL.OBJ.CT
'providing them with fishing lines'[60]

(*upernaakkut        tassa*),
*upernaaq-kkut       tassa*
spring-VIA           that.is
'in the spring, that is'

58.    (*aalisarnermi         saarullinniarnermi*
                               *atugassagut*)}

       *aalisarneq-mi         saarullik-niaq-neq-mi*
                              *ator-saq-ssaq-vut*

       fishing.industry-LOC   codfish-hunt-NOMZ-LOC
                              use-NOM.something.that-FUT-1PL.IND

       'the ones we were going to use for our future fishing, in
       codfishing.'

59.    *Taamanikkut_*}}
       *taamani-kkut*
       at.that.time-VIA
       'At that time.'


XVIII SPEAKER

       {(*saarullippassuaqarpoq*
       *saarullik-passuaq-qaq-voq*
       codfish-a.lot.of-have-3SG.IND
       '(There was a lot of codfishing'

60.    *oqarsinnaavugut        taamak*)}}
       *oqaq-sinnaa-vugut       taamak*
       talk-can-1PL.IND        like.this
       'we can say this).'


XIX SPEAKER

61.    {*Tassami_        qeqertani         imatut_*
        *tassami          qeqertaq-ni        imatut*

there             island-PL.LOC      you.know
'We could no longer, you know, in the islands'

*annertuumik*                     *aallaarfiujunnaarmat*
*annertooq-mik*                   *aallaavik-u-junnaaq-mat*
extensive/voluminous-INST         point.of.departure-COP-no.
                                  longer-3NC.SG.CAUS

'use the islands to camp [camp in the islands a lot; i.e., when we
could no longer go out to any great degree to the islands]'

62.   *taava*    *qaninnersiugaralugu_*          *Sarfannguanut,*
      *taava*    *qanik-neq-sior-saq-gi-lugu*    *Sarfannguit-nut*
      then       near-SUP-deal.with-PASS-        Sarfannguit-TERM
                 have-3SG.OBJ.CT

'then going for the nearest one, namely Sarfannguit [i.e.,
Sarfannguaq is nearest place]'

63.   (*Sarfannguit*        *eqqaannut*        *taamani*
                                               *aallaartarpugut*)}[61]

      *Sarfannguit*         *eqqaaC-nut*       *taamani*
                                               *aallaar-saq-vugut*

      Sarfannguit-REL       near-TERM          at.that.time
                                               travel.to.hunt-HAB-1PL.IND

'(we used to go hunting near Sarfannguit [in Sarfannguit's
neighborhood] at that time).'

## XX SPEAKER

64.   {*Tassani*    *siullermik*    *Sarfannguit*        *akiani*
      *tassani*     *siullermi*     *Sarfannguit*        *akia-ni*
      there         at.first        Sarfannguit-REL      other/far.side-LOC

'At first on the other side of Sarfannguit'

      "*Akisami*"_    *taamanikkut*        *tupersimasarpugut_*}
      "*Akisa*"-*mi*  *taamani-kkut*       *tupeq-sima-saq-vugut*
      "Akisa"-LOC     at.that.time-VIA     tent-PERF-HAB-1PL.IND

'at "Akisa" [name of other side of Sarfannguit] in those days we
used to set our tents up.'

**XXI SPEAKER**

65. {*Taavalu_*    *taamanikkut*    *angallaterpassuusaramik,*
    *taava-lu*    *taamani-kkut*    *angallat-(r)passuit-u-saq-gamik*
    then-and    at.that.time-VIA    vessel-a.lot.of-COP-HAB-3C.PL.CAUS
    'And then at that time there were a lot of ships'

    (*aammalu*    *piniarniat,*
    *aamma-lu*    *piniarniaq*[62]*-t*
    and-and    hunter-PL
    '(and hunters'

    *maanilu*    *nunaqarfiit,*
    *maani-lu*    *nunaqarfik-it*
    here-and    settlement/village-PL
    'and settlements here'

66. *taamanikkut*    *Sisimiut_*
    *taamani-kkut*    *Sisimiut*
    at.that.time-VIA    Sisimiut
    'and at that time Sisimiut'

    *nunaqarfippaalussuaqarami*    *aamma)_/*
    *nunaqarfik-pak-aluk-ssuaq-qaq-gami*    *aamma*
    village-many-rather-big-have-3C.SG.CAUS    and
    'had rather many settlements) [i.e., within the governing district of Sisimiut]'

67. *Ikerasakkut*    *Uummannaarsukkut*    *Saqqakkut*
        *tamakkua*    *Itillikkut_*

    *Ikerasak-kkut*    *Uummannaarsuaq-kkut*    *Saqqa-kkut*
        *tamakkua*    *Itilleq-kkut*

    Ikerasak-group    Uummannaarsuaq-group    Saqqa-group
        those    Itilleq-group

    'Ikersak Uummannaarsuaq Saqqa and this one Itilleq'

| | | |
|---|---|---|
| *tamakkua* | *inuit* | *Assaquttakkut_/* |
| *tamakkua* | *inuk-it* | *Assaquttaq-kkut* |
| those | person-PL | Assaqutta-group |

'and those people, the people from Assaqutaq'

68.
| | | |
|---|---|---|
| *aamma* | *taamanikkut* | *tappavunga* |
| *ilummut* | *kangerlummut* | *tassa_* |

| | | |
|---|---|---|
| *aamma* | *taamani-kkut* | *tappav-unga* |
| *ilummut* | *kangerluk-mut* | *tassa* |

| | | |
|---|---|---|
| and | at.that.time-VIA | up.there/to.the.east-TERM |
| inward | fjord-TERM | that.is |

'and at that time [they took] to the fjord up there (eastward), you know'

69.
| | | |
|---|---|---|
| *upernaakkut* | *tappanna* | *saarulleqarnerusarmat_/* |
| *upernaaq-kkut* | *tappa-nna* | *saarullik-qaq-neru-saq-mat* |
| spring-VIA | up.there/to.the.east-ABS | codfish-have-more-HAB-3NC.SG.CAUS |

'because in the spring up there there used to be more codfish'

70.
| | |
|---|---|
| *tappavunga* | *aallaarrattartorsuugamik_}* |
| *tappav-unga* | *aallaar-CCati-saq-soq-u-gamik* |
| up.there.(to.the.east)-TERM | go.hunting-a.lot.of people.do-HAB-PART-COP-3C.PL.CAUS |

'they were a lot of people who used to camp/hunt[63] up there.'

## XXII SPEAKER

71.
| | | | |
|---|---|---|---|
| {*Tassalu* | *Amerloq_* | *illugiillugu* | *saqqaa-tungaa* |
| *alanngualu* | *tamanna_/* | | |

| | | | |
|---|---|---|---|
| *tassa-lu* | *Amerloq* | *illugiig-lugu* | *saqqaa-tungaa* |
| *alanngoq-a-lu* | | *tamanna* | |

| | | | |
|---|---|---|---|
| that.is-and | Amerloq | be.pair-3SG.OBJ.CT | sunside-toward |
| shadow-3SG.POS.ABS-andthis | | | |

'And on both the sunshine side and on the shadow side of Amerloq'

72. taamanikkut      piniusersorfigineqartarpoq
     taamani-kkut      piniut-lersor-fik-gi-neqaq-saq-voq
     at.that.time-VIA      (fishing).equipment-equip.with-place-have-
     PASS-HAB-3SG.IND
'it was the place the hunting equipment was kept/placed in those days/where one put nets'

     saarullinnik      tamakkuninnga_/
     saarullik-nik      tamakku-ninnga
     codfish-PL.INST      these-PL.INST
'for codfish and others'

73. qassusersorfigalugu_}
     qassuser-soq-fi-gi-lugu
     set.nets-PART-place-have-3SG.OBJ.CT
'it had a place for setting nets.'

## XXIII SPEAKER

74. {Tassalu      tappavannga      imaappoq_
     tassa-lu      tappav-annga      imaaC-voq
     that.is-and      up.there-ABL      be.like.this-3SG.IND
'And so from up there, you know'

     taamanikkut      siullermik      Akisaminngaanniit_'
     taamani-kkut      siullermik      Akisa-minngaanniit
     at.that.time-VIA      at.first      Akisa-ABL
'at that time at first from Akisa'

| Utoqqaat_Utoqqaat | Saqqaanut | allaat[64] |
| | taamani-kkut | tassa_ |
| Utoqqaat | Saqqa-anut | allaat |
| | taamani-kkut | tassa |
| Utoqqaat | Saqqa-3SG.POS.TERM | others |
| | at.that.time-VIA | that.is |

'Utoqqaat, even to Saqqa [even to its south side], others in those days'

*ipuinnaq_/*[65]
*ipu-innaq-0*
oar-only-ABS
'only oars [only rowing]'

*qassusersorfigalugu,*
*qassuser-soq-fik-gi-lugu*
set.nets-PART-place-have-3SG.OBJ.CT
'setting nets [had a place for nets]'

75. *piniusersorfigisarpagut_}*
*piniut-lersor-fik-gi-saq-vagut*
[fishing/hunting].equipment-equip with-place-have-HAB-1PL.
SUBJ/3PL.OBJ.IND
'we used to have them as a place for hunting equipment [we went
hunting there].'

## XXIV SPEAKER

76. *{Tassali*　　*kisianniuna*　　*kangerluk_*　　*anorlertartoq*[66]
*tassa-li*　　*kisianni-una*　　*kangerluk-0*　　*anorler-saq-soq*
that.is-but　but-DEIC　fjord-ABS　blow.[of.wind]-HAB-
　　　　　　　　　　　　　　　　　3SG.PART

'But so the fjord was usually windy'

77. *isersarnaartartoq,*
*isersarnaaq-saq-soq*
wind.going.into.fjord-HAB-3SG.PART
'there was a wind going into the fjord'

78. *qajassuunnagu}*
*qajassuut-nagu*
be.cautious/spare-3SG.OBJ.NEG.CT
'it was very windy [i.e., not a cautious wind, it didn't spare
them].'

## XXV SPEAKER

79. *{Tassalu*　　*taamaattumik*　　*taamanikkut_*
*tassa-lu*　　*taamaatumik*　　*taamani-kkut*

that.is-and    therefore              at.that.time-VIA
'So therefore in those days'

*taamak*     *silagitsillugumi*                            *tassa,*
*taamak*     *silagik-tit-lugu-mi*                         *tassa*
like.this    good.weather-cause-3SG.OBJ.CT-INTNS    that.is
'like this, when the weather was very good, that is'

80.    (*isersarnerajuttuummat_/*)
       *isersarneq-gajug-soq-u-mmat*
       wind.coming.in.the.fjord-tendency-PART-COP-3NC.SG.CAUS
       '(because there was a tendency to have a wind coming in the
       fjord)'

81.    *piniusiornissatsinnut*
       *piniut-sior-neq-ssaq-tsinnut*
       [fishing].equipment-deal.with-NOMZ-FUT-1PL.POS.TERM
       'to go to the fishing equipment'

       *pingaartumik*     <u>*unnuk,*</u>          unnuaq
       *pingaartumik*     *unnuk-0*          *unnuaq-0*
       especially         evening-ABS       night-ABS
       'especially the evening and night'

       *piniuserinissatsinnut*              *atornerusarparput_}*
       *piniut-leri-neq-ssaq-tsinnut*       *ator-neru-saq-varput*
       equipment-deal.with-NOMZ-           use-more/all-HAB-1PL.
       FUT-1PL.POS.TERM                    SUBJ/3SG.OBJ.IND
       'we used to use the night to attend to the fishing equipment
       [because there was a tendency to have a strong wind when the
       weather was good, we used to use the good weather at night to
       get there and deal with the nets].'


XXVI SPEAKER

82.    {*Tassa*     *unnukkut_*
       *tassa*      *unnuk-kkut*
       that.is      afternoon-VIA
       'That is, in the afternoon'

*unnunnerani_*
*unnuk-neq-ani*
afternoon-SUP-3SG.POS.LOC
'in the latest afternoon'

*isersarneq_*  *qatsortarami_}*
*isersarneq-0*  *qatsor-saq-gami*
wind.going.into.fjord-ABS  die.down-HAB-3C.SG.CAUS
'when the wind going into the fjord had died down.'

## XXVII SPEAKER

83.  *{Atorsaror— -riartulernerani*  *taamatut tassa*
*atorsaror-giartor-leq-neq-ani*  *taamatut tassa*
[wind].has.died.down.a.bit-more.and.  likewise that.is
more-near.FUT-NOMZ-3SG.POS.LOC
'Likewise in the case of the wind having died down a bit you
know [i.e., 'when the wind has died down for a while]'

84.  *tappavanngaanniit*  *silammut_'*  *ipuinnaq_'*
*tappavannga-anniit*  *silammut*  *iput-innaq*
up.there.(ABL)-from  outside  oar-only
'[we go] out from there, just [using] oars/row'

85.  *tassa*  *aallartarpugut_}*
*tassa*  *aallar-saq-vugut*
that.is  travel-HAB-1PL.IND
'that is, we go out.'

## XXVIII SPEAKER

86.  *{Atorsaroriartuaaq*[67]
*atorsaror-giartuaaq*
wind.died.down-gradually.more.and.more
'The wind having gradually died down more and more'

87.  *piniutigut*  *taamaani_*
*piniut-vut*  *taamaani*
equipment-1PL.POS.ABS  at.that.time
'our things, then'

*Amerlup*       *saqqaaniit*       *uagut*
*Amerloq-p*       *saqqaa-niit*       *uagut*
Amerloq-REL       sunshine.side-ABL       1PL
'the ones from the sunny side of Amerloq — we, uh'

*saqqa —*       *saqqaa-tungaani taamaani_/*
      *saqqaa-tungaa-ni taamaani*
sunny.side-toward-LOC       at.that.time
'on the way toward the sunny side at that time'

88.       *piniuteqarajunnerusaratta_}*
      *piniut-qaq-gajug-neru-saq-gatta*
      things-have-often-more-HAB-1PL.CAUS
      'we used to have more equipment.'

## XXIX Speaker

89.       *{Saqqaanilu*       *tassa*       *atuartarlugit,*
      *saqqaa-ni-lu*       *tassa*       *atuartaq-lugit*
      sunny.side-LOC-and       that.is       follow-3PL.OBJ.CT
      'And then on the sunny side [we] used to bring them in line
      [the nets]'[68]

90.       *imaattorlugit*
      *imaattoq*[69]*-lugit*
      like.this-3PL.OBJ.CT
      'like this [gestures]'

91.       *amuartarlugit_/*
      *amuar-saq-lugit*
      haul.up-HAB-3PL.OBJ.CT
      'hauling them up'

92.       *taamanikkummi*       *qassuterpaalussuarnik*
      *piniuteqartarpugut*       *tassa_}*

      *taamani-kkut-mi*       *qassut-(r)pak-aluk-ssuaq-nik*
      *piniut-qaq-saq-vugut*       *tassa*

at.that.time-VIA-INTNS  net-many-rather-big-PL.INST
equipment-have-HAB-1PL.IND that.is

'at that time we had rather a lot of nets as equipment, you know.'


**XXX SPEAKER**

93. {*Taavalu_*  *arlalip* —
  *taava-lu*  *arlalip* —
  then-and  several/more.than.one
  'And then'

  *soorunami*    *arlalippasuusaramik*
  *soorunami*    *arlallit-passuit-u-saq-gamik*
  naturally/of.course  several/more.than.one-many-COP-
          HAB-3C.PL.CAUS
  'because of course there were a lot of'

  *tamakkua*  *qassutit_/*
  *tamakkua*[70]  *qassutit*
  those    NET.PL.ABS
  'those nets'

94. *aammalu*  *ipuinnaq*   *tassa*  *imaak*
  *angalasuugatta_/*

  *aamma-lu*  *iput-innaq_0*  *tassa*  *imaak*
  *angala-soq-u-gatta*

  and-and   oar-only-ABS  that.is  like.this
  be.on.the.road-PART-COP-1PL.CAUS

  'and by rowing [with oars] only, you know, since we moved like
  this'

95. *unnuaq*  *ilaanni*  *tamangajaat,*  *tamaat*
                  *tassami_*

  *unnuaq-0*  *ilaanni*  *tamangajaat*  *tamaq-at*
                  *tassami*

night-ABS   sometimes   almost.the.whole   the.whole/all-3SG.O
in.any.case

'sometimes almost the whole night, the whole in any case'

96.  *piniuserisarpugut_/*
*piniut-leri-saq-vugut*
equipment-deal.with-HAB-1PL.IND
'we had to deal with the equipment [i.e., make it ready to use]'

97.  *aammami_*   *imak_*   *ilarussimasartorsuugamik*
*aamma-mi*   *imak*   *ilaguC-sima-saq-soq-suaq-u-gamik*
and-INTNS   like.this   tangled-PERF-PASS-PART-big-COP-3C.
PL.CAUS
'and [it could be] they might have to be untangled'

98.  *imaalitsiaannarlugit*                     *aamma_/*
*imaali-tsiaq-innaq-lugit*                     *aamma*
has.become.like.this-a.little-only-3PL.OBJ.CT   and
'and in a short period of time/soon/fast'[71]

99.  *naammassineq*                     *ajornartaramik_}*
*naammassi-neq-0*                     *ajornar*[72]*-saq-gamik*
accomplish/finish-NOMZ-ABS     be.impossible-HAB-3C.PL.CAUS
'they were usually impossible to finish.'

## XXXI SPEAKER

100.  {*Taamalu_*   *ullaassanngoriartornerani_*
*taama-lu*   *ullaassaq-nngor-giartor-neq-ani*
then-and   dawn-become-almost-NOMZ-3SG.POS.LOC
'And then in the almost dawn time'

101.  *seqernup*[73]   *nuiartornerani*                     *tassa_*
*seqineq-up*   *nui-giartor-neq-ani*                     *tassa*
sun-REL   [sun].rises-more.and.more-NOMZ-   that.is
3SG.POS.LOC
'in the sun's rising [i.e., when the sun is coming up/rising], you
know'

102.     *uernaleriartuaaq,*
         *uerna-ler-giartuaaq*
         sleepy-nearly-gradually.more.and.more
         '[we] begin to be sleepy'

103.     *seqineq         kissakkiartuaartillugu_/*
         *seqineq-0       kissaq-giartuaaq-tit-lugu*[74]
         sun-ABS          warm-gradually.more.and.more-cause-3SG.OBJ.CT
         '[it] is causing the sun to get warmer [the sun is getting warmer]'

         *ilummut_'        assumut_/*[75]
         *ilummut          assumut*
         to.the.inside    to.windward
         'to the inside to windward'

104.     *aamma     tassa          ullaakkut        ullaassakkut*
                                                     *aamma_*

         *aamma     tassa          ullaaq-kkut      ullaassaq-kkut*
                                                     *aamma*

         and       you.know       morning-VIA      dawn-VIA
                                                     and

         'and you know in the morning, at dawn'

         *assarnaarajuttunnguugami_/*
         *assarnaar*[76]*-gajug-soq-nnguaq-u-gami*
         wind.going.out.of.fjord-tendency-PART-small-COP-3C.SG.CAUS
         'there was a tendency to be a wind going out of the fjord'

105.     {*unnukkut         silammukarutta,*
         *unnuk-kkut        silammukaq-gutta*
         evening-VIA        go/be.on.way.out.of.fjord-1PL.COND
         'if we were on the way out of the fjord in the evening'

106.     *assorluta_/*
         assoq-luta

have.wind.against.one-1PL.CT
'we were against the wind'

107. *ullaakkut*        *seqineq*        *nuilersoq*
     *ullaaq-kkut*      *seqineq-0*      *nui-leq-soq*
     morning-VIA        sun-ABS          rise-begin-3SG.PART
     'in the morning the sun rose'

108. *ilummut*        *aallassaagut*
     *ilummut*        *aallar-ssa-vugut*
     to.the.inside    travel-FUT-1PL.IND
     'we traveled to the inside'

109. *aamma*        *assumukarluta_}*
     *aamma*        *assoq-mukaq-luta*
     and           have.wind.against-go.to-1PL.CT
     'and we went against the wind.'

110. *{Taamanikkut_*        *ipuataarluni*
     *taamani-kkut*         *ipuataar-luni*
     at.that.time-VIA       row/pull.oars.through-3SG.CT
     'In those days, rowing'

111. *uernataarluni*
     *uernga-ataaq-luni*
     sleepy-entirely-3SG.CT
     'when one is really sleepy'

112. *sussaanngitsorsuuvoq_'*
     *sussaanngit-soq-suaq-u-voq*
     a.bit.rotten/bad-part-big-COP-3SG.IND
     'it was really bad'

113. *ajorluinnarpoq_}*
     *ajor-luinnaq-voq*
     not.good-complete-3SG.IND
     'it was absolutely awful.'

**Speaker 3, text 3a**

Recorded 1993 in Sisimiut
Interviewed by Kêrte Jeremiassen

**| INTERVIEWER**

1.    {*Tassa       massakkut,    Sisimiuni              D.L.-ip*
      *angerlarsimaffianiippugut_'*

      *tassa        massakkut     Sisimiut-ni            D.L.-ip*
      *angerlarsimaffik-ani-u-vugut*

      That.is    now        Sisimiut-PL.LOC    D.L.-REL
      home-3C.SG.POS-COP-1PL.IND

      'So now we are in D.L.'s home in Sisimiut'

2.    *D.L.ip_*       *imaa_*      *siuliatigut_*
      *D.L.-ip*       *imaa*       *siuleq-a-tigut*[77]
      D.L.-REL    like.this     one.that.goes.before-3NC.SG.POS-SG.VIA
      'D.L., you know, before'

      *innuttaasut*                  *illuanni*              *utoqqaat*
      *innuttaasoq-t*                *illu-anni*             *utoqqaq-it*
      community.member-PL    house-3PL.POS.LOC    old.person-PL
      'in the community [members'] house [for] old people'

      *naapisimaranni* —                        *naapisimaaratsigit_/*
      *naapi-sima-ranni* —                      *naapi-sima-uti-gatsigik*
      meet-PERF-1SG.SUBJ/3C.SG.OBJ.CAUS    meet-PERF-for/with-
                                               1PL.SUBJ/3PL.OBJ.CAUS

      'I have met her — we have met them'
      ['D.L., you know, when we have met her —, when we met with
      the old people before in the community house']

3.    *taava*    *oqaluttuassaqarunaqimmat_'*
      *taava*    *oqaluttuaq-ssa-qaq-gunar-qi-mmat*
      so        story-FUT-have-probably-INTNS-3NC.SG.CAUS
      'when she seemed to have a story [more stories to tell]'

4.  *pulaaqqillugu,*
    *pulaar-qqig-lugu*
    visit-again-3SG.OBJ.CT
    '[we] visited her again'

5.  *oqaloqatigeqqinniarparput_'*
    *oqaloqatigi-qqig-niaq-varput*
    talk.with-again-FUT-1PL.SUBJ/3SG.OBJ.IND
    'we will talk with her again'

6.  *taamani,*       *innuttaasut*          *illuanni*
    *taamani*        *innuttaasoq-t*        *illu-anni*
    at.that.time   community.member-PL   house-3PL.POS.LOC
    'at that time in the community house'

    *oqaloqatigigatsigu_/*
    *oqaloqatigi-gatsigu*
    talk.with-1PL.SUBJ/3SG.OBJ.CAUS
    'when we were talking with her'

7.  *makku*    *soorlu*     *oqaluuserivagut_/*
    *makku*    *soorlu*     *oqaluuseri-vagut*
    this-PL   for.example   talk.about-1PL.SUBJ/3PL.OBJ.IND
    'for example, we talk about these'

8.  *utoq — nunatsinni*         *ullutsinni*        *utoqqaat_*
          *nuna-tsinni*          *ulloq-tsinni*      *utoqqaq-it*
          land-1PL.POS.LOC      day-1PL.POS.LOC/    old.person-PL
                                SG or PL.POSM
    'in our land, in our days, the old people'

    *amerliartuaartut_'*
    *amerliC-giartuaaq-tut or toq-t*
    be.more.and.more-gradually.more.and.more-3PL.PART or PART.PL
    'They are gradually increasing in number [there are more and
    more old people]'

9.    *ukiortusiartuaartut*
      *ukioq-tusi-riartuaaq-tut* or *soq-t*
      year-become.bigger/more-gradually.more.and.more-3PL.PART
      or PART-PL
      'they are gradually getting older'

10.   *amerliartortut_/*
      *amerliC-giartor-tut* or *soq-t*
      be.more.and.more-more.and.more-3PL.PART or PART-PL
      'there are more and more [of them]'

11.   *taavalu*      *nammineq_*    *atuakkat_*     *soqutigalugit*
      *taava-lu*     *nammineq*     *atuagaq-t*     *soqutiga*[78]*-lugit*
      then-and       self           book-PL         be.interested.in-3PL.
                                                     OBJ.CT

      'and then she herself has been very interested in books'

12.   *aamma*      *eqqartorpai_*
      *aamma*      *eqqartor-vai*
      and          tell.about-3SG.SUBJ/3PL.OBJ.IND
      'and she tells about them'

      *kalaallit_*            *kalaallisut*       *atuakkat_}*
      *kalaalleq-t*           *kalaallisut*       *atuagaq-t*
      Greenlander-PL     Greenlandic      book-PL
      'Greenland — Greenlandic books.'

## II INTERVIEWER

13.   D._      *aallaqqaasiutigalugu* . . . [interruption in tape]
      D.       *aallaqqaasiut-ga-lugu*
      D.       beginning-have-3PL.OBJ.CT
      'D., at first/in the beginning'

14.   (*sumi*      *inunngorsimavit?*)
      *sumi*       *inunngor-sima-vit*
      where        be.born-PERF-2SG.INT
      '(where were you born?)'

### III Speaker

15.   {*Sisimiuniiunga,*
       *Sisimiut-nii-vunga*
       Sisimiut-be.from-1SG.IND
       'I am from Sisimiut'

16.   *Sisimiuni            inunngorpunga_'*
       *Sisimiut-ni          inunngor-vunga*
       Sisimiut-LOC    be.born-1SG.IND
       'I was born in Sisimiut'

       *ukioq          1914_*
       *ukioq-0        1914*
       year-ABS      1914
       '[in the] year 1914'

17.   *maj,           asanninnerup      qaammataa 17}*
17.   *maj            asanninneq-up     qaammat-aa 17*
       17th may    love-REL            month-3SG.POS/SG.POSM.ABS 17
       'seventeenth of May, seventeenth of the month of love.'

### IV Interviewer

17.   {*Aap_     tamanikkununa            innuttaasut        illuanni*
       *aap       tamani-kkut-una          innuttaasoq-t      illu-anni*
       yes        at.that.time-VIA-DEIC    community-PL     house-3NC.
                                                                      PL.POS.LOC
       'Yes, at that time in the community house'

       *aamma     ukiutit                                pigigut,*
       *aamma     ukioq-tit                              pi-givut*
       and         year-2SG.POS/PL.POSM.ABS     thing-have-1PL.
                                                                    SUBJ/3PL.OBJ.PART
       'and we were [talking] about your years [i.e., your age, how old
       you were]'

18.   *qassinimmaa              ukioqarpit         massakkut?}*
       *qassinik-maa(nna)[79]    ukioq-qaq-vit      massakkut*

how.many                  INST-now        year-have-2SG.INT now
'how old are you now?'

**V SPEAKER**

19.     {*79-it_*'
     *79-it*
     79-PL
     'seventy-nine'

20.     *majimi*     *asanninnerup*    *qaammataa*     *aappaagu*
     *maj-mi*     *asanninneq-up*    *qaammat-aa*    *aappaagu*
     May-LOC    love-REL       month-3SG.POS/   next.year
                               SG.POSM.ABS
     'In May, the month of love, next year'

     *80-sinngussagaluarpakka_/*       *massakkut_*}
     *80-si-nngu-ssa-galuaq-vakka*    *massakkut*
     80-INTRANS-become-FUT-CONSEQ-1SG.SUBJ/3PL.OBJ.IND
                                     now
     'I will be eighty now.'

**VI**

21.     {*Sulimi*         *soorlu_*       *soorluluunniit_*'
     *suli-mi*       *soorlu*       *soorlu-luunniit*
     yet-what.about   for.example   for.example-even
     'Yet for example, for example, it seems like you are'

     *70-it*     *angurit* —     *inoritit*
     *70-it*     *angu-rit* —   *inor-gitit*
     70-PL    approach —   under-2SG.SUBJ/3NC.PL.OBJ.PART
     'are approaching — , you are just under seventy'

22.     *isikkut*     *isigalugu_*}
     *isi-kkut*    *isigi-lugu*
     eye-VIA    see.well-3PL.OBJ.CT
     '[seeing well through (my) eyes].'

**VII SPEAKER**

23.     {*Tassa_*   *taama,*    *taama*    *pisarpaannga_/*

> *tassa*     *taama*     *taama*     *pi-saq-vaannga*
> that.is     like.this     like.this     thing-HAB-3PL.SUBJ/1SG.OBJ.IND
> 'That is, they tell me like this'

24. *naluara_/*
     *nalu-vara*
     not.know-1SG.SUBJ/3SG.OBJ.IND
     'I don't know [it]'

25. *tassami_*       *isikkorneran — _*     *taanna*
     *isikkuminarnersuara_'*

     *tassa-mi*                 *taanna*
     *isi-kkuminar-neq-suaq-ga*

     that.is-INTNS              that.one
     eyes-be.good.for-NOMZ-big-1SG.POS.ABS

     'that is, my being someone who is good to look at'

     *tusakataavittarpara,*                *ilaa_/*
     *tusakataavittaq*[80]*-vara*            *ilaa*
     be.quite.tired.of.hearing-3SG.SUBJ/3SG.OBJ.IND    you.know
     'I get really quite tired of hearing, you know'

26. *pingaartumik*     *peqqi—,*     *peqqippallaarneq*
     *ajorama*           *massakkut*

     *pingaartumik*                 *peqqiC-vallaar-neq-0*
     *ajor-gama*     *massakkut*

     especially                  healthy-so.much-NOMZ-ABS
     be.bad-1SG.CA     now

     'especially as I am not so very healthy now'

     *angalaniarnikkut_/*
     *angala-niaq-neq-kkut*[81]
     walk-FUT-NOMZ-VIA
     'when walking'

27.    (*imaa       soorlu_       uummaatinnik*
*patsiseqartumik)_}*

*imaa       soorlu       uummat-nnik*
*patsiseqaq-soq-mik*

like.this     for.example    heart-1SG.POS.INST
use.for.excuse-PART-INST

'(like, for example, because of my heart).'

## VIII SPEAKER

28.    {*Tusakataavittarpara*               *taanna*
*tusakataavittaq-vara*              *taanna*
be.quite.tired.of.hearing-1SG.SUBJ/3SG.OBJ.IND   that.one
'I am really quite tired of hearing that'

*isikkorinnersuara_'*
*isikku-rik-neq-suaq-ga*
view-have.a.good-NOMZ-big-1SG.POS.ABS
'[that] I look good'

29.    *Emilliannguup*       *panimma*
*Emillia-nnguaq-p*     *paniq-ma*
Emilia-DIM-REL      daughter-1SG.POS.ABS
'Emily, my daughter'

*taamaallunga*
*taamaa-lunga*
be.like.that-1SG.CT
'while I am like that'

30.    *oqarfiginikuuaanga_/*
*oqarfigi-nikuu-vaanga*
say.to-PAST-3SG.SUBJ/1SG.OBJ.IND
'said to me'

31.    "*Tassamiuna*       *illit_*    *ajoquteqarnerit_*
*tassami-una*       *illit*     *ajoqut-qaq-neq-it*

in.any.case-DEIC     2SG      sickness-have-NOMZ-2SG.POS.ABS
'"in any case your having a sickness'

*upperineq*              *ajornartoq*
*upperi-neq-0*           *ajornar-soq*
believe-NOMZ-ABS     be.impossible-3SG.PART
'it is impossible to believe'

32.   *isikkorinnersuarmit"_}*
      *isikku-rik-neq-suaq-mit*[82]
      view-have.a.good-NOMZ-big-ABL
      'because you look so good."'

## IX SPEAKER

33.   {*Naluara*
      *nalu-vara*
      not.know-1SG.SUBJ/3SG.OBJ.IND
      'I don't know'

34.   *sooq*    *taamaannerlunga}*
      *sooq*    *taamaa-ner-lunga*
      why     be.like.this-wonder-1SG.CT
      'why I am like that.'

## X SPEAKER

35.   {*Immaqa*     *baajatorneq*                *ajorama,*
      *immaqa*      *baaja-toq-neq-0*            *ajor-gama*
      maybe        beer-drink-NOMZ-ABS     be.bad-1SG.CAUS
      'Maybe because I don't drink beer [because I am not a beer
      drinker]'

36.   *naluara*
      *nalu-vara*
      not.know-1SG.SUBJ/3SG.OBJ.IND
      'I don't know'

37.   *tamakku*        *pissutaasarnersut_}*
      *tamakku*        *pissut-u-saq-ner-sut*

these-REL  reason-COP-HAB-wonder-3PL.PART
'[if] these are the reasons.'

## XI Interviewer

38. {*Tassa*  *inuunerit*    *tamaat*
   *baajartor —*      *baajatortanngilatit?*}

   *tassa*  *inuuneq-it*   *tamaq-at*
   *baaja-toq-saq-nngit-latit*

   that.is  life-2SG.POS.ABS  the.whole/all-3SG.O
   beer-drink-HAB-NEG-2SG.INT

   'That is, you haven't drunk beer in your whole life?'

## XII Speaker

39. {*Tassa_*  *imaattooq,*
   *tassa*  *imaaC-sooq*
   that.is  like.that-much.(PART)
   'That is, it was like this'

40. *suligallarama_'*
   *suli-gallar-gama*
   work-still-1SG.CAUS
   'when I was still working'

41. *soorlu_*   *kalaaliminertorlunga*
   *soorlu*   *kalaalleq-mineq-toq-lunga*
   for.example  Greenlandic-piece.of-eat-1SG.CT
   'for example, when I ate some Greenlandic food'

42. *immiaarartortarpunga*    *ataatsimik_/*
   *immiaq-araq-toq-saq-vunga*   *ataaseq-mik*
   beer-little.one-drink-HAB-1SG.IND  one-INST
   'I would drink one little beer'

43. *ilaani*   *nungunnagu_*}
   *ilaani*   *nunguC-nagu*

sometimes    finish-3SG.OBJ.NEG.CT
'sometimes not finishing it.'

## XIII SPEAKER

44.    {*Tassa    ukioq_        naluaraluunniit*
       *tassa      ukioq-0      nalu-vara-luunniit*
       that.is    year-ABS     not.know-1SG.SUBJ/3SG.OBJ.IND-even
       'That is, the year, I don't even know'

       *ukioq        massakkut,    ukioq        suna,*
       *ukioq-0      massakkut     ukioq-0      suna*
       year-ABS     now           year-ABS     what
       'the year, now, what year'

45.    *baajamik      usserama*
       *baaja-mik     usser-gama*
       beer-INST     try-1SG.CAUS
       'when I tasted beer'

46.    *naluara,*
       *nalu-vara*
       not.know-1SG.SUBJ/3SG.OBJ.IND
       'I don't know'

47.    *eqqaamasaaruppunga_}*
       *eqqaama-saq-erup-vunga*
       remember-PASS-privative.(take.away)-1SG.IND
       'I don't remember [I have lost my memories].'

48.    *baajatorneq        ajorpunga_}}*
       *baaja-toq-neq       ajor-vunga*
       beer-drink-NOMZ    be.bad-1SG.IND
       'I haven't drunk beer.'

## XIV INTERVIEWER

49.    {*Makkuami        pujortagassat                   cigaritsit?}*
       *makkua-mi        pujortagaq-ssaq-t               cigaritsi-t*

These-INTNS  stuff.that.is.smoked-FUT-PL  cigarette-PL
'What about these, tobacco and cigarettes?'

## XV SPEAKER

50. {*Pujortartorujussuugaluarama_*
*pujortaq-toq-rujussuaq-u-galuaq-gama*
smoke-consume-very.much-cop-CONSEQ-1SG.CAUS
'I used to smoke very much but'

51. *ullormut_*      20-*it*      *nungunngilaaginnartaraluarakkit*[83]
*ulloq-mut*      20-*it*      *nungu-nngit-laaq-innaq-saq-galuaq-gakkit*
day-TERM      20-PL      finish-NEG-a.little-just-HAB-CONSEQ-
                      1SG.SUBJ/3PL.OBJ.CAUS

'I finished a little bit less than twenty a day . . .'

52. 1987-*arsimi*          *tassanngaannarsuaq*
*pujortarunnaarama_*

1987 *ars-mi*          *tassannga-innaq-suaq*
*pujortaq-junnaaq-gama*

1987 years-LOC      from.then.on-only-big
smoke-no.more-1SG.CAUS

'in 1987 from then on I stopped smoking [I no longer smoked]'

53. *uanga*        *cigaritsip*        *ajuleraminga_/*
*uanga*        *cigaritsi-p*        *ajor-leq-gaminga*
1SG        cigarette-REL        be.bad-begin-3C.SG.SUBJ/1SG.OBJ.CAUS
'cigarettes didn't like me anymore [began to be bad for me]'

54. *uanga*        *cigaritsi*        *ajulinngikkaluarpara_/*
*uanga*        *cigaritsi-0*        *ajor-leq-nngit-galuaq-vara*
1SG        cigarette-ABS        be.bad-begin-NEG-CONSEQ-1SG.
                      SUBJ/3SG.OBJ.IND
'but I don't like cigarettes anymore [I began not to have/like
cigarettes anymore]'

55. *taamangaasit*        *oqartarpunga*}
*taamanga-aasiit*        *oqaq-saq-vunga*

like.that-as.usual    say/talk-HAB-1SG.IND
'that is what I usually say [I usually say like this].'


## XVI INTERVIEWER

56.   *Qanutut        ajuleramitit?*
      *qanoq-tut      ajor-leq-gamitit*
      how-EQ          be.bad-begin-3C.PL.SUBJ/2SG.OBJ.CAUS
      'Like how did they stop liking you [how did they begin to be bad
      to you/for you]?'


## XVII SPEAKER

57.   {*Tassa_         sapilerakku              ilaa_*
      *tassa           saper-leq-gakku          ilaa*
      that.is          cannot-begin-1SG.SUBJ/   you.know
                       3NC.SG.OBJ.CAUS
      'That is I just couldn't do it [i.e., smoke], you know'

58.   *millussisaraluarpunga_*
      *millu-ssi-saq-galuaq-vunga*
      inhale-do.like-HAB-CONSEQ-1SG.IND
      'I used to inhale . . .'

59.   *iserneq      saperami_/*
      *iser-neq-o   saper-gami*
      go.in-NOMZ-ABS  cannot-3C.SG.CAUS
      'it couldn't go in [i.e., smoke]'

60.   *soorlu_          ilaa_           pigisa—   maanga*
      *piumajunnaarami                             ilummut_}*

      *soorlu           ilaa                        maanga*
      *pi-juma-junnaaq-gami                         ilummut*

      for.example    you.know                    to.here
      thing-want-no.more-3C.SG.CAUS               to.inside

      'for example, you know, it wouldn't come inside anymore.'

**XVIII SPEAKER**

61. {_*Tassa*   *paasivara*                                 *ilaa_*'
    *tassa*      *paasi-vara*                               *ilaa*
    that.is      understand-1SG.SUBJ/3SG.OBJ.IND   you.know
    'That is, I understand it, you know'

62. (*pujortaqqissinnaajunnaarlunga*)_/
    *pujortaq-qqik-sinnaa-junnaaq-lunga*
    smoke-again-can-no.more-1SG.CT
    '(I just couldn't smoke anymore)'

63. *aamma*      *maqaasinngilara_*
    *aamma*      *maqaasi-nngit-lara*
    and miss-NEG-1SG.SUBJ/3SG.OBJ.NEG.IND
    'and I didn't miss it'

64. *aamma_*      *ajornartorsiutiginngilara,*
    *aamma*       *ajornartorsiut-gi-nngit-lara*
    and           problem-have-NEG-1SG.SUBJ/3SG.OBJ.NEG.IND
    'and it wasn't a problem for me [I didn't have a problem]'

65. *pujortarunnaarama_*
    *pujortaq-junnaaq-gama*
    smoke-no.more-1SG.CAUS
    'that [when] I didn't smoke anymore'

66. (*tassa*      *qujana*—_   *massakkut*    *qujaannartarpunga*
    *tassa*                    *massakkut*    *qujaannaq-saq-vunga*
    that.is                    now           thankful-HAB-1SG.IND
    '(that is, now I am thankful'

67. *pujortarunnaarsimagama_*)}
    *pujortaq-junnaaq-sima-gama*
    smoke-no.more-PERF-1SG.CAUS
    'because I have stopped smoking).'

68. *Sunaaffa,*        *uummallulerlunga_*
    *sunaaffa*         *uummat-luk-leq-lunga*

think.about.it    heart-bad-begin-1SG.CT

'Think about it, it was because my heart was getting bad'

69.   (*taamanikkut*    *tassa*    *taamaalivunga_*)}}

    *taamani-kkut*    *tassa*    *taamaali-vunga*

    at.that.time    that.is    become.like.that-1SG.IND

    'then, that is, I became like this).'

## XIX INTERVIEWER

70.   {*Qanormi_*    *illoqarfimmut_*    *akulerusimatigaat,*

    *qanoq-mi*    *illoqarfik-mut*    *aku-leri-sima-tigi-vit*

    how-what.about    town-TERM    live-be.involved.with-

                        PERF-so(equative)-2SG.INT

    'How about that you are so involved (in the society) in the town'

71.   *aneertarpiit?_*}

    *aneer-saq-viit?*

    go.for.walk-HAB-2SG.INT

    'do you go out for walks?'

## XX SPEAKER

72.   {*Kanani_*

    *kanani*

    down.there

    'down there'

    *massakkut*    *tuapannguani_*

    *massakkut*    *tuapaat-nnguaq-ni*

    now    pebbles-DIM-PL.LOC

    'now among the pebbles'

    *samani*    *itersap*    *iluanut*

    *nuunnikuugama*

    *samani*    *itersaq-p*    *ilua-nut*

    *nuuC-nikuu-gama*

    down.there.to.the.west    depression/hollow-REL    inside-TERM

    move-PAST-1SG.CAUS

'down there to the west when I moved inside the valley'

73.  *ippingiatoqaanga,*
    *ippingiatoq-qi-vunga*
    feel.uneasy/unwell-INTNS-1SG.IND
    'I didn't feel good about it [i.e., the move]'

74.  *kanani        oqaluffiup        eqqaaniikkallarama*
    *illunnguami_/*

    *kanani        oqaluffik-up     eqqaani-ic-gallar-gama*
    *illu-nnguaq-mi*

    down.there    church-REL     neighborhood-COP-still-1SG.CAUS
    house-DIM-LOC

    'when I was still beside the church down there in the small
    house'

75.  *ernerma,        uagut        illutoqarput*
    *ernerma        suliarinikuugamiuk_'*

    *erneq-ma        uagut        illu-toqaq-vut*
    *erneq-ma        suliaq-gi-nikuu-gamiuk*

    son-1SG.POS.REL    1PL.REL     house-old-1PL.POS.ABS
    son-1SG.POS.REL    work-have-PAST.PERF-3C.SG.SUBJ/3NC.
    SG.OBJ.CAUS

    'my son had fixed our old house [rebuilt it]'

76.  *nutarterlugu*
    *nutarter-lugu*
    make.new-3SG.OBJ.CT
    'making it new/modernizing it'

77.  *tamaat        nutaanngorlugu            tassami_*
    *tamaat        nutaanngor-lugu            tassami*
    everything    become.new-3SG.OBJ.CT    in.any.case
    'making everything become new/modern in any case'

78. *atortorissaarutit*    *tamaasa*        *tamaat_/*
    *atortorissaarutit*-0   *tamaq-asa*      *tamaq-at*
    technological.       the.whole/all-3PL.O    the.whole/all-3SG.O
    appliances-ABS

    'all modern things'

79. *kisiann*     *upernaaq*     *manna_*
    *kisianni*     *upernaaq*-0    *manna*
    but         spring-ABS     this
    'but this spring'

    *siornali_*       *aalisarnermik*     *ajutoorami_/*
    *siorna-li*       *aalisarneq-mik*    *ajutooq-gami*
    last.year-but    fishing-INST      unlucky-3C.SG.SUBJ.CAUS
    'but last year he was unlucky at fishing'

80. *(imaattoq_*
    *imaaC-soq*
    be.like.this-3SG.P or PART-ABS
    '(that is'

81. *qimattariaqalerakku*
    *qimaC-sariaqaq-leq-gakku*
    leave-must-begin-1SG.SUBJ/3SG.OBJ.CAUS
    'I had to leave it'

82. *qimakkakku_)}*
    *qimaC-gakku*
    leave-1SG.SUBJ/3SG.OBJ.CAUS
    'I left it).'


## XXI Speaker

83.   *{Takanani_*
    *takana-ni*
    over.there-LOC
    'There'

*inissisimalluaqigami*              *takanna,*
*ini-ssi-sima-lluaq-qi-gami*        *takanna*
room/place-do-PERF-good/well-       down.there
INTNS-3C.SG.CAUS
'it was good down there/it lay well down there'


84.  *eqqaalu*          *nuannersartarlugu*
     *eqqaa-lu*         *nuanner-saq-saq-lugu*
     around-and     pleasant/nice-AGENT-HAB-3SG.OBJ.CT
     'around it [I? he?] made it nice'


85.  *naasulersorlugulu_/*
     *naasoq-lersor-lugu-lu*
     flower-supply.with-3SG.OBJ.CT-and
     'and supplying it with flowers'


86.  *naatittarlugu*              *upernaakkut*     *naasut*
     *naatit-saq-lugu*            *upernaaq-kkut*   *naasoq-t*
     make.grow-HAB-3SG.OBJ.CT     spring-VIA         flower-PL
     'I used to make the flowers grow in the spring/make it grow
     flowers . . .'


87.  *pinikuugakkit*                  *nuannersorujussuaq*
     *pi-nikuu-gakkit*                *nuanner-soq-rujussuaq-0*
     thing-PAST.PERF-1SG.SUBJ/3NC.   nice-part-very.much-ABS
     PL.OBJ.CAUS
     'I made it very nice'


88.  *aneersuarlunga*
     *aneer-suaq-lunga*
     go.for.a.walk-a.lot-1SG.CT
     'I went for walks a lot'


89.  *aneersuarlunga_*
     *aneer-suaq-lunga*
     go.for.a.walk-a.lot-1SG.CT
     'I went for walks a lot'

90. *ullorsuaq*     *pisarpunga*
*ulloq-suaq-0*     *pi-saq-vunga*
day-big-ABS     thing-HAB-1SG.IND
'I used to do this all day long'

91. *silagitsillugu_/*
*sila-gik-tit-lugu*
weather-have.a.good-cause-3SG.OBJ.CT
'if the weather was good'

92. *assorsuaq*     *maqaasivara*     *massakkut_}*
*assut-suaq_0*     *maqaasi-vara*     *massakkut*
much-very.much-ABS     miss-1SG.SUBJ/     now
                 3SG.OBJ.IND
'I miss it very much now.'

## XXII SPEAKER

93. *{Uani_*     *allaanermit_'*
*uani*     *alla-u-neq-mit*
here     different-COP-NOMZ-ABL
'Here it is different'

94. *aneerfeqaranilu_/*
*aneer-vik-qaq-nani-lu*
go.for.walk-place-have-3SG.NEG.CT-and
'there is no place to walk'

95. *soorlu_*     *puup*     *iluani_}*
*soorlu*     *puu-p*     *ilua-ni*
for.example     bag-REL     inside-LOC
'it is like [being] in a bag.'

## XXIII INTERVIEWER

96. *{D._ oqarputit*
*D. oqaq-vutit*
D. say-2SG.IND
'D., you said'

97. *Sisimiormiuullutit_*
*Sisimiut-miut-u-lutit*
Sisimiut-from-COP-2SG.CT
'you are from Sisimiut'

98. *kikkunukua*     *angajoqaarisimavigit?_}*
*kikkut-ukua*     *angajoqaat-gi-sima-vigit*
who.PL.ABS-these.PL.REL  parents-have-PERF-2SG.SUBJ/3PL.
          OBJ.INT

'who were your parents?'


XXIV SPEAKER

99. {*Tassa_* *piniartorsuarminngooq*  *ataataqarsimavugut_*'
*tassa*  *piniartoq-suaq-mik-gooq* *ataata-qaq-sima-vugut*
that.is hunter-big-INST-reported. father-have-PERF-1PL.IND
    speech
'That is, we had a father they say was a big hunter'

100. *ullut*  *tamarluinnaasa_*
*ulloq-t* *tamaq-lluinnaq-asa*
day-PL all/every-all.the.time-3PL.O
'every single day'

*anaanakkut*  *allallu*
*anaana-kkut-0*  *alla-t-lu*
mother-family-ABS others-PL-and
'my mother's family and others'

*nunaqqatigut*
*nunaqqat-vut*
who.live.in.same.town-3PL.IND
'who lived in the same town'

101. *meeragallaratta*
*meeraq-gallar-gatta*
child-still-1PL.CAUS
'when we were still children'

102. *oqartarput,*
*oqaq-saq-vut*
say-HAB-3PL.IND
'they used to say'

103. *ataatagooq_*  *pingajungaarami*
*ataata-0-gooq*  *pingajuq-ngaaq-gami*
father-ABS-reported.speech  get.something/be.lucky-a.lot-3C.
SG.CAUS
'my father, they say, got a lot/always got something'

104. *qaammatit_*  *ullui*  *naasarpai_/*
*qaammat-t*  *ulloq-i*  *naa-saq-vai*
month-PL  day-3SG.POS.PL.  be.done-HAB-3SG.SUBJ/3PL.
POSM.ABS  OBJ.IND
'the days of the month used to be done/pass'

105. *ataasiinnaanngitsunik*  *puisinik*  *tikiussuilluni_}*
*ataasiq-innaa-nngit-soq-nik*  *puisi-nik*  *tiki-ussor-i-luni*
one-only-NEG-PART-PL.INST  seal-PL.INST  arrive-one.
after.another-
INTRANS-3SG.CT
'he arrived with not just one seal [he got more than one seal].'

## XXV SPEAKER

106. *{Kisianni*  *uagut,*  *uanga,*  *sisamanik*
*ukioqartunga,*

*kisianni*  *uagut*  *uanga*  *sisamat-nik*
*ukioq-qaq-sunga*

but  1PL  1SG  four-PL.INST
year-have-1SG.PART

'But when we — I was four years old'

107. *ataataga*  *qajaasimavoq}*
*ataata-ga*  *qajaa-sima-voq*
father-1SG.POS.ABS  die.in.kayak-PERF-3SG.IND
'my father died in the kayak.'

XXVI SPEAKER

108.    {*Taanna      eqqaamavara,*
        *taanna       eqqaama-vara*
        that          remember-1SG.SUBJ/3SG.OBJ.IND
        'I remember that one'

109.    *qajaasoq_*                              *ulloq*      *taanna_/*
        *qajaa-soq*                              *ulloq-0*    *taanna*
        die.in.kayak-3SG.PART or PART.ABS        day-abs      that.one
        'the one who died by kayak that day'

110.    *kisianni*    *ataataga*                *puijukkiutinngilara_/*
        *kisianni*    *ataata-ga*               *puiukkiuti-nngit-lara*
        but           father-1SG.POS.ABS        forget.completely-NEG-1SG.
                                                 SUBJ/3SG.OBJ.NEG.IND
        'but I always remember my father'

111.    *nalunngiinnarpara*
        *nalu-nngit-innaq-vara*
        not.know-NEG-only-1SG.SUBJ/3SG.OBJ.IND
        'I just know it'

112.    *ataataqarsimallunga_}*
        *ataata-qaq-sima-lunga*
        father-have-PERF-1SG.CT
        'I had a father.'

113.    *aqqaluara*                             *marluinnannguanik*
                                                 *ukiulik_}}*

        *aqqaluaq-ga*                           *marluk-innaq-nnguaq-nik*
                                                 *ukioq-lik*

        little.brother-1SG.POS.ABS             two-only-DIM-PL.INST
                                                 year-provided.with

        'my little brother who was only two years old.'

## XXVII Speaker

114. {(*Kisianni*    *aamma*    *aqqaluannguara*
                 *siorna*    *90-isimi_toquvoq_/*

     *kisianni*    *aamma*    *aqqaluaq-nnguaq-ga*
                 *siorna*-0    *90-mi toqu-voq*

     but       and       little.brother-DIM-1SG.POS.ABS
                 last.year-ABS   90-LOC die-3SG.IND

     '(But my little brother died last year in 1990'

115. *siornaak_*}
     *siorna-ak*
     last.year-DUAL
     'two years ago.'

116. *Aamma*    *aanaartoorluni_*
     *aamma*    *aanaartoor-luni*
     and        cerebral.hemorrhage-3SG.CT
     'And he got a cerebral hemorrhage,'

     *E.M._*}}
     E.M.
     E.M.
     'E.M.)'

## XXVIII Speaker

117. {*Anaanagaara*                   *Sisimiormiut*}
     *anaana-gi-vara*               *Sisimiut-miut*
     mother-have-3SG.SUBJ/3SG.OBJ.IND   Sisimiut-from
     'I have a mother from Sisimiut.'

## XXIX Speaker

118. {*Taanna*    *ataataga_*
     *taanna*    *ataata-ga*
     that.one   father-1SG.POS.ABS
     'That one, my father'

*Itilliminngaanneersuusimavoq_/*
*Itilleq-minngaanneeq-soq-u-sima-voq*
Itilleq-from-PART-COP-PERF-3SG.IND
'was from Itilleq'

119.   *kisianni*     *maanga*     *nuussimalluni_/*
       *kisianni*     *maanga*     *nuuC-sima-luni*
       but            to.here      move-PERF-3SG.CT
       'but he moved here'

120.   (*aleqanigooq_*                      *atsagigaluara*
       *aleqa-ni-gooq*                      *atsagi-galuaq-ga*
       big.sister-3C.SG.POS.ABS-            aunt-CONSEQ-1SG.
       reported.speech                      POS.ABS
       '(his big sister, they say, my late aunt'

       *maani*     *uinimmat_}*
       *maani*     *uiniC-mat*
       here        marry-3NC.SG.CAUS
       'got married here.'

**XXX SPEAKER**

121.   {*Inuusuttuaraalluni*
       *inuusuttuaraq-u-luni*
       teenager-COP-3SG.CT
       'When he was a teenager'

122.   *anaanaarussimagami_/*
       *anaana-eruC-sima-gami*
       mother-be.no.more-PERF-3C.SG.CAUS
       'because he didn't have a mother any more'

123.   *ilagalugu*
       *ila-gi-lugu*
       together.with-have-3SG.OBJ.CT
       'he went with her'

124.   *maanga*     *nooqatigisimagamiuk)}*
       *maanga*     *nuuC-qati-gi-sima-gamiuk*

to.here      move-companion-have-PERF-3C.SG.SUBJ/3SG.OBJ.CAUS
'she moved here with him).'

## XXXI SPEAKER

125.    {*Anaanaga*        *taamak*     *oqaluttuarpoq*}
       *anaana-ga*            *taamak*     *oqaluttuaq-voq*
       mother-1SG.POS.ABS   like.this    tell.story-3SG.IND
       'My mother tells it like this.'

## Speaker 3, text 3b

Recorded 1993 in Sisimiut
Interviewed by Kêrte Jeremiassen

## XXXII INTERVIEWER

126.    {*Qanormita*      *ateqarpaa—*
       *qanoq-mita*     *ati-qaq-vaa—*
       how-wonder     name-have-3SG.INT
       'What, I wonder, was your father's name?'

       *ateqarsimava*           *ataatat?_*}
       *ati-qaq-sima-va*      *ataata-t*
       name-have-PERF-3SG.INT   father-2SG.POS/SG.POSM.ABS
       'did his name used to be?'

## XXXIII SPEAKER

127.    {*H.,*       *H.M._*}
       *H.,*-0    *H.M.*-0
       H.,-ABS   H.M.-ABS
       'H., H.M.'

## XXXIV SPEAKER

       {*Sooq_/*   *taava_*   *anaana_*
       *anaanagaara B._*    *B.O._*'

       *sooq*       *taava*     *anaana-gi-vara*
       *B. B.*-0           *O.*-0

|  |  |  |
|---|---|---|
| so | then | mother-have-1SG.SUBJ/3SG.OBJ.IND B. |
| B.-ABS | O.-ABS | |

'So, then I have B., B.O. as a mother [my mother was B.O.]'

128. *O.iuvoq*                *inunnguutsiminik_/*
     *O.-u-voq*                *inunnguutsiminit*
     O.-COP-3SG.IND    at/from birth
     'she was O. at/from birth [i.e., her maiden name was O.]'

129. *imaattoq_}*
     *imaaC-soq*
     be.like.this-3SG.PART
     'like this.'

## XXXV SPEAKER

130. *{T. — ataatagisimavaa*                          *T.O._}*
       *ataata-gi-sima-vaa*                  *T.-0 O.-0*
       father-have-PERF-3SG.SUBJ/3SG.OBJ.IND    T.-ABS O.-ABS
     'She had as her father T.O.'

## XXXVI SPEAKER

131. *{Anaanaga*                          *kisianni,*
     *anaana-ga*                          *kisianni*
     mother-1SG.POS/SG.POSM.ABS    but
     'My mother, however'

     *aatsaat*    *uanga*    *meeqqiulereersunga*
     *aatsaat*    *uanga*    *meeqqiuC-leq-reer-sunga*
     first    1SG    have.children-begin-already-1SG.
                      PART
     'when I had already begun to have children'

132. *toquvoq_/*
     *toqu-voq*
     die-3SG.IND
     'she died'

133.  '39-*mi'anaanaga toquvoq_*
   '39-*mi'anaana-ga toqu-voq*
   '39-LOC'mother-1SG.POS.ABS die-3SG.IND
   'my mother died in [19]39,'

134.  81-*arsiliilerluni_/*
   81-*arsi-li-ler-luni*
   81-years-turn.(so.many.years)-begin-3SG.CT
   'she turned eighty-one years old;'

135.
| *tassa* | *taanna* | *ilaqutariinni* | *kisimi_'* |
|---|---|---|---|
| *tassa* | *taanna* | *ilaqutariit*[84] | *kisimi* |
| that.is | that.one | family-PL.LOC | one |

   'that is, that one, she is the only one in the family'

   *inuunertunertaasimavoq_}*
   *inuuneq-tuneq-taq*[85]-*u-sima-voq*
   life-have.a.lot.of-belong.to-COP-PERF-3SG.IND
   'who lives the longest [gets very old].'

136.  *Imaattoq}}*
   *imaaC-soq*
   be.like.this-3SG.PART
   'It's like this.'

## XXXVII SPEAKER

137.
| {*Tassa* | *anaanaga_* | *ataataarukkatta_* |
|---|---|---|
| *tassa* | *anaana-ga* | *ataata-eruC-gatta* |
| that.is | mother-1SG.POS/ | father-be.no.more-1PL.CAUS |
|  | SG.POSM.ABS |  |

   'that is, my mother — we lost my father [we didn't have my father anymore]'

| *imaattoq_* | 1918-*imi_'* | *erniinnaararsuaq_'* |
|---|---|---|
| *imaaC-soq* | 1918-*mi* | *erniinnaq-araq-suaq* |
| be.like.this-3SG.PART | 1918-LOC | soon/shortly-a.little-very/ |
|  |  | extremely |

   'like that in 1918, very soon after'

| *ukiuk* | *novemberip* | *2-ni_}* |
|---|---|---|
| *ukiuk-0* | *november-ip* | *2-ni* |
| winter-ABS | November-REL | 2-LOC |

'winter — on the second of November.'

## XXXXVIII SPEAKER

138.
| *{Taava_* | *kiguninnguatigut* | *anaanaga niuertukkut* |
|---|---|---|
| *taava* | *kinguneq-nnguaq-tigut* | *anaana-ga niuertoq-kkut* |
| then | after-little-PL.VIA | mother-1SG.POS/SG.POSM.ABS trader-family.PL |

'Then, a little bit after the trader'

*qaaqquaat_'*
*qaaqqu-vaat*
call.on-3PL.SUBJ/3SG.OBJ.IND
'came to call on my mother'

139.
*imaattoq_/*
*imaaC-soq*
be.like.this-3SG.PART
'it's like this'

140.
*ikiortigisarumallugu_/*
*ikiorti-gi-saq-juma-lugu*
helper-have-PASS.PART-want-3SG.OBJ.CT
'[he] wanted to have her help'

141.
| *tassalu* | *taamanimiilli* | *anaanaga qallunaanut_* |
|---|---|---|
| *tassa-lu* | *taamani-miit-li* | *anaana-ga qallunaaq-nut* |
| that.is-and | at.that.time-ABL-INTNS | mother-1SG.POS/ SG.POSM.ABS Dane-PL.TERM |

'and that is, right from this time, my mother was'

*kiffanngorpoq_}*
*kiffaq-nngor-voq*
maid-become-3SG.IND
'a maid for the Danes.'

## XXXIX Speaker

142.　*{Qallunaarparujorujussuit*
　　*qallunaaq-pak-ruju-ruju-ssuaq-it*
　　Dane-a.number-many-many-big-PL
　　'Many, many Danes'

　　*70-it　　sinnerlugit*
　　*70-it　　sinner-lugit*
　　70-PL　　be.more.than-3PL.OBJ.CT
　　'not before she was more than seventy'

143.　*ukioqalereerluni*　　　　　*aatsaat_*
　　*ukioq-qaq-leq-reer-luni*　　*aatsaat*
　　year-have-begin-already-3SG.CT　　first
　　'years old'

144.　*kiffartorunnaarpoq_}*
　　*kiffartor-junnaar-voq*
　　be.in.service-no.more-3SG.IND
　　'she was no longer a maid [i.e., to the Danes].'

## XL Speaker

145.　(*Taamaammat*
　　*taamaat-mmat*
　　therefore-3NC.SG.CAUS
　　'Therefore'

146.　*toqummat_'*
　　*toqu-mmat*
　　die-3NC.SG.CAUS
　　'when she died'

147.  *Bro    niuertuulluni_*
      *Bro    niuertoq-u-luni*
      Bro    trader-COP-3SG.CT
      'Bro being the trader'

148.  *kransersuarmik         naasortalerpaa_/*
      *kranse-suaq-mik        naasorta-ler-vaa*
      wreath-big-INST         flowers-provide.with-3SG.SUBJ/3SG.OBJ.IND
      'he lay a big wreath of flowers [on it, i.e., the grave]'

149.  *(tassa    kiffartorsimanera                       pillugu)_}*
      *tassa     kiffartor-sima-neq-a                     pi-lugu*
      that.is    be.in.service-PERF-NOMZ-3SG.POS/          do-3SG.OBJ.CT
                 SG.POSM.ABS
      '(that is [because] she had been in his service [he had her
      service]).'


## XLI SPEAKER

150.  *{Arnaq          imaannanngitsorujussuartut*
                       *taasinnaavara*

      *arnaq-0         imaannanngit-soq-rujussuaq-tut*
                       *taa-sinnaa-vara*

      woman-ABS        unusual-part-very.much-EQ
                       call-just-1SG.SUBJ/3SG.OBJ.IND

      'I could just call her a special woman'

      *anaanaga_/*
      *anaana-ga*
      mother-1SG.POS/SG.POSM.ABS
      'my mother'

151.  *eqiasuitsorujussuaq_*
      *eqiasuiC-soq-rujussuaq-0*
      be.diligent-PART-very.much-ABS
      'she was very industrious'

152. *sulinngiffimmigut_*     *sinissanani*
*sulinngiffik-migut*     *siniC-ssa-nani*
vacation/free.time-3SG.POS.VIA sleep-FUT-3SG.NEG.CT
'in her free time, she didn't sleep'

153. *piliniartartoq_*
*piliniaq-saq-soq*
provide-HAB-3SG.PART
'she was getting/hunting for food [for the winter]'

154. *saarulleqallarmat*     *taamanikkut,*
*saarullit-qaq-llaq-mat*    *taamani-kkut*
codfish-have-great-3NC.SG.CAUS at.that.time-VIA
'there was a lot of codfish at that time'

155. 1920-*ikkut*  *aallartilaarneranni,*
1920-*kkut*   *aallarti-laaq-neq-anni*
1920-VIA   begin-a.bit-NOMZ-3PL.POS/SG.POSM.LOC
'at the very beginning of the 1920s'

*umiaasaarannguaqaratta_'*
*umiaasaaraq-nguaq-qaq-gatta*
flat-bottomed.boat-little-have-1PL.CAUS
'we had a little flat-bottomed boat'

156. *kiffaaffini_*     *unnukkut*
*suliunnaaraangami*

*kiffaaffik-ni*     *unnuk-kkut*
*suli-junnaaq-gaa-gami*

housework-3C.SG.POS.LOC  evening-VIA
work-no.more-whenever-3C.SG.CAUS

'whenever she stopped working as a maid in the evening'

157. *unnuarsiorluni*
*unnuaq-sioq-luni*
night-deal.with-3SG.CT
'when it was night [i.e., she was doing nightshift]'

158. *illuttorluni*
*illuttor-luni*
bearing.something.in.both.hands-3SG.CT
'rowing'

159. *aalisariartarpoq,*
*aalisaq-giaq-saq-voq*
go.fishing-go.to.do-HAB.3SG.IND
'she went fishing'

160. *uanga       aqqaluaralu            tikitsiisarparput,*
*uanga       aqqaluaq-ga-lu         tikiC-sii-saq-varput*
1SG          little.brother-1SG.     arrive-wait-HAB-1PL.SUBJ/
             POS.ABS-and            3SG.OBJ.IND
'my little brother and I waited for her to come back'

161. *tassa       ikiorniassagatsigu_}*
*tassa       ikior-niaq-ssa-gatsigu*
that.is      help-try-FUT-1PL.SUBJ/3SG.OBJ.CAUS
'because we tried to help her [we had to, were to help her].'

## XLII Speaker

162. *{Taamaappoq          tassa}*
*taamaat-voq          tassa*
like.that-3SG.IND     that.is
'It was like that [that's how it was].'

## XLIII Speaker

163. *{Aana                      suli    tupinnarneq_'*
*aana                      suli    tupinnaq-neq*
here.it.is/that.one.there    yet     wonderful/unusual-SUP.ABS
'And what was most wonderful of all'

164. *aqqaluara                  apersortittussaasoq_'        (1930-imi)_'*
*aqqaluaq-ga               apersortit-sussaa-soq        1930-mi*
little.brother-1SG.POS/    be.confirmed-planned/        1930-LOC
SG.POSM.ABS               shall-3SG.PART
'when my little brother was to be confirmed (in 1930)'

165.  *illutaarpugut_'*
      *illu-taaq-vugut*
      house-get.a.new-1PL.IND
      'we got a new house'

166.  *takanna*              *suli*           *illukoq*
                             *oqaluffiup*      *kanginnguani*

      *takanna*              *suli*           *illu-koq-0*
                             *oqaluffik-up*    *kangia-nnguaq-ni*

      this.one.down.there    yet             house-former/old-ABS
                             church-REL       east-little-3SG.POS

      'this old house, still a ruin, beside [a little east of] the church'

      *taanna*    *qaqqajunnaasannguup*              *qaaniittoq_'*
      *taanna*    *qaqqajunnaqasag-nnguaq-up*        *qaani-iC-soq*
      that.one    low.hill-little-REL               top-COP-PART or
                                                    3SG.PART

      'on the top of that little hill'

167.  *tassa*      *anaana*        *taamanikkut*       *illutaarpoq_}*
      *tassa*      *anaana-0*      *taamani-kkut*       *illu-taaq-voq*
      that.is    mother-ABS      at.that.time-VIA    house-get.a.new-
                                                     3SG.IND

      'that is, my mother got the house then.'

## XLIV Speaker

168.  *{Anaanama_*               *tupinnartumik_*
      *anaana-ma*                *tupinnaq-soq-mik*
      mother-1SG.POS.REL       wonderful-PART-INST
      'It was wonderful that my mother'

      *naminneq*        *tamaat*              *akilerlugu_'*
      *naminneq-0*      *tamaq-at*           *aki-leq-lugu*
      self-REL        the.whole/all-3SG.O   pay-provide-3SG.OBJ.CT
      'paid for it all herself'

*sanasullu*           *tamaasa_*
*sanasoq-t-lu*        *tamaq-asa*
worker-PL-and     the.whole/all-3PL.O
'and all the workers'

169.   *angutitaqannginnatta_'*
*anguti-taq-qaq-nngit-natta*
man-belonging.to-have-NEG-1PL.NEG.CAUS
'because we didn't have a man [in our family]'

170.   *sanasullu*           *tamaasa*           *akilerlugit_*
*sanasoq-t-lu*        *tamaq-asa*         *aki-leq-lugit*
worker-PL-and     all-3PL.O          pay-provide-3PL.OBJ.CT
'she paid all the workers'

171.   *assigiinngitsut*        *inuit —*        *inuit*          *sanavaat*
*assigiinngitsut*[86]     *inuk-it*        *inuk-it*        *sana-vaat*
different-REL          person-PL       person-PL       work-3PL.SUBJ/3.
OBJ.IND

'different people worked on it'

172.   *angutit_'*      *sanavaat_'*
*angut-t*        *sana-vaat*
man-PL        work-3PL.SUBJ/3.OBJ.IND
'men worked on it'

173.   *tassa*        *tamaasa*                    *akilerlugit,*
*tassa*        *tamaq-asa*                  *aki-ler-lugit*
that.is       the.whole/all-3PL.O      pay-provide-3PL.OBJ.CT
'she paid them all'

174.   *taamanikkut*           *aamma*       *uanga*       *eqqarsaatigalugit*
*taamani-kkut*          *aamma*       *uanga*       *eqqarsaat-gi-lugit*
at.that.time-VIA       and              1SG              thought-have-3PL.
OBJ.CT
'and even at that time, I thought about them/these facts'

175.  *tupigisarpara_/*
      *tupigi-saq-vara*
      wonder about-HAB-1SG.SUBJ/3SG.OBJ.IND
      'I wondered about it'

176.  *imaattoq_/*
      *imaaC-soq*
      be.that.is-3SG.PART
      'that is'

177.  *taamanikkunuku*              *sioqqat*          *cementimut*
                                                       *atoqqusaanngitsut*

      *taamani-kkut-uku*            *sioqqat*[87]      *cement-mut*
                                                       *ator-qqusaanngit-sut*

      at.that.time-VIA-DEIC        sand.ABS          cement-TERM
                                                       use-must.not-3PL.PART

      'at that time sand could not be used for cement'

      *nunap*           *siorai,*
      *nuna-p*          *sioraq-i*
      land-REL          piece.of.sand-3SG.POS/3PL.POSM
      'the sand of the land [i.e., Greenland's sand]'

178.  *Ikannga*          *akitsinniit*        *siorarsuarnit*
      *ikannga*          *akitsi-nniit*       *sioraq-suaq-nit*
      from.over.there    high.up-from.ABL     piece.of.sand-big-PL.ABL

      taasartakkatsinnik
      *taa-saq*[88]*-saq-gatsinnik*
      call-HAB-HAB-1PL.SUBJ/3SG.OBJ.CAUS
      'from the place we used to call "old sand" [big sand]'

179.  *sioqqiartitsilluni*
      sioqqiar-tit-si-luni
      fetch.sand-cause-INTRANS-3SG.CT
      'she made some people get sand/she made sand be fetched'

180. *laajalerluni_'*
*laaja-leq-luni*
hired.hand-provide-3SG.CT
'getting hired hands'

181. *upanniussuaq*      *niuertoqarfiup*      *upanniussua*
*upanniussuaq-0*    *niuertoqarfik-up*   *upaniussuaq-a*
"upanniussuaq"[89]-ABS   trading.post-REL   big.whaling.
                                         dinghy-3NC.
                                         SG.POS.ABS

'she [rented] the trading post's [town's] whaling dinghy
"upanniussuaq"'

*umiatsiaritillugu,*
*umiatsiaq-gi-tit-lugu*
rowboat-have-cause-3SG.OBJ.CT
'as a transport boat'

182. *ilumut*    *tassa_'*
*ilumut*    *tassa*
true     that.is
'it is true'

183. *inersimaleriarama*
*iner-sima-leq-giaq-gama*
grow.up/become.adult-PERF-begin-go.to.do-1SG.CAUS
'now that I am an adult'

184. *kingorna*   *assut*   *eqqarsaatigisarpara*   *anaana*
*kingorna*   *assut*   *eqqarsaat-gi-saq-vara*   *anaana-0*
later       much    thought-have-HAB-1SG.   mother-ABS
                               SUBJ/3SG.OBJ.IND
'much later I thought about my mother'

185. *inuup*         *nakuusimassusia_}*
*inuk-up*      *nakuaq-u-sima-ssuseq-a*
person-REL   strong-COP-PERF-quality-3NC.SG.POS/SG.POSM.ABS
'what a very strong person.'

## XLV Speaker

186. {*Taava aqqaluataama apersortinnissaanut*
*taava aqqaluataaq-ma apersortinneq-ssaq-anut*
then little.brother-new-1SG. confirmation-FUT-3NC.
POS/SG.POSM.REL SG.POS.TERM
'Then at the time of my youngest brother's confirmation'

*illutaarpugut*
*illu-taaq-vugut*
house-get.a.new-1PL.IND
'we got a new house'

187. *nuannersorujussuuvoq taamanikkut_/*
*nuanneq-soq-rujussuaq-u-voq taamani-kkut*
be.nice-PART-very.much-COP-3SG.IND at.that.time-VIA
'it was very nice in those days'

188. *akuttugallarmata igaffillit_'*
*akuttu-gallar-mata igaffik-lik-t*
rare-yet/still/for.the.time. kitchen-provided.with-PL
being-3NC.PL.CAUS
'because it was rare to have kitchens/kitchens were rare'

189. *igaffilinnguaq_*
*igaffik-lik-nnguaq-0*
kitchen-provided.with-little-ABS
'a little kitchen'

*inilik_ nuannersorujussuaq_}*
*ini-lik-0 nuanneq-soq-rujussuaq-0*
room-provided.with-ABS nice-PART-very.much-ABS
'a little room [was] very nice.'

## XLVI Speaker

190. (*Aamma kingorna uigigaluarma*
*allivaa_*

*aamma kingorna ui-gi-galuaq*[90]*-ma*
*alli-vaa*

and              later              husband-have-CONSEQ-1SG.POS.REL
                                    grow-3SG.SUBJ/3SG.OBJ.IND

'And later my late husband made it bigger'

191.   *aqqaluara*                      *nuliaqalermat*
       *aqqaluaq-ga*                    *nuliaq-qaq-leq-mat*
       little.brother-1SG.POS.ABS       wife-have-provide-3NC.SG.CAUS
       'when my little brother got married [had a wife]'

192.       *meeqqiulerlunilu*
           *meeqqior-leq-luni-lu*
           have.children-provide-3SG.CT-and
           'and got children'

193.   *aamma*     *allinikuuaa_/*
       *aamma*     *alli-nikuu-vaa*
       and         grow-past-3SG.SUBJ/3SG.OBJ.IND
       'and he made it bigger'

194.   *sinittarfiit*                    *inilerlugit*
       *taakku*                          *immikkut_)}}*

       *sinittarfik-it*                  *ini-leq-lugit*
       *taakku*                          *immi-kkut*

       bedroom-3PL.POS/PL.POSM.ABS       room-provide-3PL.OBJ.CT
       those-REL                         own

'those ones built their own bedrooms/those ones made separate
bedrooms.'


## Speaker 4, text 4

Recorded August 21, 1995, in Nuuk

I

1.     {*Tassa_*     *siullermik*     *oqaatigissavara_/*
        *tassa*       *siullermik*     *oqaatigi-ssa-vara*

that.is      at.first        talk.about-FUT-1SG.SUBJ/3SG.OBJ.IND
'So first I am going to talk about this'

2.    *uanga*      *Nuummi*        *inunngorpunga_*
      *uanga*      *Nuuk-mi*       *inunngor-vunga*
      1SG          Nuuk-LOC        be.born-1SG.IND
      'I was born in Nuuk'

3.    *tassa*      *1928-imi_}*
      *tassa*      *1928-mi*
      that.is      1928-LOC
      'that is, in 1928.'


II

4.    *{Taamaalillunga,*
      *taamaali-lunga*
      be.like.that-1SG.CT
      'Myself, and in this way [I was like this]'

5.    *Nuup*        *eqqaa_'*
      *Nuuk-up*     *eqqaq-a*
      Nuuk-REL      near-3SG.POS/SG.POSM.ABS
      'around Nuuk'

      *meeraaninniilli_'*
      *meeraaneq-m-niit-li*
      childhood-1SG.POS/SG.POSM-from-INTNS
      'ever since my childhood'

      *angallavigiuarsimavara_*
      *angala[91]-vigi-juaq-sima-vara*
      travel-TRANSR-always-PERF-1SG.SUBJ/3SG.OBJ.IND
      I have always been traveling

6.    *piniartuinnarsuit*              *akornanni*
      *piniartoq-innaq-suaq-it*        *akorneq-ni*
      hunter-only-big-PL.POS.REL       space-3SG.POS.LOC

*peroriartornera*                                    *pissutaalluni_}*
*peror-giartor-neq-ga*                               pissut-u-luni
become.adult-more.and.more-NOMZ-                     reason-COP-3SG.CT
1SG.POS.ABS

'because I have grown up among only the great hunters [my growing up among only hunters being the reason].'

III

7.    {*Ataataga*              *nammineq_*       *piniartuuvoq_'*
      *ataata-ga*              *nammineq*        *piniartoq-u-voq*
      father-1SG.POS.ABS       self              hunter-COP-3SG.IND

      'My father himself was a hunter'

8.    (*oqarsinnaavunga*
      *oqaq-sinnaa-vunga*
      say-can-1SG.IND

      '(I can say'

9.    *piniartorsuuvoq*                     *inuusunnermini_')*
      *piniartoq-suaq-u-voq*               *inuusunneq-mini*
      hunter-big-COP-3SG.IND               youth-3C.SG.POS.LOC

      'he was a great hunter in his youth)'

10.   *kisianni_*          *pisoqasaanngorluni_*
      *kisianni*           *pisoqasaaq-nngor-luni*
      but                 one.who.is.advancing.in.years-become-3SG.CT

      'but when he got old'

11.   *tassa_*      *ajoqitut*           *tiguinnakkatut_*[92]
                                         *sulisinneqalerpoq_'*

      *tassa*       *ajoqi-tut*          *tigu-innaq-saq-tut*
                                         *suli-tit-neqaq-leq-voq*

      that.is      catechist-EQ         take-only-PASS.PART-EQ
                                         work-cause-PASS-begin-3SG.IND

      'that is, he was put to work as a catechist'

12. *allamik*      *pisussaarummat_*}
    *alla-mik*      *pisussaaruC-mat*
    other-INST      no.one.wants.to-3NC.SG.CAUS
    'because no one else could be got.'

IV

13. {*Taamaalillutalu_*'
    *taamaali-luta-lu*
    be.like.that-1PL.CT-and
    'And we were like that [it was like that for us]'

14. *meeraaffinni*      *Saarlumi_*
    *meeraq-vik-nni*      *Saarloq-mi*
    child-place-1SG.POS.LOC      Saarloq-LOC
    'in the place where I was a child in Saarloq'

    *ajoqitut*      *sulivoq_*      *ukior-passuit_*}
    *ajoqi-tut*      *suli-voq*      *ukioq-passuaq-it*
    catechist-EQ      work-3SG.IND      year-a.lot-PL
    'he worked as a catechist for many years.'

V

15. {*Oqaatigissavaralu,*
    *oqaatigi-ssa-vara-lu*
    talk.about-FUT-1SG.SUBJ/3SG.OBJ.IND-and
    'And I will talk about [him/it]'

16. *ataataga*      *aamma,*      *tamalaarpassuarnik*
                                *soqutigisaqarami_*'

    *ataata-ga*      *aamma*      *tamalaaq-passuaq-nik*
                                *soqutigisaq-qaq-gami*

    father-1SG.POS.ABS      and      a.little.of.everything-a.lot-PL.INST
                                interest-have-3C.SG.CAUS

    'and my father, he was interested in many things'

17.   *siullermik_*      *seminariami*       *atuaqataavoq*
      *siullermik*       *seminaria-mi*      *atuaqat-u-voq*
      at.first           seminary-LOC        schoolmate-COP-3SG.IND
      'the first time he went to the seminary (teacher's school)'

18.   *ima*     *kursuserpoq*
      *ima*     *kursus-er-voq*
      like      course-have.a.course-3SG.IND
      'like to take courses'

19.   *maannakkutoorlugu_'*
      *maanna-kkut-tooq-lugu*
      now-VIA-like-3SG.OBJ.CT
      'it would be called now'

20.   1929-*imi_}*
      1929-*mi*
      1929-LOC
      '[was] in 1929.'

VI

21.   {*Taava_*      *tamatuma*       *kinguningaatsiarsuagut*
                                      1942-*imi_*

      *taava*        *tamatuma*       *kinguneq-ngaatsiaq-suaq-agut*
                                      1942-*mi*

      so             this.REL         result/succession-very.much-big-3SG.
                                      POS.VIA
                                      1942-LOC

      'So then much later in 1942'

22.   *aamma*     *kingumut*     *ukiivoq*                    *Nuummi_*
      *aamma*     *kingumut*     *ukii-voq*                   *Nuuk-mi*
      and         again          winter.over-3SG.IND          Nuuk-LOC
      'and he again was one year [wintered over] in Nuuk'

23.   *aamma*     *seminariami_*      *atuaqataalluni_}*
      *aamma*     *seminaria-mi*      *atuaqat-u-luni*

and          seminary-LOC    schoolmate-COP-3SG.CT
'and he learned in the seminary.'

VII

24.     {*Taamaalilluni,*
        *taamaali-luni*
        be.like.that-3SG.CT
        'And in this way'

25.     *ajoqitut*              *sulilivinnini_'*
        *ajoqi-tut*             *suli-leq-vig-neq-ni*
        catechist-EQ           work-begin-really-NOMZ-3C.SG.ABS
        'he really began to work as a catechist [i.e., his really beginning to
        work as a catechist was authorized]'

26.     (*tassami*            *uppernarsaaserlugu_/*)}
        *tassami*             *uppernarsaat-ler-lugu*
        in.any.case          proof/certificate-provide.with-3SG.OBJ.CT
        '(in any case he got a certificate).'

VIII

27.     {*Taava_*     *oqaatigissavakkalu*                *taamanikkut*
                                                          *piniartorsuit*

        *taava*       *oqaatigi-ssa-vakka-lu*             *taamani-kkut*
                                                          *piniartoq-suaq-it*

        then          talk.about-FUT-1SG.SUBJ/            at.that.time-VIA
                      3PL.OBJ.IND-and
                                                          hunter-big-PL

        'Then I can talk about the big hunters in those days'

        *piniartuinnarsuit*          *akornanni*    *Saarlumi_/*
        *piniartoq-innaq-suaq-it*    *akornanni*    *Saarloq-mi*
        hunter-only-big-PL           among          Saarloq-LOC
        'among only the big hunters in Saarloq'

28.     *inuit_'*        (*uanga*               *meeraanerpiama*
                                                *nalaani_*)

*inuk-it*          *uanga*                    *meeraaneq-piaq-ma*
                                             *nalaani*

person-PL     1SG                    childhood-exactly-1SG.POS.REL
                                             time.period

'the Inuit (when I was just a child at this time)'

29. *Qaarusumminngaanniit*     *nuupput*          *Saarlumut_'*
    *Qaarusuk-minngaanniit*     *nuuC-vut*          *Saarloq-mut*
    Qaarusuk-ABL                       move-3PL.IND     Saarloq-TERM
    'they moved from Qaarusuk to Saarloq'

30. *taamaalillunilu,*
    *taamaali-luni-lu*
    be.like.that-3SG.CT-and
    'and it was like this/in this way'

31. *Saarloq*              *inuttusiallappoq_'*
    *Saarloq-0*            *inuttu-si-allag-voq*
    Saarloq-ABS        have/be.people-INTRANS-increase-3SG.IND
    'Saarloq became more populated'

32. *tassa,*     *immaqa*     *70-80-it*     *missaanni*     *inoqalerluni_/*
    *tassa*      *immaqa*     *70-80-it*     *missaanni*     *inuk-qaq-leq-luni*
    that.is     maybe        70-80-PL        about              person-have-
                                                                          begin-3SG.CT

    'that is it had maybe about seventy to eighty people'

33. (*Taakkulu*          *tamarmik*                  *piniartuupput_*)}
    *Taakku-lu*          *tamaq-mik*                  *piniartoq-u-vut*
    those.ABS-and     the.whole/all-3PL.S     hunter-COP-3PL.IND
    '(and those ones were all hunters).'


IX

34. {*Ataataga*                  *ajoqitut_*            *meeqqanullu*
    *atuartitsisutut*            *sulivoq_'*

    *ataata-ga*                  *ajoqi-tut*             *meeraq-t-nut-lu*
    *atuartitsisoq-tut*          *suli-voq*

> father-1SG.POS.ABS    catechist-EQ    child-PL-TERM-and
> teacher-EQ            work-3SG.IND

'My father worked as a catechist and as a teacher to children'

35.
> uangalu_             atuarfinni_
> uanga-lu             atuarfik-nni
> 1SG-and              school-1SG.POS.LOC

'and me, in my school'

> meeqqat    atuarfianni              atuarfigaara_
> meeraq-t   atuarfik-anni           atuarfik-gi-vara
> child-PL   school-3PL.POS.LOC      school-have-1SG.SUBJ/3SG.
>                                    OBJ.IND

'I had him as a teacher in the children's school'

36.
> meeraqatikka              allat        ilagalugit_}
> meeraq-qat-kka            alla-t       ilaga-lugit
> child-companion-1SG.      other-PL     together.with-3PL.OBJ.CT
> POS/PL.POSM.ABS

'together with my other child playmates.'

X

37.
> {Taava_        juumooqarpugut_'
> taava          juumooq-qaq-vugut
> then           midwife-have-1PL.IND

'Then we had a midwife'

38.
> aamma,         ilinniarsimanngitsumik,
> aamma          ilinniaq-sima-nngit-soq-mik
> and            learn-PERF-NEG-PART-INST

'and [she was] without learning [i.e., (she was) someone without learning]'

39.
> imaappoq                 tiguinnakkamik_/
> imaaC-voq                tigu-innaq-gaq[93]-mik
> be.like.this-3SG.IND     take-just/only-PASS.PART-INST

'let me say this, she was just taken [i.e., that is, she was just taken]'

40.   *kisianni*    *juumootut,*
      *kisianni*    *juumooq-tut*
      but          midwife-EQ
      'but as a midwife'

      *atorluartorujussuarmik,*
      *atorluaq-soq-rujussuaq-mik*
      use.in.a.reasonable.way-PART-very big-INST
      '[she was] a very good one'

41.   *tassaavoq*              *arnaq*        *utoqqaq: H.E._}*
      *tassa-u-voq*            *arnaq-0*      *utoqqaq-0: H.E.*
      that.is-COP-3SG.IND   woman-ABS    old.person-ABS: H.E.
      'it was an old lady: H.E.'


XI

42.   {*Maani,*    *naluneqanngittut*                J.E.-*ikkut,*
                                                     B.E.-*ikkut,*

      *maani*      *nalu-neqaq-nngit-sut*            J.E.-*kkut-0*
                                                     B.E.-*kkut-0*

      here       not.know-PASS-NEG-3PL.PART      J.E.-family-ABS
                                                     B.E.-family-ABS

      'Here the well-known [they are well known] J.E. and B.E.
      [families]'

      *aanaavat_}*
      *aanaa-at*[94]
      grandmother-3PL.POS/SG.POSM.ABS
      'their grandmother.'


XII

43.   {*Taava*    *soorlu*        *oqareersunga*
      *taava*     *soorlu*        *oqaq-reer-sunga*
      then       for.example/like   say-already-1SG.PART
      'Then, like I said before'

44. *ataataga,*              *aamma*    *soqutigisaqaqigami*
    *ataata-ga*              *aamma*    *soqutigisaq-qaq-qi-gami*
    father-1SG.POS.ABS   and       interest-have-INTNS-3C.
                                          SG.CAUS
    'because my father had many interests'

45. *kommunerådi*[95]               *Nuummi*        *ilaasortaavoq_'*
    *kommuneråd-0*                  *Nuuk-mi*       *ilaasortaq-u-voq*
    community.council-ABS   Nuuk-LOC   member-COP-3SG.IND
    'he was a member of the community council in Nuuk'

46. *taamanikkut*        *Saarloq_'*
    *taamani-kkut*       *Saarloq-0*
    at.that.time-VIA   Saarloq-ABS
    'because at that time Saarloq'

    *Nuup*            *Kommuneaniikkami_*
    *Nuuk-up*         *Kommune-aniit-gami*
    Nuuk-REL     Commune-3SG.POS.LOC-3C.SG.CAUS
    'was a part of the Nuuk Commune'

47. *kommunerådi*                  *Nuummi_'*
    *ataatsimeeqatigijuarpaa_}*

    *kommunerådi*                  *Nuuk-mi*
    *ataatsimii-qat-gi-juaq-vaa*

    community.council-ABS     Nuuk-LOC
    be.in.a.meeting-companion-have-always-3SG.SUBJ/3SG.OBJ

    'he always used to have [had] a meeting with the Nuuk
    community council.'


XIII

48. *{Taava*      *inuunermi*                  *ilaatigut,*
    *taava*       *inuuneq-mi*                 *ilaatigut*
    then          life-3C.SG.POS.REL     sometime/once/part
    'Then for a part of his life'

*aamma    Landsrådimi_'*
*aamma    Landsråd-mi*
and          country's.council-LOC
'and in the country's council'

49.  (*tassa,    qanormaannaa?_'*        *suppleant_*
*tassa    qanoq-maanna-a*        *suppleant*
that.is    how-now-INT.VOWEL.        vice.member [Danish word]
LENGTHENING
'(that is, how do we say it? as a vice member'

*tassa_)    sinnisut — sinniisussatut_'*
*tassa                sinniisussa-tut*
that.is                vice.member-EQ [Greenlandic word]
'that is) as a vice member'

50.  *aamma    Landsrådimi                ataatsimeeqataasarpoq*
*aamma    Landsråd-mi                ataatsimii-qat-u-saq-voq*
and          country.council-LOC        be.in.a.meeting-companion-
COP-HAB-3SG.IND
'and he used to be in the country council meetings'

51.  *marloriarluni                ataataga_}*
*marloq-giaq-luni                ataata-ga*
two-do.x.times[96]-3SG.CT    father-1SG.POS.ABS
'going twice, my father [i.e., as vice-member, taking over when
the chief was indisposed].'

XIV

52.  *{Taamaalilluni_*
*taamaali-luni*
like.this-3SG.CT
'In this way/like this'

53.  *politikkimut_    ataataga                iseriartuaarsimavoq,*
*politikki-mut    ataata-ga                iser-giartuaaq-sima-voq*
politics-TERM    father-1SG.POS.ABS    enter-more.and.more-
PERF-3SG.IND

'my father got more and more into politics'

54.   *aammalu*     *nalunngilara*
     *aamma-lu*   *nalu-nngit-lara*
     and-and     not.know-NEG-1SG.SUBJ/3SG.OBJ.NEG.IND
     'and I know'

55.   *inuusunnerminiit*      *soqutigisarijuarsimagaa_}*
     *inuusunneq-minit*      *soqutigisaq-gi-juaq-sima-gaa*
     youth-3C.SG.POS.ABL    interest-have-always-PERF-3SG.
                                SUBJ/3SG.OBJ.PART
     'he has always been interested in it from his youth.'

XV

56.   *{Ataataga_*
     ataata-ga
     father-1SG.POS.ABS
     'My father'

     *imaannaanngitsorsuartut*     *oqaatigineqarsinnaavoq_/*
     *imaannaanngit-soq-suaq-tut*   *oqaatigi-neqaq-sinnaa-voq*
     not.without.importance/     say.about.one-PASS-can-3SG.IND
     meaning-part-big-EQ[97]
     'he was said to be an exceptional person [i.e., was like one not
     without importance]'
     [i.e., 'My father was said to be an exceptional person; it can be
     said that my father was like an exceptional person']

57.   *aammami_*     *takisuuliorpallaarnanga*
     *aamma-mi*     *takisooq-lioq-vallaaq-nanga*
     and-INTNS     long-make-so/too.much-1SG.NEG.CT
     'and, not to make it [story] too long [I won't make it
     too long]'

58.   *oqaatigitsiarsinnaavara,*
     *oqaatigi-tsiaq-sinnaa-vara*
     say.about.one-a.little-can-1SG.SUBJ/3SG.OBJ.IND
     'I can say a little about this'

59.　*qanoq*　　*inuuneqarsimasoq_}*
　　*qanoq*　　*inuuneq-qaq-sima-soq*
　　how　　　life-have-PERF-3SG.PART
　　'how he has lived.'

XVI

60.　*{Inuusunnermini_*
　　*inuusunneq-mini*
　　youth-3C.SG.POS.LOC
　　'In his youth'

　　*suli*　　*ajoqinngunngikkallartilluni_/*
　　*suli*　　*ajoqi-nngor-nngit-gallaq-tit-luni*
　　yet　　　catechist-become-NEG-temporary/continuous-cause-
　　　　　　3SG.CT
　　'when he hadn't yet been caused to become a catechist'

61.　*ataataga,*
　　*ataata-ga*
　　father-1SG.POS.ABS
　　'my father'

　　*kunngerput_*
　　*kunngi-rput*
　　king-1PL.POS/SG.POSM.ABS
　　'our king'

　　1921-*imi_*
　　1921-*mi*
　　1921-LOC
　　'in 1921'

　　*danskit*　　*kunngiat,*　　　*Christiaat* 10.-*lingat (qulingat),*
　　*danski-t*　　*kunngi-at,*　　　*Christiaat* 10.-*lingat (qulingat)*
　　Dane-PL　　king-3PL.POS.ABS　　Christian 10th (tenth)
　　'the Danes' king, Christian the Tenth'

　　*tikeraarmat_'*
　　*tikeraar-mat*

arrive.from.traveling-3NC.SG.CAUS
'when he arrived'

62. *taamanikkut,*      *Nuup*      *eqqaani*
                                    *qajarpar— —passuit,*

   *taamani-kkut*      *Nuuk-up*      *eqqaq-ani*
                                      *qajaq-passuit*

   at.that.time-VIA   Nuuk-REL   neighborhood-3SG.POS.LOC
                                 kayak-lots.of.PL

   'at that time around Nuuk'

   *umiarpassuillu*          *piugallarmata_}*
   *umiaq-passuit-lu*        *pi-u-gallaq-mata*
   boat-lots.of.PL-and    thing-COP-continuous-3NC.PL.CAUS
   'there were lots of kayaks and umiaqs.'

XVII

63. {*Taamani_*      *qaannakkut_*
    *taamani*      *qaannat-kkut*
    at.that.time    kayak.SG-VIA
    'At that time'

   *immaqa*      *unammersuartut*      *siullerpaat_'*
   *immaqa*      *unammer-suaq-tut*      *siulleq-paat*
   maybe      competition-big-EQ      first-INTNS
   'maybe the very first kayak competitions'

64. *Nuup*      *eqqaa,*                       *tamakkerlugu_*
    *Nuuk-up*      *eqqaq-a*                    *tamakker-lugu*
    Nuuk-REL   neighborhood-3SG.POS/      all.together-3SG.
               SG.POSM.ABS               OBJ.CT
    'including the whole Nuuk area'

65. *ataatama*                *peqataaffiginikuuvai_}*
    *ataata-ma*                *peqataa-ffigi-nikuu-vai*
    father-1SG.POS.REL      be.with/take.part.in-TRANSR-PAST.
                            PERF-3SG.SUBJ/3PL.OBJ.IND

'my father took part in them.'

XVIII

66. {*Issuatsiarsinnaavaralu_*
*issuar-tsiaq-sinnaa-vara-lu*
cite-a.little-can-1SG.SUBJ/3SG.OBJ-and
'And I can cite a little of this'

67. *Aggu*   *Lyngeugaluup_'*       *allaaserigamiuk,*
    *Aggu*   *Lynge-u-galuaq-up*    *allaaseri-gamiuk*
    Aggu   Lynge-COP-late-REL    write.about-3C.SG.SUBJ/3SG.
                                  OBJ.CAUS

'the late Aggu Lynge, when he wrote about it/him [referent unclear]'

68. *ataataga*            *pisimagaa_'*
    *ataata-ga*           *pi-sima-gaa*
    father-1SG.POS.ABS    thing-PERF-3SG.SUBJ/3SG.OBJ.IND

'he did it [about my father? translation unclear]'

69. "*Pikkorinnersaallu*          *immikkut*
    *akissarsisippaa*"_}

    *pikkoriC-neq-saat-lu*        *immikkut*
    *akissarsi-tit-vaa*

    clever-SUP-means.to-and    special/individual
    get.prize-cause-3SG.SUBJ/3SG.OBJ.IND

'"And the cleverest will get a special prize"/"he will give a prize to the cleverest."'

70. (*Tassa*   *kunngip*    *Christiaap*      *qulingata_*)}}
    *tassa*    *kunngi-p*   *Christiaa-p*     *qulingat-a*
    that.is   king-REL    Christian-REL    tenth-3SG.POS/SG.POSM.ABS
'(That is, King Christian the Tenth).'

(*Christiaap*          *qulingata_*)}}}
*Christiaa-p*          *qulingat-a*

Christian-REL    tenth-3SG.POS/SG.POSM.ABS
'(Christian the Tenth).'


## XIX

71.   {*Taamanikkut*   *tassa,*   <u>*nersusaasorujorujorujoruussuuvoq*</u>

    *taamani-kkut*   *tassa*   *nersor-saq-u-soq-ruju-ruju-*
                              *rujussuaq-u-voq*

    at.that.time    that.is   praise-PASS.PART-COP-PART-very-
                              very-very.much-COP-3SG.IND

    'At that time he was very, very, very, much praised'


    *ataataga,*
    *ataata-ga*
    father-1SG.ABS
    'my father'


72.   *maannakkuusuuppat*
    *maanna-kkut-u-soq-u-ppat*
    now-VIA-COP-PART-COP-3NC.SG.COND
    'if it were today/now'


73.   *tusaamasanngorsimagaluarluni_*}
    *tusaamasaq-nngor-sima-galuaq-luni*
    famous-become-PERF-CONSEQ-3SG.CT
    'he would have been very popular.'


## XX

74.   {*Kisianni*   *taava*   *taallatsiaannarlugit_*
    *kisianni*   *taava*   *taa-llatsiaq-innaq-lugit*
    but       then   mention-little-just-3PL.OBJ.CT
    'But then just to mention these a bit'


75.   *meeraanera_*         *eqqartulaassavara_/*
    *meeraaneq-ga*       *eqqartor-laaq-ssa-vara*
    childhood-1SG.POS.ABS   talk.about-a.little-FUT-1SG.SUBJ/3SG.
                              OBJ.IND
    'I will talk a little about my childhood'

76. *taamanikkut*        *meeraanerma*              *nalaani_'*
    *taamani-kkut*        *meeraaneq-ma*             *nalaani*
    at.that.time-VIA      childhood-1SG.POS.REL      time.period-3C.
                                                    SG.POS.LOC

    'at that time, in the time of my childhood'

    *piniagassaapput_'*
    *piniagassat-u-vut*
    hunted.animal-COP-3PL.IND
    'there were animals that were hunted'

77. *piniagassatigut*              *taasinnaasakka*
    *tassa_'*

    *piniagassat-tigut*            *taa-sinnaa-sakka*
    *tassa*

    hunted.animals-PL.VIA          give.provenance.of-can-1SG.SUBJ/3PL.
                                   OBJ.PART
    that.is

    'I can give the list of the hunted animals'

78. *ukiumi_*          *terianniat_'*
    *ukioq-mi*          *terianniaq-t*
    winter-LOC          fox-PL
    'In the winter [there were] foxes'

    *aqissit_'*          *ukallit_'*
    *aqisseq-t*          *ukaleq-t*
    ptarmigan-PL         hare-PL
    'ptarmigans, and hares'

79. *taavalu*       *aamma_*       *soorunalumi*                   *puisit_'*
    *taava-lu*       *aamma*        *sooruna-lu-mi*                 *puisi-t*
    then-and        and            of.course-and-what.about        seal-PL
    'and then, of course, what about the seals'

80. *sikukkut*       *avungalu,*             *Natsilimmut_'*
    *siku-kkut*       *avunga-lu*             *Natsilik-mut*

ice-VIA       in.the.north-and     Natsilik-TERM
'across the ice up north to Natsilik'

*Saarluminngaanniit*       *ilaanni*        *sisoraaserlutik*
*Saarloq-minngaanniit*     *ilaanni*        *sisorar-uti-ler-lutik*
Saarloq-ABL                sometimes        ski-device-begin-3PL.CT
'sometimes putting skis on from Saarloq'

81.   *piniariartarlutik_}*
      *piniar-giaq-saq-lutik*
      hunt-go.to.do-HAB-3PL.CT
      'hunting.'

## XXI

82.   {*Taava_*      *upernariartortillugu,*
      *taava*        *upernar-giartor-tit-lugu*
      then           become.spring-go.to.do-cause-3SG.OBJ.CT
      'Then when spring came'

83.   *piniagassat*                 *saqqummeriartortarput_'*
      *piniagassat*                 *saqqummer-giartor-saq-vut*
      hunting.animals.PL            come.out-more.and.more-HAB-3PL.
                                    IND
      'the hunting animals used to come out more and more'

84.   *allatuulli_'*                          *taava*   *aataarpassuit_*
      *allatooq-t-li*                         *taava*   *aataaq-passuit*
      young.Greenland.seal-PL-INTNS           then      Greenland.seal-lots.
                                                        of.PL
      'and young Greenland seals, and lots of Greenland (harp) seals

      *Newfoundlandip*        *avataaninngaanniit_'*
      *Newfoundland-ip*       *avataa-ningaanniit*
      Newfoundland-REL        coast-PL.ABL

      *nunatsinnut*           *tikerallaraangamik_'*
      *nuna-tsinnut*          *tiker-gallaq-gaangamik*
      land-1PL.POS.TERM       arrive-INTNS-whenever.3C.PL.CAUS
      'arrived continually from the Newfoundland coast to our land'

85.  *sineriapput_*          *kangerluillu_*       *pulaararlugit*
     *sineriak-vut*          *kangerluk-it-lu*     *pulaar-ar-lugit*
     coast-1PL.POS/PL.       fjord-PL-and          visit-for.a.while-3PL.
     POSM.ABS                                      OBJ.CT
     'visiting our coasts, and the fjords, for a while'

86.  *aataarpassuanngortarput_/*
     *aataaq-passuaq-nngor-saq-vut*
     Greenland.seal-lots.of-become-HAB-3PL.IND
     'there used to be lots of Greenland seals [coming]'

     *meeraaffimma*          *nalaani*             *Saarluni_}*
     *meeraq-ffik-ma*        *nalaani*             *Saarloq-ni*
     child-place-1SG.        time.period-3C.SG.    Saarloq-LOC
     POS.REL                 POS.LOC
     'in the time of my childhood in Saarloq.'

     *Saarluminngaanniit_}}*
     *Saarloq-minngaanniit*
     Saarloq-ABL
     'from Saarloq'

## XXII

87.  *{Taamanikkullu*        *pissarsiornerput_'*
     *taamani-kkut-lu*       *pissaq-sioq-neq-vut*
     at.that.time-VIA-and    game[98]-deal.with-NOMZ-1PL.POS
     'And at that time our livelihood'

88.  *eqqaamasaqanngilanga,*
     *eqqaamasat-qaq-nngit-langa*
     memories-have-NEG-1SG.NEG.IND
     'I don't have any memories'

89.  *ajorsa*                          *pilluta*
     *ukiorsiorlunnitsinnit_}*

     *ajor-saq-0*                      *pi-luta*
     *ukioq-sioq-lug-neq-tsinnit*

be.bad-PASS.PART-ABS    thing-1SG.PL.CT

winter-be.out.in-bad-NOMZ-1PL.POS.ABL

'[that] we had bad luck in our bad winters [i.e., I don't remember that we had actual hardship because of bad winters].'

## XXIII

90. {*Aamakku*          *avatinnguatsinni*          *aalisagarpassuit_'*
    *aamakku*          *avati-nnguaq-tsinni*          *aalisagaq-passuit*
    [exclamation][99]    outside-little-1PL.POS.LOC    fish-lots.of.PL
    'And all this fish right outside!'

91. *suluppaakkat_'*    *eqqarsaatigalugit*
    *suluppaagaq-t*    *eqqarsaat-gi-lugit*
    redfish-PL          thought-have-3PL.OBJ.CT
    'redfish, [I] have thoughts about them'

92. *suluppaakkat*    *taakku*        *piniagaanerpaapput*
    *suluppaagaq-t*    *taakku*        *pinia-gaq-a-nerpaa-vut*
    redfish-PL          those.ABS      hunt-PASS-3SG.POS-SUP-3PL.IND
    'those redfish were most hunted'

93. *taamanimi*              *meerarpiaanerma*        *nalaani*
    *taamani-mi*              *meeraq-piaq-u-neq-ma nalaani*
    at.that.time-INTNS      child-only.just-COP-NOMZ-1SG.POS.REL
                                                        time.period.3SG.POS.LOC
    'at that time in the time of my childhood [when I was only just a child]'

    *saarulliit*        *suli*    *imat— imannarsuaq*
                        *pitsilersimanngimmata_*[100]}

    *saarulleq-it*      *suli*    *imannarsuaq*
                        *pi-si-leq-sima-nngit-mata*

    codfish-PL          yet      to.such.a.degree
                                thing-INTRANS-begin-PERF-NEG-3NC.PL.CAUS

    'the codfish weren't yet [hunted] to such a degree.'

XXIV

94. {*Kisianni_*     *taamanikkut*     <u>*saarulliit*</u>
<u>*qaffartarput*</u>     *tassami_/*

*kisianni*     *taamani-kkut*     *saarulleq-it*
*qaffar-saq-vut*     *tassami*

but     at.that.time-VIA     codfish-PL
come.higher.up-HAB-3PL.IND     in.any.case

'But at that time the codfish used to come higher up in any case'

95. *itisuuminngaanniit*     *qaffartarput*     *upernaakkut,*
*itisooq-minngaanniit*     *qaffar-saq-vut*     *upernaaq-kkut*
deep-ABL     come.higher.up-HAB-3PL.IND     spring-VIA

'they came higher up from the deep [water] in the spring'

96. *soorlu*     *eqqarsaatigigutsigu*
*soorlu*     *eqqarsaatigi-gutsigu*
for.example     think.about.it-1PL.SUBJ/3SG.OBJ.COND
'for example, if we think about it'

97. *aprili_'*     *aprili*     *majikkunni_'*
*aprili*     *aprili*     *maji-kkut-ni*
April     April     May-family-LOC
'April, in April or May'

*qaffaraangata*
*qaffar-gaangata*
come.higher.up-whenever.3NC.PL.CAUS
'whenever they came higher up'

98. *tassa*     *saarullissuit*     *piisaarutigilersarpagut*
*aamma*

*tassa*     *saarulleq-ssuaq-t*     *piisaar-utigi-leq-saq-vavut*
*aamma*

that.is    codfish-big-PL          overflow-reason-begin-HAB-1PL.
                                    SUBJ/3PL.OBJ.IND

and

'that is, we began to overflow/gorge ourselves with codfish'

99.    *piliassat*                *naammattorsuit_}*
       *piliat*[101]*-ssat*          *naamaC-soq-suaq-t*
       winter.supply-FUT-PL      good-PART-big-PL
       'the future winter supply [was] great/[there was] a very good
       future winter supply.'

## 1. Introduction

1. The term 'incorporation' for this process is the standard used in descriptions of Greenlandic, contra Baker (1988).

2. For the most part, there is consensus on the naming of the cases in Greenlandic, but some small variations exist. I will adopt P. Langgård's terminology, itself adopted for the most part from Kleinschmidt (1851).

3. In the literature, the numbers 3 and 4 are used. Because of the different uses of these two numbers to refer to coreference, especially between scholars of Greenlandic and scholars of other Inuit dialects, I will simply refer to them as 3c (3 coreferential) and 3NC (3 noncoreferential).

4. Most of the studies preceding Chomsky in the 1950s were grammatical, following the traditional format of phonological and inflectional description, minor descriptions of clause formation and word order, and examples of texts. Although this is hardly surprising, given historical trends in linguistic studies, these grammars have had a considerable effect on modern studies of the Inuit dialects, particularly in the terminology and therefore also in the understanding of the semantics of inflectional categories. There are some very comprehensive grammars of West Greenlandic, by far the best of which is Kleinschmidt's *Grammar of West Greenlandic* (1851; reprinted 1968), which has served as the basis for similar work by Rasmussen (1888), Thalbitzer (1911), and Schultz-Lorentzen (1945), among others, and almost without fail as the authoritative source for more recent studies, including those by Bergsland (1955) and Fortescue (1984). Grammars exist for many other Inuit dialects (see various works by Dorais, Harper, Mallon, Smith, Spalding, Lowe, etc.). These have tended to be qualitatively different, designed for nonacademic readers for pedagogical purposes. In many of these grammars, syntax is only superficially addressed, but they have been the starting point of many modern syntactic descriptions of the Inuit language and its dialects. The early descriptions of Inuit cases and verb moods have been heavily influenced by the traditional methods of studying Latin. For example, categories valid in Latin were applied to the Inuit case system; hence the use of terms such as terminalis, vialis, ablative, and so forth. The terms have become standard, however, despite their inadequacies. The instrumental, for example, is used not only as an instrumental but as a case assigned to modifiers of incorporated nouns, adverbs, and objects of accusative (or antipassive) constructions. The same can be said of the description of verb

moods; as with case names, the terminology applied can be misleading, especially with respect to the dependent moods, which can function independently and which often have multiple functions. Lowe (1985:202) suggests that the contemporative (or conjunctive, in his terminology) seems to have a number of very different functions largely because of the different forms needed in translation.

5. The use of the terms 'accusative' and 'antipassive' indicates the theoretical approach. 'Accusative' is used where ergative is seen as a case-marking system in opposition to accusative case-marking, and 'antipassive' where the ergative is seen as a transitive clause in opposition to a detransitivized, 'antipassive' structure. Both terms are used in the discussion here, according to the theoretical approach of the linguist described. The view maintained in this discussion, however, is that the construction in question is an antipassive. See chapter 4 for the full discussion.

6. Karen Langgård has written about incorporation, which she has called inderivation, in West Greenlandic, although her research on this topic postdates the author's work.

7. Other approaches to discourse (e.g., studies of conversation, narrative, and argumentation) have certainly included proposed units of discourse; these are of a different nature than the units I propose here.

8. The contemporative only coindexes either subject or object, but not both. The participial mood is described as a subordinate mood; in the intransitive paradigm, it does not coindex 3 noncoreferential person, as other subordinate moods do, and transitive forms with 3 noncoreferential subjects are rare today.

## 2. Topic (and theme) as discourse roles

1. Other ways of distinguishing parts of discourse, such as main point and supporting arguments, background and foreground, and so forth, are more relevant to textual or pragmatic approaches to the study of discourse, but ultimately, they seem to lead back to the concepts of topicality and thematicity.

2. "Prominence" is, like topic and theme, a term prone to various interpretations and terminological confusion. There are different types of prominence, including intonational prominence, called "information focus" by Halliday (1967a) and "emphasis" by Jones (1977); grammatical prominence of the type called "focus" by Jones, and "focus," "topicalization," and so on, by both generativists and relationalists, referring to marked word order in the sentence; and thematic or topical prominence, referring to primary referential continuity in discourse. The three may or may not overlap in any particular clause (Halliday's claim that theme is by definition not the information focus of a clause depends on a use of the term theme that is not employed in the theories presented here). Here and in the chapters to follow, unless I am discussing another's theoretical propositions, I use the term "intonational emphasis" for intonational prominence, and the term "emphasis" for grammatical prominence. I have chosen to avoid the term "focus" altogether. I retain the term "thematic prominence," however.

3. In all the texts at which I looked, the number of times an oblique nominal was later taken up as topic, either as subject or direct object, without being reintroduced overtly as subject or direct object, is exceedingly small.

4. As for so-called topic-prominent languages, like Chinese, I, like Chafe (1976:50), have no direct knowledge of them. This definition, however, does not conflict with Chafe's description of topic as a framework for the limiting of the application of a predicate to a particular domain.

5. Givón (1984) highlights and emphasizes the terms he introduces, such as thematic unity, thematic continuity, and so on, but he does not actually provide an explicit definition for "theme" and its derivatives.

6. This would explain the importance of theme, rather than topic, in the switch-reference phenomena that I examine in chapter 4.

7. Creider (1979) theorizes that languages can treat initial, preverbal, and final positions as positions associated with topicalization of focusing, and that SOV languages tend to treat initial position as topical and preverbal position as focusing. He also provides specific examples from Eskimo (1979:15) and claims that languages such as Eskimo (the dialect appears to be Eastern Canadian, possibly Inuktitut) use only changes in grammatical relations to effect changes in topic and focus, as opposed to using word order. Based on the data in my texts, I disagree with this claim (cf. text 4, clause 73, 'at that time he was very, very, very much praised, my father').

8. For other examples of indicatives and topic introduction co-occurring, see text 4, clauses 5, 11, 14, 27-28, 31, 34-35, 37, 46, 48, 55, and 78.

9. It would be interesting to see if switch-reference in clause-chaining languages with nominative-accusative are related to topic or not.

### 3. Ergativity as a reflection of topic status

1. Actually, antipassives in West Greenlandic require that the demoted object be marked with instrumental case, but Bok-Bennema (1991) considers the deep-level differences between accusative and instrumental functions in her discussion of case.

2. Kalmár (1979b:72) mentions the unpublished work of J.-P. Paillet, in which Paillet identifies sentence structure with topic status. A topic that is the sentential agent has an intransitive, accusative structure; a topic that is the sentential patient has an ergative structure if previously unknown or a passive structure if previously known. Kalmár laments the fact that Paillet did not define his terminology, but essentially, the relevant features in the determination of clause structure are topichood and givenness. Not having access to this paper, I cannot comment on it further; however, although some features of Paillet's theory are close to what I propose below, there are some irreconcilable differences.

3. Dixon (1972) identifies, for example, a particle that is used consistently at thematic boundaries and that signals topic shift. I have noted the same general tendencies in West Greenlandic (as has Schiffrin 1987 for English).

4. Equating agent with topic allows Du Bois to argue against Mallinson and Blake's (1981) analysis of topic in ergative languages. On the other hand, Mallinson and Blake (1981:86, 90) suggest that the agency hierarchy is really a topicality hierarchy.

5. Kalmár (1979b) also applies the Praguian notion of theme/rheme to the Inuit language, specifically to Eastern Canadian Inuktitut, although he specifies that exceptions must be made for pronominals on the verb in clauses with no overt nominals. However, most clauses in normal oral discourse in Inuit have no overt nominals in subject or direct object position, either because of incorporation or because of its preference for inflectional rather than independent pronouns. This effectively means that analyzing Inuit sentences in terms of theme/rheme would result in more exceptions than not. This is not to say that word order within clauses is without importance in discourse, but rather that a strict dependence on a particular ordering of information within a clause seems to be an unpromising approach in explaining ergativity and clause structure in West Greenlandic.

6. Theoretically, this notion of topicality needs more refinement: is topic a primitive, as are S, O, or A, or is it a derived category, as is subject (S and A)? Technically, it must be a discourse primitive, as S, O, and A are syntactic primitives. Syntactically, or grammatically, however, topic is indicated in West Greenlandic as an alignment of S and O.

7. I use the terms "agent" and "patient" here as they are used by Dixon (1979, 1994) and Comrie (1981).

## 4. Switch-reference or thematic coherence and topic continuity?

1. Comrie (1983:23) is careful to characterize it as a clausal property, rather than as a property specifically of the noun phrases in question. This in part explains the range of marking systems described below.

2. The subordinate verb is pronominally marked for coreference as well; see Table 4.2.

3. I follow the established convention of using 'i' for coreference and 'j' for non-coreference with another noun phrase. In the examples given, since contemporatives and participials are used in conjunction with another, superordinate, clause, subscript 'i' indicates coreference and 'j' noncoreference with the subject of the superordinate.

4. There is an interesting split here, with the participial's subject in the relative case if it is singular, and in the instrumental if it is not.

5. The participial forms -j- and -t- often alternate morphophonologically, as do -v- and -p-, as in the inflectional endings -voq and -poq in West Greenlandic.

6. Discourse functions of the verb moods have been suggested most notably by Ivan Kalmár in several studies of Inuktitut grammatical features in narrative discourse. Kalmár (1982) specifically addresses the distribution of the verb moods with respect to their function in discourse in the Iglulingmiut dialect of Inuktitut. He analyzes a number of narrative texts collected by Rasmussen, and concludes that the independent moods convey information essential to the narrative, while the causative conveys

background information (as opposed to causation, condition, or doubt according to traditional grammatical explanations); both, however, advance the development of the narrative. Contemporative (and presumably participial) clauses, on the other hand, also express background information via elaborations at a point of development in the narrative rather than through narrative development. The difference between the participial and the contemporative is one of focus, with the former being participant focus and the latter event focus.

7. See especially the use of nominals by speaker 3 in my data.

8. Fortescue (1991:64) notes the occasional occurrence in spoken discourse of switch-reference marking in indicatives. How acceptable or prevalent this is, and in what circumstances it is found, are unknown.

9. It is on the basis of the medial/final distinction that Longacre (1985:239) suggests that the subordinate/coordinate distinction in such languages is irrelevant. A sentence would consist of a chain of medial verbs and end with a final verb clause, the latter being the only independent clause structure in the chain. However, the data I collected shows that in spoken discourse, clause chaining is often only partially realized, and multiple juxtapositions of independent clauses do occur frequently, as do sentences consisting only of dependent forms. Further, the Inuit languages do have different forms for subordinate and coordinate structures. Givón (1984: chapter 8) discusses a continuum of finiteness with respect to subordination and coordination, in which all clauses are interdependent but vary according to the level of finiteness. Subordinate structures are less finite in that they have fewer features of finiteness, including tense, modality, aspect, and negation, these features being more predictable in structures that depend on others for interpretation. To what extent West Greenlandic can be shown to have less finite subordinate forms will be discussed later in chapter 4.

10. The hierarchy Cole describes, where 1, 2, and arbitrary reference are higher than nonagentive 3, is reminiscent of Silverstein's ergativity hierarchy (as Cole himself points out, 1983:11). This makes sense if ergativity is a marker of local topic as object, as I have shown in the previous chapter, since there is a tendency for the speaker or some other human to be the subject and the inanimate noun to be the object.

11. In my data, clauses are grouped based on high-level intonation features rather than on grammatically correct clause chains. This is a reflection of the oral nature of my texts. However, within each intonational group, one can often distinguish subgroups (subparagraphs), sometimes based on intonation (as in the parenthetical paragraphs), and sometimes based on syntactic or semantic grounds, such as verb mood, aspectual indication, and so forth. Thus, if a clause chain reports on a single occurrence in the past, and one clause indicates habitual activity (e.g., 'once we went to Narsaq and I saw these piked whales' versus 'we used to go there every summer'), one might reasonably propose that the latter has a separate level of textual organization than the chain.

12. In an indirect way, the fact that the speaker lacks health is repeated in clauses 52–69, in a discussion of the speaker's reasons for having stopped smoking. Thus, the contemporative in clause 68 may refer more to the theme of the section, the fact that she is unhealthy, than to the more exact reference in clause 27. In any event, the unhealthy heart has been mentioned already and is consequently not elaborated upon.

13. This discussion must bring up questions of gap length and givenness status; seventeen clauses is substantially more than many people allow for the maintenance of given information. The example should show, however, that gap length is unpredictable.

14. Incidentally, speakers 1 and 4 also differ greatly in the development and organization of their discourse. For example, whereas speaker 1 shows development in his use of the participial, from being a minute marker of switch-topic/theme (from clause to clause) to a general marker of topic/theme at paragraph level as the recollection progresses and becomes clearer and more organized, speaker 4 shows a high-level interpretation of switch-topic/theme right from the beginning.

15. If so, then the difference between the literary and oral uses of the contemporative and participial verb moods must lead one to speculate on the rise of prescriptivism in literary West Greenlandic.

## Appendix

1. Inuit nominal endings mark both number and case. Where number of possessum is unmarked, possessum is singular.

2. Inuit verbal endings identify number, person, mode, and transitivity. There are separate personal endings for transitive and intransitive verb forms, and separate affixal forms for the different modes. Number and person, however, are often fused. Person, number, and modal categories will generally be given; where number is not indicated, the singular and plural forms are indistinguishable and meaning is derived from context. Where unmarked for transitivity, forms should be understood as intransitive.

3. All sources used in analyzing the affixes mention the nominal affix *-rujussuaq* 'very much'; Fortescue (1983) mentions the verbal affix *(pilu)rujussuar* 'enormously'. *-Rujussuuvoq* consists of the same elements: *-rujussu* without the now obsolescent abbreviated form of the nominalizer *-aq*, the copula *-u-*, and the 3SG indicative ending *-voq*.

4. According to Per Langgård (personal communication), *-galuaq-* is a syntactic marker and consequential sememe, indicating a following paratactic or hypotactic construction. With future tense, it can be understood as irrealis, or perhaps a form of politeness. It can indicate the speaker's reservations about what has just been said, and so on.

5. This word form is not attested in the various lexicons used for this analysis. The morphology is as follows: *inuk-u-riar-usiq-at* human-COP-INTNS-NOMZ-3PL.POS. ABS. It is essentially lexicalized in this meaning.

6. The form *ullumikkut* shows a relatively common but recent change in word structure involving the reinterpretation of original case endings as part of the stems of certain words and the resulting addition of new case endings as required by the syntax. *Ullumikkut* consists of the word *ulloq* 'day', *-mi*, a locative, and an additional but nontraditional *-kkut*, a vialis. Both the older *ullumi* and the newer *ullumikkut* are currently used in West Greenlandic.

7. *Silattoq-* is a way of saying 'grow up', and refers to the development of memory and consciousness in children. The speaker is suggesting something like 'one of the first things I remember'.

8. This was transcribed as *oqaluttoq*, but it seems to be *oqaluppoq* on the tape; the difference is one of verb mood, the former being a participial, the latter indicative. The indicative would signal a clear parenthetical thought on the part of the speaker (P. Langgård, personal communication).

9. The affix *-ssaq-* generally indicates some future aspect; when attached to nouns, the meaning of the construct becomes 'a future N'.

10. Equalis *-tut* is the same in both singular and plural.

11. The stem *tamaq* belongs to a very restricted remnant class of words that have a separate set of inflectional case endings; they may be the last and only traces of true adjectives in Greenlandic (P. Langgård, personal communication; he suggests that they refer to some spoken or unspoken topic.). Unlike the rest of the system, they seem to function on a nominative-accusative basis, but they all take relative case endings:

| Person | ABS.F. | REL.F. |
|---|---|---|
| 1SG | *tamarma* | *tamarma* |
| 2SG | *tamarpit* | *tamarpit* |
| 3SG | *tamaat* (3nc) | *tamarmi* (3c) |
| | | |
| 1PL | *tamatta* | *tamatta* |
| 2PL | *tamassi* | *tamassi* |
| 3PL | *tamaasa* (3nc) | *tamarmik* (3c) |

Example: *tamarmik sinipput* 'all of them are sleeping'; the verb is intransitive.

The main difference is in the third-person forms. The third-person noncoreferential is only used as an object; the third-person coreferential form is used as subject of intransitive and transitive clauses. Other members of this class include the stems *kisi* 'alone', *nammi* and *immi* almost synonymous reflexives, and *ilunngaq* 'entirely, all of' (for less physical concepts than *tamaq*). The basic meaning of *tamaq* is 'all', but different shades of meaning are acquired in context (e.g., 'all together', 'every', etc.).

12. *Oqaatsit* contains a lexical entry for *ineriartorneq*; the addition of *-sima-* within the word simply adds a perfective meaning to a word which is perhaps semilexicalized.

13. *-Nit*, *-niit*, and *-ninngaanniit* are all interchangeable allomorphs indicating ablative case.

14. The last morpheme of this word, *-suaq-*, actually derives from two, *-suk-* and *-aq*. The *-aq* is found on a number of morphemes and its provenance is unknown. In word formation, the *-aq* disappears, and all derivational and inflectional affixes are appended to the preceding morpheme (in this case, *-suk*), which then undergoes the usual morphophonemics. In *ilinniarfissuaninnganniit*, *ilinniarfissuk-* is the base to which the third noncoreferent possessive ablative is appended. There is one word in Greenlandic that does not function in this way, and that retains *-aq* in derivation: the word for the building that now houses the University of Greenland is known as *Norlliit illorsuaat*, from *Nuuk-rleq-it illu-rsuaq-at* 'promontory-farthermost-3PL.REL house-big-3PL.POS/SG.POSM', or 'the German's house' (i.e., the house of the ones who live in the furthermost point of land). This example was given to me by P. Langgård, who suggests that the German missionaries spoke Greenlandic so badly that they added the inflectional ending to *-aq*.

15. The two words *ilisimasassanik tiguinnarissanik* were explained by the translator as a metaphoric expression meaning roughly 'to take in what will be learned'. The translation 'to spread knowledge' is his. The use of the word *tiguinnariaq* is standard in speaking of 'lay' catechists.

16. *Eqqarsaatersuut* is lexicalized as 'aphorism' but is parsable as *eqqarsar-uti-rsur-uti* 'thought-device-use/deal.with-device'.

17. *Oqaatsit* lists *sineriak* 'coast' and the combining form in *sinerissap silaa* 'coastline'.

18. *-Ssuu-* is a dialectical variant of *-ssaa-*.

19. *Illussaq* is a house that is being built but is not completed, or it is a house that will be owned (by the relevant participant) but is not yet inhabited.

20. *Sinnerlugu* appears in *Oqaatsit* as a lexical entry, meaning 'more than'; if lexicalized, it may function more as an adverb than as a verb.

21. *Oqaatsit* translates *nersunarpoq* as 'to admire him because he can last'; my translator rendered *nersunartarsimaqaat* as 'to be badly off'.

22. This is apparently the only form left of a paradigm with *-gaa-* and the participial endings.

23. The use of certain morphemes, such as *-tit-*, *-tariaqaq-*, *-qqu-*, and others, with intransitive inflectional morphology on a transitive stem, automatically entails passive semantics (P. Langgård, personal communication).

24. The gloss 'and fellows' is taken from Fortescue (1984:129); *-kkut* in this meaning is not to be confused with the vialis inflectional ending *-kkut*. Examples are translated as '*x* together with *y*'. With kin terms, it signifies the person named and his or her household members; in these cases, it is glossed simply as 'family'.

25. The vialis is used for frequentative (Fortescue (1984:240).

26. The use of the future morpheme here signals narrative style and functions as a habitual. The combination of narrative future (i.e., habitual) and negative in some contexts has the semantics of 'never'.

27. The word *asi* is translated as 'out of the way place' in *Oqaatsit* but as 'nature' by the translator.

28. *Ilagiit* is a plural form.

29. The final [i] in the affix *-tigi-* is really a schwa, and the inflectional ending of verbs with a schwa preceding the inflectional ending is slightly modified: the intervocalic /v/ is lost and both the schwa and the inflectional vowel are realized as /a/'s.

30. The use of *-sai* for 3PL.POS is a recent development; the older form is *-saat*.

31. In clause 115 the syntactic function of *ullut tamaasa* is as the object of the contemporative, and it is thus syntactically an absolutive case, but *tamaasa* itself is in the relative (or non-subject case, reflecting the old nominative-accusative inflection). See note 11, text 1a.

32. *Qayaq* 'kayak' has an irregular plural, *qaannat*, sometimes also used as a singular form, that is the result of a phonological rule slowly becoming obsolete, in which a continuant becomes long when followed by a nonuvular consonant in the next syllable; /j/ becomes /n/ when geminated. *Qaannat* is being replaced by the regularized form, *qayat*; in fact, this is the standard plural form in South Greenlandic. The speaker of this text uses both forms interchangeably: cf. line 125, *qaannamik*, which consists of *qaannat* and the singular instrumental ending *-mik*. *Qaannat* or *qajat* can also refer to the person paddling the kayak.

33. Every summer, large pieces of ice break off from the frozen stretches of the Arctic Ocean near the North Pole and drift down the east coast of Greenland, around Cape Farewell, and up to Qaqortoq and Narsaq on the West Coast (and in cold years, occasionally as far north as Nuuk), before being carried by the current out to the east coast of the North American continent, by Labrador and Newfoundland. These are not icebergs, which break off from glaciers from the inland ice, but rather flat ice floes from the Arctic sea ice; hence the term *sikorsuaq*, from *siku-rsuaq* 'big sea ice' rather than *iluliaq* 'iceberg'.

34. As with the use of the future morpheme *-ssa-*, the conditional here does not have conditional but iterative semantics. It is typical of narrative style. The unmarked form would be *aallarsimallutik*, from *aallar-sima-lutik* 'go-PERF-CT'.

35. *Sinnerlugit* is lexicalized and means 'more than'; it is formally 3PL.OBJ.CT.

36. Most, if not all, grammar books of Greenlandic list the 3C.PL.SUBJ/3PL.OBJ. CA as *-gamikkik*. This was originally a dual, which left its trace here in the plural. This form has not been used for years, however, and current usage is *-gamikkit* (which is, in fact, the plural rather than old dual).

37. This word was transcribed as *orsutalerlugu*, although it is in all probability *orsoqtalerlugu*.

38. *Tunisit-* is derived from *tuni-tit*, meaning 'to be given', from the stem 'give' and the agentive *-tit-*, which here acts as a reflexive in combination with the intransitive inflection on a transitive stem. Another example of this was provided by P. Langgård: *Perimut ilinniartippunga* 'I was taught by Per', from *Per-mut ilinniar-tit-vunga* 'Per-TERM learn-agent-1SG.indic', as opposed to *Per ilinniartippara* 'I taught Per'. Note the use of the stem *ilinniartit-* 'to teach' in both cases.

39. At this time, there was an American military base, Bluie West 1, in Narsarsuaq, not far from Narsaq.

40. The inflectional ending in this clause shows the lack of assibilation characteristic of South Greenlandic: *-gamitigut* instead of *-gamisigut*.

41. The /v/ is epenthetic, because of the impossibility of having three identical vowels in a row.

42. This was transcribed with the inflectional ending *-gamiut*, although it should be *-gamiuk*. Final consonants are not always clearly distinguished in normal speech, and final syllables are often left inarticulated by speakers, as in clause 155, where the speaker does not actually say the final syllable of *oqartarpoq*. Rischel (1974) suggests that although it is normal not to enunciate case endings in oral Greenlandic, hearers can distinguish meanings from intonation patterns at word endings.

43. *-Neq* is a nominalizing affix and can convert a clause to an object or subject noun phrase, taking normal nominal inflections but losing markings of mood, person, and number. With certain verbs, however, including *ajoq-*, the transitivity of the nominalized verb is preserved in the superordinate verb, the underlying subject and object of the nominalized verb is marked by the superordinate verb, and the nominalized verb is not inflected for case (Fortescue 1984:47).

44. The transcriber explained that the speaker should have said *issiavimminut*, from *issiavik* 'chair' and *-minut* 3c.sg.pos.term.

45. There is a palatalized quality to the /i/ in *pattagiaq*; when followed by a nonuvular consonant in the following syllable, single voiced consonants are geminated. In this case, a geminated /j/ is realized as /ss/, whence *pattagissa-minut*.

46. The transcriber suggested that the speaker may not have finished his first thought; the sentence should consist of at least two parts, 'he went to the piano' and 'he sat down [at the piano]'.

47. According to the transcriber, *issiavikulu* is South Greenlandic for 'armchair', whereas in Nuuk it is *issiavissuaq*.

48. *Oqaatsit* glosses *tussiut ullaarsiut* as well as *ullarsiut* as 'morning prayer(s)'; the transcriber also translated this passage as 'morning psalm'.

49. Although it had been transcribed as *pappiliaq* here, *Oqaatsit* lists it as *pappiala* or *pappiara* 'paper'.

50. *-Vagut* is the standard dialectal form for *-vavut*; *-vavut* is the form found in all grammars and in the old writing system, but it has not been used in oral form for many years.

51. *Assigiinngitsut* is a plural form.

52. The word *ima* appears in various forms in the text: *imaappoq* (verb), *imatut* (participial), *ima* (particle), and so forth. The verb is formed from the particle *ima* and the copula *iC-+* inflectional ending. In the morphological analyses here, it is given as lexicalized *imaa-+* inflectional ending. In most cases, it can be translated as 'it's like this', 'that is', or 'you know' as these phrases are used in English. The translations in general follow those provided by the translator. In the other texts, the form *imaattooq* is also found; in contrast to the verb *imaappoq*, it is used as a filler particle, meaning roughly 'well' or 'uh'.

53. *-Ssaq-* + *-liaq-* contracts to *-ssiaq-*.

54. There are several ways of indicating agentive function in Greenlandic: *-tit-* as in *ilinniartippoq* 'he causes to learn; he teaches', and *-sar-* as in the example in clause 18, or as in *eqeersaasoq* 'something that causes one to wake up; alarm clock'. There is apparently no clear distinction in meaning between the morphemes; they are not interchangeable, however. A word that normally takes one agentive morpheme will not also take the other.

55. *Illugaatsiaq* was translated by the translator as 'a house not too small, not too big' (i.e., a medium-sized house). The house in question was a fish plant, bigger than a residential house.

56. The stem is *nalu-* 'to not know'; *nalunngit-*, consisting of the stem and the negative affix *-nngit-*, means 'to know' and takes the negative form of the personal endings.

57. The only prefix in West Greenlandic, *ta-* is commonly attached to deictic markers such as the stem *pav-*. The directional deictic stems all have an inflectional system separate from that of other nouns. Thus, as a noun, the nominative of this stem is *panna* 'the place up there/the place to the east/the place to landward', the relative *passuma*, the terminalis *pavunga*, and so forth. A list of the members of this restricted class of words can be found in Kleinschmidt (1851:21).

58. *Qassutit* is listed as a plural form in the lexical sources.

59. The construction here involves an incorporated noun repeated in the instrumental. *Saarullinnut qassutissatsit* is a compound noun modifying the incorporated noun; its absence would change the meaning of the phrase: *saarullinut qassutissiortarpugut* would mean 'we are making nets to catch cod', whereas the construction in clause 52 means 'we are making a certain kind of net, codfish nets'. This is a normal way of constructing clauses with compound nouns (e.g., also *Petap atuagaataanik atuagaatsiqarpoq*, 'he has Peter's books', literally 'he has books, Peter's books').

60. Codfishing involved the use of long ropes attached to the net and extended in a line from the beach or from a buoy. The nets were generally placed in a line, one after the other.

61. The narrator is probably talking about directions in this passage. Since the fishermen could no longer go in one direction to fish, they had to go the other way; and in the other direction, Sarfannguit was the closest place to set up camp.

62. The lexical sources do not have a listing for *piniarniaq*. *Piniarpoq* is cited as 'to hunt', and Fortescue (1980:269) claims that *piniarniarpoq* is lexicalized as 'to set out hunting'. The translator glossed the word in question as 'hunter', whereas *Oqaatsit* glosses *piniartoq* as 'hunter'. The text is in Sisimiut dialect, and most glossaries are in the dialect of the Nuuk area.

63. This was glossed as 'hunt' in the lexicon but translated as 'camp' by the transcriber/translator. Both activities are traditionally related.

64. *Saqqaanut allaat*, meaning 'even to Saqqa', or more probably 'even to its south side', is an idiomatic construction; *allaat* generally means 'others'. The speaker is describing the setting of nets, but to understand these and the following clauses, some background in fishing techniques, weather patterns, and topography is necessary. In this paragraph, the speaker says they started with Akissa and moved to Utoqqaat, even to Saqqa. Saqqa can be interpreted as a place name, as the transcriber did, or as 'south side [of a fjord]', as does P. Langgård. There is generally one bad side of a fjord, where no one would put a net because of its shallow slope (and therefore danger to boats and unlikelihood of holding big fish).

65. It is common to find *-innaq* as an abbreviated form of a verb (without verbal inflection). The speaker, by emphasizing the use of oars, indicates that the boats used were simple (probably dinghies).

66. In the following paragraphs, the speaker makes reference to certain well-known (locally) weather patterns in the Greenlandic fjords. In the summer, the land warms up faster than the sea, especially where the water is deep. In the afternoon, there is a strong upcurrent of warm air, leaving a vacuum. Cold air rushes in from the surface of the sea, creating a strong late afternoon wind, known as an *isersarneq* (+-*aq, isersarnaaq*). The warmer the day, the stronger the wind. This fades away when the sun sets and the land cools down. In the winter, the opposite phenomenon occurs. The sea is warmer than the land, and the wind goes from the land to the sea, out of the fjord; this is called an *aniserneq*. The same is true of the night. In the summer at night, the land cools down, and towards dawn the wind rushes out of the fjord.

67. This is an absolute construction.

68. See note 60.

69. *Imaattoq* is originally a participial form; it has, however, become lexicalized both as a particle and as a verbal base, and can therefore be found with verbal inflectional endings.

70. *Tamakkua* is one of the deictic class of words with separate inflectional endings; in modern speech, the relative and the absolutive forms are often confused and switched, such that *tamakku(a)* (relative) is used instead of *tamakku* and vice versa. *Tamakku(a)* is the plural of *tamanna* (Fortescue 1984:262).

71. The translator suggested 'it was not that easy' as the translation here.

72. *Ajornar-* is glossed in *Oqaatsit* as 'to be impossible'. -*Nar-* + transitive stem turns an underlying object into a passivelike stem, according to P. Langgård; compare

*nammassineq ajorpaa* 'he couldn't finish it'. *Ajor-* 'not good' is one of a limited number of stems that derive their transitivity from a nominalized verb as part of a compound verbal construction, as illustrated here.

73. *Seqinerup* becomes *seqernup* by metathesis and deletion.

74. *-Tit-* + contemporative in effect converts the grammatical object to the functional subject (see Fortescue 1984; also P. Langgård, personal communication).

75. See note 66. At night, the wind is going out of the fjord. Thus, the rowers row out with a headwind at night, work all night, and go back in the headwind.

76. *Assarneq* and *anisarneq* are both used to mean 'wind going out of the fjord'. *-Aq* is also added to the noun stem.

77. A present-day variant of *-kkut* is *-gut,* or *-tigut* when possessed (Fortescue 1984:209). For example, *illuagut* or *illuatigut* both mean 'through his house'.

78. This can be parsed *soquti-gi-,* where *-gi* has the special form *-ga-*before the contemporative; *soquti* is not listed as an independent word in lexical sources.

79. Fortescue (1984:13), includes *maa(nna)* as an "enclitic" (or *anhangspartikel*); he does not define it, but on its own, *maanna* is glossed as 'now'. Its function as an enclitic is to render the question more speculative.

80. *Tusakataavittaq* is lexicalized (M. Fortescue, personal communication); it is built from *tusar-katag-i-saq-vara* 'hear-be.tired.of-intrans-really.quite-hab-1sg.subj/3sg. obj.ind'. The intransitivizer or semitransitiviser -i- has adversarial semantics here, a function that is now quite lexicalized in West Greenlandic.

81. Nominalized clauses can function as temporal adverbs, most commonly those with the nominalizer *-neq-* and a personal possession affix and a case inflection, normally either locative or vialis (Fortescue 1984:61). In the form given here, no personal possession affix is present.

82. *-Neq-* nominalized verbs with the ablative case are used for adverbs expressing causation (Fortescue 1984:65).

83. The /g/ between *-laaq-* and *-innaq-* is epenthetic (P. Langgård, personal communication).

84. *Ilaqutariit* is a mass noun meaning 'family'.

85. There are several ways of expressing possession in Greenlandic. *-Gi-* indicates inalienable possession, as in *arnagivaa* 'he has a woman', meaning in essence 'he has a mother'; *-utigi-* indicates alienable possession, as in *arnaatigaa* 'he has a woman', meaning 'he has a girlfriend'; and *-taq-* indicates collective possession, always with a specific context, as in *arnatavoq* 'she is a woman member of a given group' (given by context). The morpheme *-qaq-* is sometimes given as the intransitive form of *-gi-,* but it also has existential meanings, as in *qimmeqarpoq* 'there are dogs, there is a dog'.

86. *Assigiinngitsut* is a lexicalized plural form (*Oqaatsit*).

87. *Sioqqat* is a lexicalized plural noun, lexicalized, according to *Oqaatsit*.

88. All verb stems with final vowel apparently take two habitual markers rather than one (P. Langgård, personal communication).

89. The translator identifies this is as the name of a boat; the term *upanniut* means 'whaling dinghy'; *upanniussuaq* means 'big whaling boat'.

90. There are several ways of expressing the concept of 'late' or 'former' state: *-gigaluaq-* is used to indicate late possession, as in *uigigaluaq* 'late husband', and *-ugaluaq-* to indicate the former state of a nonpossessed entity, as in *Peterseniugaluaq* 'the late Petersen' (P. Langgård, personal communication).

91. The stem is *angala-*; the morpheme *-vigi-* always geminates a preceding consonant (P. Langgård, personal communication).

92. *Ajoqi tiguinnagaq* is a compound construction, meaning 'lay catechist'. The same sort of construction is found in clause 39 (with incorporated head noun in clause 37).

93. /g/ + noncontinuant consonant becomes /kk/ when following syllable begins with /m/.

94. The /v/ in *aanaavat* is epenthetic; the same vowel cannot occur more than twice without a consonant in Greenlandic.

95. Long words and compounds, strange words, and so on generally suspend all case endings in Greenlandic. Thus, *kommunerådi* does not take the instrumental ending. However, note the locative case in *Landsrådimi*, in line 48.

96. *-Giaq-* refers back to noun stem for its meaning: *N -giaq-* 'do *N* times'.

97. The equalis here is used in its predicative function.

98. The term *pissaq* refers to 'game' in a hunting economy; otherwise, it means 'income' in contemporary usage.

99. *Aamakku* is an exclamatory, demonstrative, or vocative particle.

100. The derivation and meaning of this word are unclear. The two possibilities suggested by P. Langgård are *pitsip-*, meaning 'buy something for someone', and *pitser-*, meaning 'little by little'.

101. *Piliat* is a lexicalized plural noun.

## REFERENCES

Austin, J. L. 1962. *How to Do Things with Words: The William James Lectures Delivered at Harvard University in 1955*. Cambridge MA: Harvard University Press.

Baker, Mark C. 1988. *Incorporation: A Theory of Grammatical Function Changing*. Chicago: University of Chicago Press.

Bechert, J. 1976. Ergativity and the constitution of grammatical relations. In Plank 1979, 45–59.

Berge, Anna. 1999a. A preliminary analysis of discourse particles in West Greenlandic texts. Paper presented at Seventy-third Annual Meeting of the Linguistic Society of American, Los Angeles, January 7–10, 1999.

Berge, Anna. 1999b. Preliminary studies of the distribution of *Aamma* in West Greenlandic. *Proceedings of the Second Workshop on American Indigenous Languages*. Santa Barbara Papers in Linguistics. Santa Barbara: Department of Linguistics.

Bergsland, Knut. 1955. A grammatical outline of the Eskimo language of West Greenland. Mimeo., Oslo.

Bittner, Maria. 1987. On the semantics of the Greenlandic antipassive and related constructions. *International Journal of American Linguistics* 53:194–231.

Blake, Barry J. 1990. *Relational Grammar*. Croon Helm Linguistic Theory Guides. London: Routledge.

Bok-Bennema, Reineke. 1991. *Case and Agreement in Inuit*. Berlin: Foris Publications.

Brown, Gillian, and George Yule. 1983. *Discourse Analysis*. Cambridge Textbooks in Linguistics. Cambridge: Cambridge University Press.

Brugman, Claudia, and Monica Macaulay, eds. 1984. *Proceedings of the Tenth Annual Meeting of the Berkeley Linguistics Society, February 17–20, 1984*. Berkeley: Berkeley Linguistics Society.

Cartier, Alice. 1985. Discourse analysis of ergative and non-ergative sentences in formal Indonesian. In *Relational Typology*, ed. Frans Plank, 31–45. Berlin: Mouton Publishers.

Chafe, Wallace L. 1976. Givenness, contrastiveness, definiteness, subjects, topics, and point of view. In Li 1976, 27–55.

Chafe, Wallace, ed. 1980. *The Pear Stories: Cognitive, Cultural, and Linguistic Aspects of Narrative Production*. Norwood NJ: Ablex.

Chafe, Wallace. 1994. *Discourse, Consciousness, and Time: The Flow and Displacement of Conscious Experience in Speaking and Writing*. Chicago: University of Chicago Press.

Cole, Peter. 1983. Switch-reference in two Quechua languages. In Haiman and Monro 1983, 1–15.

Comrie, Bernard. 1978. Ergativity. In *Syntactic Typology: Studies in the Phenomenology of Language*, ed. Winfred P. Lehmann, 329–94. Austin: University of Texas Press.

Comrie, Bernard. 1981. *Language Universals and Linguistic Typology: Syntax and Morphology*. Chicago: University of Chicago Press.

Comrie, Bernard. 1983. Switch-reference in Huichol: A typological study. In Haiman and Munro 1983, 17–38.

Comrie, Bernard. 1984. Subject and object control: Syntax, semantics, and pragmatics. In Brugman and Macaulay 1984, 450–64.

Comrie, Bernard. 1989. Some general properties of reference-tracking systems. In *Essays on Grammatical Theory and Universal Grammar*, ed. Doug Arnold, Martin Atkinson, Jacques Durand, Claire Grover, and Louisa Sadler, 37–52. Oxford: Clarendon Press.

Cooreman, Ann. 1983. Topic continuity and the voicing system of an ergative language: Chamorro. In Givón 1983, 425–89.

Creider, Chet A. 1979. On the explanation of transformations. In Givón 1979b, 3–21.

Daneš, Frantisek. 1964. A three-level approach to syntax. In Vachek 1964b, 225–40.

Daneš, Frantisek, and Josef Vachek. 1964. Prague studies in structural grammar today. In Vachek 1964a, 21–32.

de Beaugrande, Robert-Alain, and Woflgang Ulrich Dressler. 1981. *Introduction to Text Linguistics*. London: Longman.

Dixon, R. M. W. 1972. *The Dyirbal Language of North Queensland*. Cambridge: University of Cambridge Press.

Dixon, R. M. W. 1979. Ergativity. *Language* 55:59–138.

Dixon, R. M. W. 1994. *Ergativity*. Cambridge Studies in Linguistics. Cambridge: Cambridge University Press.

Dorais, Louis-Jacques. 1988. *Tukilik: An Inuktitut Grammar for All*. Inuit Studies Occasional Papers 2. Quebec: Association Inuksiutiit Katimajiit Inc. and Groupes D'Etudes Inuit et Circumpolaires.

Dorais, Louis-Jacques. 1990. *Inuit Uqausiqatigiit: Inuit Languages and Dialects*. Arctic College–Nunatta Campus.

Du Bois, John W. 1987. The discourse basis of ergativity. *Language* 63:805–55.

Egede, Paul. 1760. *Grammatica Grönlandica Danico-Latina*. n.p.: Hauniae.

Fillmore, Charles J. 1968. The case for case. In *Universals in Linguistic Theory*, ed. Emmons Bach and Robert T. Harms, 1–88. New York: Holt, Rinehart and Winston.

Firbas, Jan. 1964. On defining the theme in functional sentence analysis. In Vachek 1964b, 267–80.

Fleischman, Suzanne, and Linda R. Waugh, eds. 1991. *Discourse-Pragmatics and the Verb: The Evidence from Romance*. London: Routledge.

Foley, William A., and Mike Olson. 1985. Clausehood and verb serialization. In Nichols and Woodbury, 17–60.

Foley, William A., and Robert D. Van Valin Jr. 1984. *Functional Syntax and Universal Grammar*. Cambridge Studies in Linguistics 38. Cambridge: Cambridge University Press.

Foley, William A., and Robert D. Van Valin. 1985. Information packaging in the clause. In *Language Typology and Syntactic Description 1*, ed. Timothy Shopen, 282–364. Cambridge: Cambridge University Press.

Fortescue, M. D. 1980. Affix ordering in West Greenlandic derivational processes. *International Journal of American Linguistics* 46:259–78.

Fortescue, Michael. 1983. A comparative manual of affixes for the Inuit dialects of Greenland, Canada, and Alaska. *Meddelelser om Grønland* 4. Copenhagen: Nyt Nordisk Forlag.

Fortescue, Michael. 1984. *West Greenlandic*. Croom Helm Descriptive Grammars. London: Croom Helm.

Fortescue, Michael. 1991. Switch-reference anomalies and "topic" in West Greenlandic: A case of pragmatics over syntax. In *Levels of Linguistic Adaptation*, ed. J. Verschueren, 53–80. Amsterdam: John Benjamins.

Fortescue, Michael. 1992. The development of morphophonemic complexity in Eskimo languages. *Acta Linguistica Hafniensia: International Journal of Linguistics* 25:5–27.

Fortescue, Michael. 1995. The historical source and typological position of ergativity in Eskimo Languages. *Études/Inuit/Studies* 19:61–76.

Friedman, Lynn. 1976. The manifestation of subject, object, and topic in American sign language. In Li 1976, 125–48.

Garcia, Erica. 1979. Discourse without syntax. In Givón 1979b, 23–50.

Givón, Talmy. 1976. Topic, pronoun, and grammatical agreement. In Li 1976, 149–88.

Givón, Talmy. 1979a. From discourse to syntax: Grammar as a processing strategy. In Givón, 1979b, 81–112.

Givón, Talmy, ed. 1979b. *Syntax and Semantics 12: Discourse and Syntax*. New York: Academic Press.

Givón, Talmy, ed. 1983a. *Topic Continuity in Discourse: A Quantitative Cross-Language Study*. Amsterdam: John Benjamins.

Givón, Talmy. 1983b. Topic continuity in discourse: The functional domain of switch-reference. In Haiman and Munro, 51–82.

Givón, Talmy. 1984. *Syntax: A Functional-Typological Introduction 1*. Amsterdam: John Benjamins.

Givón, Talmy. 1990. *Syntax: A Functional-Typological Introduction 2*. Amsterdam: John Benjamins.

Grimes, Joseph E. 1975. *The Thread of Discourse*. Janua Linguarum Series Minor 207. The Hague: Mouton.

Haiman, John, and Pamela Munro, eds. 1983. *Switch-Reference and Universal Grammar: Proceedings of a Symposium on Switch Reference and Universal Grammar, Winnipeg, May 1981*. Amsterdam: John Benjamins.

Halliday, M. A. K. 1967a. Notes on transitivity and theme in English 1. *Journal of Linguistics* 3:37–81.

Halliday, M. A. K. 1967b. Notes on transitivity and theme in English 2. *Journal of Linguistics* 3:199–244.

Halliday, M. A. K. 1968. Notes on transitivity and theme in English 3. *Journal of Linguistics* 4:179–215.

Hammerich, L. L. 1951. Kleinschmidt centennial 1: The cases of Eskimo. *International Journal of American Linguistics* 17:18–22.

Hopper, Paul J., and Sandra A. Thompson. 1980. Transitivity in grammar and discourse. *Language* 56:251–99.

Hopper, Paul J., and Sandra A. Thompson. 1984. The discourse basis for lexical categories in universal grammar. *Language* 60:703–52.

Hymes, Dell. 1981. "In vain I tried to tell you": Essays in Native American ethnopoetics. In *Studies in Native American Literature 1*. Philadelphia: University of Pennsylvania Press.

Johns, Alana. 1993. Symmetry in Labrador Inuttut. *MIT Working Papers in Linguistics* 18:43–38. Papers on Case and Agreement I. Cambridge MA: MIT, Department of Linguistics.

Johns, Alana. 1995. On some mood alternations in Labrador Inuttut. In *Grammatical Relations: Theoretical Approaches to Empirical Questions*, ed. Clifford S. Burgess, Katarzyna Dziwirek, and Donna Gerdts, 131–51. Stanford CA: CSLI.

Johnson, Marion R. 1980. *Ergativity in Inuktitut (Eskimo), in Montague Grammar and in Relational Grammar*. Bloomington: Reproduced by the Indiana University Linguistics Club.

Jones, Linda Kay. 1977. *Themes in English Expository Discourse*. Edward Sapir Monograph Series in Language, Culture, and Cognition 2. Lake Bluff IL: Jupiter Press.

Kalmár, Ivan. 1979a. The antipassive and grammatical relations in Eskimo. In Plank 1979, 117–43.

Kalmár, Ivan. 1979b. Case and context in Inuktitut (Eskimo). National Museum of Man Mercury Series, Canadian Ethnology Service Paper 49. Ottawa: National Museums of Canada.

Kalmár, Ivan. 1982. The function of Inuktitut verb modes. In *Tense-Aspect: Between Semantics and Pragmatics: Containing the Contributions to a Symposium on Tense and Aspect, held at UCLA, May 1979*, ed. Paul J. Hopper, 45–64. Typological Studies in Language 1. Amsterdam: John Benjamins.

Keenan, Edward L. 1976. Towards a universal definition of "subject." In Li 1976, 305–33.

Kleinschmidt, Samuel. 1851. *Grammatik der grønlœndischen Sprache: mit teilweisem Einschluss des Labradordialekts*. Hildesheim: Georg Olms Verlagsbuchhandlung, 1968.

Kuno, Susumu. 1987. *Functional Syntax: Anaphora, Discourse. and Empathy*. Chicago: University of Chicago Press.

Labov, William. 1972. The transformation of experience in narrative syntax. In *Language in the Inner City: Studies in the Black English Vernacular*, 354–96. Philadelphia: University of Pennsylvania Press.

Levinson, Stephen C. 1983. *Pragmatics*. Cambridge Textbooks in Linguistics. Cambridge: Cambridge University Press.

Li, Charles, ed. 1976. *Subject and Topic*. New York: Academic Press.

Li, Charles, and Sandra Thompson. 1976. Subject and topic: A new typology of language. In Li 1976, 457–90.

Longacre, R. E. 1976. *An Anatomy of Speech Notions*. Lisse: Peter De Ridder Press.

Longacre, R. E. 1979. The paragraph as a grammatical unit. In Givón, 115–34.

Longacre, Robert E. 1983. Switch-reference systems in two distinct linguistic areas: Wojokeso (Papua New Guinea) and Guanano (northern South America). In Haiman and Munro, 185–208.

Longacre, Robert E. 1985. Sentences as combinations of clauses. In *Language Typology and Syntactic Description 2: Complex Constructions*, ed. Timothy Shopen, 235–86. Cambridge: Cambridge University Press.

Longacre, Robert E. 1996. *The Grammar of Discourse*, 2nd ed. New York: Plenum Press.

Lowe, Ronald. 1981. *Analyse Linguistique et Ethnocentrisme: Essai sur la Structure du Mot en Inuktitut*. National Museum of Man Mercury Series, Canadian Ethnology Service Paper 70. Ottawa: National Museums of Canada.

Lowe, Ronald. 1985. *Uummarmiut Uqalungiha Ilihaurrutikrangit: Basic Uummarmiut Eskimo Grammar*. Inuvik: Committee for Original Peoples Entitlement.

Lyons, John. 1977. *Semantics 2*. Cambridge: Cambridge University Press.

Mallinson, Graham, and Barry J. Blake. 1981. *Language Typology: Cross-linguistic Studies in Syntax*. North-Holland Linguistic Series 46. Amsterdam: North-Holland Publishing.

Mallon, S. T. 1974. *Inuktitut Phase One and Phase Two*. Rankin Inlet Version. Yellowknife: Inuktitut Learning Services, Department of Education Northwest Territories.

Mallon, S. T. 1990. *Introductory Inuktitut*. Victoria: Linguistics Programs Victoria.

Mathesius, Vilém. 1964a. On linguistic characterology with illustrations from modern English. In Vachek 1964b, 59–67.

Mathesius, Vilém. 1964b. On the potentiality of the phenomena of language. In Vachek 1964b, 1–32.

Mathesius, Vilém. 1964c. On some problems of the systematic analysis of grammar. In Vachek 1964a, 306–19.

McCune, Grace Anne. 1983. On thematic structure in English exposition: A study of news commentary texts. PhD dissertation, University of Michigan, Ann Arbor.

Menovscikov, G. A. 1969. Les constructions fondamontales de la proposition simple dans les langues Eskimo-Aleoutes (en liason avec la construction ergative). *Langages* 15:127–33.

Merlan, Francesca. 1976. Noun incorporation and discourse reference in modern Nahuatl. *International Journal of American Linguistics* 42:177–91.

Mithun, Marianne. 1984a. The evolution of noun incorporation. *Language* 60:847–94.

Mithun, Marianne. 1984b. How to avoid subordination. In Brugman and Macauley 1984, 493–509.

Munro, Pamela. 1983. When "Same" is "Not Different." In Haiman and Munro 1983, 223–44.

Nichols, Johanna. 1983. Switch-reference in the northeast Caucasus. In Haiman and Munro 1983, 245–66.

Nichols, Johanna, and Anthony Woodbury, ed. 1985. *Grammar Inside and Outside the Clause: Some Approaches to Theory in the Field*. Cambridge: Cambridge University Press.

Nowak, Elke. 1993. Through the looking glass: Syntactic structures of Inuktitut and ergativity. *Études/Inuit/Studies* 17:103–16.

Oqaatsit. 1990. *Oqaatsit Kalaallisuumiit Qallunaatuumut: Grønlandsk Dansk Ordbog*, ed. Chr. Berthelsen et al. [Nuuk]: Atuakkiorfik.

Payne, Doris L. 1987. Information structuring in Papago narrative discourse. *Language* 63:783–803.

Perlmutter, David M., ed. 1983. *Studies in Relational Grammar 1*. Chicago: University of Chicago Press.

Perlmutter, David M., and Carol G. Rosen, ed. 1984. *Studies in Relational Grammar 2*. Chicago: University of Chicago Press.

Pike, Kenneth L. 1981. *Tagmemics, Discourse, and Verbal Art*. Ann Arbor: Michigan Studies in the Humanities.

Plank, Frans. 1979a. Ergativity, syntactic typology, and universal grammar: Some past and present viewpoints. In Plank 1979b, 3–38.

Plank, Frans, ed. 1979b. *Ergativity: Towards a Theory of Grammatical Relations*. London: Academic Press.

Rhodes, Richard. 1992. Scope in discourse: Pragmatics or syntax? In *Cooperating with Written Texts: The Pragmatics and Comprehension of Written Texts*, ed. Dieter Stein, 589–606. Studies in Anthropological Linguistics 5. Berlin: Mouton de Gruyter.

Rischel, Jørgen. 1974. *Topics in West Greenlandic Phonology: Regularities Underlying the Phonetic Appearance of Wordforms in a Polysynthetic Language*. Copenhagen: Akademisk Forlag.

Sadock, Jerrold M. 1980. Noun incorporation in Greenlandic: A case of syntactic word formation. *Language* 56:300–319.

Sadock, Jerrold M. 1991. *Autolexical Syntax: A Theory of Parallel Grammatical Representations*. Chicago: University of Chicago Press.

Schiffrin, Deborah. 1987. *Discourse Markers*. Cambridge: Cambridge University Press.

Schultz-Lorentzen, Christian Wilhelm. 1945. *A Grammar of the West Greenland Language*. Meddelelser om Grønland 129, No. 3. København: C. A. Reitzel.

Silverstein, Michael. 1976. Hierarchy of features and ergativity. In *Grammatical Categories in Australian Languages*, ed. Robert M. W. Dixon, 112–71. New York: Humanities Press.

Smith, Lawrence R. 1981. Passive as a two-cycle process in Inuktitut. In *The Language of the Inuit: Historical, Phonological, and Grammatical Issues*, Etudes/Inuit/Studies 5, Supplementary Issue, 101–13. Quebec: Inuksiutiit Katimajiit Association, Inc.

Stirling, Lesley. 1993. *Switch-Reference and Discourse Representation*. Cambridge: Cambridge University Press.

Swadesh, Morris. 1946. South Greenlandic (Eskimo). In *Linguistic Structures of Native America*, ed. Harry Hoijer et al., 30–54. Viking Fund Publications in Anthropology 6. New York: Viking Fund.

Swadesh, Morris. 1951. Kleinschmidt Centennial 3: Unaaliq and Proto-Eskimo. *International Journal of American Linguistics* 17:66–70.

Swadesh, Morris. 1952a. Unaaliq and Proto-Eskimo 2: Phonemes and morphophonemes. *International Journal of American Linguistics* 18:25–34.

Swadesh, Morris. 1952b. Unaaliq and Proto-Eskimo 4: Diachronic notes. *International Journal of American Linguistics* 18:166–72.

Toolan, Michael J. 1988. *Narrative: A Critical Linguistic Introduction*. London: Routledge.

Trask, R. L. 1976. On the origins of ergativity. In Plank 1979, 385–404.

Vachek, Josef, ed. 1964a. *A Prague School Reader in Linguistics*. Bloomington: Indiana University Press.

Vachek, Josef, ed. 1964b. *Travaux Linguistiques de Prague 1: L'École de Prague d'Aujourd'hui*. Prague: Editions de l'Académie Tchécoslovaque des Sciences.

Vachek, Josef. 1966. *The Linguistic School of Prague: An Introduction to Its Theory and Practice*. Bloomington: Indiana University Press.

Vaxtin, N. B. 1976. Nominal and verbal ergativity in Asiatic Eskimo: Splits in the person and mood paradigms. In Plank 1979, 279–89.

Woodbury, Anthony C. 1977. Greenlandic Eskimo, ergativity, and relational grammar. In *Syntax and Semantics 8: Grammatical Relations*, ed. Peter Cole and Jerrold M. Sadock, 307–36. New York: Academic Press.

Woodbury, Anthony C. 1983. Switch-reference, syntactic organization, and rhetorical structure in Central Yup'ik Eskimo. In Haiman and Munro 1983, 291–315.

Young, Linda W. L. 1994. *Crosstalk and Culture in Sino-American Communication*. Studies in Sociolinguistics 10. New York: Cambridge University Press.

# Topic and Discourse Structure in West Greenlandic Agreement Constructions

# Topic and Discourse Structure in West Greenlandic Agreement Constructions

ANNA BERGE

University of Nebraska Press | Lincoln and London

IN COOPERATION WITH THE AMERICAN INDIAN STUDIES
RESEARCH INSTITUTE, INDIANA UNIVERSITY, BLOOMINGTON

Library of Congress
Cataloging-in-Publication Data
Berge, Anna.
Topic and discourse structure
in West Greenlandic agreement
constructions / Anna Berge.
p.   cm.—(Studies in the native
languages of the Americas)
"In cooperation with the American
Indian Studies Research Institute,
Indiana University, Bloomington."
Includes bibliographical
references and index.
ISBN 978-0-8032-1645-7
(cloth: alk. paper)
1. Kalâtdlisut dialect—Discourse
analysis. 2. Kalâtdlisut dialect—
Syntax. I. Indiana University,
Bloomington. American Indian
Studies Research Institute. II. Title.
PM62.B46   2011
497'.12—dc22
2011001962

Set in Minion Pro by BookComp, Inc.
Designed by Nathan Putens.